RACE

Julie M. Fenster

 Crown Publishers / New York

of the CENTURY

THE HEROIC TRUE STORY

OF THE

1908 NEW YORK TO PARIS

AUTO RACE

The author gratefully acknowledges the following for permission
to reprint photos which appear in this book:

New York Times
The National Automotive History Collection, Detroit Public Library
The Library of Congress
Omaha World-Herald
University of Washington Libraries, Special Collection

Other photos in this book were first published in the following:
Im Auto Um die Welt (Berlin: Verlag Ullstein, 1909)
La Vie Au Grand Air (Paris) vol. 11, no. 499, April 11, 1908
The Story of the New York-to-Paris Race reprint by Floyd Clymer, 1951
The Story of the New York-to-Paris Race (Buffalo: Thomas, 1908)
Round the World in a Motor Car (London: Grant Richards, 1909)

Published in the United States by Crown Publishers, an imprint of
the Crown Publishing Group, a division of Random House, Inc., New York.
www.crownpublishing.com

Crown is a trademark and the Crown colophon is a registered trademark
of Random House, Inc.

Library of Congress Cataloging-in-Publication Data

Fenster, J. M. (Julie M.)
  Race of the century: the heroic true story of the 1908 New York to Paris auto race /
Julie M. Fenster.
—1st ed.
  1. New York to Paris Race, 1908.   I. Title.
  GV1029.2.F46 2005
  796.72—dc22   2004026644

ISBN 0-609-61096-1

Printed in the United States of America

DESIGN BY ELINA D. NUDELMAN

10 9 8 7 6 5 4 3 2 1

First Edition

FOR RICHARD HARFMANN

CONTENTS

Contents

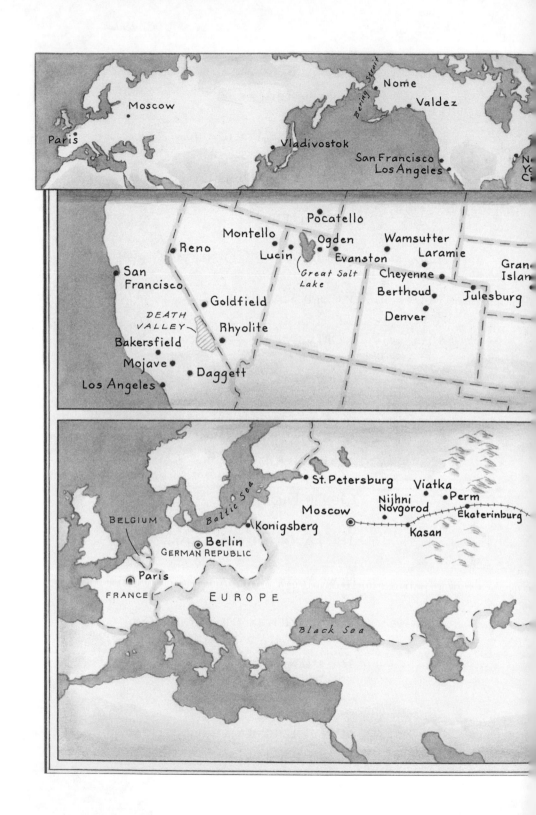

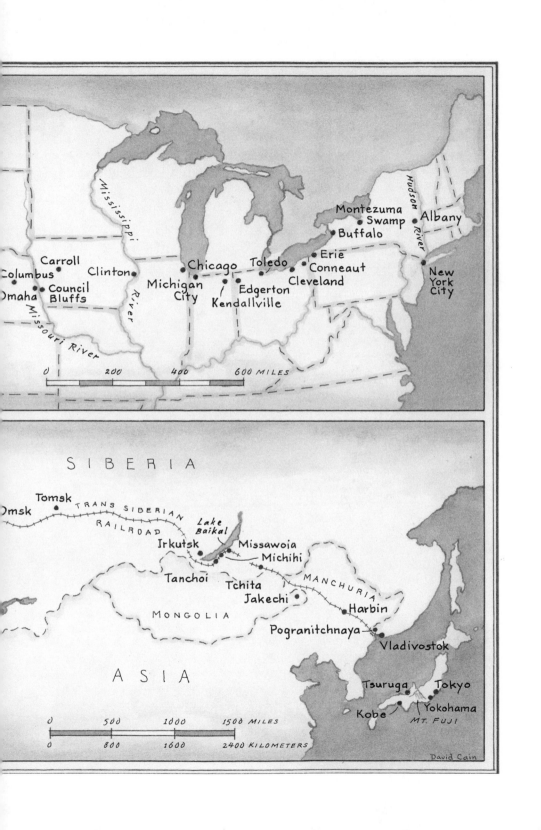

Mississippi River

Hudson River

Montezuma
Swamp
Albany

Buffalo

Carroll
Clinton
Chicago
Toledo
Erie
Columbus
Michigan
City
Edgerton
Cleveland
Conneaut
Omaha
Council
Bluffs
Kendallville
New
York
City

Missouri River

0   200   400   600 MILES

SIBERIA

Omsk
Tomsk
TRANS SIBERIAN
RAILROAD
Lake
Baikal

Irkutsk
Missawoia
Michihi

Tanchoi
Tchita
Jakechi
MANCHURIA

MONGOLIA
Harbin

Pogranitchnaya
Vladivostok

ASIA

Tsuruga
Tokyo

Kobe
Yokohama
MT. FUJI

0   500   1000   1500 MILES
0   800   1600   2400 KILOMETERS

David Cain

Chapter One

Holiday

The newsboys of New York could hardly wait for February 12 in 1908. It may have been just another Wednesday to some people, but not to the urchins and orphans who swarmed over the sidewalks every morning to hawk the *World* or the *Sun,* the *Herald,* the *Tribune,* or the *Times,* fanning out again in the afternoon to sell the *Press,* the *Telegram,* the *Globe, Mail,* and *Evening World.* In the days before broadcasting, the news of the world didn't move any faster than the sweaty little boys who carried it—but they didn't waste a second. They couldn't. A big city had a couple of dozen newspapers in 1908. And what is more, the leading papers issued four or five editions per day. It was a daily deluge that made newsboys run as fast as they could with each succeeding bundle of papers, getting rid of the old news just before the new news came along.

When the day finally came to a close, New York City's orphan newsboys could look forward to decent surroundings at the Newsboys' Lodging House on Chambers Street in Lower Manhattan. On February 12 in 1908 about three hundred of them were also looking forward to a special feast for Lincoln's Birthday: turkey, cranberry sauce, celery, potatoes, turnips, pie, and coffee, all courtesy of a patron named Delano Weekes.

Robert T. Lincoln, the son of the sixteenth president, was on the list of guests invited to share the newsboys' bounty. As a resident of Chicago, he'd already sent his regrets, though. So had another Union leader's son—one with a less convincing excuse. George B. McClellan, namesake of Lincoln's early favorite among Yankee generals, was the mayor of New York City in 1908. Bookish and a little vague under the best of circumstances, McClellan had a long list of appearances to make on Lincoln's Birthday, and he sent word in advance that Chambers Street wasn't among them.

In the early morning, while the newsies were bleating for business and wondering just exactly what kind of pie they'd be having later on for dessert, the next round of headlines was sprouting all around them. In

2

Brooklyn, a twenty-eight-year-old tailor from Italy lay dying; he had been shot five times by the mafia, which was surging to new heights of influence in 1908, dumbfounding even hardened Americans with its capacity for violence. "The Black Hand wrote to me demanding money," the tailor was telling police early that morning from his deathbed, "and I refused. Last night, they sent two men after me. They got me."

He wasn't the only one in trouble. The organizers of the *Grande Redoute Rose*—the Pink Ball—were under siege from all of the women on the guest list who didn't happen to own a pink gown, and who couldn't get one in time for the February 14 dance. The committee spent the morning debating whether or not to allow white.

No one in New York, however, or anywhere else, had a worse day than John J. Grant, a printer by trade. He swallowed poison, slit his wrists, and then jumped off the Brooklyn Bridge—and lived. As soon as he was rescued, he was arrested.

Because schools, government offices, brokerages, and other businesses were closed for Lincoln's Birthday, the stores were crowded right from the start. Macy's celebrated its fiftieth anniversary by putting nearly everything on sale, selling eight-rib umbrellas for $5.00 each. Anyone who bought one could have brought it home in a bag, though; the morning was perfectly clear, with temperatures in the mid-thirties. Automobiles were also on sale in mid-February. "This is bargain time," confided one agency in boldface type in the newspaper. Those who believed it could visit the showroom on Broadway north of Times Square, the same neighborhood in which most of New York's car dealerships were located.

The Broadway Mammoth Automobile Exchange, on Fifty-sixth Street near Broadway, about ten blocks up from Times Square, declared in its own ad, "Swell rich man's cars can now be bought cheaper than inferior new ones." Since swell rich men at the time were paying between $6,000 and $12,000, equivalent to about $150,000 to $300,000 today, there was some incentive to look for an overlay. "Pierce-Arrow, $850," advertised Broadway Mammoth. "Thomases, all models, 1905, 1906, 1907, $600 to $1,500." One reason for the drastic depreciation in price was that a car in those days didn't have a long life on the road; after

3

about ten thousand miles, a customer was presumed to have had his or her money's worth. But then, it would take the average customer three years to log as many as ten thousand miles in 1908.

In practical terms, the typical secondhand Thomas in the Broadway Mammoth lot had progressed a mere seven blocks, since the Thomas Agency, where the new cars were sold, occupied a building on Broadway at Sixty-third Street. A New Yorker out walking on the brisk morning of the twelfth couldn't fail to notice the Thomas Agency. Nearly every inch of its four-story facade was draped in decoration, with banners at every window. Something special was in the air—along with the flapping of a great many flags. All down Broadway, the buildings were decked out in colors and patriotic signs. Lew Dockstader, a popular comedian, was inspired by the display to assume the persona of Abraham Lincoln taking a walk in New York: "I was much surprised as well as gratified when I arrived in New York," he said, "to find myself so well-heralded. I walked up Broadway, and flying from many hotel fronts I noticed bunting and flags telling the glad news that I was here." But then Dockstader's Mr. Lincoln finished by adding, in a rather perplexed way, "Someone just told me that the decorations were not for me—but for a car race."

The crowds gathering on Broadway all morning were not out to honor Abe Lincoln, either. They were on the avenue to catch sight of the start of the New York-to-Paris Automobile Race. There would only be one—one race round the world, one start, and one particular way that, for the people who lived through it, the world would never be the same. The automobile was about to take it all on: not just Broadway, but the farthest reaches to which it could lead. On that absurdity, the auto was about to come of age.

"By ten o'clock," reported the *Tribune,* "Broadway up to the northernmost reaches of Harlem looked as though everybody was expecting the circus to come to town." The excitement was generated by the potential of the auto to overcome the three challenges most frustrating to the twentieth century: distance, nature, and technology. First, distance: in the form of twenty-two thousand miles of the Northern Hemisphere, from New York west to Paris. Second, nature: in seasons at their most unyielding. And third, the very machinery itself, which would be pressed hard by the race to defeat itself. Barely twenty years old as a contraption and only ten as a practical conveyance, the automobile couldn't reasonably be expected to be ready to take on the world. But there were men who were ready and that was what mattered.

The six cars entered in the race were parked in Times Square, facing out of the wide end of the triangle formed by Forty-third Street, Seventh Avenue, and Broadway (which slashes diagonally across Seventh Avenue). For the moment, the cars were separated from the rest of the world by a crowd of a thousand people, who not only wanted to see the start, but touch it. After nine o'clock, another thousand or more pressed into Times Square every five minutes.

"The crowd was one of the worst that the police have had to handle in years," reported the *Globe*. "It was one black mass." Three hundred policemen were on hand all morning, charged mainly with keeping a one-lane road open along the route laid out for the cars. If the crowd had its way, after all, the cars would never budge. When a gaggle of women waiting in front of the Cadillac Hotel on Broadway at Forty-third Street grew too merry and spilled over the curb, a detachment of mounted police arrived in seconds to herd them back.

Times Square wasn't yet a theater district in 1908, but a neighborhood of hotels, watched over by the New York Times Building, the lone skyscraper in the middle of it all, and the source of its name. Ultimately, the race was to head north out of the city. But for the six racecars facing the Times Building across Forty-third Street, the route started south on Broadway for a block, making a turn around the base of the square, before heading north up Seventh Avenue to the intersection at Forty-fifth Street where crooked Broadway barged into Times Square. The cars would then follow Broadway out of the city.

In the square, the north-south avenues were lined by a double row of cars, two hundred of them in all colors and sizes. Their owners had received special permission to accompany the racers at the start, and for that purpose each had been assigned an immensely valuable parking space well in advance. Once the six racers started moving, the enthusiasts were to peel away from the curb in their autos and join the convoy.

By 10:30, the crowd surrounding the racecars numbered fifty thousand. In photographs taken from high up in the Times Building, the scene looked as though a blanket had been spread over the square, a blanket made up of black overcoats. Faces popped up out of the black, looking every which way to see something of the cars or the spectacle they had created. Even those people who couldn't see the racers at the starting line could smell gasoline. All the while, the music of a brass band filled the air.

Celebrities had a special place, as they always do in New York. A grandstand had been erected directly across Forty-third Street from the cars, so that those on it would have a view both of the start and of the cars as they made their way up Seventh Avenue, after the initial lap of the square. In the meantime, the celebrities could see the cars, and the crowd could see the celebrities. Colgate Hoyt was bustling back and forth on the grandstand, a solidly built man recognizable by his thick moustache and the thin hairline just then disappearing over the horizon of his head. Originally from Cleveland, Hoyt specialized in railroad finance—and good connections. His wife, Lida, was a niece of General William T. Sherman, and he counted John Rockefeller and steel magnate Charles Schwab among his closest friends. Robust by nature, Hoyt was on the board of directors of the Aero Club of America, a group dedicated to the airplane, which had been invented only five years before. The club was so riddled with infighting that a wit of the day credited it with originating aerial warfare. At the time of the race, Hoyt was also president of the Automobile Club of America, and that gave him a place on the grandstand.

Jefferson DeMont Thompson was there, too. A developer and landlord, Thompson was not as rich as Hoyt, but he was likewise interested in airplanes and automobiles and was a member of all the concomitant clubs. Thompson was also in the much more rarified Motor Scooter Club of America, the scooter of 1908 being a vehicle for use on ice whenever people couldn't toy with their yachts. Thompson served as president of the Broadway Association, which guided the development of the Times Square neighborhood, and so his place on the grandstand was practically deeded.

Keeping to themselves on the grandstand were Miss Theodora Shonts, the most famous young woman in New York in mid-February 1908, and her friends from France, the Duc de Chaulnes, the Duchesse d'Uzes, Prince Galitzine, Baron Louis de Conde, and the Baron de la Boullere. They were not in black overcoats, but in as much fur as they could arrange around themselves. In Paris, the Duc de Chaulnes was known as a penniless boulevardier who was always trying to get himself married to a rich girl. But in New York, he had finally crossed his own finish line. Engaged to the very rich Theodora Shonts, he was the toast of the town, regaled as the veritable heir to the mantle of Charlemagne. Theodora was the most envied woman in the city, standing with her arm draped through that of the duc she'd brought home from Paris. No one knew or cared that the Duc de Chaulnes had owed his tailor $1,345 since 1901. Nor did the throngs pointing out the duc to one another in Times Square know that he had gone on a morphine binge just before leaving Paris—and that, purely for love of Theodora or possibly in fear of her father, he had made it a long, unrestrained bender that lasted for days. With that, he had sworn off drugs forever.

The race was due to begin at 11:00 A.M., when Mayor McClellan was scheduled to fire the starting pistol. As the time drew near, some observers detected a somber atmosphere bestilling the crowd, as bystanders looked at the racers and realized just how treacherous a trip lay in store for them. Everyone couldn't be contemplative, though. "Send me a cake of ice from Siberia," shouted one observer. "See you in Paris," exclaimed another. Not all of the comments were even in English.

Some people were in Times Square to see history—or at least news—in the making; some to join in the celebration of automobile sport. Some were only there to catch sight of the duc and future duchesse. But many of those who cheered loudest were caught in a patriotic fever, brought on by the sight of the German, Italian, or French entries. Or the American one. The New York-to-Paris Race struck them all as a holiday that was set to move west across the world. Excitement would well up wherever the race arrived; a person had only to look up from an average day to see it and hear it and get jostled in the streets by it. That's what was happening in Times Square on February 12, 1908.

"Undoubtedly the sternest test of men and machines that has ever been undertaken," reflected an editorial in the *New York Times*. "This stupendous undertaking is almost on a par with the dash for the pole," observed the *Baltimore American*. "It shows how deeply seated the spirit of adventure and of emulation is in the human race."

The *Denison (Iowa) Bulletin* was more practical. "You think that automobile race doesn't amount to anything?" the editor would write. "Well, now, how much more have you thought about and studied autos the past few weeks than you ever did before? And what you have been doing 50,000,000 other people have been doing also, and of that fifty millions, many have the money to spend for machines of their own. See?"

A person along the way in Kendallville, Indiana, would express the spirit of the New York-to-Paris Race best of all, holding up a sign for the benefit of the racers, reading, "Good Luck in the Kendallville-to-Paris Race!"

The race would be new, as long as it kept moving, and so would the people it passed.

With the start set for 11:00, the police in New York began clearing a path, once and for all, using their billy clubs to press the crowd back onto the sidewalks. "They pushed and shoved," reported the *New York Globe*, "until they succeeded in making a lane about thirty feet wide up the square and Broadway." Just before the top of the hour, members of the Automobile Club of America formally inspected the cars, and then F. J. Wagner, the official starter, made sure they were lined up evenly, as though he were absolutely determined that no entrant steal the advantage of a foot or two at the outset of twenty-two thousand miles. In truth, he was more sternly directed by the photographers than the race officials.

At 11:00 on the dot, a horn blasted a long, shrill note, and when it stopped, the square was quiet. The band struck up the "Marseillaise." That was a cue. A man at the front of one of the three French cars jerked the handcrank and started the engine. One by one, the national anthems played and the cars revved up. Apart, the engines were loud. Together, the six of them made a noise that pounded through the air, growing bigger than any of the buildings that had been looking down on

8

them. People wiped tears from their eyes, either stirred by the moment or else vibrated to the point of springing leaks. And yet, when Wagner approached the lineup and said to the teams, "All right?" his voice was, in the words of one of the entrants, "as clear and distinct in the enormous square as if he were talking in a small closed room."

The drivers—even those who didn't speak English—replied, in unison, "All right!"

With that, Wagner turned to the grandstand. And with that, no one knew what to do, because Mayor McClellan had yet to arrive. The .22-caliber pistol provided for the great moment lay on a table, while the dignitaries and celebrities stood around it, trying not to look confused. They were entirely confused, though, and after a few minutes, so were fifty thousand other people. The mayor's assistants peered hopefully into the crowd for some sign of the boss. The drivers worked the throttles on their cars. Policemen dug in and kept up the pressure against the surging crowd. And then Colgate Hoyt leapt forward, grabbed the gun, and shot it into the air. At precisely 11:14, the racers started to move, and the cheering even drowned out the engines.

Chapter Two

A Race Course

Oberlieutenant Hans Koeppen of the Fifteenth Prussian Infantry didn't know much about automobiles when the New York-to-Paris Race was announced in late November 1907. His favorite sport was tennis. And in terms of transportation, he was more at home on a horse than in a car, but that didn't stop him from taking part in the first of the prerace formalities: widespread speculation as to who would enter. At German army headquarters, known as General Staff, where Koeppen was posted, his fellow officers insisted that a German car, either a Benz or a Daimler, would undoubtedly and almost necessarily finish first. Benz or Daimler: that was the only question. Daimler or Benz. Koeppen couldn't add much to that particular discussion, though. The two were just names to him.

Most Germans were in the same fog. Their country delighted in building vehicles but barely knew what to do with them next. Benz, for example, produced magnificent automobiles but sold more of them in France than at home. It wasn't a question of price. Inexpensive cars like Opel trickled gamely into the German market. It was more a matter of contentment with things just the way they were.

Hans Koeppen, for one, didn't miss having a car. And anyone would think that he was leading an utterly charmed life. He'd grown up near Hanover, a pastoral part of Germany, the only child of a retired army colonel and his wife. At seventeen, Koeppen followed in his father's footsteps and joined the Prussian army. Coursework and training came easily to him and he was selected for a post on the General Staff. All by itself, a rank in the Prussian army made Koeppen a busy man in Berlin in 1907, peppered with invitations to balls and outings, tennis matches to his heart's content, and excursions to the mountains or the sea. There was always something to do in Berlin in those years, especially among the elite who drew Oberlieutenant Koeppen into their circle.

A solidly built six-footer, Koeppen sometimes wore a moustache, which, with his close-cropped dark hair and rather straight bearing, should have lent him the severity so much in vogue among junior officers—Prussian ones, in particular. But there was nothing severe about Hans Koeppen, at least nothing that showed itself in and around Berlin in 1907.

Humorous by nature and polite to a fault, Lieutenant Koeppen was, after all, a soldier in peacetime, whose lot was to study the defeats of the past, while enjoying the fruits of its victories. Though the world in which he grew up, the old Germany, wouldn't last long into the twentieth century, it cast a certain glow with its aura of plenty, of heavy dinners and light conversation, and schools, factories, scientists, and hospitals without equal in the world—holidays without equal, either, and concerts for free, lectures for all, and fairs; hard work but not long hours. For a young officer it made for the most pleasant life imaginable, or it should have, until the New York-to-Paris Automobile Race was announced.

Koeppen's initial interest in the race wasn't sporting, despite the fact that he was a good athlete himself. It was purely patriotic and, in that, there was a kind of severity that even Koeppen didn't realize he possessed, that even easygoing fellows can have when they turn a corner to see that they are no longer merely wanted, but actually needed.

The frustration in Germany, such as it was in relation to automobile racing, was that no German car had participated in the arduous Peking-to-Paris Race, which had captured the attention of Europe over the summer of 1907. The whole idea for the New York-to-Paris Race grew out of the excitement left over by the Peking race. The Italians had been in it; the French, and even the Dutch, had had an entry, but not the Germans. That was about all that Hans Koeppen knew about automobile racing of any kind.

When the Peking-Paris Race was first suggested in January 1907, it was largely intended as a slap at track races, which were then just taking hold. "The supreme use of the automobile is that it makes long journeys possible," Paris's *Le Matin* newspaper proclaimed. ". . . But all we have done is make it go round in circles."

"What needs to be proved," *Le Matin* insisted, "is that as long as a man has a car he can do anything and go anywhere. *Anywhere.* Yes, anywhere."

In principle, the automobile was limitless. It didn't need rails as a train did, and it didn't need to rest, as a horse would. The only thing it did seem to need as of 1907 was more time. The very first road vehicle powered by an internal combustion engine—a Benz—had made its debut in 1886. More of a three-wheeled motorcycle than anything resembling a car, it did not so much launch the automobile age as end almost a hundred years of tinkering in which various inventors mounted power plants onto wheels, pushing the result onto the road. Any one of a half dozen such conveyances could be cited as "the first car," but the Benz was the one that finally amounted to something, inspiring others, especially with the versatility of the internal combustion engine. Progress was slow in the beginning, as automobile enthusiasts were regarded as juvenile, at best. When Albert de Dion, a French count, announced his intention to build automobiles in France in the 1880s, his family committed him to a rest home.

What eventually started the revolution was not science, anyway, but commerce. The invention may have been born in 1886, but the much vaunted automobile age should properly be traced to 1892, when a French manufacturer issued a catalog of its current models. That simple, nontechnical act was the start of the industry, of makers selling cars on the open market: not to sympathetic neighbors or to fellow engineers, but to total strangers, of which the world offered a practically infinite supply. Competition immediately stretched up and out to find them. Boasting followed, in order to keep them.

As the center of the world's automaking in 1900, France was also out in front in boasting, an activity that led directly to the staging of city-to-city races there. Competitors drove at a frantic pace from one point to another—from Paris to the city of Bordeaux, for example—in some of the most sizzling race action ever seen. French roads were exceptionally good, due to the country's mild weather and engineering tradition, so drivers lived the dream of going as fast as they wanted, or could, over varied terrain. Auto-racers were hailed as pioneers for going 30 or even 40 mph, but nineteenth-century cows, dogs, and pedestrians proved less successful in facing traffic at those speeds. Race fans enthusiastically judged city-to-city races according to the average miles per hour of the winners. Everyone else, however, judged each race by how many bystanders had been killed along the way.

After France outlawed city-to-city races within its borders, going round and round in circles came into fashion. Closed tracks sprang up, and fast cars were banished to them. *Le Matin* and a great many fans, however, never quite relegated themselves to that new reality or to the fake challenge of racing in a tea saucer. To them, *anywhere* meant a lot of things, but one thing it didn't mean was *nowhere.*

"Is there anyone who will undertake to travel this summer from Paris to Peking by automobile?" challenged *Le Matin* on January 31, 1907. Most people who read *Le Matin* that morning were amused with the notion, but declined the invitation. China didn't have many cars then— fewer than two hundred in the whole country—and as to the rest of the Asian part of the course, Mongolia didn't have any cars and neither did central Russia. Although local tribespeople riding in carts might not have noticed it, the roads in those countries were unfit for automobiles, being narrow, rutted, and, in many cases, barely detectable. What the three countries did offer in abundance were bridgeless rivers, nameless swamps, and desert plains. And mountains.

The rumor was that the Peking-to-Paris challenge originated with Albert de Dion, the early automobilist. He had not only outlived his doubting relatives, but inherited his father's title of marquis along the way. In 1907, Marquis de Dion was a highly respected businessman, presiding as a founding father over French automaking and racing. At fifty-one, he was almost entirely bald, with a square face, kindly eyes, and a wide moustache that curved to a point at the ends. De Dion was the head of France's largest car company, producing opulent cars that carried his name throughout the world. If Peking-to-Paris (the route had been reversed early in the planning) wasn't the marquis's idea, he was at least quick to embrace it, writing to *Le Matin* to say that his cars would participate, if any others would. "This is a real Jules Verne affair," de Dion mused. "But nothing is impossible."

In helping to sell the public on the idea of the Peking race, de Dion was probably only repeating the pitch just as he got it from his most vociferous employee: his nephew, Bourcier St. Chaffray. Compact and dapper, St. Chaffray was a lively Frenchman and a very witty one. Certainly he was facile. No matter how fast a car could go in 1907, Bourcier St. Chaffray could go even faster in the melee of the average conversation. Tossing off implications for others to pick up and embrace as facts, he left the general impression that he had been involved in practically every long-distance race ever organized. One way or another, he was an insider within race circles and served as the emissary between Marquis de Dion and *Le Matin* during the running of Peking-Paris. Clean-shaven at a time when most European men had moustaches, St. Chaffray had short, dark hair, large, expressive eyes, a thin Gallic mouth—and ears like jug handles. Except for his ears, he was at least streamlined. It was St. Chaffray who convinced the marquis to enter two cars in the Peking-to-Paris event, with company-sponsored teams to drive them. The marquis agreed, but only if other cars entered, too.

Almost immediately, a competitor stepped up in the form of a handsome race driver named Auguste Pons, who would be in command of a little three-wheeled car called a Contal. Dark in complexion, with deep-set eyes, Auguste Pons presented even in repose an expression chiseled with intent—what would later be termed a "game face." Probably because Contal was the only company that would agree to sponsor him, Pons was zealous in his insistence that a flyweight three-wheeler was indeed the very car to take on a six-thousand-mile journey across two continents. On close inspection, the Contal he would take to Peking was little more than a motorcycle with two wheels in the front, and a bucket seat for a passenger positioned between them. With a little jimmying, two or three Contals might fit in the backseat of one big De Dion, but Pons was young, and, moreover, he was a mountain of muscle, which might just insulate his bones from the jarring effect of a motortrike ride across Asia. Pons was also impetuous, winning track victories through sheer fearlessness as he darted through any glimmer of an opening, surrounded by tons of speeding iron on every side.

Drivers like Pons will always need luck, not so much to win races, but to survive them. What was surprising about Pons's choice of a profession, and his decision to enter the arduous Peking event, was that he had a wife and two little girls at home. (One of his daughters, Lily Pons, would grow up to become the most beloved opera star of the 1930s.) Even a charming family couldn't make Auguste Pons stay home, though. He meant to drive.

The fourth entrant in the Peking race was a mysterious Burgundian named Charles Godard. Stocky but fit, he was neither average-looking nor particularly attractive at first glance, with features that were large and mismatched. That didn't stop Godard from putting himself in the center of attention, whenever possible. If his face wasn't pretty, it was supple and prone to exaggeration. He was an extrovert—glib, kinetic, and perfectly willing to sacrifice his dignity for the sake of any joke that might pop into his head. On the ship taking the teams to Peking for the start, he decided that there wasn't enough excitement and so he organized a cabaret. No sooner had it started than he decided that it wasn't exciting enough, either, and he jumped up onstage to serve as emcee. Yet Godard's playful nature didn't make him any less mysterious. Despite the fact that he almost never remained quiet, very little was known about him. The rumor floated around behind him that he had served a short term in prison for some sort of fraud. More definitely, it was known that he had raced cars regularly, racking up his share of wins, yet he gave the impression that he didn't prepare and, what's more, that he didn't really care, not the way his stone-faced competitors did. Between races, he had a daredevil motorcycle act that played at carnivals.

The fifth entrant to sign up for Peking was a brittle Italian prince named Scipione Borghese, driving an Itala automobile. In Italy, he was called "the Englishman," which was supposed to be an insulting reflection on his lack of warmth. In addition to all of the other meticulous preparations Prince Borghese made for Peking Paris, he remembered to bring along a sycophantic newspaperman to report on the *raid,* as it was originally known. In French terminology, a *raid* was not a race, but a sporting intrusion into foreign territory, intended only to see who could finish—not who would come in first.

In the spirit of the *raid,* the contestants, driving in teams of two to three men to a car, were supposed to stay together on the road from Peking and generally assist one another, but once in China, sportsmanship almost immediately dissolved. Prince Borghese was off like a shot, with his fancy car and even fancier bankroll. For a time, Charles Godard was the only one in the race willing to wait for Auguste Pons, gamely bouncing through desert terrain in his overblown trike. Finally, though, with the *raid* having become a full-fledged race and the Gobi Desert closing in all around, the other racers left Godard and Pons far behind, and then, even Godard had to give up on Auguste Pons.

Eight days into the race Pons and his mechanic, Octave Fouccalt— the human hood ornament who rode up front between the wheels— were in grave trouble. Somewhere in the middle of the Gobi Desert, they were lost and out of provisions. Unbeknownst to the other contestants, or to any other human beings on earth, the Contal had broken down. As a matter of fact, Pons and Fouccalt were broken down, too, in desperate need of water and food. Following the line of a faint track in the sand, they walked twenty miles without finding any sign of life. With that, Pons decided to return to the vehicle, twenty miles back again. He and Fouccalt fell asleep next to the Contal and didn't awaken for almost a day. What happened next was typical of the overwrought young Pons. On waking, he decided to go off the track in order to find people—any people, even the Gobi pirates of whom he'd been warned time and again. He didn't want to die alone in the sand. Yet that was just what Fouccalt told him was the likely result of wandering around in the dizzying expanse. Pons trudged out anyway and by a stroke of improbable but welcome luck, he soon spotted a nomadic camp in the distance. He had two choices: to continue to the camp and then hope that the inhabitants would go back for Fouccalt or to return for the other man himself.

Pons went back, but not so much for the exhausted Fouccalt as for the motorbike. He was obsessed with the idea of continuing to Paris— actually, it is hard to say what idea was in Pons's head. But he wanted the vehicle enough to insist that Fouccalt help him push it toward the encampment. When the wheels lodged in the sand, the two men started to dig it out, pushing, shoveling, clawing, and tugging each wheel by the spoke. That is when they collapsed, their strength finally broken. Just far enough off the trail to be invisible to it, they ought to have perished there.

Before the day was out, a posse of nomads happened on them. Miraculous as that seemed, it wasn't necessarily good news. Many of the people living off the land, such as it was in the Gobi Desert, would have just as soon killed them as looked at them. And then there were others—who would only barely have looked at them. When Charles Godard was stranded farther on in the desert, a band of tribesmen simply plodded by, blandly ignoring his pleas for help. Pons and Fouccalt were not only scooped up by the nomads who found them but nursed back to health and saved from certain death. They were no longer on their way to Paris, however, at least not by automobile.

Prince Borghese, the first contestant to drive into Paris the following August 10, was hailed a hero. His newspaperman wrote a book on that very point. The two De Dion teams also survived to see Paris again, arriving on August 30. Charles Godard, haunted by the worst luck of any car in the quartet, managed by his own Herculean efforts to finish alongside the De Dions. Or nearly so: at the very end, when the battered clown was about to make his triumphal entrance into Paris, he was arrested for taking money on false pretenses from Dutch diplomats in Peking. The charges, however true they were, didn't register in the world of Charles Godard, nor in the suspended reality of the Peking-to-Paris Race. Of *course* he took money, if he needed it: people who entered races like Peking-Paris started out desperate. The ones who finished grew worse, not better, with every mile that went by.

Within hours of reaching Paris, Charles Godard was pulled from his car and hauled off to jail, denied his moment of glory. Though Godard was French, his car was not. Ever afterward, he was convinced that *Le Matin* had orchestrated the arrest solely to reserve the remaining accolades for the two De Dions. Peking-Paris never broke Charles Godard's will to win, but it did defeat his sense of humor, at least temporarily. In his case, that was an even more significant surrender.

Three months later, in November of 1907, a great many people were still talking about the Peking-to-Paris Race—but Bourcier St. Chaffray was not one of them. He bobbed up with an even better idea: a test that would leap over the baby steps of racing to yank the cars of 1908 into the longest, toughest race ever devised. *Le Matin* immediately picked it up and announced the new competition in its editions of November 24. The superlative of all races—ever, even up to the present day—"New York-to-Paris" succinctly described the route. Bored with track racing, the French people had decided to make a new racing oval out of the entire Northern Hemisphere.

The cars were, of course, to travel west from New York, not east into the ocean. Nonetheless, the race promised something just as preposterous: except for the jump across the Atlantic, the cars were supposed to go round the world "without use of a boat," as the first descriptions explained. The route started by crossing the United States, which had been traversed only nine times before by automobile, each time an arduous adventure. It then led north through Canada and made a left turn at Alaska, fifteen hundred miles wide, which the cars were to cross before arriving at the Bering Strait, a narrow body of water that separates the American wilderness from the Russian one—sometimes. Occasionally, the choppy waters of the strait freeze over, and when that happened, the racers were to drive across to Russia. "The most difficult stretch of the journey," predicted Roald Amundsen of the dash across the Bering Strait, in a letter to the *New York Times*. "The loss of a machine at that point should be considered by the contestants." Amundsen may have sounded rather callous, calmly weighing the odds of a car and its occupants falling through the ice, but that same imperturbability would help put him first at the South Pole four years later, in 1911.

The course was not much easier on the other side of the strait. The peninsula that stretches into northeastern Russia was only a little more fully explored than the moon in 1907. Practically every outsider who had ever made the trip got a book out of it: in fact, there had been just three. The consensus was that the only thing meaner than the sudden blizzards that racked the area were the inhabitants. And the only thing scarier than they were was their food—bits of meat or meal that generally ran the gamut from rancid to rotted—should they be in a truly rare frame of mind and offer to share any.

The course of the New York-to-Paris Race led next through Siberia, four million square miles in total, and five thousand miles across. No one had ever traveled across it by car; the only road through much of it was the track of the Trans-Siberian Railway, slicing through forests with no room to spare on either side of the ties. It may as well have been a subway, the woods were so thick.

The twenty-two-thousand-mile trek would include Moscow, perhaps even make a detour to St. Petersburg, and definitely run through Berlin, before ending finally in Paris.

Just describing the New York-to-Paris Race took longer than it did to run some races, start to finish, in 1907. Even in a modern car on today's highways the trip would be daunting. In a world without highways, it was regarded as suicidal. "The cars," explained Carlton Mabley, a New York automobile importer who passed for a voice of authority under the circumstances, "will have to climb mountains several times to an altitude of over 10,000 feet and drop down the sides of mountain ranges on passes and roads that are well-nigh impassable even to the sure-footed beast of burden. The drivers will have to go through rivers which in many cases will completely cover the wheels and flooring of the car, and the motor will have to do its work at a temperature of 100 degrees as well as at 50 below zero." The prospect of such an endeavor certainly started people talking—and rifling through atlases.

The *New York Times* could stand only three days of the buzzing excitement before bursting forth, on November 28, with the announcement that it would join *Le Matin* as cosponsor. In an era that glided along without any overarching news story, such as a war or some pestilence to dwell on, the *New York Times* realized that the world's longest race would not only be news, but a turning point in the young twentieth century. Besides, it would fill up a column on page one every day, and a lot of page two for at least six months running.

The good gray *Times* was not often in the habit of generating news, like some common tabloid churning up controversy where none existed before, but "this big undertaking," it enthused, "a year or two ago would have been termed the wildest dream of automobile imagination." If someone was willing to snatch a story that rightly belonged in 1925 and plunk it down in 1908, a good paper was bound to be intrigued.

One hundred and four years before 1907, Thomas Jefferson underwrote the Lewis and Clark expedition. Fifty-three years after, John F.

Kennedy launched the initiative to put a man on the moon. In 1907, though, the U.S. government was very much out of the business of paying for exploration. That didn't stop a whole generation of people determined to stretch the limits of the world as they knew it, flying a balloon higher than anyone ever had before, swimming a longer distance in rougher waters, or finding the source of a South American river not even named on the maps. The newspapers were full of such scientific and sporting adventures in the first ten years of the new century: strictly amateur but entirely serious. And those newspaper accounts were integral to the spirit of the explorers—they didn't get any money, and didn't really want any. What was important was personally and individually expanding the realm of the possible. The role of the newspapers lay in convincing them that success wouldn't be for naught.

The fact that the first decade of the twentieth century was an era of individual records and accomplishments played right into the appeal of the automobile. The man who drove a car across Florida for the first time received national attention in November 1907, while those who pioneered local routes all over the country were guaranteed space in the hometown papers. Everyone who ever forged a new route in a car—and in 1907, that included practically every living driver—would be going along in spirit on the New York-to-Paris Race.

The question for the first few months was whether anyone would go on it in the flesh. There was the expense, figured to be something like $50,000 per car, along with the bother of working out fifty thousand details, all along the way. For car companies, there was the risk that a bad showing would actually hurt sales in such a well-publicized affair. And for the drivers, there were concerns about things not usually related to car-racing, things such as frostbite and starvation, wild animals and violent natives. And there was that chance that the ice would break in the Bering Strait. Even Auguste Pons had to think twice about that.

Chapter Three

Heroes Wanted

All of Italy turned to Prince Borghese, expecting him to enter the New York-to-Paris Race, to win it as he had Peking-Paris, and to bring home the crowning honor for his nation. However, presuming to expect anything of Prince Borghese was fraught with risk. The Italian government had learned that several years before when, without warning, he quit his post as a diplomat in order to become an outdoorsman. His wife, Princess Borghese, had learned it too, when she was abandoned to raise their daughters alone while he roamed around the world. As to long-distance racing, the prince had apparently had enough of falling through bridges for one lifetime. He flatly refused to enter the New York-to-Paris event.

Other entrants came and went during December, in both European and American automobile circles. "This latest race has surely set motorists to thinking as never before," said a ranking member of the Automobile Club of America. "It is so bold that we have to stop and think what it means." Not everyone stopped—all that the race meant to some people in the auto business was free publicity. A simple announcement from a car company, at the cost of a telegram to the *New York Times* or *Le Matin,* was rewarded with full coverage and the chance for the sales manager to expound at length on the merits of his product. After that, he could get back to his desk and forget all about the New York-to-Paris Race. The papers knew that they were striking a deal with the devil by publicizing any willing comer, but it was worth it to them, if such articles fired public interest.

Meanwhile, many automobilists—and explorers—did stop and think carefully about the race. One of the more intriguing problems revolved around the availability of gasoline. Even in cities burgeoning with automobiles, obtaining fuel was a matter of good planning. Service stations were rare, and drivers were used to buying gasoline in tin buckets at hardware stores. In the frontier regions of Wyoming, Utah, Nevada, and Alaska, let alone Siberia, there was no gas at all to be had. Only one company had the means to change the situation: Standard Oil, the global oil company based in New York City.

"Everyone knows that it is a monster society," *Le Matin* wrote of Standard Oil. "It is incarnated in the personality of the gold king, John D. Rockefeller." As of 1907, Rockefeller had been retired for more than ten years, but that didn't trouble *Le Matin,* which was typical in its vitriolic hatred of the oil company he created. Nonetheless, a monster society had its uses, in the race as well as in the overall development of a new automobile age. Within a week of the announcement of the race, Standard Oil agreed to help out by making gasoline available over all of the American territory and several of the foreign countries on the twenty-two-thousand-mile route. *Le Matin* promised to make arrangements for the fuel supply in Russia. In wilderness areas, the fuel would be shipped in barrels, which would await the autos at train stations. Standard Oil chemists also set immediately to work creating motor oils that would withstand the temperature extremes that the racers would encounter along the way. If the air was cold enough, conventional oil would freeze stiff.

"Why, in some parts of Alaska," explained Jefferson M. Levy, a former congressman from New York State with investments in Alaska, "a gun cannot be fired in extreme cold weather unless every particle of grease has been either wiped clean out or boiled out with hot water . . . for the grease would jam the different parts of the gun to such an extent that it could not be used. What show would an automobile in the arctic region have under such conditions? None at all." Standard Oil's chemists were working diligently to overcome that very problem.

Congressman Levy, a bachelor, happened to have the finest address in America, when he wasn't wandering around Alaska or boiling guns there. He lived in Thomas Jefferson's former home, Monticello, in Virginia. As a young man, he inherited the property from his uncle, a navy officer who had purchased it as a favor to the impecunious heirs of the Jefferson estate.

"Man can overcome nature to a certain point," Levy maintained. "Beyond that he is helpless. The difficulties of the proposed race are so great that I doubt if human beings can surmount them."

Most people were inclined to agree. Urbanites who couldn't drive their own cars on any but the fairest of days in the summer could barely fathom driving a car through the bitter temperatures and drifting snow of a true arctic climate. For that reason, most of the speculation regarding the race concerned Alaska and Siberia.

To most people outside of Russia, Siberia was just a word, a cliché meaning "cold" and "lonely." An Ohioan named George Kennan was one of the first outsiders to make it his business to know the place firsthand. "You can take the whole of the United States of America," Kennan wrote in 1891, "from Maine to California and from Lake Superior to the Gulf of Mexico, and set it down in the middle of Siberia without touching anywhere the boundaries of the latter's territory; you can then take Alaska and all the countries of Europe with the exception of Russia, and fit them into the remaining margin like the pieces of a dissected map. After having thus accommodated all of the United States, including Alaska, and the whole of Europe, except Russia, you will still have more than 300,000 [square] miles of Siberian territory to spare."

Another ranking expert on Siberia was an Englishman named Harry de Windt. In 1896, under the sponsorship of a London magazine called the *Pall Mall Gazette,* he had undertaken to travel from Paris to New York without the benefit of a boat. He didn't use an automobile, of course, but instead hitched rides on conveyances ranging from donkey-carts to horse-drawn sleighs to dogsleds to trains. The first person ever to attempt such a journey, he didn't have any choice in his mode of travel out in the hinterland; he was just lucky not to have to walk. De Windt's journey was sometimes compared to that of Phineas Fogg, the fictional adventurer in Jules Verne's *Around the World in Eighty Days* (1873), but Fogg did indeed travel on boats. He also clung to the balmier climates, looping through southern Asia and India. Harry de Windt wanted to use the northern route. After he completed the expedition across Siberia, though, his trip was cut short when he broke through the ice at the Bering Strait. He almost drowned before a whaling ship made a daring rescue.

In 1902, de Windt tried again to travel from Paris to New York—the long way. He made his second trip under the sponsorship of the *London Daily Express* newspaper, leaving his record in a book that discouraged any sane person from going to northern Siberia, even if it might seem absolutely necessary. Describing a Tchuktchi village along the Arctic Sea in northeast Siberia (an outpost through which the racers would have to pass), he wrote:

> Two or three woebegone creatures, in ragged deerskins, crawled out of the huts and surveyed us with such suspicion and distrust that I verily believe they took us for visitors from the spirit world. As a rule the Tchuktchi costume is becoming, but these people wore shapeless rags, matted with dirt, and their appearance suggested years of inactivity and bodily neglect. I noticed, however, with satisfaction that their churlish greeting was not unmingled with fear, although they obstinately refused the food and shelter begged for (by means of signs), pointing at the same time, to a black banner flapping mournfully over the nearest hut. This I knew to be the Tchuktchi emblem of death. Our sulky hosts then indicated a dark object some distance away upon the snow, which I sent Stepan [a horseman] to investigate, and he quickly returned, having found the corpses of several men and women in an advanced stage of decomposition.

De Windt would have starved among the Tchuktchis if he hadn't finally managed to trade some vodka for food, but then, he was often on the verge of starvation in Siberia, even when staying at a post house along the road, in one of those parts of Siberia that had roads. Post houses, intended as rest stops for travelers, were "dens of filth and squalor," in de Windt's recollection: "Vermin was everywhere; night and day it crawled gaily over the walls and ceiling, about our bodies, and into our very food." He hated the fact that most of the food offered to visitors was putrid; that even in the good season, bad weather erased the roads with ease; that there was an average of one murder per day in Irkutsk, a town of eighty thousand otherwise regarded as "the Paris of Siberia"; and that practically every haggard village was equipped with a jailhouse for the political prisoners who were constantly being moved around Siberia.

Most of all, de Windt deplored the monotony that was part of any journey in Siberia, especially one that dared to cover the whole length of the place. After days upon days of watching the same scenery glide past the sleigh, he couldn't tell whether he was awake or asleep. Siberia demanded a preternatural quality of patience: "Patience," de Windt said, "without which commodity no traveler should ever dream of visiting Asiatic Russia. He is otherwise apt to become a raving lunatic." Yet it was the impatient who were drawn to conquer Siberia.

"I'll go the instant the word is given to get ready," said twenty-five-year-old race driver Montague Roberts in early December, when he was asked whether he would be willing to take on the New York-to-Paris challenge. He needn't have been in a hurry. If Siberia demanded patience all the time, so did New York City in December 1907. No American companies had firm plans to enter the race and so, for the time being, none of them needed drivers.

Roberts was young for a race driver—too young according to some people, including the organizers of the premier closed-road race in the United States, the Vanderbilt Cup, run annually on Long Island. Even after Roberts qualified in the elimination trials for the 1905 running, the officials banned him, solely because of his age. Two years later, at twenty-five, Monty Roberts had become a fast-rising star. Tall and trim, he carried himself with the careless grace of an athlete, which was unusual among racers of the day. They were more often stiff and even limping, either from injuries or the lingering exhaustion of battling with heavy controls on broncolike cars. Roberts's physique was no accident, though. He actually trained for races—which was a first, at least in American racing. Cloistered out on a farm, he had two sessions a day with a trainer, running, throwing a medicine ball around, punching a bag, and taking rubdowns in between.

"Has automobiling come to the point of training as one would for a boxing match or a football game?" grumbled a veteran driver when word of Roberts's regimen leaked out. "Well, that's the latest. I suppose we'll be having swimming pools next and be put to bed at 9 o'clock at night, as college football teams are."

If a swimming pool would have helped Roberts, Harry S. Houpt would have had one delivered to the farm. Houpt, the agent for Thomas cars in New York City, was Roberts's mentor, as well as his boss.

Monty Roberts had been born in Pittsburgh, but he was raised in Jersey City, New Jersey. After high school, he served as a mechanic in the army's Ordnance Department, and in 1900, he built the first gas-powered artillery truck ever used by the army. He also won medals for marksmanship. After two years, Roberts left the army and took a job delivering cars built by the United States Long Distance Car Company of Elizabethport, New Jersey. In those days, a company representative, called a demonstrator, would drive a new car to a customer's home, and then remain for up to a month, giving the owner (or the chauffeur) a course in how to use it. On one occasion, Roberts was assigned to deliver a car to a judge in Deal, a town on the Jersey shore, about one hundred miles away by the best routes available in those days. A hundred miles, though, was a long distance to drive in 1902, even in a Long Distance car. Roberts later recalled that it took him a week to make the trip. In his spare time, away from the job, he went racing, scoring a record-breaking success in his debut at Newark's Waverly Track in 1904. More wins followed.

Because Harry Houpt managed one of the most active race teams in the country, and certainly in greater New York City, he heard early on about the young man from Jersey who was ripping up the area tracks. Roberts accepted a job with Houpt's agency and delivered Thomas cars between race assignments, taking them to celebrities including the Broadway stars Elsie Janis and Fred Stone. Roberts was not only an expert driver and mechanic, but a thoroughly presentable young man When a Hudson River landowner named James Roosevelt traded in an old, belt-driven Benz on a Thomas, Roberts received the assignment to take the new car to him at his estate in Hyde Park, New York. While he was there he gave driving lessons to Roosevelt's son, Franklin, the future president. He later characterized FDR at twenty-two as a good pupil, very "flexible . . . a real fellow." But at the time, Roberts was more impressed with the Roosevelts' estate, overlooking the Hudson.

"In 1906, I continued my racing career at Empire City track, Brighton Beach and on the Point Breeze track, Philadelphia," Roberts wrote in a roundup of his young career a few years later. "On the latter track I succeeded in lowering Barney Oldfield's record for that track." The new mark may have interested Roberts, not to mention Oldfield, but the feat that set all the fans talking took place in Brighton Beach late in 1907. Houpt had entered a six-cylinder Thomas in a twenty-four-hour race there, assigning Roberts and another man to drive it. In a twenty-four-hour race, the car ran continuously, with two alternating drivers; the vehicle that notched the most laps won. As of race time in Brighton Beach, though, the other man had yet to show up. Roberts started anyway. As the hours dragged by, his substitute still failed to appear. Roberts drove the entire race by himself, taking first place, setting a record, and gaining a legion of fans.

Harry S. Houpt counted himself chief among them. He gave Roberts the six-cylinder Thomas car used in the Brighton Beach heroics, a gift worth about six times the salary of an average automobile demonstrator. He also promised him a shot at the French Grand Prix in the spring of 1908.

Like a boxing manager, Harry Houpt had carefully groomed Roberts for the big time, and along the way, the easygoing young man grew to be a local favorite. Friendly in appearance, with wideset eyes and a wide mouth to boot, Roberts turned out to be a natural salesman for the automobile in general, and for racing in particular, flashing a confident smile that was marked but not marred by a single brown tooth in the front corner. Funny and frank, Roberts appeared to race fans to be the all-American boy—and just the man to take on the world in the New York-to-Paris Race. The fans, however, would not pay the tab for such an undertaking and as of December, neither would E. R. Thomas, head of the Thomas factory in Buffalo.

By the beginning of January, the Marquis de Dion had already committed himself to sponsoring an entry, and his engineers were at work preparing a thirty-horsepower De Dion touring car for the twenty-two-thousand-mile trip, installing extra gas tanks, equipping it with an array of tools and even stuffing wood into the frame to combat brittleness in frigid temperatures. Bourcier St. Chaffray, plying his trade, had not only convinced the marquis that the De Dion would sweep to victory, he had talked himself into a place on the team. He even prevailed in nominating himself as captain of the team. At the same time, St. Chaffray also wanted to be considered captain of the whole race. To that end, he made himself useful at the offices of *Le Matin,* overseeing the planning of the route.

Charles Godard had been just as busy. On returning from the Peking race in the summer of 1907, he had been clapped into jail, but only temporarily, until he found someone new from whom to borrow money— money with which to settle the debts he'd left behind in China. Being one of the heroes of an international race had lifted his reputation immeasurably, and so Godard not only made restitution on his old debts, he even found people who were willing to invest in him and his ideas about cars. With the change of fortune, he organized an automobile company called Moto-Bloc. One of the investors was said to be Charles Schwab, the Pittsburgh steel magnate whose former chauffeur was also a partner in Moto-Bloc. Godard and his associates began manufacturing quite a good car, in small numbers, in their Paris factory. Predictably, Godard envisioned much greater things for the company after one of its cars won the New York-to-Paris Race, but in order to win, he had to enter, and to do that, he had to make use of company funds, as well as one vehicle. After the Moto-Bloc won the race, though, everything would be paid back many times over, so everything would be all right.

For a few weeks, the only serious entries in the New York-to-Paris Race were the two French cars. Bourcier St. Chaffray and Charles Godard even traveled in a convoy with their respective entourages to a glacier in the Alps, where they tested the De Dion and the Moto-Bloc in ice and deep snow. They also worked on techniques for shoveling the cars out of drifts.

While St. Chaffray and Godard were away in the Alps, another car was entered in the race. It too was French. And it was set to carry yet another veteran of Peking-Paris—eight days' worth of it, anyway. Auguste Pons signed on to drive a tiny Sizaire-Naudin two-seater in the New York-to-Paris Race. He had at least graduated to a four-wheeler, but he was still philosophically insisting that it was the light vehicle that was best suited to heavy going. To anyone who would listen, he explained that the smaller the car, the less the strain on both it and those occupants who would occasionally find themselves pushing it. Pons may have had no choice but to defend the kind of cars he was able to get, but in the case of the Sizaire-Naudin, he genuinely seemed to believe that he was right and all the others were wrong.

The Sizaire weighed thirty-three hundred pounds and had a one-cylinder engine capable of generating fifteen horsepower. By way of contrast, the De Dion weighed sixty-six hundred pounds and had a four-cylinder, thirty-horsepower engine. In terms of a power-to-weight ratio, they were evenly matched, yet they were very different cars. In most road races, such as the Vanderbilt Cup, such disparate entries were sorted into divisions, in part for safety reasons and in part because the different cars reflected very different styles of racing, the lightweights scooting around turns like beads in a tube and the big cars showing their best stuff by gathering a head of steam on the straightaways. The New York-to-Paris Race, however, was open to any type of car. For all of the talk, no one could say for certain which one would have the advantage on the toughest course in the world.

With the new year, the race finally had a firm starting date. The planners had discerned that, in general terms, the racers had to leave New York in mid-February to reach the Bering Strait in spring, when it might still be frozen, and cross Siberia in summer, when it might not be. The *New York Times* suggested February 12, Lincoln's Birthday, which fell on a Wednesday in 1908. Once the starting date was set, there didn't seem to be much time to spare. To reach New York on schedule, the European teams would have to be onboard transatlantic liners by February 4, little more than a month away.

As 1908 began, though, there was no way to argue with that government official in Paris who claimed that the New York-to-Paris Race would serve to show the absolute supremacy of the French automobile. Since the only three entries were French, he was bound to be right. Just six years before World War I turned nationalism into a word worth dying for, companies—and race fans—in the other automaking countries had to decide whether to let France win the most heroic of car races before even a single engine was cranked. They had the month of January left to do so, and to prepare for a twenty-two-thousand-mile journey across three continents. Montague Roberts, anyway, was ready.

Chapter Four

Race to the Starting Line

From the French point of view, no advantage could be too flagrant. Provoked by the daily proddings of *Le Matin* and the sting of France having been an also-ran in the Peking-Paris race, Bourcier St. Chaffray, Charles Godard, and Auguste Pons each made a full-time job of preparing for the start. One of the crucial chores during January was engaging teammates. Prince Borghese may have brought a mere writer on the trip from Peking, but Godard had a much more modern idea for 1908: movies. His Moto-Bloc team would include a cameraman, R. Maurice Livier. St. Chaffray wouldn't be so generous with his spaces. He had the dream, the moxie, the push, the guts—and all of the other intangible elements of ambition that do nothing to get a car out of a mudhole. What he needed was someone with practical abilities.

Hans Hendrik Hansen was the man. He could drive well, and moreover, he had been educated as an engineer. Norwegian by birth, he was married to a Russian woman, and they actually made their home in Siberia: he knew the region firsthand. That was not all. Hansen was fluent in every major language to be encountered between New York and Paris: English, Russian, Chinese, German, French. He also spoke a couple of Siberian dialects. And he knew Spanish, just in case.

Dedicated to adventure, Hansen had engineered railroads in South America; he had explored for oil in Siberia; he'd spent five years in New Mexico; and he'd served as a commissioner of the Columbian Exposition World's Fair in Chicago in 1893. He arrived there in a Viking ship that he had sailed from Norway, across the ocean and through the Great Lakes. In between his other pursuits, he made a minor specialty of searching for people who were lost while trying to reach the North Pole. In his most famous case, the Russian government hired him in an urgent attempt to find and rescue Salomon Andree, an intrepid professor who had tried to float to the North Pole in a balloon in 1897. Unfortunately, the effort to locate him failed. (A Norwegian fisherman would come across Andree's remains on an outlying island in 1930.)

Hans Hansen stood out in a crowd, in part because he usually wore a dark blue military uniform and an officer's cap. The uniform and the title he used, "Captain Hansen," were souvenirs of his part in putting down a revolution in Argentina. Hansen had fought on the side of the Argentine navy. He cut a fine figure in his uniform, being on the tall side and angular in build. There was a very bright, intelligent cast to his face, with a stroke of fun that was indicated by the opulent reddish moustache he wore. The general impression was that he had a comfortable personal fortune, derived from his mining interests in Siberia. "He is a remarkably well informed and educated man," beamed a reporter for the *New York Times* who met Hansen in Paris just before the New York-to-Paris Race.

If Hans Hansen took care to present an appealing persona, he also took care not to waste the benefits. The captain was a deft man with the ladies. Anyway, his wife was far away in Siberia, if distance would unbind fidelity. Even when the cars passed through Siberia, she was likely to be far away, that place was so big. And so the New York-to-Paris Race held out a rare opportunity for Captain Hansen. Lionized at every turn, he would make his way west, mile by mile during the day and parlor by parlor at night.

"Mr. Hansen is 42 years of age," observed a reporter, "and long past the period where the exuberance of youth leads to all sorts of extravagance." Whether or not that was quite accurate, the Marquis de Dion formally hired him to serve on the team with Bourcier St. Chaffray. The third member of the team was a mechanic/driver named Autran. In all of the many published accounts of the race, Autran never once listed a first name. He was simply "Monsieur Autran," a dashing-looking, dark-haired man of twenty-five, taller than St. Chaffray and huskier than Hansen. (Though he seemed not to want the world to know it, his first name was Alphonse.)

In Italy, the early attention surrounding the race was focused on organizing a team for an Itala car, perhaps even the same vehicle that had finished first in Peking-Paris. However, it was another company, Brixia-Züst, that finally put the country in the race, with the help of a newspaper called the Milan *Mattino*, which promised to sponsor the entry.

Züst, as it was commonly known, was an established firm, turning out hefty, respectable cars along the lines of Buick in the American market. That American market was of keen interest to Züst in 1908, since the company had established a fairly ambitious U.S. sales organization the year before, headquartered in New York and managed by an aggressive American businessman named Arthur Ruland. Calculating that the New York-to-Paris Race was just the medium by which to introduce Züst cars to the broader market, Ruland pushed hard for the factory to sponsor a car. The home office was certainly interested. To match the panache of the Itala effort the year before in the Peking race, Züst tried to engage one sporting compte or marquis after another, but apparently none had Prince Borghese's appetite for hardship and so the Züst effort seemed to be beached in early January, with just one recruit.

Antonio Scarfoglio, of Milan, was twenty-one years old, a poet, and imbued to the point of overflowing with the "exuberance of youth that leads to all sorts of extravagance." He was also the son of the man who owned the Milan *Mattino*.

Alberto Pirelli, in the Italian plan as the supplier of tires for the Züst entry, was well acquainted with young Scarfoglio. "He is a courageous gentleman," Pirelli observed, "but not an experienced automobilist." Nonetheless, when Antonio decided that the New York-to-Paris Race was a story that he had to tell, he convinced his father that he should act as the paper's correspondent on the car. He also contracted to send dispatches en route to the *London Daily Mail*. With that, and his father's influence, Scarfoglio secured a place on the team—if there was a team. Every time a Züst car seemed absolutely certain to be entered, the company dithered a little bit longer in choosing drivers. And so the general picture of the Züst in mid-January was rather peculiar. No one was in the front driver's seat. No one was in the front passenger's seat, where the mechanic would sit. However, all packed and ready in the backseat was Antonio Scarfoglio, an elegant if callow young man with thick black hair, smooth skin, and the look of wide-eyed skepticism that is the special province of a young poet.

In Germany, the outlook for an entry was even more bleak in early January. The emperor sat in the palace, as frustrated as any race fan in the empire. In 1907, Kaiser Wilhelm's nation had failed to mount an entry for Peking-Paris, and in 1908, it seemed doomed to sit out the even more important New York-to-Paris Race.

Great Britain, the other European automaking country to have missed the Peking race, didn't appear likely to have a car in the New York race, but no one in the kingdom seemed to care. The British had their own long-distance races, grueling tests on the Isle of Man or in the wilds of Ireland, and anyway, they had yet in their long and storied history to feel the need to rush from anywhere to France. Perhaps if the event had been the New York-to-London Race, feelings wouldn't have been mixed. A British Rolls-Royce Silver Ghost would have been an interesting entry, though, with its claim that the engine only needed service every 18,750 miles. Unfortunately, that was not to be.

Kaiser Wilhelm, however, was never one to remain oblivious to nationalistic challenges. He was headstrong to say the least. And he had a sincere love for automobiles, with garages full of them. Yet even when word spread through the realm that His Highness was interested in seeing Germany enter the New York-to-Paris Race, car companies shuffled backward with excuses. Only the army seemed to heed the call.

The less interest that other Germans exhibited in the race, the more determined Oberlieutenant Hans Koeppen became to enter it himself. He believed that the round-the-world race was a wholly appropriate activity for an officer. It takes a battle of some sort to push young officers upward. After fourteen years of serving the army during peace, thirty-one-year-old Lieutenant Koeppen regarded the New York-to-Paris Race as an opportunity to brevet himself up to a captaincy, if only of a three-man outfit sitting in a racecar. First, though, there was the matter of the car.

Inquiries to major automakers in Berlin and Mannheim elicited nothing. Finally, Koeppen made an appointment to see the director of the Imperial Automobile Club, Herr de la Croix, who listened politely— and very patiently, considering that he already understood the problem. For months, he had withstood boasting from men who liked to hear themselves say that they wanted to enter the New York-to-Paris Race. Lieutenant Koeppen, in his blue uniform, managed in the course of their conversation to separate himself from the rest. He was quietly intent, willing to admit all that he didn't know, but unyielding on the subject of his own fitness to undertake the dangerous journey. Herr de la Croix began to take Koeppen seriously. He knew of two other young men who were as intent on putting themselves in a German entry: one was Hans Knape and the other was Ernst Maas. The director of the auto club told Koeppen about them and then suggested a car company called Protos, which might just be as desperate as he was, in a different way.

Protos was a newly organized firm, located in Berlin, turning out sturdy cars and in critical need of publicity to boost it into a league with its well-established competitors. Koeppen met with the head of Protos, who readily agreed to enter a car, just as de la Croix had predicted. But he would do nothing else. The company wouldn't pay for the trip or contribute any of the supplies, except for spare parts that it manufactured itself.

Koeppen rushed out of the Protos offices, finally certain that he would be in the race. However, he still only had one part of any entry. In 1908, just as today, the car itself was one-half of a racer; the money to keep it and a team going was the other, and it was just as important as any other kind of fuel. The next morning, he made an appointment to see Rudolf Ullstein, publisher of one of Berlin's newer afternoon papers, *Zeitung am Mittag*. "As soon as I stepped into his office and explained that I came to him about an especially interesting sports-related matter," Koeppen later wrote of Herr Ullstein, "he looked at me wide-eyed and said: 'When you rang early this morning, I racked my brain for quite a while, trying to figure out what you would want from me. Now, as you stand before me, I know it: You want to drive New York-to-Paris!' "

Koeppen didn't deny it. And Ullstein didn't deny that he thought the trip was impossible. Still, he was intrigued. "Many more difficult problems have been solved," he allowed, "whose solution no one believed possible, and which were still solved, because of the strong will to see it through and the unshakable belief in the value of success." He talked a little bit about the airship invented against all odds by Germany's Count Ferdinand von Zeppelin in 1900. Still, Ullstein worried about the trip through Siberia. Koeppen had his answer for that, as curt as a good headline and just as dramatic.

"Either I make it through," he said, "or I'll never be seen again." Ullstein seemed ready to make a commitment to sponsor the team, and then suddenly he demurred. Growing cold, he said that he'd have to speak with his brother. Koeppen presumed that all was lost, but the next day he received an invitation to attend another meeting at the newspaper. Ernst Maas and Hans Knape were also there. Herr Ullstein explained that the newspaper would foot some of the expenses, if Lieutenant Koeppen filed stories about the race for the *Zeitung am Mittag*. However, he said, if the three men really wanted to go, they would have to meet the balance of the expenses, a cost of at least 6,000 marks each (equivalent to about $50,000 in today's currency). The Ullsteins specifically wanted them to use their own money. None of the other participants in the New York-to-Paris Race had to pay their own way, but for the three Germans, it was that or nothing at all. They probably should have balked, complained, and kicked up a fuss, but there wasn't time. They leapt at the chance. "The conference," Koeppen wrote, "came to a fortunate conclusion."

Ernst Maas immediately drove to Paris in an attempt to meet with Bourcier St. Chaffray, newly anointed as the "Commissionaire General" of the New York-to-Paris Race.

Commissionaire General St. Chaffray was working in an office at *Le Matin*, struggling under a mountain of maps and reports, with more arriving daily, trying to settle on a firm route for the race. At the same time, he was struggling to frame a set of rules. Maas didn't learn as much from St. Chaffray as he would have liked, but his appearance in Paris did confirm that a new car, and a new country, had been added to the competition. Meanwhile, Hans Koeppen was still in Berlin and in a hurry.

"On January 10th," Koeppen wrote, "we found out the boat that would be transporting us from Hamburg to America would be leaving on the 29th at the latest, so we would have to leave Berlin by the 26th at the latest and have everything taken care of before then." Gasoline and oil deliveries had to be investigated and ordered, where possible; clothing and tools had to be purchased; maps had to be located; letters of credit had to be arranged; passports and visas had to be in order. Those were major concerns, but there were a few others. Lieutenant Koeppen, for example, had yet to secure a leave of absence from the army. Normally, that required a month. There were only sixteen days left.

And of course the car had to be built. The Protos company wasn't yet big enough to have stock on hand; all of its cars were built to order. Without any unexpected problems, it would take five or six weeks to build a car as large as a Protos, including time spent waiting for component parts, making sure they fit, and returning them for adjustment. Koeppen begged the head of the company to double the pace, or triple it if he could. Joining in the race to get a Protos to the race were the employees of the company and the dozens of factories that supplied it with components. In all, six hundred men entered into the effort to build the best possible Protos in the smallest feasible amount of time. At the center of the beehive was Hans Knape.

Knape, a crisp Berliner, was assigned to do most of the driving in the race. In appearance, he looked something like Koeppen and could have passed for his rather impatient older brother. In fact, he was three years younger than the lieutenant. Knape had also started out in the infantry of the Prussian army, although he later transferred to the engineering corps, where he was first officer. In that capacity, he was an expert in road- and bridge-building, arts that observers wryly predicted would be more valuable than driving in the New York-to-Paris Race. As an amateur, Knape had driven in several long-distance car races, but really made his mark as a pioneer in motorboat racing, twice winning Germany's top prize in that field, the Komer Cup. Lieutenant Koeppen may have been the motivating force behind the Protos team, but Knape was its celebrity. And Koeppen was expected to remember that fact. He had never been on a long-distance car trip, after all, and he didn't even know how to drive.

One would have thought that the race would only appeal to men with gasoline in their veins, but quite the opposite was true. It meant the most to some of those who had never taken a long automobile trip before. Duty-bound, adventurous, vain, or all three at once, they craved the chance to pit themselves against every obstruction, including their own ignorance. "The men who are entered in this race," said Alberto Pirelli, "are men of the stripe who declare the greater the difficulty the better they like the prospect, since there is the greatest honor in achieving that which many declared to be impossible."

As of Thursday, January 23, however, Lieutenant Koeppen didn't seem to be going anywhere. He still didn't have permission to leave his post in the army. With or without him, the Protos was scheduled to leave from a spot in front of the Berlin offices of *Zeitung am Mittag* at 8 A.M. on Sunday, January 26. By Thursday evening, not even Koeppen was as frantic as his superior officers in the Fifteenth Infantry. They didn't want to deny him the right to leave, though they would have to do just that or arrest him if he tried.

But then, if he tried to leave, he would have had to take a streetcar. The Protos wasn't ready, and every time he stopped at the factory, in the midst of his other darting errands, it looked even less like an automobile. Sometimes, he couldn't tell if the workmen were building it or taking it apart. By turns, they were doing both, as they fit components to the chassis, found problems, and removed parts for further examination.

On Friday afternoon, Koeppen was at the General Staff offices, awaiting the last delivery of army mail. It finally arrived, but with no leave of absence. There was nothing left for Koeppen to do. Action was taken, though, by his commanding officers—and the ones above them and the ones above them. Late in the day, a messenger arrived at General Staff, carrying a message from the Kaiser. Inside was a leave of absence personally signed by Wilhelm II, granting Koeppen six months away, but no more. The Kaiser felt that even apart from the excitement of the race, the competition might allow Germany and the United States to become better acquainted and more friendly.

Koeppen rushed out of General Staff headquarters, only to find that while he may have been ready to go, the car wasn't. The workmen were still wrestling with it as of Saturday, the day on which it had to be finished. To leave late was to risk missing the ship and to miss the ship meant there would be no Protos at the start in New York. Koeppen stood in the shop for a while, watching the process and trying to discern some progress. When the sun went down, he went home.

Of course, deadlines are always subject to interpretation. And even the meaning of a word as simple as "Saturday" has its nuances. Activity at the factory didn't pause until 2 A.M. Saturday night, or Sunday morning, technically, when the car was finally set: packed and prepped and ready to race. For the next five hours, it sat in the dim light of the Protos factory, and all was quiet and still around it.

Chapter Five

To Defend America
Against the World

Early on Sunday morning, Knape and Koeppen climbed into the front seats of the Protos as true racers, and the unmuffled roar of the engine was theirs for the first time. The third teammate, Ernst Maas, had arranged to meet them in New York, after sailing from France with the other entrants. In the chill of the morning, as the car eased out of the factory, Knape and Koeppen were finally moving forward, at home in the car. They didn't know quite what would face them next, and wouldn't for months on the road toward Paris.

"At eight o'clock in the morning, the 26th of January, a Sunday, everything was in order," Koeppen wrote. "It was done! The day was cold and windy and the road was filled by the press, members of the Imperial Automobile Club and people who got up early that morning to wish us well on our trip."

For its part, the Protos looked for all the world like an army truck—although no army was yet using trucks in 1908. It was long and gray, with a custom-made canopy top for the back. For the departure, the car was festooned with German, American, and French flags, but they did little to cheer it up. It still looked like an army truck. The well-dressed ladies who turned out to cheer it on didn't seem to care, and neither did the race fans, the children held up for a look at history, and the patriots who lined the streets surrounding the newspaper office. Koeppen was astounded by their sheer numbers—the first surprise of the trip. The size of the crowd made him feel as though he had already won the race. As the Protos pulled up to the newspaper building, he saw his fellow officers from the Fifteenth Infantry lined up in their blue-and-gold dress uniforms. A choir, the Maennerchor Society, was also waiting there, having begged the chance to sing a farewell to the Protos team.

Knape stopped the Protos in front of the *Mittag* office building. Other automobiles, including one containing the brothers Ullstein, lined up behind it, ready to escort the two racing men out of town. Knape made no secret of the fact that he was in a hurry to keep going.

Oblivious to the celebration—and to the way that Koeppen was reveling in it—he was only looking around for the signal to start. The members of the Maennerchor Society, sensing that they were about to lose their chance, suddenly burst forth with "Soldier's Farewell." At the first strains, the crowd quieted down and the drivers in the retinue stopped gunning their engines. Even Knape listened.

"The most beautiful song," Koeppen wrote. "These people weren't hired or anything, making the presentation that much more touching." According to a reporter on the scene, there wasn't a dry eye within blocks of the Protos. With that, the cars started to roll forward, meeting more crowds along the way. In a village about forty miles west of Berlin, though, the convoy slowed to a halt. The escort cars were due to return to Berlin. "I said good-bye to my parents and relatives," Lieutenant Koeppen recalled. "It was indeed not an entirely easy moment."

My seventy-nine-year-old father didn't make it difficult at all. "Boy, be good," he said curtly, "you'll carry it out. If I were a little younger, definitely, I would gladly take part myself."

But my mother! I'm her only child. She didn't want to hide her most lively concern from me, even up to the last moment.

A resolute man should not be influenced by the soft-heartedness of a mother's tears. Consequently, I had to think in this moment of the words that a high officer and sportsman who was a former teacher of mine at the War Academy said: "A modern man is born to face obstacles. Whether he perishes in the process or reaches his goal, is simply a matter of fate, because if one sees only danger ahead, he'll never have the energy to conquer something that is difficult and bring it to a good end."

I saw the pain in my mother, the silvery-white of my father's hair—would I see them again? The next second, my teammate dashed away.

That same day, Antonio Scarfoglio had his own rather pale leavetaking in Milan, as the Züst team boarded a train for Paris, the gathering point for the cars leaving from Le Havre. "A hurried good-bye through the carriage window," he wrote, "the train is off; and we are definitely launched on our prodigious adventure. There are three of us in the compartment, Haaga, Sirtori and myself, as yet unknown to each other. Until this moment we have not had time to think. We have lived in a state of exhilaration which seemed to paralyse our mental faculties. For the last fortnight, occupied with all the minute but indispensable details of the preparations, we have lived in a sort of trance."

Amid the frenzied excitement in Milan, the three new teammates had only barely been introduced to one another. Emilio Sirtori, a beefy professional car driver of twenty-six, regularly worked for Züst but had been engaged for the New York-to-Paris Race with only about a week to spare. Henry Haaga, a German-born mechanic, just twenty-two, was hired even later. And so the three were alone together for the first time as they settled into their seats in the train compartment. The conversation probably didn't advance their camaraderie much; Henry Haaga couldn't speak Italian. Antonio Scarfoglio wasn't concerned with any such minor issues, though.

"Shall we ever return?" he was thinking. "Whither are we going? The mind forms a picture of a wide, easy road, a happy journey across America; then—farewell to everything, silence for months and months." He went on with his daydreams, entirely wrong in most of his conceptions, until he was thoroughly depressed and pessimistic. He wasn't alone. Near the Italian border with France, Emilio Sirtori perked up just enough to ask, "Do you think we shall pull through . . . and get back?"

Scarfoglio shrugged. Haaga, slight and even delicate in appearance, was slumped in his seat as though he were already exhausted by the race. The three teammates rode along in silence, far more interested in their own thoughts than in each other. Fixated on outsized images of the danger to come, they may not have been modern men according to Koeppen's old instructor, but nonetheless, they didn't stop. They meant to start.

A few days later, the farewell in Paris was as festive as that in Berlin. The Italians in the Züst lined up next to the De Dion and the Moto-Bloc in front of the offices of *Le Matin*. The little Sizaire-Naudin was on the end, looking like a punctuation mark next to the other three. After a hero's send-off, they traveled in a parade to the seaport of Le Havre. By the first of February, all of the European participants were on the ocean, making their way to New York City, the Germans having previously set sail from Hamburg on the *Kaiserin Augusta Victoria.*

Those who left from France sailed on the *Lorraine.* Antonio Scarfoglio was aboard, along with his teammates, Sirtori and Haaga. Bourcier St. Chaffray was traveling with Captain Hansen and Monsieur Autran. Charles Godard was there, with his chosen mechanic, Arthur Hue, and more important, his cameraman, Maurice Livier. And so was Auguste Pons, along with his teammates, Maurice Berthe and Lucien Deschamps. The only report to emerge from the ship divulged the fact that nearly all of the entrants were seasick and confined to their cabins. Only Captain Hansen, veteran of the Argentine navy, felt fine, holding forth at the captain's table on nearly any subject of interest.

While the Frenchmen and Italians, the Germans, and the stray Norwegian were making their way to New York during the first days of February, a certain panic was setting in among the Americans. The United States had no entry in the race. The three or four companies that had rushed in with heroic plans had backed out just as quickly and a lot more quietly. Every so often during January, Montague Roberts's name had been bandied about as the driver of a Thomas car to be entered in the race—only there was no Thomas in the race. Harry Houpt, as the New York agent for Thomas cars, had been campaigning without success for a factory entry. He couldn't sponsor it on his own. He could, however, offer up the driver, based on his contract with Roberts. Even that failed to ignite so much as a flicker of intent in Buffalo, where the Thomas factory was located.

The Thomas Motor Car Company was headed by the notably conservative, normally predictable Edwin Ross Thomas: "E. R." to friends and headline writers alike. E. R. had been born in 1850 and grew up in Kentucky, where his father owned a coal mine, but with the outbreak of the Civil War eleven years later, the family sold out of the Confederacy and moved north to Indiana. E. R. eventually made a small fortune as an executive in the bicycle business. Proving as nimble as his dad, he wriggled out just before that industry suddenly contracted in the late 1890s. Like other middle-aged refugees from the bicycle market, Thomas turned to automobiles, and with a capital investment from E. W. Statler, the hotel magnate based in Buffalo, he started his car company in 1902. The automobile industry counted two kinds of leaders in those days. There were car men, dizzy with pride in the go-devils they produced, and then there were businessmen, who were never dizzy about anything. E. R. was one of the latter.

Automaking in Buffalo was a world apart from the rapacious industry in Detroit. E. R. Thomas ran a factory that was innovative, but steady. Steadiness was a revered quality in Buffalo business circles. The industry was just as competitive for E. R. as for any of the young turks rushing to the fore in Detroit, but for the time being, Thomas was building up his business on basic principles—not on tempting risks.

E. R. couldn't decide which of those two categories the New York-to-Paris Race fell into. There had never been anything like it before: an undertaking that would surely reap national publicity for the Thomas car at the start, and also at the finish, assuming the car was in at the wire. But in between, there were only expenses projected to average five hundred dollars a day. Harry Houpt and his Chicago counterpart, Charles Coey, didn't look at the bottom line; they did their jobs as sales executives and argued that the race would ignite interest in Thomas cars as it rolled out across the country: New York City, Buffalo, Cleveland, Chicago, Omaha, Cheyenne, Ogden, San Francisco—prime markets, all. E. R. didn't doubt that but wondered how many sales would bubble up in Nome, Irkutsk, and Nizhni Novgorod. With no decision forthcoming from him, there was no car from Thomas, and with no car from Thomas, there was no entry at all from the United States.

Other burgeoning companies refused even a flirtation with the New York-to-Paris Race. Cadillac might logically have entered a car, but it didn't have much of a sporting sense, operating under the aegis of Henry Leland (a man who started his career building rifles during the Civil War). Packard had the money for the race but generally veered clear of mud in any form. A Thomas car was comparable in quality to either a Cadillac or a Packard, but with a rebellious streak neither of them had. For one thing, Thomas cars were at home in all kinds of races and were anything but ashamed of it. At a time when Cadillac and Packard were naming their models after horsepower ratings—the Packard "Thirty," for example—nomenclature that left nothing of interest to the imagination, the top-of-the-line Thomas was called the "Speedway Flyer," a name that came with its own rush of wind. Thomas cars sold quite well, but commercially they weren't in a league with Cadillac or Packard. While those two were each passing sales of five thousand per year, the Thomas Motor Car Company was striving to crack through one thousand. Some people thought the race would help the company break into the front of the sales pack, but as time wound down toward the start on the twelfth, the one person who counted most at the company still couldn't say for sure.

On February 7, Lieutenant Koeppen and Engineer Knape arrived in New York and spent most of their first day in America infuriated because the Protos had been dented by dockworkers. The next day, when the *Lorraine* docked with its cargo of racing men and cars, the waterfront became a carnival, crowded with too many fans, flags, and decorated escort cars—and too few customs agents. The ones who were on hand held up the party for most of the day while they decided whether or not the United States, which had imported all of 1,305 cars in 1907, should admit four more foreign autos on that February day in 1908.

Koeppen and Knape were on hand to meet their teammate, Ernst Maas, who plunked a suitcase down on the dock and flicked open the locks, allowing the case to burst open from the impatience of the "Eskimo suits" that he'd squashed inside. In the midst of the melee, word came through the customs office that there was a telephone call for the foreign entrants in the race. Someone answered the phone and found Jefferson DeMont Thompson, president of the Broadway Association, on the other end. He had wanted to be on hand to greet the intrepid sportsmen, and so forth, but his chauffeur had been arrested for speeding on the way to the pier.

All eighteen of the foreign racing men had accommodations at the Knickerbocker. The most fashionable hotel in the city, it was the temporary address in New York for the faster types of celebrities from the world of entertainment and sports. It was also the permanent address of opera star Enrico Caruso—and New York's edgy "in" set never strayed too far from where he was. The Knickerbocker was located across Seventh Avenue from the Times Building at Forty-third Street, so that the racing cars, which were eventually parked in front of the hotel, remained conveniently close to the starting line.

Settling into the Knickerbocker on Saturday morning, the foreign drivers professed to be interested only in working on their cars in preparation for the start Wednesday. New York City wouldn't be New York City, however, if it were to let its favorites eat alone.

"There will be little time for entertaining with so much to do in the matter of preparing the cars for the start," clucked the *New York Times* in an article published Sunday. "Tonight, however, the Italian Club will give a banquet to the contestants, while the afternoon will be spent sightseeing. Tomorrow night they will attend a dinner at the Times Building, and on Tuesday, at noon, they will go to Martin's [restaurant] for luncheon with the Importers' Automobile Salon. On Tuesday night, the Automobile Club will dine them." And that apparently reflected a schedule with "little time for entertaining" in the robust city of New York in 1908. On Wednesday, the racers were due to start for Paris.

Over the course of the weekend, millions of Americans had been celebrating the arrival of the European entrants, but with a strange aura of detachment, as though they were the hosts of a stupendous party—to which they were not invited. E. R. Thomas was one of the many who realized that the United States desperately needed a car in the race. Sometime between the arrival of the *Lorraine* and the salad course at the Italian Club, word spread that he had made his final decision about the race. Apparently the swirl of excitement surrounding the eighteen foreigners had helped make up his mind.

The Thomas company didn't issue any special announcement. Other companies had done that, without any follow-up. Thomas said nothing to the outside world.

Inside the factory, a brick building on Niagara Street in Buffalo— that's where it happened. The decision to enter the race created a minor explosion of activity. First, there was the car, which was to be a Thomas Six, the "Speedway Flyer" model. It had to be taken from finished stock and prepared for its journey—not the twenty-two thousand miles it would attempt under its own power, but the four hundred miles to New York City that it would make by train. The car that was selected was a Flyer originally intended for a customer in Boston and fitted out according to his preferences. Another car could be built for him later. The company needed a Flyer without delay.

The crush of the race deadline left no time to do anything to the car except check it out in a general way, and then take it on the night of Sunday the ninth to the freight yard, where it was loaded onto a flatcar and sent on its way. Once it arrived, Harry Houpt could complete arrangements for the entry.

While the other European entrants were attending the first of their banquets Sunday night, Hans Koeppen and his teammate Ernst Maas returned to the Fatherland, in spirit, being entertained by Madame Johanna Gadski, the star of the Metropolitan Opera House. At thirty-six, Madame Gadski was a tall, winning blond soprano who was regarded as the ultimate interpreter of Wagnerian roles such as "Brünnhilde," the warrior princess. Madame Gadski was the foremost German citizen in America, a position she took very seriously—too seriously as it would turn out eight years later. She was summarily dropped from her pinnacle at the Met during World War I for piping up with the thought that she would happily blow up an American ammunition factory if she thought that it would ever produce bombs for use against Germany. With that, she was sent back to her beloved homeland. In New York in 1908, though, Madame Gadski towered over all things German.

Madame Gadski was known as a surpassing hostess, and the invitation to dine with her was not only an honor for Koeppen and Maas, but something of a command. Hans Koeppen was particularly well trained for it, chatting away the hours just as though he were back in Berlin. On one tour or another with *Siegfried,* Madame Gadski had spent time in all of the major American cities on the route of the New York-to-Paris Race, and she gave the men a preview of the landscape, social and geographic.

On Monday morning, the European teams were still uncertain as to whether a Thomas would actually enter the race, or not. They busied themselves testing their vehicles in the snowdrifts of the countryside outside of New York. At least, most of the entrants were testing the cars; Bourcier St. Chaffray was testing one of his arctic outfits, a long brown coat complete with a hood, lined in wool and a mystery material said to seal in warmth. The honor of leading the cars out of New York for their test had been assigned in advance to the owner of a Peerless automobile, which was festooned with signs and flags to let pedestrians know just exactly what, and who, was coming next. The Peerless was followed by the long and large De Dion, with St. Chaffray at the wheel, peering out of his gigantic coat; the Moto-Bloc driven by Charles Godard; the tiny Sizaire with burly Auguste Pons at the wheel; the huge Züst carrying Sirtori, Haaga, and Scarfoglio; and the Protos with Knape and Maas in the front and Lieutenant Koeppen in the back, looking bemused. When the parade slowed down for the sake of a streetcar crossing Broadway, a little boy approached the Moto-Bloc and shouted, "Will you ever get to Paris?"

Without missing a beat, Charles Godard responded, "Sure!" As he added a wave, he asked one of his companions what the boy had said. The only English word Godard knew was "Sure."

It was while the European teams were out in the snow that Harry Houpt stood up in his office and danced a jig, after finally receiving a telegram containing the message he had been trying to coax out of the Thomas factory for months:

Harry S. Houpt Co., 63rd & Broadway, N.Y.:
Shipping to-day by express the Thomas sixty-horse power stock car entered in New York-to-Paris race to defend America against the world.

Houpt could hardly wait to get his hands on the car and stock it with supplies for the trip. Montague Roberts was engaged to drive it, of course, though Houpt still wanted him to drive in the French Grand Prix and several domestic races in the spring, meaning that Roberts would start the race but leave the car sometime in March. With that start fast approaching, Roberts himself was more worried about finding someone to accompany him on the trip . . . someone who was robust and resourceful. Not only resourceful, but diabolical when necessary. And both expert in machinery and experienced in navigation. Someone wise to the ways of the world, but unspoiled by civilization, and certainly without any stubborn predilections, such as the need to have a steak dinner every Saturday night. There would be steak dinners along the way. There just wouldn't be any Saturday nights until the car reached Paris. Finally, Roberts needed someone willing to leave within forty-eight hours for approximately six months on the road, where there was a road.

By the time the convoy to the snowy suburbs returned to midtown Manhattan in the afternoon, the mechanical version of stage fright seemed to have gripped the foreign cars. The Protos was groaning under the weight of the veritable hardware store that had been crammed into its storage compartments. Paring down the supply of tools and spare parts didn't occur to anyone on the team; instead, Maas and Knape tore the car down and installed heavier springs. Lieutenant Koeppen couldn't help with that, knowing very little about car repair. So he went out and bought more supplies to load as soon as they were through.

The Züst, parked in the Brixia-Züst company garages, had developed more serious problems. Several of the other entrants dropped by, listened to the car's rattling cough, and told Scarfoglio and Sirtori very graciously that it was hopeless; the car was as good as dead.

All afternoon, Henry Haaga scrutinized the components, dismantling, cleaning, and inspecting each system carefully. Word spread rapidly through the city that the Züst was ailing. Italians soon gathered around the door of the garage, waiting in the cold for news.

"The Italian psychology is a curious thing," Scarfoglio concluded, as he regarded the subdued mob on the sidewalk. "Sceptics, pessimists, unpatriotic while under the shade of their own houses, distance makes the Italians lovers, desperate lovers, of the far-off sun, the pure sky, the limpid air of their native home. A fierce homesickness fills their eyes with tears; and at the fluttering of an Italian flag, the sound of an Italian voice, they become sentimental, tender, and indulgent towards the distant land. And the Italians of America more so than any others. . . . And that is the reason why, trembling with anxiety, as though round the bed of a beloved invalid, these Italians watch, outside the garage where Haaga and Sirtori are working. Every workman that leaves the place is taken by assault, anxiously questioned, implored to tell the truth and hide nothing."

According to Scarfoglio, the cause of the trouble was a "broken tube of the injector." That was the English translation of Scarfoglio's Italian report, based on a diagnosis direct from Haaga, who only spoke German. He was probably referring to the carburetor. While Haaga toiled on Monday and then again on Tuesday, the Italians outside remained, many of them missing two full days of work so that they could stand as near to the Züst as possible, anchoring the hope of a much wider family.

As the sun began to set, the Thomas Flyer was on a flatcar, clattering over the tracks alongside the Hudson River, headed toward New York City. That the *New York Times* was relieved to have an American entry in the race was an understatement. Without the Flyer, the paper would have been in the uncomfortable position of covering a wholly European story on American soil. It wouldn't have sold many papers that way. The presence of the Thomas brought the adventure much closer to the *Times'* own readers, and the paper gave it an extra push, arranging to send a reporter in the American car. T. Walter Williams received the assignment. Round and robust, he was not exactly an outdoorsman, looking as though he would be more at home in the lounge car of any westbound train than in the backseat of the Flyer. Williams only had to cover as much of the race as he could take, though. Whenever he wanted, the paper would send a replacement.

That left the question of the riding mechanic. With one day to spare before the start, the *New York Times* printed a roster of each team, rather lamely listing Roberts's codriver as Harold Brinker, another Thomas demonstrator.

Brinker was scheduled to drive the Thomas, all right, but not until March, when Roberts was to return to New York to prepare for the French Grand Prix. On the day before the start of New York-to-Paris, Harold Brinker was relaxing at home—in Denver.

As a choice for a working teammate, Monty Roberts had requested the services of George Schuster, a mechanic and part-time demonstrator he knew from the factory. On one of Schuster's visits to New York over the winter, the two had discussed the possibility of taking on the race together. Schuster hadn't heard anything else, though. No one except Roberts was enthusiastic about the choice; Schuster was too low in the factory hierarchy to receive any attention or very much respect, yet he was just high enough to be considered indispensable for the anticipated six-month duration of the race. The factory stalled, awaiting Roberts's second choice, but none was forthcoming.

"A telephone call put me into the longest automobile race in history," George Schuster wrote in his memoir:

The date was February 11, 1908. I was then chief roadtester of Thomas Flyer automobiles for the E. R. Thomas Motor Company of Buffalo, New York, and on that winter day happened to be in Providence, Rhode Island. I demonstrated a new Flyer there that morning to the owner of a Pope Toledo who wanted a car of greater power. When I returned to our local distributor just before noon, E. C. Morse, the Thomas sales manager, was calling me from the factory in Buffalo.

"We are entering a car in the Paris race," he told me. "Will you take the night train and be in New York tomorrow morning? You will be the mechanic and Monty Roberts will be the driver. He wants you and says you are willing."

Schuster threw his suitcase together and hopped on a train for New York.

THE CARS THAT STARTED THE RACE

Sizaire-Naudin
FRANCE

Protos
GERMANY

Moto'-Bloc
FRANCE

De Dion
FRANCE

Thomas Flyer
UNITED STATES

Brixia-Zust
ITALY

Chapter Six

One Down in New York

At the crack of the starter's pistol at 11:14 in Times Square, hats went into the air, along with shouts and wide smiles. And with that, the cars began to inch forward, illustrating for all to see that the longest journey really does begin with but a single turn of the wheel. Millions more of them and the same six cars would be in Paris.

"Montague Roberts had been leaning on the steering wheel, to the point that it seemed ready to collapse, but he calls out 'All Right!' " wrote Stephen Lausanne, a senior editor of *Le Matin,* who was present at the very moment of the start. "Captain [*sic*] Koeppen makes a dry gesture, moving his hand to the visor of his cap. Scarfoglio sends a kiss to the crowd. Pons shakes his shoulders. As for St. Chaffray, he doesn't move, but his face seemed even more pale than usual."

A detachment of police horses led the way up Broadway and cleared a path. The first car to follow was the Sizaire-Naudin, with Auguste Pons at the wheel. Long and low-slung, the Sizaire was not much more than a sportscar. No windshield, no dash: just a long column leading from the engine compartment to the steering wheel. The Sizaire didn't even have a body. The seats were surrounded by air. The only sheet metal on the car covered the one-cylinder engine, with the help of two leather straps, while a pair of mudsplashes bent over the front wheels. Like each of the other racecars, the Sizaire-Naudin was painted gray. Gray paint—the kind used on battleships, in boiler rooms, and on the bars in prison—went on thick and remained so, to resist chips. As a result, the rainbow of colors in the New York-to-Paris entries ran all the way from slate to mist. The Sizaire-Naudin was somewhere in the middle range, a medium gray.

The second car to pass the crowds in Times Square was the dark gray Moto-Bloc, with the "stout and genial" Charles Godard driving. The Moto-Bloc was the second-biggest car in the race, arriving like a movable stage, with four hefty kerosene spotlights arranged on the hood. It did have a windshield, though it was made of leather and only protected the passengers up to the chest. Long before the introduction of safety glass (which crumbles into bits rather than shattering into daggers), windows were regarded as a suicidal luxury for rugged vehicles or sporting ones—and the New York-to-Paris cars were both. The leather windshield had an added benefit; it doubled as a posterboard, with "Moto-Bloc" written in large letters across the front. "Tour du Monde" (*world tour*) was written across the back of the storage compartment at the rear of the car. On each of the boxes attached to the sides was an advertisement reading "Louis Vuitton: Trunks . . . Bags."

The American car was third in the starting parade, and if the crowds had any reserve of gusto, then the morning's din increased as it passed. But no reporter could say that it did. The crescendo had long since reached its maximum. In response, the drivers revved their engines, and so the cars and the crowds roared at each other, on a day like no other in Times Square.

The Thomas Flyer was lithe, if not quite lightweight. It was built as a gentleman's roadster, a style normally fitted with only two seats, though the original customer, the man in Boston, had ordered two more constructed onto the back, where the trunk would normally have been strapped. The factory had painted "Thomas Flyer" in eye-catching, diagonal print on the sides, but by the time the running boards were loaded with boxes of supplies and long planks (for crossing creeks) were strapped on top of them, running the length of the car, all that passersby could see was *MAS LYER*. Anyone who was there that morning knew what they were looking at: the newly famous Thomas Flyer, though a few people had the gall to say it looked like a hook-and-ladder firetruck. It did—but it was still a racecar underneath the planks and suitcases. Montague Roberts and his team sat under a metal framework built to hold the canopy top, for use when the weather was wet. A rifle hung from the empty framework, swinging gently with the vibration of the car.

The Protos was the fourth car in the rollout. Whitish-gray and burly from any point of view, it was wider than any of the other cars in the race. It had been specially built that way back in Berlin, to allow ample room for a canvas top over the back, making it look like a covered wagon, according to nearly all who observed it. "New York: Paris" was written across the side of the cover. In Berlin, the Protos factory had also fitted the racecar with six fuel tanks, carrying 176 gallons of gasoline, more than any other car in the race. (Most of the cars separated their fuel into isolated compartments, in case a puncture or fire affected any one of them.)

The De Dion was the next to glide by, carrying Bourcier Chaffray and the "De Dionites," as *Motor Age* called the team. The biggest, heaviest car in the race, the De Dion had a split personality. The front half looked like a car—rather a modern car for the day, with headlights in front of the grille. The back, however, was nothing more than a payload, like that of a dump truck today, filled with a mountain of crates and bags. Somewhere in the midst of it was a third seat. "Above the layer of [gas] tanks," explained *Motor Age*'s reporter, "is what appears to be a square delivery body; on climbing up on the running board it is seen that a circular well has been left of just sufficient size to allow of the accommodation of spare tires, the center being the seat for the third man. In the chests built round the well are spare parts, tools, clothing, a Nansen [portable] kitchen, sufficient food for 1 month, and the thousand and one things necessary for an Arctic exploration." The one thousand and first of those things was the sail that Captain Hansen had devised to propel the vehicle across the Arctic tundra.

The sixth and last car to pass the crowds was the Italian car, the Züst. Or "Zost," as some spectators must have thought, with the umlaut crowding the "u" on the painted grille. The Züst was not as large as the Protos or the De Dion. It was a long car, still retaining the appearance of a car, though, with two seats in the front and a bench seat for two in the back. The only concession to the mileage stretching out ahead was the construction of shelving along the sides toward the back, to hold extra trunks.

The New York-to-Paris racecars may have been gray like burros and overladen like mules, but most of them had high-horsepower engines and were capable of speeds of up to 70 mph. Where the course would let them—that is, where there were decent roads—they could set speeds that would not be seen again in the same vicinity for decades. It was all a question of being ready for anything, which is the most thoroughbred trait of all.

Following the group of six racers along Seventh Avenue was a touring car containing Miss Theodora Shonts with her gaggle of French aristocrats. Two hundred cars passed after that, in a parade of honking horns and waving flags representing the United States, France, Italy, and Germany. As the cars made their way up Broadway and through Automobile Row, the Pope car dealership, which was normally in bitter competition with Thomas Motors, rang a loud siren in celebration. Along Broadway, people hung out of every window, taking in the "Little Storm of Colors," as the *New York Times* called its creation, the start of the New York-to-Paris Race.

"There goes 'Get-There' Roberts," shouted a man from an office building near Sixtieth Street. Fifty blocks on, the crowds were still thick on the sidewalk. At Columbia University, many of the late-morning classes were suspended and eight hundred students stood with their professors awaiting the cars. At Barnard College, a physics course was the only class dismissed entirely for the sake of the race, but the screaming engines making their approach soon overruled even the strictest professors. The students rushed without permission to the windows to meet the sound and wave. The cars saluted them back.

"Never in the history of automobiling," observed the *New York Times,* "and rarely in the history of any sport has so much excitement been known in the streets of New York." It was true. But then, the *New York Times* might have said it even if it weren't. The newspaper was like the father of the bride: proud as punch even before the thing began. More objective accounts, though, were just as impressed by the city at its most lighthearted. "By 10 o'clock Broadway up to the northernmost reaches of Harlem looked as though everybody was expecting the circus to come to town," marveled the normally staid *New York Tribune.* "The mild day made it possible to stand and wait for the racers without special discomfort and apparently everybody who could turned out to see them pass."

Likewise, the other papers had no choice but to give the *Times* credit for a magnificent moment, instantly understood by hundreds of thousands of people. "It was all spectacular," wrote the special correspondent for the *Chicago Tribune*.

The cheering barely stopped until the cars reached Yonkers (about twelve miles north of Times Square), where the long procession halted and most of the two hundred escort cars turned around to go back to New York. Miss Shonts turned her attention back to her own business, her Saturday wedding to the Duc de Chaulnes.

After the other cars receded, the excitement died down and the silence of a winter countryside encircled the cars. Of course, it was a silence cut to ribbons by the sound of the engines, but still, there was no longer any response to those engines, only the space that made the earth seem so large and that made a race from New York to Paris worth waging in the first place. If the hard part—covering the remaining 21,988 miles—began in Yonkers, the race also bore down on the entrants starting there, with the snow lying deeper the farther north the cars traveled, and the roads increasingly neglected. Only a few well-shod horses went out in such snowy weather, and they were pulling sleighs. Most country folk just stayed home, leaving the roads unmarked, unplowed, and barely detectable in most places.

The fun part, quite obviously, was over. In retrospect, the celebration at the start was perhaps rather extravagant, considering how little the participants had actually accomplished up to that point. Had anyone realized just how exuberant it would be, the starting line might have been more crowded with entries. Anyone yearning to be an immediate celebrity, trailing applause, admiration, and invitations to dine, anyone with more of an appetite for merriment than adventure—every person in Manhattan, in other words—would only have had to enter the race and then drop out somewhere around Tarrytown to enjoy a most memorable Lincoln's Birthday.

Auguste Pons, for his part, made it as far as Peekskill, at the northern border of Westchester County, about forty-five miles north of New York. Driving the Sizaire-Naudin, the pipsqueak of the race, Pons was already separated from the other racers when he realized that something was very wrong—not with his car, but with the sun. It was on his right, when it should have been on his left. Either it was a historic anomaly or he was heading south, back to New York City. He turned the car around and headed north again.

The other five cars made better progress. The Italian Züst made a conspicuous stab at taking the lead, trying to lose the others on Westchester County's snowy roads. Antonio Scarfoglio and Emilio Sirtori were of one mind: to push for the lead from the first. Arthur Ruland, the American manager of the Züst business, was in the car, too, and he concurred. To lead the race was to win the headlines.

Oberlieutenant Koeppen had the opposite inclination: to run slow and steady in the early going. He had to finish the race, to win it, if at all possible, but he had to finish, no matter what. If Koeppen had been in the Sizaire-Naudin, outmatched against its very first steep hill, he would have picked the car up and carried it to Paris. The Kaiser was watching him. So were the Prussian army and all Germany—and Koeppen would not escape that fact for a second until he got his car to Paris. He advised Knape to drive conservatively and see who dropped out. If everyone else did, after all, there would be no hurry to Paris. And so Koeppen watched the Züst zoom ahead. He wasn't worried.

But Scarfoglio was. The snow was catastrophic. "At Poughkeepsie (seventy miles from New York)," he wrote to the *London Daily Mail,* "it was crackling against our tyres. At Hudson (120 miles), it was burying our rims and beginning to cause us trouble. At Albany (150 miles), it was up to the nave of the wheel. At Schenectady (177 miles) it was over the radiator."

Told by the local papers that the New York-to-Paris racers were expected at 2:30 on the first afternoon, residents of Poughkeepsie were waiting downtown on Market Street, near Cannon, arrayed in cars or standing on foot. In either case, they were shivering. Poughkeepsie was a typical small city circa 1908, at least for an automobilist trying to transverse it in the dead of winter. The downtown streets were well paved with bricks, cement, or macadam; moreover, they were wide enough for the streetcar to run down the middle, along with the horse-drawn traffic and an occasional auto. But the lanes leading out to the country were made of dirt and gravel. At best, they were recently graded; at worst, badly rutted. In addition, they tended to be narrow. Road signs were practically unknown in the countryside, and there were few direct routes to anywhere.

All over the country, people who wanted to travel from one town to another, especially in the winter, took the train. Oddly enough, American highways were much better in 1808 than they were in 1908. In the first decades of the 1800s, on the eve of the railroad era, a good many commercial turnpikes and plank roads smoothed the way between cities. By 1908, though, the railroad ruled city-to-city travel.

Portable road maps didn't exist in most regions; they just weren't needed. Train schedules were the only necessity. And so country roads were left to country folk, and at that, they were mostly just for reaching the nearest town and its all-important train station. Even on dry summer days, many automobilists were wary of rustic lanes. As an alternative, the city of Poughkeepsie had its own driving park: an open field, like a rink for fair weather, where cars could go round and round and never get lost.

The New York-to-Paris teams collected maps wherever possible, even those that didn't show routes. But most of the time, they did as everyone did and stopped frequently to ask for directions. If they were lucky, though, it never came to that. To help the New York-to-Paris racers find their way, a delegation of Poughkeepsie automobile enthusiasts drove south to meet them and guide them into town. Such guides were awaiting the racers in many American towns and cities.

In Poughkeepsie, built on a rise overlooking the Hudson, local entrepreneurs reveled in the very weather that was beginning to torment the racers. The most active spot in town on Lincoln's Birthday was the river itself, where men with saws were harvesting ice a whopping twenty-two inches thick—sixteen being the norm. Vassar College, where the college girls were in the midst of midterm exams, was the second-busiest place in Poughkeepsie that Wednesday, the girls walking around like zombies; one particularly fragile student lost her temper when she was bumped on the way to her history class. "Don't joggle me, or I'll lose the history dates," she exclaimed.

Downtown on Market Street, Poughkeepsie was alive, too, as "the necks of all were strained," looking south for any sign of a great car. At exactly 3:10, the Thomas Flyer turned a corner and whisked up the broad avenue, Monty Roberts at the wheel, beaming. Since leaving New York three hours and fifty-five minutes earlier, he'd donned a leather football helmet, for protection from the wind. He made for a strange sight, but a welcome one.

Forty minutes later, Bourcier St. Chaffray, covered in white arctic clothing from head to toe, arrived in the De Dion to find that Roberts, Schuster, and the reporter Williams were in a restaurant, thawing out and finishing a relaxed lunch. St. Chaffray, Hansen, and Autran had just begun to take their hoods off when, according to a reporter, "the Italian car Züst came rushing along like an express train. It never began to slow down until it reached Cannon Street and then rushed through the crowd so fast that no one could get a good look at it." Sirtori, directed by Scarfoglio, then made a mistake, turning up Main Street, the wrong route. A bystander flagged him down to redirect him north toward Hyde Park, Albany, and Paris.

"It continued on up the Hyde Park road, without stopping at all in this city," wrote the reporter, reflecting the indignation of all Poughkeepsie. Monty Roberts refused to rush away from the table just to catch up, but nonetheless, within a very few minutes, he was back out on the road, chasing the Züst, followed by St. Chaffray, who had had to hurry his own lunch, something he was loath to do.

Roberts and the Thomas Flyer soon caught up to the Züst, snow whirling behind both cars. In general terms, Roberts knew where he was going—the route went right past the Roosevelt estate in Hyde Park, where he'd been the year before—and so he took the lead. If someone wanted to race, Monty Roberts was always glad to oblige. As the cars moved north, however, and the drifts stood deeper, he realized that leading an automobile race through the snow is hardly a gratifying honor.

As the Thomas picked its way forward, there was often no sign at all of the road. Over long stretches, Schuster was compelled to walk in front of the car with a long stick, probing for the ground underneath the snow. Whenever possible, Roberts steered around the drifts. It wasn't always easy. If Schuster and Williams had to take apart fences on adjoining farms, they did so without compunction, and the Thomas diverted through frozen fields. All the while, the Züst and the De Dion were somewhere behind—sometimes close, sometimes lost in the distance. The other two racecars, the Moto-Bloc and the Protos, were nowhere to be seen.

It wasn't rip-roaring action. Nonetheless, the *Buffalo Express* refused to be disheartened by reports detailing the adventures in slow-motion racing. It ran its story of the first leg of the race under the headline "This Going Is Terrific," with the subhead "Drifts Are Hard to Get Through, and It's Fight, Fight, Fight from Morn' till Night." The *New York World,* nemesis of the *New York Times,* was more restrained in its cheerleading; "Racing to Paris Pretty Slow Work" was its headline.

The original idea was to reach Albany on the first night, but that goal was set before the leaders found themselves in the village of Churchtown, New York. According to Roberts, a local farmer there—an old St. Nick of a man with a white beard and the faint Dutch accent of the Valley—pushed through a snowy field, hailed him down, and very generously told him about a shortcut. It was a shortcut, as it turned out, to nowhere, on a road undulating with three-foot drifts. Apparently the kind-mannered St. Nick was one of those many farmers who hated cars and meant to do them in, one at a time. In some places around the country, ruralists held off the auto age by leaving nails on the road or even by taking shots at motorists from a hidden distance. Roberts cursed the man later, and had plenty of time to do so, since he spent most of the next four hours shoveling snow on the so-called shortcut. St. Chaffray and Hansen in the De Dion were likewise stuck on the same road, and the Italians were stopped just behind, in the Züst. As it grew dark, the engines were stopped and the only pistons in motion were the arms of the men, working their snow shovels up and down. Finally, "an intelligent native" (the distinction being Williams's) trudged out with a lantern to let Roberts know that the best way to get to Albany was to go back to the village and take the road behind the schoolhouse. That sounded like better news than it was: it took the ten men two hours to shovel a path to the schoolhouse.

By then, it was getting dark out, and if it was easy to get lost in the daylight on the unmarked roads of the countryside, twilight made it inevitable. As it turned out, though, Auguste Pons, struggling along fifty miles behind the leaders, didn't have to worry about being lost. Heading up a steep incline called Spitlock Hill near Peekskill, the Sizaire-Naudin's engine died. The Frenchmen had no choice but to set out on foot. Knocking on the door of the first farmhouse they saw, they roused a woman named Mrs. Andrews, who came to the entry with a lantern. Rather taken aback at first, especially since she didn't know French and they barely knew English, she regained her composure and took them in for the night. Mrs. Andrews's front parlor was just about as close to Paris as Auguste Pons would get in the Sizaire-Naudin. The next day, he was on a train back to New York, and though he later fixed the car and made his way a little farther up the Hudson Valley, the Sizaire was out of the race by the end of the week. Auguste Pons got to France before any of the others—on a transatlantic liner.

Driving through the same night air at the vanguard of the race, at the close of its very first day, Monty Roberts left his rivals behind—because they refused to use tire chains, so he claimed. Scarfoglio and St. Chaffray feared that chains would slow them down and used studded tires instead. Roberts had no such illusions; he accepted the fact no one was going to set a landspeed record in the Hudson River Valley that night and, like the tortoise going faster than the hare, he cruised into the river town of Hudson at about 8:30 P.M. Ten streets long and ten streets wide, Hudson was one of the oldest settlements in the state. Overlooking the river, it looked quaint, but it had a reputation as a libertine town with its eye out for river rats, both rich and poor.

No crowds in Hudson were waiting for the racecars. It was too dark and too cold to stand around outside. Anyway, the talk of the town that Wednesday night was not about cars, but cocks, the fighting roosters. A whole fight-card full of them had been confiscated a few days before from an illegal, inhumane pit. Birds, cages, and crowing filled the Hudson police station to overflowing. As Roberts and Williams wearily checked into the Lincoln Hotel, Schuster parked the Flyer in a commercial garage, and all around them, people were much too busy talking about the cockfight, the police, and the respectable men pretending not to have been there, to pay a lot of attention to three mumbling, stumbling automobilists. Nothing could have been a greater relief to the racing men: a quiet end to a noisy day—one of the noisiest days ever known in New York.

Chapter Seven

Towpath Sprint

Car	Miles	Place	Team
Thomas Flyer (U.S.)	116	Hudson, New York	Roberts, Schuster, Williams
Züst (Ita.)	116	Hudson, New York	Sirtori, Scarfoglio, Haaga
De Dion (Fra.)	116	Hudson, New York	St. Chaffray, Hansen, Autran
Protos (Ger.)	74	Poughkeepsie, New York	Koeppen, Knape, Maas
Moto-Bloc (Fra.)	44	Peekskill, New York	Godard, Hue, Livier

Someone frightened a horse in Hudson. It might have been Roberts in the Thomas Flyer, arriving in the dark on Wednesday night, or Emilio Sirtori in the Züst, a short time later, or Bourcier St. Chaffray in the De Dion, but whoever it was, the horse broke its harness and ran away. The owner immediately went to the stationhouse and complained to the police, over the sound of crowing cocks.

On Thursday, the first full day of racing, Roberts was ready to leave Hudson early. George Schuster, however, was in the midst of an exchange of telegrams concerning his wife, back in Buffalo, who had fallen seriously ill. Schuster thought about abandoning the team, to take a train back to Buffalo. With the advance of messages, though, he changed his mind. His wife's health was of paramount concern, of course—but if he left the Flyer, it would inevitably lose a day awaiting another mechanic and with that kind of handicap so early in the race, the factory might be tempted to withdraw the car. He decided to wait another day before making any decision to leave the team. With Schuster ready to go, the Thomas car left Hudson for Albany at about 6 A.M. The other two teams were still at breakfast.

So was Charles Godard, eating ravenously at a hotel in Peekskill, a long way back down the Hudson. Not far away, there was a certain ditch, covered cunningly by a snowdrift, that the Moto-Bloc had found the afternoon before. The car was said to have been airborne at the time. For hours on end, Godard and his two teammates worked to dig the car out, but they didn't succeed until 1 A.M. Starved for dinner in the midst of the evening's exertions, they hadn't found anything in their luggage but a couple of bottles of champagne, intended for the finish in Paris. They polished them off before nightfall and then there was nothing at all to sustain them. At one o'clock in the morning, when they finally arrived at the hotel in Peekskill, the manager wouldn't bring them anything to eat, not even so much as a mint. Godard barely survived until breakfast.

By the time the Hudson police pressed their investigation of the frightened horse, two of the prime suspects were already gone, St. Chaffray having left in the De Dion not long after Roberts in the Thomas Flyer. And so the law circled in on Scarfoglio, sitting alone in the Züst and awaiting the others on his team. Deeming the Züst bizarre enough to spook a horse, an officer charged him and assessed a fine of three dollars. Scarfoglio was outraged, but it took more than a hot lecture in Italian to impress the law in Hudson. The fine was paid.

"Thus we traversed a country uniformly dreary," Scarfoglio wrote dolefully, "an immense snowy land with trees stretching their bare, skeleton arms to the grey sky, and here and there a frame house barred [shuttered] and silent." Perhaps it was the three dollars that ruined his day. The snow was coming down hard, though, snaring the Züst in one predicament after another. Most of the day, the three leading cars traveled single file and close together. Along one stretch, the De Dion went off the road. Roberts stopped the Thomas and backed up to tow his rival out. Sportsmanship was expected of the drivers, part of a code that belonged to the tradition of amateurism still evident, in patches, in 1908. A true sportsman benefited only from his own efforts, not from the misfortunes of opponents.

At midday, with a break in the snowstorm, the Züst made one of its impulsive dashes to the lead, but for naught. "After two hours of travel," St. Chaffray wrote, "we found the Züst crew in front of the road working hard in the snow with shovels. They made a tunnel eight feet deep under their car, and the auto was steadily sinking deeper, no matter what the Italians would do. They worked with all the more obstinacy."

"Capt. Hansen," St. Chaffray continued, "on seeing Scarfoglio, suggested luncheon. He opened a bottle of white wine and a box of hard-
boiled eggs and sandwiches, and stopped work. The luncheon in the
snow was a merry one."

The good spirits didn't last long. Someone came along from a house
down the road to tell the racers that they'd been driving, or more accurately, digging in the wrong direction.

In the Hudson Valley, it was a snow day, if ever there was one. Traffic
was almost completely stopped on country roads, and people were actually trapped in their homes. Only those well-prepared types who had
"sharp-shod" horses, ones with specially cut shoes, were on the road,
and they were continually flagged down by hungry country dwellers in
need of supplies from town.

The conditions were so bad that the Albany Automobile Club's guide
cars, driving south to greet the racers, couldn't even make it out of town
on the first try. In late morning, they left again and managed to meet the
three leaders in the town of East Greenbush, not more than ten miles
away. Even then, East Greenbush was notorious as a speed trap for
autos—but not in February. With the snow still coming down, only
sharp-shod horses and New York-to-Paris racecars were moving on the
roads around Albany. The guide cars led the three leading racecars, the
Thomas Flyer, the Züst, and the De Dion, into downtown Albany.

As the state capital, Albany was in the midst of a drama that same
Thursday that would reverberate through the rest of the century. The
case of Chester Gillette, whose story would be told in Theodore
Dreiser's novel *An American Tragedy*, had recently been heard on its
final appeal in the state's highest court. The socially ambitious twenty-
year-old from central New York had already been convicted of drowning his lower-class girlfriend in the Adirondack resort of Big Moose
Lake. He was in Auburn State Prison, awaiting the court's decision. In
Albany, the judges were discussing his fate on the day the racers arrived.
At the same time, the state legislature was discussing a bill that should
have been of particular interest to Roberts, Scarfoglio, St. Chaffray, and
even Koeppen and Godard, who were still flogging away somewhere
along the Hudson. The prospective law would permanently prohibit

cars of more than twenty horsepower from state roads. That would include the Thomas (60 hp), the Züst (40 hp), the De Dion (30 hp), the Moto-Bloc (30 hp), and the Protos (40 hp).

Albany did its best to honor the automobile racers, starting with a banquet lunch at the finest hotel in town, the Ten Eyck. St. Chaffray loved it. Captain Hansen did, too, but then, he liked gatherings, saying in his remarks at the luncheon that it was well worth digging through the snow to meet the kindly people of Albany. Then there was Antonio Scarfoglio, who was only thinking all the while that "we literally fought our way inch by inch, and foot by foot over the twenty-two miles between Albany and Hudson." Apparently, he didn't consider it worth the effort. "We were received in triumph in Albany," he began, before going on to explain what was so bad about that:

> There were bands, flowers, and banquets, and naturally speeches; for the Americans dine only as an excuse for speech-making. Albany is one of those pompous little cities furnished with a Capitol and a Pantheon, which the Americans are so fond of dumping in the midst of a waste to remind the land and all travelers of their domination.

Scarfoglio was unfortunately disinterested in the only luxury offered by the New York-to-Paris Race: the unlimited opportunity to attend banquets. Frustration often welled up as outright anger in a young man such as he: as sensitive as a racehorse and not much better at controlling his emotions. Nor did he try to disguise his disgust at the conditions and the progress of the race, detailing his opinions in dispatches to the *London Daily Mail* and *Il Mattino.* The Züst managers in New York started looking for a less candid man to take his place.

By two o'clock, the Ten Eyck was emptying out and the three New York-to-Paris leaders were on their way due west for the first time, heading away from the Hudson River and toward the Great Lakes city of Buffalo. It was a logical route west, the same one traced by the Erie Canal, a "ditch" four feet deep and twenty to forty feet wide completed eighty-three years before. The Erie Canal wasn't used in the winter, but in fair weather, it was still the backbone of the state.

As Roberts led the way out of Albany, temperatures warmed up, which should have been good news for the racers. It wasn't. Warm temperatures brought melting drifts and slushy mud. If the cars slowed down, they became stuck; if they kept up a realistic speed, they tended to skid. Under the circumstances, the heavier cars were no longer pack mules, but bucking broncos, jerking the steering wheel suddenly, in response to minor changes in the road surface or contour. Long before power steering let the frailest of drivers turn the wheel with a fingertip, the job of controlling a large car was exhausting. Roberts managed to drive the relatively light Thomas by himself, but at times, both St. Chaffray and Captain Hansen had to keep their hands on the steering wheel of the six-thousand-pound De Dion.

The city of Schenectady, only about twenty miles from Albany, gave the racers a rousing welcome, which was generous, considering that the city was due to open an almost absurdly sumptuous new train station a few days later. The New York-to-Paris cars sped right past it. Whatever symbolism the moment might have reflected, however, was dashed about fifteen minutes later when the automobilists made their way out of town, leaving the downtown roads, where the snow had been cleared, and heading for the main road to the west. It was then that they realized that there was no road west out of Schenectady, not on that day. With the main route impassable, one of the local guides suggested turning down an embankment to an orchard. At the bottom of the incline, the teams had to build a bridge in order to get across a ravine. Captain Hansen went at that chore with his usual gusto, clearing trees and laying the framework for the bridge with stones. ("We call Capt. Hansen 'Gaston,'" St. Chaffray said, referring to a French hero of the 1300s, "not because he makes good speeches all the day, but because of his fondness for hard work.") With the bridge built and the cars across it, the drivers realized that the orchard was just as impassable as the road.

"What human forces can dig through a snowdrift three or four feet high a corridor twenty miles long and six feet wide?" Scarfoglio despaired. "It is impossible! It is impossible to go any further. Our arms have no power over the spades and our feet cannot resist the cold which seizes and turns them to ice. The skin of our hands and faces is completely cracked." The course seemed close to claiming three more cars, and the men who went with them. They were not only stranded in the orchard, but wedged into it by wet, heavy snow. Perhaps Scarfoglio was right; it was a moment well suited to reflection. And to feeling foolish. They had spare parts and rifles, Arctic maps and desert clothing, gray food that came in tins (and allegedly lasted forever), thermos bottles in Russian leather pouches, pickaxes, sails, flags, and ID cards, stoves, tents, and tuxedos. They had six-thousand-pound automobiles. What they didn't have was a road.

The Protos was still picking its way up the Hudson River Valley with long pauses for snow shoveling and roadside repairs. Somewhere in the snow or the wind, the German flag fell off the back of the car, leaving only the Stars and Stripes—fluttering away on the pride of Berlin. A bystander in Poughkeepsie, waiting for the Protos and holding a large German flag, handed it to Koeppen on his brief stop. As spontaneous gestures go, it was fairly touching and according to the Poughkeepsie evening paper, "Koeppen went up the Hyde Park Road in a happy frame of mind." That was what they thought in Poughkeepsie. Just outside of town, the Protos hit a drift that seemed like the worst in the whole valley until Koeppen, Knape, and Maas extricated the car from it and then found their way into another farther on that was six feet high.

The Protos arrived in Albany in late afternoon and Koeppen was taken to dinner at the private Albany Club. It was no banquet, just a table full of very interested automobilists, but he was called upon to describe his trip for the table and responded with two days' worth of pent-up stories, cheerfully rendered. Just digging out of the six-foot drift took the Germans two hours, he said.

"Lieutenant Koeppen of the general staff of the Kaiser's army," marveled a reporter, "wielding a shovel with the others." A low whistle may well have punctuated his sense of awe.

Another Albany reporter was only a little less breathless. "Lieutenant Koeppen," noted the *Albany Evening Journal,* "is making himself extremely popular along the route. His quiet dignity and earnestness has made a great impression." One of Koeppen's unintended bon mots was repeated up and down the Hudson River for days. "Why, I expect

Siberia will be a picnic compared with what we have experienced!" he said with only half a smile. In finishing his talk at the Albany Club, Lieutenant Koeppen said firmly, "We will be in at the finish, that is certain." The table practically struck him down with the explosion of applause that greeted that remark.

Koeppen's teammates, Knape and Maas, were undoubtedly invited to the dinner at the Albany Club, but they didn't attend. While Koeppen was holding his audience rapt over dinner, Knape sent a telegram to the *New York Times,* telling the story his own way, in its entirety: "The Protos stopped here at 9:30 o'clock P.M. Roads bad. Weather fine. [Signed] Knapp, driver." In reprinting the dispatch, the *Times* didn't even get his name right.

As for Charles Godard in the Moto-Bloc, he was still on his way north somewhere near Poughkeepsie. When asked if he was worried to be lagging by a whole day after only a day and a half of competition, he replied, "I travel far, not fast."

The Thomas, the De Dion, and the Züst weren't doing either that afternoon: not far, not fast. They were in the orchard near Schenectady and everything was still and quiet, the way it is off the main route and away from the commotion of people going places. The only sound to break the silence was the voice of a local resident, repeatedly suggesting that they couldn't do much but wait for the snow to melt. After a protracted discussion, an automobilist who lived in Schenectady advised the racers to abandon the roads altogether, in favor of the towpath along the Canal. As there was no other choice, Roberts, St. Chaffray, and Scarfoglio opted for the towpath, though they had an ordeal making their way to it, having to build another bridge along the way.

In fair weather, the towpath was used by the mules and horses that pulled the canal boats along. In winter, it would be empty.

The *Utica Dispatch* provided a description of the towpath in winter conditions:

The canal towpath does not drift except in isolated places. It is high and the drifting snow falls in the canal bed and leaves less snow on the towpath than anywhere else in the locality. But with even a slight covering of snow on the towpath, it is a dangerous place upon which to run motor cars at the present time. The snow is so soft and treacherous that it offers little support to the wheels and might easily cause the car to slide into the canal itself.

A guide car did slide into the canal. It was an Oldsmobile, following after the racers to make sure nothing happened to them. Occupied by two auto enthusiasts, a pair of brothers from Schenectady, the Olds skidded for an instant and then rolled off the towpath into the half-frozen water of the canal. One of the brothers broke three ribs.

The New York-to-Paris racers made fairly good time on the towpath, but they couldn't possibly thread their way along it in the dark. Stopping overnight in the town of Fonda, Schuster received a message that his wife was "much better." Meanwhile, Monty Roberts had the hotel operator place a long-distance telephone call to E. R. Thomas. If the boss was losing heart because of the delays, Roberts wanted to hear it firsthand and assuage the problem, if he could. According to rumors in the automobile industry, E. R. didn't plan to keep the car in the race past Buffalo, anyway. Or past Chicago or San Francisco, depending on the impatience of the rumor. Even Monty Roberts couldn't be sure that one of those rumors wasn't true.

Right after speaking with Roberts on the long-distance connection, E. R. met with members of the powerful Automobile Club of Buffalo. They were openly impatient. "When do you expect the cars to get here, Mr. Thomas?" one of them asked.

E. R. grinned. "As the Dutchman says, 'They get here when they get here.'" E. R. was disarmed, at least for the present. Or seemed to be.

The next day, the three leading cars were back at work, clinging to the towpath, when suddenly, there was rejoicing in the Züst. It wasn't manifested by laughter or waving. It was just a car shooting ahead, because it finally could. The towpath had dried out. Everything Scarfoglio had thought impossible the day before was not only possible, but beckoning. The Züst was no longer a sledge, it was a car, and it responded to the command to go—and go faster. And that's what cars were for, as far as he was concerned. Roberts kept up in the Thomas, but St. Chaffray didn't.

As his teammate, Captain Hansen, explained, "Life is too short to go at that pace in such a dangerous spot. Our car will take things more calmly."

For the first time, the drivers flirted with breaking the state law, which limited traffic in downtown city districts to 10 mph, in other populated areas to 15 mph, and on country roads to 20 mph. The law didn't specify any limits for canal towpaths, but the Züst and the Thomas were averaging 50 mph. Even when it began to rain, they kept it up.

Roberts knew the pace was reckless. "Idiotic" was the word he used. "But I simply had to follow the Züst," he said. He didn't want the other car to arrive first in Utica, the next city on the course. Local people standing on bridges over the canal gasped when they realized how fast the cars were moving. They were used to seeing mules plod the path. "A slip of the wheel and zipp—you are in the canal bed and probably dead with the machine on top of you," said one race fan. Sirtori, driving the Züst, opened a gap over the Thomas Flyer.

"Get after him, boy," a man hollered at Roberts from one of the bridges over the canal. "Hold him down!" shouted another. Roberts and Sirtori hurtled toward Utica as though it were Paris.

Utica was well known as a mill town, relying on power provided by the Mohawk River, which ran parallel to the canal near the city, sometimes only leaving a narrow track in between the two for the towpath. While the mills in town were mostly constructed of red brick, the houses were made of wood, painted all different colors: from that point of view, it was much like other prosperous, small cities in the United States in 1908. But it was changing. In 1890, there were only five hundred Italians in Utica; as of 1902, that number had grown to six thousand—one-ninth of the population—and by 1908, the proportion was higher still. Raffaele de Rosa was among them, having walked to Utica from another city. "It was easy to move in those days. You see, we had nothing to move but our legs," he recalled a half-century later. "We had no clothes to move except those we had on our backs."

"In those days they called us 'dagos,'" recalled another Italian-born Utican. "I used to go to a skating rink on Seymour Avenue. I would be the only Italian there. When I got there they would say: 'Here is the little dago again.' But then they would try to teach me to skate." Few other

Uticans had even that much to do with the Italians in town. Roy Van Denbergh, a principal, took a job in the Italian section of town in 1911. "It seemed to me that I had entered a foreign city in East Utica," he said. "The Italian people were a unit unto themselves with very little intercourse with the rest of the city." When Italy's own Brixia-Züst came roaring onto Broad Street ahead of any other car in the New York-to-Paris Race, though, it seemed that the East Uticans owned the whole city.

The police estimated that three thousand Italians were waiting in the streets for their car and they made more noise than all of the other seven thousand people on hand. Shouts of "Brava! Bravissima" for the car and "Viva Italia!" rang out until the voices were noticeably hoarse. Someone stepped forward to place a floral horseshoe on the front of the Züst.

Utica even pleased Antonio Scarfoglio. And it was the first thing in the United States that did, aside from an episode with a couple of bold girls in Fonda who presented him with two wrenches and a giggling insistence on fixing the car for him. (It wasn't broken at the time.) But Utica was different, a respite from the depressing effect New York State had had on Scarfoglio. He called it "that peaceful, delicious town, shining with water and paint."

"When we reach Utica the rain stops," he elaborated. "We are offered flowers, banquets, and addresses. The fact of our arriving first sends the Italians in Utica almost delirious."

Once the Züst was parked in a local garage, though, the delirium turned toward disaster. The Italians followed the car into the building, packing in more and more densely. And they kept coming in. There was no way to shut the garage doors at the front of the building; the cluster of people coming through them was too thick. A huge Italian flag, hanging from the rafters for the day's celebration, swayed over the car, and over the hundreds of faces around it. Just as a sense of panic began to take hold, a young attorney jumped on a car, pointing to a small door in the back of the building and shouting with great authority, "This way to see the egress. Don't miss seeing the egress!" It was a little trick he had heard of P. T. Barnum using, but it worked. The temptation to riot receded, along with most of the crowd.

When Roberts and the Thomas team arrived in Utica, followed a short time later by St. Chaffray with Hansen and Autran in the De Dion, the leaders of the city repaired with them all to a hotel, the Butterfield House, for a luncheon, of course. "Everywhere they receive us with ovations," reported St. Chaffray from Utica. "They want to know who are the Americans, who the Italians, who the French. But we are so smothered in mud that we do not know ourselves."

All of the racers were in good spirits, if out of place, standing around awaiting their luncheon in the formal lobby at the Butterfield House, with its high ceiling and classical decor. Constantly surrounded, they went about their own business, sending telegrams on race business, writing postcards for fun, and catching up on the papers. Among the news stories that day was one concerning deadly flooding in Ohio and Indiana, where the cars were due to pass within days. Someone asked if they had already seen much snow along the way. Without missing a beat, Hansen replied, "Sure, most of it up to there," and he pointed at the ceiling.

At 2:30 in the afternoon, the racers climbed back into the cars and left Utica. One man who was watching from the sidewalk was shaking his head. "If those daring fellows ever live to reach Paris," he said, "I shall have greater admiration for the men than for the machines."

In the city of Buffalo, it was jokes that were racing around the city, while fans nervously awaited the cars. The city's *Illustrated Times* repeated one such funny:

> *Question:* What will bring the New York-Paris race to an end: impassable ice or the failure of supplies?
>
> *Answer:* I don't know about the others, but I think the French cars will stop when the wine supply gives out.

The most distracted place in the whole city was the Thomas factory on Niagara Street. And Roberts knew it, even from afar. At every opportunity, he sent telegrams assuring E. R. that he would bring the Flyer into its hometown first. But nothing in the New York-to-Paris Race was certain.

On Saturday—known over most of the East Coast as the day Miss Shonts married the duc—the three leading cars were mired at a place called Dismal Hollow in the great Montezuma Swamp. The Swamp extended about twelve miles north of Cayuga Lake, one of the larger of the crystal-clean Finger Lakes. It was the wetland that kept Cayuga's waters both pristine and predictable. The Swamp was neither. Eight miles wide, it was regarded as a year-round mess, except by herons, tadpoles, and a thriving community of other animals. For round-the-world racers stuck in the middle of it all, it was unworldly, and rather menacing.

The Züst, the Thomas Flyer, and the De Dion were lined up next to one another, facing a steep, slippery incline of about twelve feet. Arthur Ruland set off in search of a farmer willing to bring his biggest horses into the swamp for a towing job. Twenty horses would not be too many to extricate the cars from their soggy predicament, but whether Ruland could find any help at all was still uncertain. In the meantime, the others pulled their oilskins closer around their necks and stood in the rain, waiting.

Scarfoglio, drenched from the steady downpour, lost his temper all of a sudden and accused Roberts of cheating, and of forcing the Italians to go first so that they would break the trail for him. Roberts lashed right back, reminding all the others that they'd followed his trail through the Hudson Valley happily enough. Hansen spoke up for his own hard work, and a few of the others spoke in his defense—and then their own, as the bickering continued and the Dismal Hollow became a little more of both.

The teams came to a tense agreement that as soon as they were moving again, they would alternate leadership every five hours. With that, the men returned to their cars to get out of the rain and wait in the swamp for the farmhorses. The patter on the canvas tops was the only sound they heard. Then Captain Hansen broke into a song. "We're Here . . . Because We're Here," he bellowed, in some key or other.

Chapter Eight

Act of War

Car	Miles	Place	Team
Thomas Flyer (U.S.)	471	Buffalo, New York	Roberts, Schuster, Williams
De Dion (Fra.)	471	Buffalo, New York	St. Chaffray, Hansen, Autran
Züst (Ita.)	390	Rochester, New York	Sirtori, Scarfoglio, Haaga
Protos (Ger.)	352	Geneva, New York	Koeppen, Knape, Maas
Moto-Bloc (Fra.)	299	Syracuse, New York	Godard, Hue, Livier

The Civil War had been over for more than forty years in 1908, or so it seemed when James Hogan slipped out of the Old Soldiers Home in Bath, New York, and paid a visit to Buffalo. He arrived on Friday, February 14, a day when the city was waiting impatiently for the Thomas Flyer to arrive. In the meantime, he gave it a show.

After a few drinks, and then a few more, Hogan marched down Main Street with his cane slung over his shoulder like a rifle: chest out, head high. Main Street leads from the east straight into the center of the city, easing gracefully from fashionable homes to bigger and yet bigger businesses. Hogan made quick time past them, stepping to the beat of the battle songs he'd learned in the war, songs he was belting out again, with his white hair bouncing on the collar of his overcoat.

Two days later, a convoy of cars zoomed back up Main Street, in the opposite direction of Hogan's march and at about twenty times his pace. Buffalo's leading automobile enthusiasts filled the cars, looking formal, but actually feeling rather faint. Like expectant fathers, told that the moment had arrived and finding themselves unready for it, they had learned only minutes before that Montague Roberts was approaching Buffalo in the Flyer. The best estimates had figured on his arriving the following day, Monday, but road conditions in western New York turned out to be better than predicted. At last report, Roberts was in Batavia,

82

only thirty miles away, "passing through in a spray of slush and without taking time to inquire the way."

Walter Williams, the reporter for the *New York Times*, was in his usual place in the back of the Thomas, but the car was going faster than ever before and he was holding with a locked grip to the brass handle on the back of Roberts's seat. By some estimates, the Thomas was traveling at a mile a minute, 60 mph. Roberts wasn't owning up to that and later rated his mad dash for home at an average of 45 mph.

The De Dion was not far behind the Thomas. It had paused longer in Rochester, where Hans Hansen had given an impromptu interview to a reporter from the *Herald*. Everyone along the route of the race commented on the fact that Captain Hansen was always smiling or volunteering for extra work or doing something else with which the other racing men could not be bothered. He was far and away the most cheerful man in the New York-to-Paris Race—and so perhaps it follows that he was also the first to crack.

Unburdening himself to the *Herald* reporter, he charged Monty Roberts with cheating and promised to lodge a formal complaint with the *New York Times*, just as soon as he reached Buffalo. In Hansen's view, Roberts continually connived to avoid a fair share of the work in breaking the trail in the snow.

From Rochester to Buffalo, though, there was no trail to break. With a dip in the temperature, most of the roads had frozen hard. They could still be slippery, but a driver who could maintain control over the car could make good time. And Roberts did. Along the way, he whizzed past a church where a gaggle of boys was waiting outside, all decked out for Sunday morning in their choir gowns—and cheering so loudly that George Schuster could even hear them over the growl of the engine.

Schuster, sitting in the front passenger seat of the Thomas, had spent most of the previous two days shoveling snow, relieved only occasionally by other chores, such as lying on his back in a half-foot of slush, making adjustments to the chassis. With the Thomas finally moving fast, though, he was keenly aware that every mile brought him closer to his own house in South Buffalo, where he would see his wife and learn for himself whether she was really getting better—and whether he could leave again for the rest of the trip. As far as Schuster was concerned, Monty Roberts couldn't drive fast enough to Buffalo. And Roberts knew it.

Frank B. Hower, a local oilman, was leading the charge up Main Street toward the approaching Thomas team. Pudgy in appearance and rather dour in countenance, Hower nonetheless had his fun, with a 110-foot yacht in New York City and a quail preserve of his own in North Carolina. At the time of the New York-to-Paris Race, he was taking himself very seriously as the chairman of the American Automobile Association. That made him a personage on the national scale. He was also president of the Automobile Club of Buffalo, a private enclave.

Dai Lewis was riding in the lead car with Hower. In his native Wales, Lewis had been a rugby star, but that didn't make anybody rich in the 1880s, when he arrived penniless in Buffalo. Parlaying success in bicycle racing into a bicycle repair shop, he moved with the revolution into his own automobile dealership, and then combined his experience there with a natural affability to become the full-time secretary-manager of the prestigious Automobile Club. By 1908, though, when Lewis was driving up Main Street with Frank B. Hower, he was no longer the athlete, humming with energy in his tight-fitting rugby shirt. He was a round little man, listening to Hower shouting orders over the snapping wind. Just such men, earnest and efficient, stepped up to assist the New York-to-Paris racers in cities all across the United States. But in Buffalo, there was a difference.

Frank Hower was driving a Pierce car, made by the company that would be renamed Pierce-Arrow the following year. In fact, one of the other men riding in Hower's car was the sales manager for Pierce, Edward C. Bull. The city of Buffalo launched fifteen auto companies through the years, but Pierce and Thomas were easily the most renowned, two crosstown rivals in 1908, warily coexisting. Under the circumstances, Edward Bull couldn't have been happy about the fact that the Thomas Flyer had already been glorified on the front page of practically every newspaper in the country, and a great many others around the world. Or that, even as he sat in Frank Hower's "Little Six" six-cylinder Pierce hurtling down Main Street, the Thomas Flyer was on the verge of its greatest triumph yet: first into Buffalo.

Rushing through the outlying village of Williamsville "at a clip that made a mile-a-minute seem like walking," Montague Roberts came upon a sight that made him wish he had better brakes. In a 1908 car, though, brakes were for slowing to a stop, not screeching to one. That left Roberts with a problem. On one side of the road before him were dozens of cars, including Hower's, waiting to meet the Flyer. The other side of the road was thick with reporters and photographers, along with the Twelfth United States Infantry bugler corp, blowing tattoos. There was no room down the middle for a Thomas car, certainly not one doing sixty.

In a split second, Roberts slowed as much as he could and then turned sharply off the road, bouncing into a field, largely on two wheels. The Flyer crashed through a fence, circled past the throng, and then hopped up onto the road again, leaving another hole in another fence. Even the buglers were dumbfounded. Roberts's feat was the most daring and expert driving ever seen by any of the people present, many of whom would have been dead if Roberts had tried and failed to keep to the middle. It was a fabulous way to arrive: a cowboy galloping into town and then spurring his horse to rear up in the square. Unfortunately, the Thomas Flyer finished its grand entrance with a flat tire. It was soon fixed, though, even with too many volunteers trying to help.

Main Street was jubilant as the Thomas headed downtown, the American flag at the back snapping in the air. Thousands of people lined the street, but the most determined fans of all were waiting in front of the Iroquois Hotel, headquarters for all of the New York-to-Paris Race teams, and they packed tightly around the car as soon as it pulled up. All the while, they cheered Roberts loudly. Roberts put his hand on Schuster's shoulder, to share the ovation. The moment didn't last long, though. A Thomas employee paused only long enough for the occupants to climb out before settling into the driver's seat and taking the car to the factory for service. As to Schuster, he ducked out and went home to see his wife, who was recuperating nicely.

The crowds along Main Street didn't go anywhere, though. They waited patiently and were rewarded, two and a half hours later, when the De Dion made its own dash up Main. It was also led into town by the Pierce Little Six, containing Frank Hower, Dai Lewis, and Edward Bull. "We want to help these foreign racers all we can," Bull explained later. "They don't know the roads and we intend to help them while it's in our power." The Pierce company opened its factory shops to the De Dion and each of the foreign racecars that followed, assisting with service and overhaul—anything at all that needed to be done.

E. R. Thomas wasted no time, hosting a late-afternoon luncheon at the Iroquois. Dai Lewis was there, along with Hower and the other auto men, but the guests of honor were Roberts, Williams, Hansen, and Autran—all of those who had made it so far from New York City. St. Chaffray didn't attend, having already gone to his room to rest. Schuster was also missing, but someone spoke on his behalf. Starting with E. R.'s luncheon, the racers settled in for a break, to warm up, rest, and work on the cars in Buffalo. They figured on leaving Tuesday morning, by which time the other cars would probably have straggled in.

Charles Godard still had a long way to go. He made it only as far as Syracuse on Sunday night, about 170 miles and at least two days behind the leaders in Buffalo. His Moto-Bloc had broken down near Utica. It had also broken down near Peekskill, Hudson, Albany, and Schenectady, but in Utica, the fuel line broke, which took most of a day to fix. Godard was understandably weary when he walked into the Yates Hotel in Syracuse—considered one of the best hotels in the northeast—and even more weary after he went through the process of registering, with that veil of confusion that hovers over any man in Syracuse, New York, who can't speak English. Just as he turned away from the desk, the French chef at the hotel rushed up to greet him, "and an animated conversation began, each man being pleased to find one of his countrymen who could talk the language of Gay Paree," noted a reporter for the Syracuse *Post-Standard*. "In the lobby they stood while a crowd collected and watched with great amusement the Frenchmen, who were pouring forth words in a torrent."

Another Parisian who was staying at the Yates entered into the conversation and offered to serve as Godard's translator during the stop in Syracuse. Godard would need one. In the midst of all the chatter, he ordered his dinner and a cocktail to be served in the dining room. A few minutes later, when he espied the waiter taking the drink from the barroom into the dining room, he suavely backed up and scooped the glass off the tray. No sooner did he touch it to his lips than several Yates employees started shouting at him. His new friend from Paris explained that by city ordinance, there was no drinking allowed in the lobby on Sundays. Godard smiled "and made a beeline for the dining room." Privately, he couldn't understand why such a high-class hotel let mudspattered race drivers in the door, anyway. He assured all those present that looking the way he did, he wouldn't have been allowed near any fine French hotel.

The Protos was only about fifty miles ahead of the Moto-Bloc, having had its own mechanical problems, including four flat tires since leaving New York. Apparently, its rather slender tires couldn't handle the estimated seven thousand pounds they were expected to carry. Lieutenant Koeppen was appalled at the conditions of the route. "Roads?" he exclaimed on his stop in Utica. "What terrible roads we have met. Why, if we were in Germany, we would be in Chicago now!" In Syracuse, Koeppen had done his best to lighten the car, sending supplies ahead to other cities along the route. He stopped Sunday night in Geneva, a college town on one of the Finger Lakes, where the greeting was as enthusiastic as any along the route, despite the Protos's being the fourth car through town. The fact that the Protos was German and not American didn't matter to Geneva, either.

St. Chaffray, of the De Dion, was continually fascinated by the response the racers received in small towns and big cities, and even along lonely country roads, where farmfolk often traveled long distances and waited hours, just to see the cars and wave. "It looks to me America is the very country in which to start such a contest. Everybody understands that this is something outside of the ordinary," St. Chaffray reflected. "It is a dream which passes, and the dreams are one of the best parts of men who wish to make progress."

If Koeppen was heartened by the jubilation he encountered along the way, his car was even more obviously marked by it. The body of the

Protos and the canvas cover over the back were growing dark with names, scribbled whenever the car stopped long enough for someone to wield a pen.

The Züst, running in third place, had a terrible time in Rochester and was delayed there for more than seven hours. On the way into the city, while passing through the old canal town of Pittsford, it flipped over. Sirtori lost control negotiating a slippery hill and, in an instant, the car was upside down in a drift. The occupants all leapt to safety in the soft snow. Although six horses had to be called in to set the car right, it was still viable after the accident and limped into Rochester under its own power. After that came the long delay. According to the newspapers, the time was spent repairing the car. According to Antonio Scarfoglio, there was another reason.

All of the cars in the race got mired down in mud and snow. Only the Italian Züst also had to slog through love. "In every village," Scarfoglio wrote, "in every house almost we find members of the enormous Italian colony of America, who receive us as if we bore our Fatherland in our car. To Italy in our persons, they daily offer sacrifice.

"If this be splendid patriotism," Scarfoglio continued, "it does not help our progress, particularly when the enthusiasm takes the form of banquets and receptions. Much valuable time have we lost, time essential to maintain a leading place in the race. At Rochester, we arrived two hours late, and seven hours more we stayed to digest banquets and speeches and songs."

On the other hand, when the Züst first arrived in Rochester on Sunday afternoon, broken-down and deposited in a garage with no workmen on duty, it was the Italian Americans who saved the day. "The Italians offered themselves en masse," Scarfoglio admitted more gracefully almost a year later, when he wasn't quite so tired of being Italian. "Doctors, lawyers, and workmen all laboured with us, discarding their jackets and rolling up their sleeves. A little banker and a lawyer, Cappellino and Calagero, worked the bellows with all their might; others helped Haaga by fetching coal for the fire; others, again, brought food, roasted chicken, wine and cigars. And those who did not enter the garage waited outside and froze in the snow. At midnight, the repairs were finished."

It is hard to say whether the Züst would have made better progress or worse had it represented some forgotten little country and not Italy, but the Züst team created a unique phenomenon as it crossed the United States, an upsurge of national pride and longing that Scarfoglio could neither ignore nor control. If anything was to blame, it was probably the year: 1908. Many Italians had been in America just long enough to realize that they were not really Italian anymore. That gave them something to long for.

At midnight, the Züst team ought to have trundled off to some hotel in Rochester, but instead Sirtori took the wheel of the car with a new vengeance, simply because Roberts and St. Chaffray had not waited in Rochester, as previously agreed. And so Sirtori drove west, despite the icy conditions and the fact that it was dark—and that he barely knew where he were going. For all of that, he made good time and at dawn, the Züst rolled into Buffalo, where it was supposed to stop along with the others for a break of a few days. After a quick breakfast, and a detour to the Iroquois Hotel, headquarters for the race, the car rolled right back out, entirely unnoticed except for the newsstand it demolished downtown. Emilio Sirtori, after all, hadn't slept in twenty-four hours.

At the Iroquois Hotel, Arthur Ruland, the sole American on the Züst team, left a note for Walter Williams, the *Times* reporter overseeing the progress of the race in the field:

Car turned turtle at Pittsford, six miles east of Rochester, yesterday. Dragged out of ditch by six horses. Repairs completed . . . Very meagre information here at this early hour. Understand Thomas and De Dion cars have gone on. Sirtori and crew had hasty breakfast and left at 6:45 a.m. for Erie.

—Ruland

An hour later, when Williams sauntered downstairs for his own breakfast at the Iroquois Hotel and read Ruland's note, the race faced a crisis. Williams leapt to action, trying by every means he knew to intercept the Züst along the route south to Erie, Pennsylvania, and tell it to return to Buffalo, where Roberts and St. Chaffray were awaiting its arrival. The cars were supposed to be having a break. And the New York-to-Paris Race was supposed to be a polite affair. Williams struggled to make all of those points in the truncated language of telegrams. He sent cables to every station between Buffalo and the state line.

At noon, Williams was still looking for the Züst. He was also promising local officials that in any case the Thomas and the De Dion wouldn't leave Buffalo until the following morning, Tuesday. Dai Lewis continued to plan a truly memorable banquet for that evening at the Automobile Club headquarters. Frank Hower continued to work on his keynote address for the occasion. And Bourcier St. Chaffray continued to give interviews, including one in which he described the wilds of Asia. "Even there, are the roads in better shape than they are here," he said, adding, "I do not complain. The more hardships, the bigger the triumph for the car."

The Protos faced a new kind of hardship when it arrived in Rochester at about noon, as the sense of worship it inspired turned larcenous. While Koeppen and his teammates were in the Powers Hotel having lunch, reported the *Rochester Union & Advertiser,* "the crowd busied itself stealing everything movable about the car. Even the extra shoes of the automobilists were taken." Koeppen was less than happy about it, when he came out of the hotel. But under the circumstances, only one thing would have upset him even more: if the people had put shoes and supplies *into* the overweight car, rather than taking them out.

Every time Scarfoglio and Sirtori read one of Williams's urgent telegrams in the bigger towns south of Buffalo, they only chuckled. Somehow, Captain Hansen seemed to hear the laughter. He bolted down to the Pierce garage, where St. Chaffray was overseeing the job of cutting down the lofty payload, or "box," on the back of the De Dion. In no uncertain terms, he told St. Chaffray that they had to leave immediately to chase the Züst.

St. Chaffray replied, rather casually, that he had heard that the Thomas team had already decided to wait until the next day. The De Dion might as well do the same. He was utterly offhand about the whole thing, speaking with the ennui of an aristocrat, a tone used by the wealthy—but perfected by their penniless relatives.

"I would rather see the Thomas at the bottom of the Arctic Ocean," Hansen said vitriolically, "than wait over a day for it."

St. Chaffray was unmoved. Infuriated, Captain Hansen and Monsieur Autran joined forces. They were tired of doing all the digging, while St. Chaffray sat behind the steering wheel, giving orders and eating. "You may be the nephew of the Marquis de Dion," Hansen said excitedly, "but we'll put you off this car in Chicago, unless you stop giving so many orders and pitch in with more work." St. Chaffray didn't exactly cede that point, but he finally did agree to leave without delay, in hot pursuit of the Züst.

In early afternoon, the De Dionites were ready to leave Buffalo only about six hours after Sirtori had driven off in the Züst. The Pierce company supplied a car to pilot the Frenchmen through the country roads as far as Erie. Hansen climbed with agility into the De Dion's backseat, which was tucked into what was left of the box. He lit his pipe. Back in Rochester, he had made one of his eminently quotable statements for the sake of the car enthusiasts there. "We will either reach Paris," he vowed, "or our bodies will be found by the side of the car." As he was about to leave Buffalo, he echoed that sentiment and in a way clarified it, amid the new realities. "If we don't catch the Italians before we strike Erie," he muttered to a reporter, "I'm going to throw St. Chaffray off this box as a hoodoo." Then he bit down on his pipe.

Hansen didn't file any complaints against Roberts while he was in Buffalo. In fact, he recanted his previous comments about the American driver and praised him profusely in several interviews with Buffalo papers. As long as Hansen's real problems were with St. Chaffray, he meant to stay on good terms with everyone else.

With the news that the De Dion had sped away after the Züst, the Thomas team had no choice but to follow, and as soon as possible. At 3:30, the Flyer was parked outside the Iroquois, along with a Thomas pilot car. The New York-to-Paris racer had been overhauled at the factory, with a few cosmetic changes that made it look less like a prairie schooner. And more like a fishing trawler. The fenders had been removed and the long planks on each side secured at the height of the passenger compartment, like a rim. From the back, and ignoring the artillery wheels, it looked like a boat, and something of a tub at that. Extra tires had been fastened behind the luggage, but the American flag was still attached to a short pole at the very back. However awkward the Flyer was, fitted out for its expedition, that flag and the jaunty angle at which it stood gave it the dash of a firecracker.

Schuster regretted the quick getaway, but he left with the knowledge that his wife was nearly back to her usual health. In midafternoon, he was at the car, ready for the long second leg of the race. When he arrived, he greeted George Miller, another factory mechanic, who was sitting in the car, trying not to look self-conscious. It would have taken someone far more deft than poor George Miller to succeed in not looking self-conscious, though, sitting by himself in the car with a crowd staring his way. A quiet man and a resourceful mechanic, Miller was joining the Flyer as the third official member of its racing team.

George Miller was only twenty-five, but looked older with his stocky, barrel-chested build. Like a hound, he had a face that in repose tended to look worried. He had another side and loved to get laughing with his friends, letting the jests pile up upon each other, but he didn't anticipate much fun of that sort on the race. George Schuster was a good steady man, but if he had a lighthearted side, Miller had never seen it. Shy around most other people, George Miller didn't know Roberts or Williams, the *Times* reporter, and didn't expect that they would have much to say to him. He intended simply to take orders; counting on that fact, Schuster had made him his first choice as a second mechanic.

E. R. Thomas was also hovering around the car as it prepared to depart Buffalo, looking as though he wished he had something substantive to do. Schuster took a moment to assure the boss, a man he'd only rarely met before, that he would stay with the car through Paris and that he would leave nothing undone in bringing it through first.

"We'll catch the Italians before they cross the state line!" Montague Roberts told the fans packed ten deep around the car. They cheered, of course. They probably would have cheered if Monty Roberts had said he was going to ditch the car right around the corner.

Just as the Flyer started to inch away, E. R. reached out and plucked up the corner of the American flag, hanging limply from its pole in the back. He held it out, until the speed of the car snapped it out of his hand—and kept it aloft in the air.

About a hundred miles down the road, the De Dion was the first to arrive before one of the most gratifying sights imaginable. The Züst was at the side of the road, badly broken down. "Never mind," Sirtori said as he, Scarfoglio, Haaga, and Ruland watched the De Dion fly by, without even slowing, let alone offering to help. Roberts paid the Italians the same compliment when he drove by a little later.

The New York-to-Paris Race had started anew in Buffalo. It was a competition, not an endurance test; finally and openly, it was imbued with all of the vanity and desperation intrinsic to a race. "The 'after-you-my-dear-Alphonso' spirit which has existed—or is supposed to have existed—among the rival drivers in the race was knocked gaily west yesterday," chortled the *Buffalo Express* on Tuesday morning.

Tuesday was also the day that a great blizzard moved into the Midwest, paralyzing Chicago and heading east, to meet the men who had so proudly decided that they were battling one another—the men who forgot for the moment that every race, ultimately, is against some force of nature.

Chapter Nine

Snow Spray

Car	Miles	Place	Team
Thomas Flyer (U.S.)	566	Erie, Pennsylvania	Roberts, Schuster, Miller, Williams
De Dion (Fra.)	566	Erie, Pennsylvania	St. Chaffray, Hansen, Autran
Züst (Ita.)	542	Ripley, New York	Sirtori, Scarfoglio, Haaga
Protos (Ger.)	471	Buffalo, New York	Koeppen, Knape, Maas
Moto-Bloc (Fra.)	352	Geneva, New York	Godard, Hue, Livier

J ust before the Thomas Flyer left Buffalo, a race fan visiting from Cleveland was invited to take a place in the backseat, while Williams went ahead by train. For months, the Clevelander had dreamed of finding a place on an American team. Originally, he wanted to go all the way from New York to Paris. That was never seriously considered, but unexpectedly, he did get a chance to ride at least a little way with the Thomas Flyer, and he wrote about it as soon as he got out of the car.

Wrapped in heavy clothes, with fur-lined gloves, cap and face mask, I felt like a cold storage egg when we hit Erie after six hours of nerve-racking, bounding, swerving, digging and pushing over the highways.

Somebody ought to take Roberts out and tell him a few things in a fatherly sort of way, to point out the dangers of going so fast that the front wheels hit only the high places . . . It was a wild dash onward, the smiling-faced Viking at the wheel intent only on overcoming the lead of his dearest rival, the De Dion.

The mad pace could be maintained for short distances only, for the road was bad and, time and again, it became necessary to pile out and lay planks under the wheels to get the car over big holes or build bridges to cross streams which had broken from their banks. And it was HARD work. The hardest sort of work, although welcome to the benumbed and stiffened human beings, who had been huddled down in the car.

Then it was on again. The dizzy pace made the icy blasts cut through clothing like steel knives.

The afternoon's ride cured the "fever," as the Clevelander described his infatuation. "I'd just as soon hang onto the tail of a comet," he wrote, "as ride another hundred miles in the rumble seat of Monty Roberts' space-devouring Thomas Flyer."

When Roberts climbed out of the Flyer in the city of Erie, though, he didn't feel rattled at all. He wasn't even tired. After a hearty dinner, he even went for a ride—in someone else's car—around the city and its finest park, a peninsula curling into Lake Erie, which was frozen as hard as the teams hoped the Bering Strait would be.

The evening's respite in Erie only emphasized the hardest aspect of the New York-to-Paris Race. No effort so arduous, so heroic in the Homeric sense of the word, was ever so easy to quit. All that an entrant had to do to drop out was order breakfast in bed at the hotel—and stay there. Unlike mountain climbers or polar explorers, who are long beyond the pull of comfort, the New York-to-Paris racers had to fight the constant temptation to opt for sense and civilization, both of which beckoned from very close range. The fan from Cleveland happily surrendered to them after only six hours. He explained quite succinctly why. He didn't like daggers of cold air and treacherous speeds and WORK. The question smoldering in the cold of the New York-to-Paris Race was just who would like those things. And why.

The morale in the Thomas Flyer was easily the best of any car on the road to Paris. Roberts was the star, and Schuster was his willing sidekick. In fact, as far as anyone could tell, George Schuster didn't possess an ego. It was Roberts, after all, who had made the surprising choice to tap him for the run from among all the other Thomas employees. Few people had ever seemed to notice George Schuster before and so, no matter how many repairs he had to make under the car on soaking wet roadbeds, and no matter how much snow he shoveled, or ate, in trying to clear a path for the Flyer, Schuster never lost his gratitude toward Montague Roberts.

To anyone who asked, Roberts was entirely confident about the race, explaining that his plan was to put the Thomas so far into the lead that by the time it reached the Rockies (where he was due to leave the team), the other cars wouldn't have a chance. In actuality, Roberts couldn't be certain that the car would even be in the race past Chicago. The fear that really drove him to make good time was that the factory would lose heart, and then money and then all incentive, if he weren't in first place. It was a race for Roberts, all right, a race to get past all those places where the car might logically be pulled from the competition.

The car with the worst morale in the race might seem to have been the De Dion, where Bourcier St. Chaffray and Captain Hans Hansen were confined to the same coop. They were each bright, convivial, and amusing. And they each had the same underlying intensity regarding the race. In terms of intensity, though, St. Chaffray could be hard to take. And so could Hansen, in terms of conviviality. After a particularly grueling day when the teams were forced to stop for the night in the tiny town of Canastota, New York, St. Chaffray prepared to go to bed early. Slightly built, he was usually exhausted at the end of each day's driving. Before leaving the other De Dionites, he directed that they do the same and get right to sleep. For Captain Hansen, though, one thing led to another, which led to his navy uniform and a dance and staying out until the middle of the night. It wasn't his fault that there was no town small enough to bore him.

Hansen's prowling that night led to a continuing fight with St. Chaffray over just exactly what kind of tour of the world he was taking. By comparison to Captain Hansen, St. Chaffray was rather prissy, but then, by comparison to Hansen, everyone was. Having broached the idea of mutiny to Autran back in Buffalo, Hansen was still mulling over the possibility in Erie. In one respect, though, he couldn't hope to get around Bourcier St. Chaffray. Both men were equally determined to come in first in the toughest race ever run.

The worst morale out of all the cars, however, was not in the De

Dion. The men in the De Dion were at least speaking to one another. In the Protos, there was less said with each passing day. Observers during the first few days of the running often commented on the military bearing of the three Germans, and the way they went about their chores as though under orders. It made for an impressive show, as they spoke to one another in the formal, clipped speech of officers in a war zone. But all analogies aside, there wasn't any war. They barely spoke because they didn't want to. A rift was developing between Koeppen, on one side, and Maas and Knape, on the other. But Lieutenant Koeppen couldn't figure out why. He knew they'd be first in Paris, and sometimes he watched his teammates from his place in the back, trying to figure out what else they could possibly want.

When Roberts went to bed in Erie on Monday night, he wasn't worried about the De Dionites, sleeping down the hall—or dancing someplace down the road. He knew they'd leave at about the same time as the Thomas team the next morning. Roberts barely slept at all, however, worrying that the Züst car would sneak through Erie in the dark, the way it had Buffalo. Tossing and turning in bed, he ran to the window every time he heard a car go by, which fortunately wasn't very often in Erie in February in 1908. At 3 A.M., though, someone from the hotel awakened Roberts, Schuster, and Williams and told them that the Züst was on its way. While the three of them stood half-dressed in the lobby, trying to wake up enough for a fast ride in the cold night air, the hotel manager called telephone stations along the route north.

Operators were the best source of information, because each time a New York-to-Paris racer made its way through the countryside, day or night, a rise in telephone traffic followed, as those who'd seen the car phoned their friends up ahead. To place a call, a person had to contact the exchange first and would often add the purpose of the call, as in "Get me Silver Creek-38, the French car just went by." Nothing momentous happened in a small town, especially at 3 A.M., without the "telephone girl" knowing all about it. The telephone operators whom the hotel manager woke up, however, denied that the Züst was en route.

The Züst team wasn't coming. The Italians might have wanted to make another moonlight flit, but the car was having recurring trouble with the radius rod, a result of the accident in Rochester. The radius rod kept the power to the rear axle fully engaged. The Züst could putter, but it couldn't zoom. There was no use traveling at night until it could make good time, and that would only be after proper repairs were made.

After another couple of hours of sleep and a full breakfast, the Thomas team was ready to start out again. Almost a hundred people had gathered to see it off. With particular interest, they watched Walter Williams, the beefy reporter for the *Times,* climb into his place in the back. Before starting, he turned to the crowd and warned everyone who was smoking to stand well back. His seat was located directly over the main gas tank. Not exactly a graceful man under the best of circumstances, he was especially careful as he climbed up the side, over the tools and luggage, and finally lowered himself into his spot.

"Bravo, Fatty!" someone shouted. There were other calls, as well, "familiar expressions," as Williams put it, "that street crowds are wont to shower upon public performers." He didn't care what they said, though, as long as they didn't light any matches.

St. Chaffray pulled away in the De Dion about forty minutes later, both he and Roberts dashing out, intent to be the first in Toledo, 180 miles away. Judging by their previous progress, though, they would be lucky to make Cleveland, only 107 miles west.

The first checkpoint in Ohio was the railroad town of Conneaut, barely a mile across the border, where the roads were so hilly and the turns so sharp that Williams, for one, was in fear of losing his breakfast. Unlike fashionable Lake County, which was next on the way to Cleveland, Conneaut and the rest of Ashtabula County was unprepossessing, plain country. The previous Halloween, the talk of the town, as longtime Conneaut resident Edna McMahon Loucks recalled, was that "the big boys tipped over Jim Kitchen's outhouse.

"Unfortunately," she continued, "Jim was in it." Edna was only five at the time, walking around town with her sister. "We had muffs made of sheepskin with coin purses on the top," she said. "If we had a few coins in them, the Carnegies had nothing on us."

The Carnegies did have something on the gentlemen farmers of Lake County, but not very much. Located just to the west toward Cleveland, it was Ohio's richest county, where orchards tucked themselves into the gaps between the estates of Cleveland's millionaire class. Roberts drove through it with his head bent over the steering wheel, looking at the road out of the top of his eyes. He couldn't drive with the cold air cutting into his face—not only was it painful, it made his eyes water, whether or not he wore goggles, and slowed him down. Only rarely did he straighten up. One of those times was near an isolated farmhouse, where a mother was waiting on the porch, with her four children. As the Flyer approached, she lifted a rifle from her side and fired it into the air in salute: sixteen shots in all. Roberts didn't stop to ask the significance of the number.

St. Chaffray was less than an hour behind, stopping at each town only long enough to ask about the Thomas and drop off a telegram form for transmission to the *New York Times.* He didn't even stop for lunch, rushing through Cleveland as though it were just another village, in order to keep up the chase after Roberts or Toledo, whichever he came to first. Only four years before, Cleveland had been the nation's motor city, leading all others in automobile production, and it still fancied itself a car town, second to none. Unfortunately, the racers were at a low ebb for social graces when they passed through Cleveland. The Thomas team did take advantage of an offer from a sturdy young enthusiast, Jack Sperry, to drive a pilot car through to Chicago. Unfortunately, Sperry wouldn't last long. He returned home by train from Indiana, a day and a half later, ill and shaken from the exertion.

Monty Roberts and Bourcier St. Chaffray were within minutes of each other as they arrived in Elyria, thirty miles past Cleveland. A well-known car called the Garford was made there by a company owned by an industrialist named Arthur L. Garford. Each of the cars pulled into the Garford factory for a pit stop but continued on within minutes.

The Thomas car arrived at Norwalk, another twenty-five minutes farther west, at 4:30 P.M., stopping at E. D. Cline's grocery store to fill up the gas tank, one bucketful at a time. The men went to a restaurant for lunch and then sped away at 4:54. At 4:57, the De Dion swept down Main Street, but it didn't stop at all, St. Chaffray still being obsessed with catching Roberts before he reached Toledo. The snow was thick on the ground and the ride rough as the De Dion bounced from one frozen rut to another. A little later, as the sun went down, St. Chaffray slowed to a stop so that the headlamps could be lit. It was then that Monsieur Autran, ready with his match in hand, made the discovery that the headlamps had fallen off. The best guess was that it had happened during the hard going from Norwalk. The darker the sky became, the more the De Dion slowed down.

Not the Thomas. Monty Roberts was still headed hard to Toledo. He had his headlights.

Twenty-nine miles away from the city, St. Chaffray found himself in the comfortable small town of Fremont, a port on the Sandusky River. There he gave up on Toledo, and on catching Roberts, with only a small shrug. Not only was it dark outside and snowing heavily, it was seven o'clock and St. Chaffray remembered that dining rooms in America nearly always closed at 7:30.

"We are heroes, but we eat," wrote St. Chaffray that night. "The Thomas people are under the snow at this very time when I have the pen in hand. We shall drink to their health a glass of water. [Fremont was a temperance town.] They drink now the snow."

Roberts brought the Flyer into Toledo that evening, but not without leaving his breezy, easy athleticism somewhere behind on the snowy roads. While local Thomas employees took the car to a garage, Roberts and the others checked into the Boody House. The Boody was an old-fashioned hotel, with its 1870s mansard roofline, but it was a bustling place, especially when the first of the New York-to-Paris racers walked into the lobby. As usual, Roberts was the center of attention.

"Those who saw the Yankee at the Boody last night wondered how he is standing the strain," noted a reporter. "He was nearly frozen." Luckily for him, the Boody was a worldly place, meaning that its dining room was open past 7:30. As soon as Roberts came down for dinner, he ordered a two-inch-thick steak and all the trimmings. While he revived, he fielded questions. Toledo's race fans simply stood around the table and watched Roberts eat, as though he were some twelfth-century king. "It is no play for boys," Roberts said of the driving. "It is business, even if it is exciting every minute. Unknown roads, of course, lend hazards which keep a fellow guessing every minute. No matter if a driver did feel like sleeping, the constant thought that any second may throw him to death keeps him stimulated to wakefulness."

Roberts methodically cut chunks off the steak and devoured them. "We set out from Cleveland to make Toledo, if it snowed rocks, and we did it," he said, pausing for only an instant before adding, "Did you ever see anything disappear like that little meal?"

Monty Roberts went to bed determined to draw farther ahead of St. Chaffray the next day. St. Chaffray had his sights on taking the lead from his "American friends." As for Sirtori, of the Züst, he didn't go to bed at all. He, Scarfoglio, and Haaga, men not known for their patience, had spent most of the day confined to a machine shop in Erie, trying to arrange a permanent repair for the radius rod. As soon as it was fixed, they put it to good use. Arriving in Cleveland near midnight and learning that Roberts was in Toledo, they just kept going, chasing him all through the night.

The German Protos was only just lumbering into Erie. The Moto-Bloc was behind that, still struggling to make Buffalo. Heading through the flat countryside of East Pembroke, New York, Charles Godard suddenly spotted an elderly man standing in the very middle of the road. He only barely avoided knocking him over, as he came to a stop with the best braking he could muster. The old man's arms were full of red apples, and as soon as the car stopped, he placed them carefully into the back of the car. Then the man shook hands with the racers, wished them all luck, and stood back.

"In France, you find not that," Godard said, telling the story later.

As each of the racecars passed through Buffalo, the question lingered in the air as to whether the Pierce crowd was purposely helping the Thomas's opponents in order to try and defeat the Flyer—or whether Buffalo automobilists, as a group, were simply trying to assist all of the entrants driving from New York to Paris. When Godard and the Moto-Bloc team left Buffalo, after a night of rest, the answer was apparent. The Buffalo Automobile Club duly supplied a pilot car to escort the Frenchman to Erie. It was a Thomas. And E. R. Thomas was driving.

As the leaders woke up in Ohio, three hundred miles farther west on the road to Paris, they were met by the news that Indiana was in a state of emergency. Headlines such as "Death Follows in Wake of Storm," "Thirteen Trains Stuck in Snow," and "Seven Doctors Thought to Have Perished" only began to describe the effect of the blizzard—the worst one in many years, according to the papers. On the sunniest summer day in 1908, there was nothing mundane about crossing northern Indiana by car, the roads were so rugged. Driving through on the worst day of the whole year, and possibly of the decade, was plain foolhardy according to the experts. According to race fans, though, it was sublime and perfectly in keeping with the whole idea of driving to Paris from New York.

Nonetheless, the reports confirmed that the blizzard had shut down the region. People in an endurance run would have agreed to hold back for a day or two, until the storm eased and at least some traffic resumed. People in a race, however, don't want to agree.

The last stretch of western Ohio was navigable for Roberts and St. Chaffray, and for Sirtori, closing fast in the Züst. It was the border that seemed to exact a toll. In the well-named town of Waterloo, just a few miles into Indiana, they hit a wall.

For the next three days, absolutely nothing moved on the roads of northern Indiana, except the New York-to-Paris racers and their respective pilot cars. And they didn't move very fast. The unplowed snow was four feet deep and drifted much higher. Even within towns and cities, the roads were barely passable. The state was completely paralyzed by the snow. "The weatherman has a right to discourage those auto racers if he wants to," groused an Indianapolis sports writer, "but it is pretty blamed tough on the rest of us."

Having been through upstate New York at its wintery worst and having even survived the Montezuma Swamp there, the drivers had to reach for new superlatives to describe Indiana in a blizzard. The average miles per hour of the cars was sinking to much less than one, down from about 30 mph in the Ohio snow. When the Thomas Flyer left Waterloo for the village of Corunna, a distance of seven miles, it plunged into a battle that lasted for the next thirteen hours.

The treachery of the blizzard wasn't the primary concern for the drivers, though. One would think that in the midst of a world buried in white, there couldn't be any other concerns. But Roberts was convinced that Sirtori and St. Chaffray were conspiring against the Thomas. Sirtori and Scarfoglio, in the Züst, believed the same of Roberts and St. Chaffray. And St. Chaffray, for his part, detected a conspiracy between Roberts and all of the farmers of Indiana.

"Yer ahead of the Frenchy!" called out a well-meaning farmer to Roberts, with every intention of lending encouragement. "But be keerful of the drifts clear into South Bend." South Bend was over a hundred miles away.

According to one account, St. Chaffray pulled up behind Roberts, even as the Thomas team was clearing a canyon through a long drift. " 'Gwan, shovel your head off,' " St. Chaffray is supposed to have taunted, " 'You can't get through unless you do, and when you do get through, I can, too.' " In terms of accuracy, the story had liabilities—"gwan" not being in the average Parisian's vocabulary, for example—but more than that, it implied a certain naivete that the racing men had long since lost on the road from New York.

The New York-to-Paris racers certainly did shovel for each other in Indiana, but in a way that showed just how tough a competition can be, whenever human beings are involved. Archie McDonald was eighteen years old when the three leading cars struggled through Corunna. When he was in his nineties, he still remembered it, all of it:

> These drivers had a helper with them, two of them in each car, and they drove the roads and snow, it was in the dead of winter, and snow from four to six foot deep. They stopped over, two or three of those cars, they drove in to Corunna. That's when the hotel was quite popular. They would load up with gas and oil here and take off.
>
> When they'd get into a snowbank out on the road, they would shovel the snow back of them, so the man that was following would have to do the same thing to get through.

Chapter Ten

Combustion

Car	Miles	Place	Team
Thomas Flyer (U.S.)	987	Michigan City, Indiana	Roberts, Schuster, Miller, Williams
Züst (Ita.)	949	South Bend, Indiana	Sirtori, Scarfoglio, Haaga, Ruland
De Dion (Fra.)	921	Goshen, Indiana	St. Chaffray, Autran, Hansen
Protos (Ger.)	865	Edgerton, Ohio	Koeppen, Knape, Maas
Moto-Bloc (Fra.)	854	Bryan, Ohio	Godard, Hue, Livier

O n February 19, when the three leading cars were in Indiana, the Protos was just leaving Erie, Pennsylvania. With Hans Knape at the wheel, Ernst Maas beside him, and Lieutenant Koeppen in the back, the team had high hopes of reaching Cleveland by nightfall—not a particularly lofty ambition. Monty Roberts had covered twice that distance three days before.

They made it only twenty-three miles, as far as Conneaut, before the snow stopped them. The next day and another twenty miles on, it was a fence post that captured them by insinuating itself into the wheel. Some of the spokes were knocked out, but rudimentary repairs, rendered in a livery stable, made the car ready again.

Setting out early the next morning, Knape tried to rush and lost control of the car. Just as it stopped skidding, it fell off an embankment. Once it was righted again, he drove it another eighteen miles before it was caught in a bog of ice and slush, and the repairs to the wheel gave way. As if being towed into Cleveland at 1 A.M. wasn't ignominy enough, the Protos was passed by the Moto-Bloc. It was last, it was broken, and there were 21,834 miles to go.

In the opinion of Captain Hansen, the Protos was nonetheless the most intimidating car in the race. Hansen didn't have anything to say about the vehicle itself, but the men inside were Germans, he reasoned, of the type who would not quit. That concerned him more than all the engine horsepower in the world.

On Friday afternoon, the twenty-first, the Protos left Cleveland and covered fifty miles—all the way to Norwalk or, more specifically, to Sly's Machine Shop on Woodlawn Avenue there. By then, the residents of Norwalk were used to seeing cars heading through their town on the way to Paris and so the Protos could be described very succinctly. "It was equipped similar to the other cars in the contest, only 'more so,' " the morning paper explained. The Protos was overhauled at Sly's and the next morning, promptly at 9:00, it sped away. Promptly at 9:01, it broke down. But the problem was minor and it left Norwalk for good at 9:30.

Charles Godard in the Moto-Bloc was never far from the Germans in Ohio, sometimes ahead, but usually behind. With the race separating into two divisions, the Protos and the Moto-Bloc might have engaged in a warm competition to be first among the laggards: fourth in the overall reckoning. Another sport, however, was distracting the men in the Protos.

Knape and Maas, the ones who drove the car and who very often fixed it, decided after almost ten days of racing that it was time people knew that they were in the car. Oberlieutenant Koeppen had a way of attracting all of the publicity. For one thing, he was the only one of the three who spoke English. For another, he liked people and chatted with them along the way, unlike his companions. Knape and Maas were all business. They generally disappeared on stops, without bothering to search out Americans who spoke German—of whom there were many in 1908. With nothing else to go on, reporters typically described the Protos team as "Lt. Koeppen and his fellows." That sort of thing brought his fellows to a rage, especially if they thought about it while they were shoveling.

Hans Koeppen, earnest and friendly, couldn't help being the center of attention on the team—until Ohio, where he deliberately stood back, giving no interviews at all. It was too late, though, too late to change his bearing or the impression he left, even in silence. The *Toledo News-Bee* ran a short article on the Protos's appearance in the city, which started "Lieutenant Koeppen, the driver, and his assistants . . ."

That might have been the last straw.

Koeppen wasn't the driver, and Knape and Maas weren't his assistants. The snow reduced the importance of titles, though, and the next day, all three of them worked frantically to press the Protos forward all of thirty-five miles, ending in the town of Edgerton, along the Indiana border. The story of the trip was familiar; the car went only about as fast as the men could shovel snow.

Edgerton, so fiercely won, happened to be one of the few towns in Ohio in which the Protos was in good working order. It was the team that broke down there. After a short discussion, Hans Koeppen abruptly left on a train for Chicago. According to his memoir, the decision was entirely amicable, the team realizing that it needed certain parts for the car and Koeppen being the logical person to go ahead and collect them. The others regarded the situation differently, and said so, as soon as they came across a reporter who spoke German and was buying the beers.

"It was all very nice for the Herr Lieutenant as long as things went well," Maas told a newspaperman in Indiana. "He loved to pose for the newspapers and allow us to do all of the shoveling and we had plenty of it to do."

If nothing else, the New York-to-Paris Race proved early on in the automobile age that there is no test of compatibility like a long car ride. In an overweight car slogging through deep snow for six or seven hundred miles, the conclusions were especially acute. According to the same reporter:

> Maas and Knape were highly indignant at the conduct of the lieutenant and declared that when they reached Chicago there would be an understanding or they would abandon the race. They say they were deserted at just such a time as they needed all the assistance they could possibly get. The roads between Edgerton and Kendallville they describe as the worst highways an automobile ever traveled.

And so Koeppen took that option that constantly hung over the New York-to-Paris racers. He packed his suitcase and hopped a train, cozying into a seat as he shot across the breadth of northern Indiana—or "Siberiana," as the region was being called that week. In a matter of four hours, he arrived in Chicago. Somewhere along the way, he whisked by St. Chaffray, Captain Hansen, and Autran, who were in the middle of a "shovel party," in St. Chaffray's words. Outside of South Bend, he whizzed past Sirtori, Scarfoglio, Haaga, and Ruland. They were eyeing the clearance and barely daring to breathe as the Züst crept across a bridge built for rail cars. It was only just wide enough to accommodate an automobile. To the west, in a farmer's field, Montague Roberts was shouting orders into the frozen air, driving nothing more advanced than the team of black horses that was hauling the Flyer out of a drift.

To Maas and Knape, Lieutenant Koeppen was a shirker. In his own mind, he was an officer, and he didn't have to fight the battles himself to win them.

Captain Hansen arrived in Chicago by train soon after Koeppen did, another example of a man who could take anything that the earth could muster, but not one more word from his teammates. He really was in Chicago to collect parts, though, the De Dion having been completely disabled due to a broken transmission shaft in Kendallville, in the eastern part of Indiana. Hansen informed automobilists in Chicago that St. Chaffray had been driving the De Dion when the shaft broke, and he added with emphasis that thenceforth, Monsieur Autran would drive the car, except on the easy spans.

The broken shaft was a disaster that would cost the De Dion three days, but in the wider scheme of the New York-to-Paris Race, the third week of February was as good a time as any for a disaster, since neither of the other two leaders was moving very much, due to the snow. After Hansen took off for Chicago, St. Chaffray remained with the car in Kendallville.

"I know the social life of Kendallville," he announced after just one day. "Twelve members of the Kendallville Club were at their club yesterday. The people of Kendallville . . . are fond of news, of sewing machines, of agricultural news and of big business contracts." While living, temporarily, as a Kendallvillian, St. Chaffray learned what it was like to be on the other side of the excitement, awaiting a New York-to-Paris racing car. He was awakened by the engine of the approaching Züst at 5 A.M. on his first night. "The noise of an auto in the night can be heard by the most tired contestant for a distance of one mile," he reported. St. Chaffray rushed down to the street, along with the rest of the town, to meet the car. The temperature was zero, but that seemed to discourage no one.

Even St. Chaffray was shocked by what he saw in the Züst: four men who had not stopped for rest in four days. They were dirty, frozen, bearded, and stony with exhaustion. Sirtori had been driving almost continuously for thirty-five hours; the one time he let Haaga take over, the huge car, bucking around in the snow, proved too much for the young German. Sirtori climbed behind the wheel again and drove until he had no choice but to drop. That was in Kendallville. After checking into a hotel, the four members of the Züst team immediately went to sleep.

The next day, Scarfoglio went shopping for a typewriter. As a correspondent, as well as a participant, he haunted telegraph offices everywhere the Züst made a stop. Some of the clerks, though, claimed they couldn't decipher his Roman-style handwriting and so, starting in Kendallville, he no longer scribbled into a notebook as he sat in the back of the Züst. He typed into the machine balanced on his lap.

While Scarfoglio was in Kendallville, Monty Roberts was thirty miles ahead, pulling into the county seat of Goshen. The enthusiasts who crowded his car leaned forward to hear his first words, once the engine stopped. Someone wrote them down for posterity. "I am tired of shoveling snow," he said.

Roberts had every right to complain. The worst storm in Indiana in twenty years had whipped the snow into drifts as high as seven feet. In Michigan City, a little boy walking home from kindergarten climbed over a fence at the back of an alley and fell into one such drift. He couldn't right himself and might have perished there if his older brother hadn't found him, after searching for hours. The main line trains ran on schedule, with the tracks cleared by frequent plowing, but one small passenger train was stuck in the snow for three days. As for the roads, none of them were plowed, except in the biggest cities, where unemployed men earned a dollar a day by shoveling downtown streets.

Driving a car in unbroken snow was a constant wrestling match—demanding, but eerily monotonous. Sirtori had buckled in Kendallville. It was only a question of time before Roberts gave in, too, though he struggled on valiantly. In the hamlet of Rolling Prairie, midway between South Bend and Michigan City, it happened. A representative of the *Chicago Tribune* was present. His article (signed "By a Frozen Stiff Photographer") described what happened. Like most of the newspapermen covering the race, though, he noted first and foremost the scarcity of liquor in the hinterlands:

> Two miles out of that gay—but dry—little Indiana village Roberts, who was driving, went to sleep. He slept at his post—the lobster! The wheel made a quick turn of several points of the compass, the "Flyer" gave a frantic leap to the "stabboard," and buried its nose in an eight foot drift with such reckless abandon that the connecting rod of the steering gear was badly twisted.
>
> Here's where I found out what Mr. Mechanic [George Schuster] had been taken along for. With a muttered curse or two he got out his jimmies and other tools and crawled under the car. He kept tinkering away for two hours steadily, stopping at intervals to use more ungentlemanly language.
>
> When we got the steering business fixed up we plowed slowly ahead.

Roberts, Schuster, and Miller were far from alone in their efforts to pull, slide, drive, push, carry, or drag the Thomas Flyer across the state of Indiana. They knew they could depend at every turn in the road on battalions of farmers and countryfolk, who abandoned their warm kitchens to help devise ways to move the Flyer through the snow. They could depend on them and what is more, they could depend on their draft horses—at one point it took fourteen Clydesdales to budge the car forward, with at least twice that many men shoveling the snow in front of the wheels, or pushing the bodywork from the back and sides. As the

Frozen Stiff Photographer reflected, "we had to dig the horses out every few lengths."

"Get there we must!" Monty Roberts shouted as a twelve-horse team prepared to tug the Flyer through the fields near Michigan City. According to the rules, of course, each car was supposed to go from New York to Paris under its own power. Being hauled by horses for a few yards was one thing, being dragged around for miles at a time like a fancy pull toy was another. When the foreign teams heard about the Thomas's new method for beating the snow—horses-power, as one wag called it—they lodged vociferous protests, and so did a good many American observers. The protests lost their piquancy a day or so later, though, when reports came in that the others had given in, too, that the Züst had been pulled by fourteen horses and the De Dion by eight. Later on, the Züst set a record for the whole race, when it called upon seventeen horses to pull it through a bad patch near Michigan City.

The foreign teams, however, still resented the fact that they had to pay, and pay a lot, for the efforts of horses and men, while the Thomas was invariably surrounded by Hoosiers anxious to volunteer. What's more, the foreigners reported that in some places, Indianans refused them help at any price, on the grounds of patriotism. Holding back the Züst and De Dion was apparently the next best thing to helping the Thomas.

The ultimate gratuity handed to Monty Roberts and the Thomas team came from the Northern Indiana Railway, an electric trolley line that connected several cities along the race route. The president of the company was E. S. Mulholland, who gave the Thomas special clearances to drive over the track laid out for the electric cars. By the time the Züst and the De Dion reached the same vicinity, however, Mr. Mulholland was nowhere to be found, or so his office said, and the general manager blandly explained that he couldn't possibly extend special permissions without explicit authorization—from Mr. Mulholland. Emilio Sirtori was furious, but he had no choice except to continue to wend his way through the snow. St. Chaffray and Captain Hansen, rolling again in the repaired De Dion, complained as loudly as Sirtori.

No one was as indignant, however, as Paul Picard, a Frenchman and a well-known race driver in the Great Lakes area. Picard had been assigned by the Chicago Automobile Club to escort the racers from Michigan City over the last thirty miles to Chicago. The roads in that corner of the state were easy to confuse, especially in winter. Nor could the racers rely on anyone in the city of Gary for directions. It didn't exist yet, except as a plan on a piece of paper.

Picard wielded a certain degree of power as the designated guide on the Michigan City–Chicago leg of the race, and he decided in one swoop to make up for all the favoritism accorded the Americans in Indiana. "I will help only the men who are racing fairly," he said, adding that he did not consider Monty Roberts to be on that list. When Roberts arrived in Michigan City to start the last leg to Chicago, Picard told him that he would have to wait a day or two for the Züst and the De Dion. Then the three of them would be led into Chicago together. Roberts's reply is not recorded, except that he declined to delay another minute. Unfortunately, while he refused Picard's offer to provide an escort, he didn't refuse his directions, which turned out to be dastardly, sending the Thomas down a tertiary road clogged with snowdrifts. Charles Coey, the Thomas dealer from Chicago, was riding in the pilot car accompanying the Flyer out of Michigan City, but even he didn't know the roads well enough to be of any use.

With the Thomas so near to Chicago on February 24, the celebration had begun to unfold. At midday, Michigan Avenue was lined with cars and people, waiting to welcome "Get There" Roberts. At two o'clock, the telephone rang at Coey's dealership back in Chicago. "Is this Coey's?" the voice on the wire asked.

"Yes, it is," said the man who answered.

"This is Coey! We're stuck in a snowdrift two hundred feet deep."

The celebrations were postponed. After hours of work, the Thomas was sprung from the drift, which was probably a little less than two hundred feet high—for anyone who wasn't inside of it.

At four o'clock the next day, February 25, a quartet of pilot cars from the Chicago Automobile Club met the Thomas in Hobart, Indiana, about ten miles beyond the city limits. By the time the racecar drove up Michigan Avenue, fifty cars draped with American flags were following behind it. Chicago turned out just as New York had. To the banners, crowds, and loud cheers, it added music, in the form of a band riding in the car preceding the Flyer. It also added sleet, but at least that was a sign that the temperature was rising. When the Thomas came to a stop in front of the automobile club, it was surrounded by at least a thousand enthusiasts. Monty Roberts pulled off his head gear and smiled for the first time in days. "It was an awful pull," he said of the first twelve hundred miles of the race.

The next day, when the De Dion and Züst cars arrived together, the reception was even more exciting. Sirtori had waited for St. Chaffray in Hobart, so that their two cars could parade into town together. For that reason, his Züst was in front of St. Chaffray's De Dion in the processional wending its way up Michigan Avenue. Suddenly, at the intersection of State and Michigan, St. Chaffray had a burst of enthusiasm or ego or insanity. He passed the Züst on the crowded street. Sirtori was ill-amused. "I got up speed," he said and then added, looking for the words in English, "—and made a noise with my accelerator." For half a block, the two cars were racing through a game of "chicken" in downtown Chicago. Sirtori had been first to Hobart, though, and he meant to be first in Chicago. He was.

The greater part of Indiana may have been prejudiced in favor of the Thomas, but Chicago loved all of the cars and showed it, with the windows of the Chicago's skyscrapers dotted with women in white shirtwaists waving flags and handerkerchiefs at the De Dion and Züst teams. All of the teams planned to rest for a day or two in Chicago. The men were worn out and so were the cars. And at that stage of the race, outsiders were in a position to mandate an occasional respite.

While Monty Roberts was alternating steam baths with long naps at the hotel in Chicago, Hans Knape and Ernst Maas were in Elkhart, Indiana, fixing the latest trouble with the Protos engine and seeing, of course, to the tires. The tires were always overworn on the heavyweight Protos.

Charles Godard, at the wheel of the Moto-Bloc, was not far behind and driving hard to close in on the German car. On February 25, Tuesday night, he and his crew stopped for the night at the village of

Wawaka, about one-quarter of the way across northern Indiana. They parked the Moto-Bloc in Lawrence Tyler's Livery Stable, locked in a shed of its own, and then went to a farmhouse to spend the night. The next morning, Godard opened the door of the stable and found the car—and little else. "Cameras, films, guns, tools, automobile supplies, and even our extra changes of linen had been taken and we were left here absolutely destitute of possessions, save the car, which could not be carried away, and those clothes which we wore," he wrote that night.

In New York City, Jefferson DeMont Thompson, ever ready with his checkbook, immediately offered a reward of $250 for information leading to the arrest of those involved. Back in Wawaka, the sense of outrage was more tempered. "The representatives of justice," wrote Godard, "declared they could do nothing to apprehend the culprits, could aid us in no way. Indeed, with our difficulty in making ourselves thoroughly understood, they seemed to regard us in as bad a light as if we were ourselves guilty. Finally, the attitude of the people of the town was such that we determined to go ahead in spite of our lack of every necessity for such travel.

"We are going on in that condition to the next stop," Godard added, "where we may be able to obtain such aid as we need to fit us to go on." The next stop was even worse, in what became Godard's dreamless Indiana nightmare. In the town of Ligonier, he engaged a farmer named Calvin Fisher to accompany the car with a team of horses, ready to tow it as necessary. They agreed on $3 per mile, which was $3 more than the Thomas had ever had to pay, but $5 less than the De Dion had once paid. Fisher duly left for his farm to fetch the horses, but he never came back. Godard waited, but finally, with no time left to spare, he hired another team from another farmer and made it through to Goshen.

In Goshen, Charles Godard was met by a constable named Dwight, who didn't know anything at all about the robbery in Wawaka. He was on the scene to arrest Godard. Calvin Fisher, the slow-footed farmer, had lost no time in telephoning a complaint against the Moto-Bloc team for nonpayment of $21. His claim was that he had followed Godard for seven miles out of Ligonier. Seeing that Godard was winding up to vent a protest, Constable Dwight quickly explained that he wasn't paid to straighten out disagreements, only to take defendants into custody. A small committee of Goshen automobilists arrived to intervene on Godard's behalf, but the constable was stubborn. He had to have the money or make an arrest.

During the impasse in Goshen, someone put through a telephone call to Colonel G. C. Conn of Elkhart, the next town to the northwest and the place where the constable planned on incarcerating Godard. The title of "Colonel" was no honorary blather; Conn had earned the rank in battle in the Civil War and then returned to Elkhart to start the band instrument company that still bears his name today. Colonel Conn, in his sixties, was an enthusiastic motorist. Moreover, he was a candidate for governor, having announced his intention to run less than a week before. Conn gave his personal promise to oversee the claim as soon as Godard arrived in Elkhart.

On the basis of Conn's guarantee, Constable Dwight let Godard go. And Godard went, straight through Elkhart, without stopping to see the judge or Colonel Conn. It wasn't his smartest move, but it did brighten Constable Dwight's day, as he dashed off for an old-fashioned chase, on horseback.

A little while later, Dwight rode into the village of Osceola, leading his prisoner: a touring car. Godard was allowed to go into a bank and when he came out, he surrendered $23.75, which included the cost of the pursuit. Charles Godard would be deceived by other farmers in Indiana, and even accosted by other constables. Yet none of those astute lawmen could learn who stole his supplies, tools, cameras, and underwear in Wawaka. Godard, usually the most buoyant of men, was incensed.

Captain Hansen, on the other hand, was more relaxed than he had been in weeks, as he put on his uniform and groomed his moustache at the hotel, in anticipation of the banquet: the requisite New York-to-Paris Automobile Race banquet, at the Chicago Automobile Club. In its own way, Indiana had been as hard on Captain Hansen as it had been on Godard. In one village, a farmer jumped him and tried to beat him up, after mistaking him for a crooked Norwegian sewing-machine salesman who had been through the territory years before. Hansen punished the man, first by wrestling him into a snowbank, using a tricky maneuver he'd learned in the mines of Umtilikavitch, Siberia, so he said, and then by holding him down and reciting the story of his life. The farmer, according to a witness, went into a trance—he'd only been braced for a bloody nose, not an account of the Argentine rebellion from the naval point of view. However, the fight with the farmer was generally light-hearted, and it made for yet another good story. Hansen's next confrontation in Indiana would not be as amusing. In fact, Hansen wouldn't even talk about it, or anything else, when the car finally arrived in Michigan City. One observer there went so far as to describe him as "gruff." That just wasn't Hansen.

A couple of days in Chicago had given Captain Hansen a new sense of perspective, though. He went to the banquet looking fine, and he took a place right next to his old nemesis, Montague Roberts. St. Chaffray was a few seats away. About fifty invited guests dined with the racers. Charles Coey had contracted a terrible cold as a souvenir of his efforts in the snow, but he'd undergone an unusual cure, involving electricity, during the afternoon and managed to make it to the banquet. Monty Roberts pretended to receive a shock every time he touched him.

As the meal ended, there were toasts, which translated into calls for short speeches. Hansen rose quite suavely to respond to his toast. "Besides telling you how much I appreciate your hospitality," he began, "I also have something more serious to say. You all know that I have come this far on the French car De Dion with G. Bourcier St. Chaffray. It is bitter sometimes to tell the truth and sometimes the truth is bitter, but I want to tell the truth. I am no longer with the French car in this race." Everyone in the room reacted to Hansen's bombshell, gasping or murmuring—eyes widened and heads tilted quizzically forward. Hansen held his pause. Then he continued.

"I have been the only man on the French car who is not a Frenchman and Monsieur St. Chaffray has said that because I am not a Frenchman, I must go. Is that not the fact, Monsieur St. Chaffray?"

St. Chaffray only nodded.

Further investigation, along a long line of whispers in the halls outside the banquet, turned up the fact that the end had actually come three days before, when the De Dion car had plowed into a particularly vengeful snowdrift somewhere to the south of Michigan City and sometime in the middle of the night. Brute strength was always required in extricating one of the cars from the snow, but so was clever engineering. Hansen, the Arctic expert, was supposed to be in charge of such operations, but his first efforts failed. So did his subsequent ones. St. Chaffray finally pointed that out and then began giving the orders himself. Hansen countered and the words and gestures between them escalated into an all-out screaming match. On the verge of throwing punches, they agreed to settle the fight with a duel. They were going for their pistols, packed away in the baggage, when St. Chaffray made an administrative decision, telling Hansen that he was fired. Hansen immediately said that he quit. With that, the duel was regarded as unnecessary.

The day after the banquet, St. Chaffray told reporters that Hansen had been working as a waiter in a cheap bistro in Paris when he signed up for the race. That probably wasn't true.

"Why, I could go afoot over the Siberian route and beat the De Dion car," Hansen told his own confederates the next day.

That probably wasn't true, either. Then he added, "A Norwegian cannot get along with a Frenchman, when the latter treats him like a serf." That much was indisputable.

Chapter Eleven

Gumbo

SATURDAY, FEBRUARY 29, 6 A.M.: LATEST OFFICIAL STANDINGS			
Car	Miles	Place	Team
Thomas Flyer (U.S.)	1118	Rochelle, Illinois	Roberts, Schuster, Miller, Williams
Züst (Ita.)	1043	Chicago, Illinois	Sirtori, Scarfoglio, Haaga, Ruland
De Dion (Fra.)	1043	Chicago, Illinois	St. Chaffray, Autran
Moto-Bloc (Fra.)	963	New Carlisle, Indiana	Godard, Hue, Livier
Protos (Ger.)	963	New Carlisle, Indiana	Koeppen, Knape, Maas

A s the break in Chicago stretched toward its third night, Montague Roberts was increasingly anxious to leave. If it were up to him, he would have started west again with only a day and a half of rest, but he and the Flyer were generating a wave of interest in Thomas motor cars. Charles Coey, one of the boosters from the very beginning, convinced Roberts to stay for one more night and one more banquet, an important one for sales. The next day, though, Roberts, Schuster, and a factory representative named Mason Hatch were in the car early in the morning, along with Walter Williams, ready to push on to the vaunted American West. George Miller took a longer break and arranged to meet the team by the train farther on.

Almost four thousand people turned out to see the Thomas make its start. Roberts stood up in his place in the driver's seat to lead everyone in three cheers and a tiger—a communal holler—as a gesture of gratitude to the Chicago Automobile Club. One of those in the crowd was Emilio Sirtori, who had learned just enough English to step forward and bid Roberts good luck. He added that he hoped they would meet again soon.

Roberts didn't share the sentiment. "It was the foreigners who first failed to keep their agreements," he said later, out of earshot of Emilio Sirtori. "I am through with them and hope I shall never see them again."

Roberts was still bitter that Sirtori and Scarfoglio had made their dawn slingshot run through Buffalo. His opinion of those in the De Dion wasn't much better. "The French drivers seem to think that they can make new conditions every three hours," he complained. "They say, 'We are the race.' " He was referring specifically to St. Chaffray, of course.

Whatever Roberts said to Sirtori in front of the Chicago Automobile Club, his real response was a heavier foot on the accelerator all through Illinois. Roberts was a born racer. The only way he knew to fight was to leave his enemies behind. And with spring conditions in northern Illinois, he was finally able to leave the snow shovels in the baggage.

The Thomas was the first of the New York-to-Paris cars to cross the Mississippi River, by way of the bridge at Clinton, Iowa. At the other end of the state, with about three hundred and ten miles of Iowa in between, the car was to cross another great river, the Missouri. The route bypassed Des Moines, the state's biggest city, but encompassed even more people, in all, with a central route that included the state's second-biggest city, Cedar Rapids; the farm center of Marshalltown; and several college towns, including Ames. Iowa had two kinds of roads, those that were curved and sometimes steep in the eastern part of the state, where the bluffs overlooked the Mississippi, and those that were mindlessly straight in the farming sections farther west. Both types of roads were left scarred by the spring thaw, with rivulets of melting snow crisscrossing the old wagon tracks sagging into the drenched soil.

As of February 29, when Roberts and Schuster crossed the Mississippi, they were already more than a week behind schedule, with little hope of arriving in Seattle by March 5, a crucial pivot point in the interest of reaching Alaska in decent weather. Roberts and Schuster had been on the Flyer for every single one of the 1,150 miles since Times Square. Seventeen days had passed since then, fourteen of them on the road. With something like twelve hours' worth of driving time each day, the Thomas was averaging all of 7 mph. It was an excellent record, given the roads and weather, and the amount of time devoted to digging. At that rate, though, the Thomas would take a century to reach Paris, or so it would seem to the men inside it. And the Thomas was leading the race.

The average speeds had to rise, and they did. With only a little extravagance, Roberts called the roads in Illinois and eastern Iowa "boulevards" compared with the going earlier in the race. They were sharply rutted and pocked with puddles, which slowed the car to an average speed of about 12 mph, but it kept moving, and that was the point. "It's a cinch we'll win this race," Monty Roberts said after he arrived in Iowa. "The European machines are too high and too heavy to compete on bad roads." Relatively light and decidedly strong, the Thomas was well suited to mud. In fact, even as the Flyer was picking its way through the countryside in the late winter of 1908, Henry Ford was in Detroit, huddling with C. Harold Wills to incorporate the same basic qualities of lightness and strength into the chassis of the Model T, the car that would be introduced later in 1908 to become the gamest mudder of them all.

The condition of the roads worried Iowa's race fans, whose numbers were fast swelling to include practically every person residing along the race route. None was more decisive than a banker named Henry Haag in the town of Jefferson, in western Iowa. He took it upon himself to pay crews with teams of horses to drag the main roads in his county, in much the same way that tractors today comb horse tracks between races (or baseball infields between innings), to ensure a smooth surface. In anticipation of the New York-to-Paris Race, the country lanes around Jefferson were said to be in "elegant condition." That was good, but the rest of the state was still a total mess. The cars came anyway, and nothing dampened Iowa's enthusiasm for them.

"The City of Boone Has Gone Nearly 'Automobile' Crazy," blazed a headline in the local *News-Republican*. Another city labeled its residents "daffy" on the subject. All Iowa was a little bit daffy, anticipating the racers. And it would be noticed. The foreign racers probably could have withstood another blizzard but not another state like Indiana for antipathy and insult, and unresisted profiteering. Indeed, Iowans, who liked to be contrary, or at least to make up their own minds, were acutely aware of what had happened in Indiana. The state seemed to have decided to give the racers the best three hundred and ten miles of the whole route from New York to Paris. Towns made plans not only for celebrating the teams, but for storing the cars, with round-the-clock guards assigned in advance. Guides and pilots were selected, too, to help the cars with navigation. Even before the Thomas nosed across the Mississippi, Dr. T. B. Lacey was sitting in his big touring car in Council Bluffs—on the Missouri River at the other end of the state. With his chauffeur behind the wheel, the car left "with a roar like that of a muffled gatling gun" to travel east and meet the Thomas. The next day, Dr. Lacey telephoned home from a town called Denison, eighty miles away, to announce that he'd thought it all over. Roberts could find his own way; Lacey planned to look out for Scarfoglio and St. Chaffray. When asked why he had changed his mind, he was furtive, promising to explain in a telegram—in French. "I have to write my messages in French for some very good reasons," was all he would say. Whatever his secretive reasons, it was by no means a good sign for the foreign cars that French was regarded as an uncrackable code in western Iowa.

It was in eastern Iowa that Walter Williams, the former war correspondent and world traveler, decided that he'd had enough. He couldn't write stories for the *New York Times* in a bouncing and frigid automobile, and he was sick and tired of standing in telegraph offices, scratching out an article on a pad just in time to send it and then climb back into the car again. Williams had shoveled and pushed with everyone else to keep the Thomas moving, chores well outside of the usual responsibilities of an ace reporter. But after almost three weeks, he was out of sorts.

When the rest of the team stopped for the night in the village of Clarence, in the hills of eastern Iowa, Williams kept going by train to Cedar Rapids and a suite at the first-rate Montrose Hotel. Overly relieved, perhaps, by his return to room service and all the rest of civilization, he turned vindictive and told the millions of readers of the *New York Times* that Clarence was a one-horse town, where there was no hotel.

Williams's comment was a direct insult to the town's spic-and-span Cottage Hotel. The proprietor of the Cottage, Miss Jennie Mehan, was crushed. Fortunately, the weekly *Clarence Sun* came to her defense against the mighty *Times*, testifying that a traveler could not possibly get a better supper than Miss Mehan served at the Cottage. "Williams gave the town a roast it does not deserve," snorted the editor, "and if this is a fair sample of his writings, his reports are not worth the cost of the telegraphic service." Apparently Williams agreed, at least for the moment.

He had a choice and, understandably, he took it, quitting the team in Clarence. He didn't want to devote his life to the New York-to-Paris Race. That is what made him different from the men who continued.

On the morning of March 1, one day after Williams's catharsis, Monty Roberts was making fairly good time on the approach to Cedar Rapids, though by then, he no longer regarded the roads as "boulevards" and was grousing that he would do better with a canal boat than with a car on Iowa's soggy lanes. Still, the Thomas Flyer was moving fast as it passed through the town of Marion, about five miles to the north of Cedar Rapids.

As word spread that the American car was on the way—within minutes—Cedar Rapids was elevated to a kind of ecstasy. And that presented a problem on a Sunday morning in the heart of the Bible Belt. "It seemed hardly possible that so many persons could congregate in such a short time in a city where nearly everybody attends church," observed a resident, "but when the word was flashed down from Marion that the car had started, men, women and children flocked from all directions to see it enter the city."

That still left a problem. "Mindful of the decorum of the day," the report continued, "there was no cheering." That didn't mean people weren't excited at the sight of the famous car. They were said to be thrilled beyond measure. They just couldn't make a sound.

"Forward! Forward!" wrote Antonio Scarfoglio of the Züst's first day on the road, on the westerly road out of Chicago. "A kind of frenzy has seized us. The race, the speed are intoxicating us . . . We are only living for the race."

St. Chaffray was only about a half hour behind in the De Dion, with Autran and a replacement for Captain Hansen. The new man was Emanuel Lascares, a lawyer by profession and a member of the Chicago Automobile Club. French by birth, he had been swept up in the zeal for the race and climbed into the car without quite affirming just how long he'd stay. When the De Dion arrived at the bridge spanning the Mississippi River, St. Chaffray stopped so that he and the others could take souvenir pictures. One of the American guides separated from the group and sidled up to a reporter. "The Frenchmen and the Italians in the race are suspicious of everybody," he confided. "They are afraid they will be directed over the wrong road."

That was just what Iowans didn't want to hear. By the time the Italian and French cars pulled into Cedar Rapids a day later, the reception was even more enthusiastic than it had been for the American Thomas. Anyway, it was louder.

On an afternoon regarded as a general holiday, the schools had been let out and the children joined everyone else in cheering the Frenchmen and Italians. The moment the De Dion was safely stashed at a garage, St. Chaffray, mud-spattered from head to toe, ducked into the Hotel Montrose. "What a splendid building," he exclaimed on his way in. On his way out of the lobby a few hours later, he was a new man, courtly and dignified. "Please print in your paper that the French motorists are sometimes clean," he said to a reporter with a smile.

Antonio Scarfoglio was overwhelmed with the reception. Perhaps the intoxication of the road had unleashed his gratitude for small kindnesses; perhaps he had been scarred by the trip through Indiana. Or perhaps there really was no finer place on earth than Cedar Rapids in 1908; Scarfoglio thought so. "I have travelled a great deal," he said through a translator. "But I have never seen a city which impressed me as more beautiful and more hospitable than Cedar Rapids, as we came down your beautiful boulevard and First Avenue this afternoon, with its trees and handsome homes, while thousands stood at the curbings and cheered." When the merriment died down a bit, he went to the telegraph office and set the whole town talking again by sending a telegram of 1,954 words—at a time when most people composing telegrams considered the standard minimum of ten words more than enough to express any aspect of the human experience. Scarfoglio's telegram to the

Julie M. Fenster

London Daily Mail cost almost $100, a heady figure, about a third of what a teacher in Iowa earned in a year.

Bourcier St. Chaffray of the De Dion was just as effusive as Scarfoglio, and possibly more so. "In Cedar Rapids, everybody is a millionaire," he reported to *Le Matin*. "That was my first impression." He based his judgment on the preponderance of palatial homes, any of which would have cost a fortune in France. It was just as well that St. Chaffray did like Cedar Rapids. He was going to be there for a week, his car having developed mechanical problems hopscotching ruts. The most severe of them had started with a faulty spring. To brace the suspension, in a roadside sort of way, St. Chaffray or one of his teammates had wedged a block of hardwood between the spring and the frame.

By the time the car reached Cedar Rapids, it not only had a broken spring, but a hole in the frame where the block of wood had been hammered down by the rough roads. In addition, the steering gear was shorn. To make repairs to the frame, the De Dion had to be completely dismantled. Some of the replacement parts could be fashioned in Carmody's Machine Shop, the factory in which the De Dion took up residence, but a new spring had to be ordered, and that kept the team in Cedar Rapids. It was a disaster in a race that fought for every hour's advantage.

The delay wasn't a total loss, though. St. Chaffray learned to eat puffed rice in Cedar Rapids, where the cereal was made, shot out of industrial cannons that boomed throughout the day. He entered into the fray of an upcoming mayoral election and campaigned on behalf of one of the candidates (Carmody, to be exact, in whose shop the De Dion was being repaired). He also found time to sully the name of Captain Hansen in Cedar Rapids. "Hansen is ze grand, what you call in this country, ze bluffer," he said to someone who recorded his comments phonetically. "Hansen knows nothing about ze country we shall pass through in ze north. Zat is one of his big bluffs. He's come from Manchuria, where he used to sell ze wine, and is just a poor man who is looking for what you call ze job."

Despite all the many things that there were to do in Cedar Rapids, Bourcier St. Chaffray was still temporarily out of the New York-to-Paris

Race. Not only wasn't he speeding toward Paris, his car was in hundreds of pieces, neatly lined up on the floor of Carmody's shop. Yet St. Chaffray wasn't discouraged, he wasn't depressed. He and Autran simply went at the job of fixing the car as quickly as possible. In the midst of the repairs, someone handed St. Chaffray a telegram from the Marquis de Dion in Paris. "Take your car," the cable began, "when you have it repaired, over all the road to San Francisco and over all the road through Alaska, Siberia and on to Paris, no matter if it takes you three years to do it." It was a gratifying vote of confidence. But the thought of slogging through Alaska and Siberia for three years must have been stultifying.

In the college town of Ames, almost exactly in the middle of Iowa, Montague Roberts and the Thomas crew made only the briefest of stops. "Biff, zigg, chug," was how one reporter summed up the visit. Someone else said that Roberts and his team "stopped long enough to be photographed, light cigarettes, and flirt with the ladies in the crowd, and were then off to Boone and beyond." The mayor only had time to open his mouth and draw a breath for his speech. Then two train whistles drowned out whatever it was he'd been practicing to say. The moment was lost and there was no speech.

The reception in towns and small cities across America was not waning from the first days of the race; quite the opposite, it was growing larger as the cars moved west. When the Züst arrived in Ames a few days after the Thomas Flyer, the crowd surged, packing so tightly around it that Sirtori couldn't hope to park it for the night. The manager of the local garage finally turned a hose on the throng. That broke it up in a hurry on a cold March evening. Emilio Sirtori responded to the crowd with a cheer of his own. "Hip, Hip, Hip—A-mare-i-kay!" he cried. But that was before he met the Smiths.

The next morning, Sirtori took a brother and sister named Smith for a ride up and down the main avenue in town, Onondaga Street. Cheerfully, they told Sirtori that in honor of Scarfoglio and him, they had renamed it "Onon-dago Street."

Despite the guards—and the hose—a gang of students from the University of Iowa made it their business to steal the Italian flag from the Züst. Somehow, they succeeded, to the abject disgust of their elders across the state. "The men [in the Züst] characterized it as a college prank, but it could be easily seen in talking with them that they did not enjoy the treatment," observed a newspaper from the nearby town of Boone. In the wider realm, flag-stealing was nothing; the Protos lost flags regularly to souvenir hunters. Loyal Germans stole them and then even more loyal Germans donated new ones. In Iowa, the Züst wasn't without its flag for long. A woman by the name of Mrs. Pina sewed a new one and presented it to Sirtori, Scarfoglio, Haaga, and Ruland when they passed by her hometown in Iowa.

An automobile man from Des Moines was asked by a friend about the interest in the New York-to-Paris Race:

Interest? Why, my dear fellow, let me tell you something. When the American car was going through Iowa I went out to meet it. While waiting some six miles out from the town I went into a farm house to telephone down the line to find out where the American car was and this is what I got from the mother of eleven children, the youngest a babe in arms and the oldest just able to do the chores and milk the cows:

"Why are you one of the automobile men? When is the American car coming? I am so excited I don't know what to do. Here, Johnny, quit pulling Susie's hair and go out doors and get the big flag up. The kitchen is real dirty, but I have been looking for the car and have not had time to clean it up. I am—

"Beg pardon?"

"Why certainly. Isn't it just splendid that the American car is so far ahead? I just know it will win."

When the car came within a mile, the whole party, including the mother and all eleven boys and girls, went out to the road waving American flags.

The Thomas Flyer, grinding out the miles in central Iowa, was ahead of the Züst by a solid day. Having traded smiles with the college girls in Ames, Roberts and his crew were ready to reach the bigger city of Boone. All day, people there exchanged information and rumors about when the car would arrive. It was too much excitement for a young scamp named Willie Johnson. Or else it was not enough. Taking a car out of his father's commercial garage, he drove it out to the country and piled the back with bags, tools, and shovels. He dangled two American flags off the back and enlisted two other boys, Jack Harper and Oliver Hora, to ride with him, covered in winter clothes and hidden behind goggles. When the set piece was perfect, Willie climbed behind the wheel and sped off toward Boone, honking and waving all the way. By the time he reached town, a cheering crowd was waiting, formed into "hedges of humanity," as Antonio Scarfoglio once put it. Willie stopped the car and barely moved, until he heard people disparaging the car as being rather dinky compared with the photos. Then Willie and his friends pulled off their goggles so that their neighbors could recognize them, and laughed themselves silly. The people in the crowd had no choice but to laugh a little, too.

When the real Thomas Flyer arrived in Boone, it couldn't have been mistaken for any other car. Roberts sped forward by zigzagging down the road. Even he found the car hard to control at a goodly speed over the mud. The Thomas tended to leap sideways with even more zest than most cars when one of the wheels hit a hole. In addition, as Roberts admitted, he didn't have much experience driving on rough roads. Nonetheless, he pushed the car hard to open up its lead on the others. He had had only one mishap, though, and it didn't start with the mud—but it ended with it, of course. While the Flyer was crossing a creek near the village of Belle Plaine, the bridge buckled and the car slipped into five feet of "gumbo." No one was hurt from the bridge breaking, but Roberts, Schuster, Miller and Hatch, the factory man who joined the team in Chicago, were all in agony after working the rest of the day to extricate the car from the clutches of the mud.

When Roberts stopped the car for the night in the little town of Ogden, to the west of Boone, people surrounded the car, crying, "Speech, speech." Roberts was too tired for tact. "I don't like your roads," he said in response. "The mud is something awful. The hospitality of the people of the west is splendid to behold and I like the people, but your towpaths—" With that, he stopped talking, extricated himself from his mud-stiffened overcoat, and ambled into the Ogden House hotel to check in.

The next day, the Thomas finally reached Jefferson, in Greene County. It was the moment that Henry Haag, the banker, had been waiting for. He had met the Thomas in Ogden and sat in the car as an honored guest, a pilot, guiding the team over the very roads he'd had dragged. On arriving in Jefferson, Roberts pronounced them the best country roads he'd encountered since starting the race in New York. Haag beamed.

The next day, March 3, the Thomas was out of the state, having entered it on February 29. Despite the kindness of the people, Roberts wasn't sorry to leave, saying on his way out that it was no state, anyway, but just a streak of mud.

The Züst, which had only been one day behind the Thomas upon entering Iowa, was losing time. On the fourth, the telephone rang at the Johnson Garage in Boone, with "a voice at the end of the wire sounding like a piece of the prairie." It was Willie Johnson, the prankster, calling to report that a wheel had fallen off the Italian car, out on a road to the west, toward Denison. Once again, everyone believed him. Unfortunately for the Züst, they were right to do so. It wasn't just another of Willie's jokes. Altogether, Sirtori and Scarfoglio would lose two days to that wheel—and to the mud. The Züst team walked the last few miles into the small city of Denison; in fact, they did it several times, carrying loads of supplies from the car, which was overloaded and sinking in the mire. Scarfoglio had to convince Emilio Sirtori not to quit in Denison.

Still despondent, Sirtori took to the wheel of the Züst as soon as it had four wheels again, and they headed southwest toward Council Bluffs and the state line. Slogging through the mud on an otherwise empty road, they saw a woman standing alone at the side of the road, waving them to stop. Once the car was at a standstill, she brought out a set of small American flags that she had made herself, one for each of the men in the car. In the conversation that followed, she said that she'd walked a mile to meet them. Their gratitude for the flags, which they didn't really need, and for her enthusiasm, which they did, was profuse.

Escorted by Dr. Lacey, the Italian team finally made it to Council Bluffs, the last stop in muddy Iowa. Sirtori was feeling better by then, in part due to the decision of the Illinois Central Railroad to let his car take to the tracks. "We go straight ahead to the coast," he said just before leaving Iowa, "and do not forget it. We may stop at one or two points en route, but we will get there—depend on that." Sirtori didn't like to stop, not even to sleep.

The only thing worse than battling the muds of Iowa was sitting in an easy chair in Chicago. It was rather sad and pathetic that by the end of the first week of March, when Roberts in the Thomas and Scarfoglio in the Züst had so many fresh road miseries to relate, Charles Godard had only just pulled into Chicago, talking almost incessantly about Indiana.

Monsieur Godard was lively, even when he was destitute and depressed. "Parbleu!" he cried, momentarily confounding his translator. "But I have had a long time in Indiana. Snow, we have had it in plenty and expense—whew—we have plenty, too. Every place they want to charge us $5 to sleep on the ground, and I say 'What for?' I will pay nothing. If I must pay to sleep on the ground, I will buy one lot for $500 in the cemetery, and I can sleep on the ground for always.

"One other place we stop for dinner at the house of a peasant—I think you call him farmer," he continued. "They give us one good dinner of some chicken and make us one fine welcome." The charge was five dollars [about eight times what it should have been]. " 'What for you charge me $5,' I tell the peasant. 'Yes,' the farmer say, 'you folks eat my two chickens; they are my pet chickens; they play in the kitchen with my children.' Oh! That is too much. His pet chickens! What for he cook his pet chickens?

"We go to one other place, and we come late, and the inn door is open, but the people inside are all asleep. We make a noise and the landlord he comes down very mad, and say, 'If you don't stop the noise I will have you put in one jug [jail].' I tell him all right, if we must take one jug it must be the one jug of wine. He laugh himself all over, and say, 'Oh, yes, you are the foreigners with the horse-o-mobile. Well, strangers, make yourselfs at home.' "

The charge for the room the next day was five dollars, at least twice what it should have been. "It is one strange country, that Indiana," Godard said. "Everything you buy is $5."

The following day, the Germans arrived in Chicago. Lieutenant

Koeppen had already been there, of course, but he had returned to the Protos in northern Indiana and so his entry into the city was triumphal, or as triumphal as it could be in a car that could only barely move under its own power. He, Maas, and Knape practically ditched the car in the garage at the Automobile Club and immediately repaired to the banquet room of the club, where they were received as honored guests. Koeppen seemed relaxed, as usual. When called upon to speak, he didn't say anything about the dissension in the team. He didn't even want to talk about the snow in Indiana. Instead, he responded to rumors that the lagging teams would be allowed to ship their cars by railroad to Seattle, in order to stay on schedule and ship out on the Alaska-bound freighter on or about March 5. Koeppen said that any such shortcut was entirely against the rules, unsportsmanlike and in violation of the spirit of the race.

The next day, Knape and Maas quit. They had just given Lieutenant Koeppen an ultimatum, that either he leave the car or they would. They believed that Koeppen would have no choice but to withdraw, since he did not, after all, know how to drive. But Hans Koeppen surprised them. He didn't need time to think about that or any other threat. He wouldn't leave the car. And so Knape and Maas made plans to return to Germany. None of the three said anything rancorous in public. Maas told the papers that he had to tend his business interests in Berlin. Knape said that he was returning to engineering and an idea that had come to him, probably many times of late: a motorized plow for the front of passenger cars. "I feel that we have a fortune in this invention," he said.

Maas and Knape departed Chicago almost immediately, leaving Lieutenant Koeppen in silence in his room at the Illinois Athletic Club. He didn't know anyone in Chicago. He barely knew anyone at all in the United States. He was in possession of the Protos, which was badly broken. He also had debts, which were mounting; he had fifth place in a five-car race; and he had no choice but to win the New York-to-Paris Automobile Race.

Chapter Twelve

A Single Room
in Chicago

Car	Miles	Place	Team
Thomas Flyer (U.S.)	1536	Omaha, Nebraska	Roberts, Schuster, Miller
Züst (Ita.)	1458	Vail, Iowa	Sirtori, Scarfoglio, Haaga, Ruland
De Dion (Fra.)	1262	Cedar Rapids, Iowa	St. Chaffray, Autran, Lascares
Moto-Bloc (Fra.)	1043	Chicago, Illinois	Godard, Hue, Livier
Protos (Ger.)	1043	Chicago, Illinois	Koeppen

As of the first week of March, the *Boone County Democrat* in western Iowa had already seen the Thomas and the Züst go by and it was keeping close track of the De Dion. But the other cars had disappeared, as far as the *Democrat* could tell. "The German and the other French car are thought to be lost somewhere," the paper offered, "and nobody appears to know where they are."

They weren't lost. They were in Chicago. But with the Thomas opening a lead of almost a thousand miles, the Protos and the Moto-Bloc were beginning to seem as though they were in some other New York-to-Paris Automobile Race, the one in which the contestants had only three-quarters of a working car at any given time.

Fortunately, Chicago suited Charles Godard. It was a city sometimes disparaged for its hardworking ways, "devoted to nothing but Mammon and pork," as an English author put it, but another visitor caught the spirit of the place more hauntingly: "Chicago is only America," he wrote.

The country's second-biggest city, but its most innately theatrical, Chicago was naturally interested in a titled Frenchman—which is what Charles Godard became during the course of his stay. Perhaps someone called him "Baron Godard" by mistake and he was too exhausted to interrupt with a correction. Perhaps he fibbed one day and introduced himself as a baron. It is true that he invited the entire membership of the Chicago Automobile Club to visit him at his "chateau in Neuilly-sur-Seine, near Paris." If Godard had a chateau, that was news, too, but then, if he was so well-to-do, why did he earn money riding a motorcycle in carnival shows? A great deal about Charles Godard remained stubbornly mysterious. Only one thing was absolutely certain: he wasn't a baron until he arrived in Chicago.

Lieutenant Koeppen should also have been warmly welcomed in Chicago, where the Germania Club was so fervently patriotic that it celebrated the Kaiser's birthday every January 28. People weren't even that devoted in Germany. Koeppen, however, was not available during his four days in the city to serve as a centerpiece at banquets or beer gardens. As a most unusual tourist, one with six thousand pounds of deadweight to move, he had two worries: first, fixing his car and, second, finding someone to drive it. For a long time, he sat in a chair in his hotel room at the Illinois Athletic Club, just thinking.

The Protos was unquestionably a mess. Two of the gears, reverse and high, were torn to shreds. In addition, the gasoline pump failed more often than it worked.

Unsure of what to do, Koeppen first sent a telegram to Madame Gadski in New York, asking if she knew anyone who could drive a Protos automobile from Chicago to Paris and keep it running along the way. In the meantime, through the members of the Chicago Automobile Club, he managed to find a local garage where the mechanics were expert and the owner sympathetic. Koeppen also heard about a couple of Americans who were interested in driving for him. In the afternoon, he was walking back to the athletic club from the garage, still thinking out his options, when he noticed a woman standing beside a broken car. It was an electric car. With nothing left to do for the Protos, Koeppen asked if he could help her. She worried aloud that he'd get his clothes muddy, but he waved that concern aside.

Crawling under, Koeppen somehow fixed the car. Whatever was wrong with it fell into the very narrow category of things he understood about automobile mechanics; maybe a wire was hanging loose with an empty connection beckoning right beside it. In any case, Koeppen hopped up from the ground, brushed his clothes off, and then noticed that people were standing around the car staring at him. Word had spread quickly through the street that the German racing man was helping a damsel in distress. He ignored them and spoke for a few minutes with the woman. Then she drove off, which was unfortunately more than he could do.

While Koeppen was out, a cable from Madame Gadski had arrived. It said that her favorite chauffeur happened to be living in Chicago. According to her glowing recommendation, O. W. Snyder could not only drive beautifully, but fix practically any car ever made. In addition, he was a native-born German. Koeppen had already spoken with the two Americans about making the trip, but he telephoned Snyder and arranged to meet him at the athletic club. Lanky and rather convivial, Snyder spoke easily about cars and appeared to know how to maintain and fix one like the Protos. He seemed to be ideal, yet Koeppen was reserved throughout their conversation. He decided to wait before accepting him.

Some Europeans, as Koeppen knew full well, emigrated to America for opportunity; but a great many of the young men onboard every westbound ship did so just to escape army service. Koeppen sent an urgent inquiry about O. W. Snyder to the War Office in Berlin. The only thing more damaging to a young oberlieutenant's career than failing to finish an internationally heralded race would be hiring a deserter to drive the German entry.

Within a few hours, the War Office responded. Snyder had put in his three years in the infantry and received an honorable discharge. On reading that, Koeppen arranged to hire him. In the space of twenty-four hours, Snyder quit his job and prepared for four months of driving, or portage, with the Protos. He also had to find time to help with the repairs to the car, which were finished late the next day, March 6.

On March 7, both the Protos and the Moto-Bloc were scheduled to start west from Chicago. Baron Godard was originally supposed to wait for Lieutenant Koeppen and the Protos, so that the two round-the-world laggards could travel in tandem. Even in the rear guard, though, the spirit of a race bears down. When Godard heard that the magneto on the Protos was acting up on the morning of the seventh, he couldn't be bothered to wait for it to be fixed. He was ready to leave Chicago, and the Protos, behind.

Maurice Livier not only had purchased a new movie camera, to replace the one stolen in Wawaka, he had built a temporary platform over the hood of the car. As the Moto-Bloc left the Chicago Automobile Club, Livier was perched out on the hood with the camera, taking movies of people waving, traffic halting, and the tall buildings of Chicago receding slowly in the distance.

Five hours after Charles Godard set out from Chicago, Koeppen and his new driver departed, the last of the racers to leave the city. In losing his teammates, Knape and Maas, Lieutenant Koeppen did at least get to sit in the front for the first time. It was an expensive seat, though, because with Maas and Knape gone, he also lost two-thirds of the expense money. Henceforth, all of the costs were Koeppen's. To keep the Protos going, he made arrangements to back his letter of credit with all of his life savings and a substantial loan from his parents. For Koeppen, the first quarter mile in Chicago represented a brave start, or restart. An old gentlemen waving right along with hundreds of others at the Automobile Club waited for the roar of the Protos's engine to grow faint. "They are last," he said, "but they will get there, for they never give up."

Thirty-five miles out of Chicago, the Protos was stopped by engine trouble. And about a hundred miles after that, it was stopped by an oversized pretzel. The German society in Clinton, Iowa, the first city across the Mississippi River, surprised Koeppen with a lively dinner, as soon as he arrived in town. Just before it ended, Otto Korn, the proprietor of Korn's Bakery, brought out an unexpected souvenir for the lieutenant. With all eyes on him, he walked solemnly to the head table with a wide tray in his hands and on the tray lay a mammoth pretzel, decorated with flags. When the applause died down, Koeppen promised to send it home to Berlin, so his relatives could see it.

Snyder proved to be a good driver, and the Protos made steady progress. The German car had long since passed the Moto-Bloc, which hadn't even been able to get through the relatively innocent mud of Illinois. Set closer to the ground than the Protos, it was broken by the effort and actually arrived in Iowa on a railroad car—a shortcut vigorously protested by Lieutenant Koeppen, when he read about it. Race officials in Paris took a dim view of piggyback rides, too, and disallowed the short railroad trip. As soon as the Moto-Bloc was repaired, Godard was ordered to backtrack (by train if he liked) and make up the mileage he'd bypassed.

The result was that as the second week in March began, Baron Godard was going backward, courtesy of the train. Lieutenant Koeppen, when he was in the Protos, was struggling to keep moving in the mud. And St. Chaffray was taking up residence in one Iowa town after another, awaiting parts and repairs for the faltering De Dion: first in Cedar Rapids (cracked frame) for six days, then in Marshalltown (broken driveshaft) for two, and in Crescent (failed driving-gear) for three. Altogether, St. Chaffray would spend eleven days in Iowa just sitting still. Each one of those days counted: by the time he finally exited the state, he would be exactly eleven days behind the Thomas Flyer, the car with which he had left Chicago. The frustration of inertia finally took a toll, first vanquishing all signs of jaunty humor.

"Pardieu," St. Chaffray cried, as he sat awaiting a meal in one Iowa town. "Such roads. Such mud. Such people." He blew rings with his cigarette smoke to complete his thought.

The cost was not only emotional, though. Telegrams that could express the disappointment and anger contained in a smoke ring tended to be extensive; St. Chaffray claimed that he spent $1,000 a day on cables from Iowa. Among other things, he learned via the transatlantic cable that the Iowa mud had notched one notable victory: no driveshaft had ever broken on a De Dion car before.

In his spare time, the eleven days' worth of it, Bourcier St. Chaffray often criticized Montague Roberts and the Thomas team, contending that the Americans had replaced the engine of their car twice and, worse, that it had been pulled by streetcars in northern Indiana. "What mattair if ze car get to Paris first," St. Chaffray fumed. "Eet will not be given honor. It will be deescredited, yes." And he was always interested in reflecting on his former teammate, Captain Hans Hansen. "As soon as we left Buffalo, he commenced to act up," St. Chaffray confided to a reporter (one who resisted the temptation to denote St. Chaffray's accent). "He was fond of the girls and was always asking for money. When we looked into the lunch basket for our noonday meal, it was always empty and Hansen always full."

Captain Hansen, on the other hand, chose to be magnanimous about the squabble. "I hope that no one in the west will be prejudiced against St. Chaffray," he said in an interview, "for he is a good fellow at heart." By then, Hansen could afford to be generous. After a snap trip to Buffalo to see E. R. Thomas, he had secured a place in the Flyer. Hopping a train back to the west, he met the American car just before its entrance into Omaha, Nebraska. "I was glad to see the Captain," Roberts reported. "He proudly produced a silk flag and waved it as his credentials." With that, Captain Hansen was back in the race and hundreds of miles ahead of his old comrade, that good fellow, Bourcier St. Chaffray.

Omaha was a fast-growing city in 1908, built across a rumpled terrain of hills and hollows. It was a cattle center, and that made it a railroad town, as well: the starting point for the Union Pacific Railroad, omnipotent in the west. Behind the scenes, the city was home to the UP shops—cavernous factories where much of the railroad's equipment was built or repaired. On the day that the Thomas Flyer was expected in Omaha, the word went out in the papers—and the soda fountains and barbershops—that a special siren had been attached to one of the UP's mogul locomotives (the railroad equivalent of a tugboat), which was parked across the Missouri River in Iowa. As soon as the car came into sight, the siren would blast a signal, piercing the air over the river and letting a hundred thousand people in Omaha know that the moment was at hand. Or giving them apoplexy.

After two days of waiting for the Flyer to crawl out of the Iowa mud, the man in charge of the siren finally got to pull the cord on March 4. Tens of thousands of people were watching for the car when it arrived downtown at noon. Whatever it was that they were expecting, though, they found themselves facing what one person called "a pterodactyl after a prehistoric mudbath." When the car was hosed off later and returned to its true color, many people were confused, wondering when there had been time to give it a coat of grayish-white paint.

○ ○ ○

The greeting in Omaha was the best of any city to the east, according to those on the Thomas team, speaking for the benefit of the local dignitaries. On the race route, hyperbole seemed to be in the air whenever the aroma of a hot meal was. Nonetheless, Omaha was a memorable stop for the Thomas team. After lunch, the team members went shopping at the M. E. Smith store, where everything was free for them, courtesy of Mr. Smith. And the team members loaded up, departing with sheepskin-lined overcoats, corduroy trousers, matching blue flannel shirts, caps, and gloves. Back at the hotel, they were at the center of a rollicking party, hosted by the most famous man in the state. Even Roberts couldn't resist a bit of name-dropping in a dispatch, sent from the hotel that afternoon: "Col. William F. Cody, 'Buffalo Bill,' was on the Reception Committee, which accounts in a large measure for our good time," Roberts scrawled. "The Colonel is about to buy a drink for the crowd, and I must end this story." Buffalo Bill was then drawing six million people per year to his Wild West shows. It was nothing for him to entertain four auto racers from the east.

Then, after a banquet dinner in the evening, the racers were taken for some real fun—to go roller skating. The city had set up an indoor rink at the Auditorium Building downtown. A roller-skating rink represented spoiled city living for 1908. It was so avant-garde that Captain Hansen, who had been everywhere and done everything, couldn't get the hang of it. He and Roberts staged a race, but "Get There" Roberts won easily when Hansen could barely remain upright. By the next day, the roller rink was gone, completely dismantled, as the Auditorium opened to a state convention of Democrats, frenzied over the presidential candidacy of Nebraska's own William Jennings Bryan.

Even before the chants for Bryan began at the Auditorium, Monty Roberts was already on his way out of Omaha, having spent almost twenty-three hours there—quite a lot for any one city, considering that the car wasn't broken. Roberts was ahead of Scarfoglio and the Züst team by two days and he meant to stretch the lead, not lose it. Monty Roberts had become downright irascible on the subject of the foreign drivers. "We hear nothing but protests," he said, "and I am sick of the word. I never won an automobile race yet but there were protests. In this race, however, it is a go-as-you-please and we are conforming to the rules as much as we know them."

Before leaving Omaha, though, Roberts had a pang of conscience. He asked reporters to qualify the fact that although he had personal differences with some of the foreign drivers, he hoped that Omahans would show them all the same enthusiasm shown to the Thomas Flyer. Roberts was irascible, but in his own even-tempered, amiable way. "Mr. Roberts is a pleasant looking fellow, with a winning smile and a glad hand for everybody," wrote a Nebraskan who met the American driver. "He couldn't look otherwise, because he isn't built that way."

Nebraska, which was dismissed as "the Great American Desert," on maps until a few decades into the nineteenth century, was slightly higher and a little bit drier than Iowa and consequently a great deal less muddy in March of 1908. Roberts sped through the state in a little more than three days—almost exactly five hundred miles, on the arcing course laid out for the race. That was far better than the four full days it had taken to cover 310 miles through Iowa. Nor was the pace slowed by another of the hazards of American roads in 1908: utter confusion. H. E. Frederickson, the prosperous young Thomas dealer in Omaha, drove a pilot car to the west for Roberts, and unlike some of the enthusiastic guides Roberts had encountered along the way, Frederickson actually knew where he was going. Describing the situation with his usual exaggeration, but only a little of it, Roberts said that Frederickson was the first pilot who had stayed with the Flyer for more than two miles, all the others having been scared off by bad roads. Not only was Frederickson made of sterner stuff, he had a vested interest in making the Thomas look good. And anyway, the roads really weren't very scary in Nebraska.

"Listen for the siren whistle again today," advised the *Omaha Daily News* on March 6. The Züst was coming—but not that day. To extricate the Italian car from Iowa and its mud, Scarfoglio and Sirtori had resorted to driving over the tracks of the Illinois Central Railroad, with a special locomotive assigned to it as an escort. According to Scarfoglio, they would have turned back otherwise. The mud was impossible. On the seventh, the Züst finally arrived in Omaha, heralded by "the shrieking of sirens, the booming of cannons and the cheers of the throng"—

an even more boisterous reception than the one that had greeted Roberts in the Flyer. Meanwhile, though, Roberts was more than halfway across the state. "The American car is two days ahead, but what is that?" Scarfoglio said. "It is a long, long ways to Paris and we have lots of time to catch him." Unfortunately, the Züst arrived in Omaha with a "disarranged" suspension system, including several broken springs, after its ride on the rails or, more accurately, on the ties. Under normal circumstances, new parts would have had to be ordered from New York.

Omaha, however, happened to be home to the only factory in the west equipped to roll and fit new springs. The Union Pacific shops generously took on the job of repairing the Züst. Even there, with all of the best equipment and a team working around the clock, the job took more than one full day. The only benefit of the delay was that with each day, spring weather took hold even more firmly on the roads of Nebraska.

On March 8, while the trainmen were using their heavy tools on the undercarriage of the Züst, the Thomas Flyer was making a one-hundred-mile dash for Cheyenne, Wyoming. Scarfoglio and Sirtori were stuck in Omaha at the other end of the state. St. Chaffray was sojourning near Marshalltown, Iowa. Godard and Koeppen were far behind him.

The Flyer was on a streak. It would be disparaging to call it a "lucky" streak, but the American car had traveled hundreds of miles without the breakdowns and mishaps that continually hobbled the others. Montague Roberts was driving brilliantly, pressing the car hard but always within the limits of its capability under the prevailing conditions. Judging those limits is an unending calculation for a driver in any road race, but especially in a race that was trying new territory in every sense of the word. Roberts and the Thomas Flyer made for a seamless combination: strong, smart, and flexible. But the streak was almost over. A new driver was waiting in Wyoming to take over the car.

"My trip ends at Cheyenne," Roberts wrote within days of reaching the city, "which I regret, as I have long fostered a great regard for my car, which has stood the strain so well, and carried us this far in safety. I hate to leave 'old baby,' and turn her over to strange hands, although my rugged companion, George Schuster, assures me that he will see she is not mistreated." Schuster, however, had to be wondering just how much of the car's treatment would be up to him. He and Roberts had made as good a team as there was in racing; the next driver only presented a question in that regard.

All that Roberts could do to help the team was to keep pressing the Flyer toward Cheyenne. The car didn't pass many houses in the ranch-land of western Nebraska, and not many people, either. Occasionally a cowboy loped along next to the car, tossing a conversation back and forth with the occupants.

One cowpoke started out at a slow pace next to the Thomas and insis-tently urged his horse on, faster and faster. Roberts matched the speed and they raced that way for two miles over the flat grassland, before the horse tired out and it was the Flyer that disappeared into the west.

Cheyenne

Car	Miles	Place	Team
Thomas Flyer (U.S.)	1908	Julesberg, Colorado	Roberts, Schuster, Miller, Hansen
Züst (Ita.)	1536	Omaha, Nebraska	Sirtori, Scarfoglio, Haaga, Ruland
De Dion (Fra.)	1262	Cedar Rapids, Iowa	St. Chaffray, Autran, Lascares
Moto-Bloc	1093	Maple Park, Illinois	Godard, Hue, Livier
Protos (Ger.)	1078	Geneva, Illinois	Koeppen, Snyder

In the gray light of early morning on March 8, Floyd Clymer was driving to Cheyenne from his hometown of Berthoud, Colorado, a trip of about sixty miles. He was hoping to make it in about five hours. Like hundreds or even thousands of others descending on Cheyenne that day, Clymer wanted to see the Thomas Flyer round-the-world racecar and perchance to meet Monty Roberts. The roads from Berthoud, pocked and crooked, were hard to follow, but Clymer knew the way, having driven it with his father, a country doctor, dozens of times. He was all alone except for the jackrabbits startled off the road by the approach of his car.

Clymer was only thirteen years old. Driving himself to Cheyenne, he was a prodigy of a sort. Some children play the violin with symphony orchestras. Some earn advanced degrees. Floyd sold cars. The "Kid Dealer," as he was known, had a storefront office in Berthoud and was the recognized dealer for Cadillac, Reo, and Maxwell, among other makes. In those years, a smalltown dealer didn't keep cars in stock but merely took orders. A general store could be a dealership or a postmaster could be a dealer, all on the basis of a few catalogs left open on the counter. Clymer went further, though, placing ads and constantly seeking better makes to sell. He was, after all, one of the most experienced automobile dealers in northern Colorado, having sold twenty-six vehicles in two years. He knew the ropes—he'd been in the business since he was eleven. Like all the other kids, though, including the ones who scrawled their names on the New York-to-Paris racers, Clymer wanted to be a part of the race, at least for an instant. Unlike the others, he also intended to come home with some new business, in the form of a Thomas Motor Car Company dealership agreement.

A man from Denver, H. B. Buckwalter, had taken much the same trip as Clymer the day before. A still photographer by profession, he had packed a movie camera in his luggage, along with almost a thousand feet of film. The motion picture was just about the same age as the automobile, each having been launched commercially in the early 1890s. Fifteen years later, they were both established, but not yet predominant, at least not in the Rocky Mountain region. Buckwalter gave both a shove forward with his trip to Cheyenne in early March. He had developed a side business making movies of local events, especially those including plenty of action. He then leased his films to the local movie houses. By his reckoning, Monty Roberts and the Thomas Flyer were likely to be popular attractions in the Rocky Mountain region and even farther afield. As he headed north to Cheyenne, he wasn't thinking about movies, though. He was cursing the fact that to drive between Denver and Cheyenne, a fairly straight line topographically, he had to make his way through a tangle of local roads that could make a compass dizzy.

"The roads between Denver and her sister capital," asserted a report printed that very week, "are a network of winding highways in places. In stretches over the prairie there is hardly any road to be distinguished, while in other places, the ordinary driver would take the road which is seriously deceiving and which leads after about ten miles of smooth sailing over almost impassable plowed fields."

Carloads of other Denver residents were already waiting in Cheyenne in anticipation of the great moment, the arrival of the Thomas Flyer. One of those in the contingent was H. G. Colburn, an automaker by trade who walked around saying to anyone who would listen, "Next time, a Denver-built car, a Colburn, will be in the big race." He helped pass the time, but missed the point. A Colburn was all right—especially for a Denver-built car, of which there were not many over the years. But there would never be a *next time* for the New York-to-Paris Race. There wouldn't be any point in another. Charles E. Van Loan, a gregarious newspaperman from Denver, reveled in that very fact. He was in Cheyenne to cover the race for the *Denver Post*. Van Loan had been a sportswriter in Los Angeles and liked to put his readers in the thick of the personalities involved in any competition. Later, he would turn the same trick in fiction, and a little while after that, in scripts for silent movies. Van Loan, a burly, fair-skinned man of thirty-one, was out to soak up the atmosphere, stir it up where he could, and work on getting himself a seat in the Flyer for the leg to Ogden, Utah.

Another man up from Denver already had his seat. Three days before the Thomas was due to arrive, E. Linn Mathewson, the son of the general agent for Thomas cars in the west, had received a telegram from Buffalo notifying him that he would replace Montague Roberts in Cheyenne and drive the Flyer through Wyoming to Ogden. Harold Brinker, the professional driver originally scheduled to take over in Cheyenne, would go along in a pilot car and take command of the Thomas in Ogden.

Brinker was famous in the west for surviving a spectacular crash the previous September at the Overland Park track in Denver. Another driver was killed, but Brinker avoided the wreckage by steering into the fence, and through it. His orders from Buffalo were to stay ready, because his job was still "to take car through to Paris." For the moment, though, Linn Mathewson was to be the star of the show.

Wealth had come easily to Mathewson Junior and it showed in his self-important demeanor; he was all business, just like his father. He was also a respected amateur in races around Colorado. He knew the terrain through rural Wyoming, and he certainly knew Thomas cars. At twenty-three, he was two years younger than Roberts. There were those who said that the only reason Mathewson was included as a late addition was to make up for the fact that the race bypassed Denver, the biggest car market in the Rocky Mountain region. At any rate, he was a good driver. And if Mathewson Senior wanted him to drive, then so did the Thomas Motor Car Company.

All morning on Sunday, the eighth, crowds of people were milling around downtown Cheyenne, looking for notices of the Thomas's progress on the bulletin board outside the Union Pacific offices; watching city workmen string electric globes of red, white, and blue along the race route; and listening to Colburn brag. The best perch in town was the sidewalk in front of the Industrial Club, the men's club to which the Thomas was heading. That's where the jostling was heaviest all morning. A lot of the less aggressive sorts just found somewhere else to sit, or lean, and read the newspapers.

There were plenty of papers to choose from that day. Cheyenne's *Daily Leader* was uncontainable: "Monte, You Winner, The Town's Yours," read the banner headline. But the Denver paper, the *Rocky Mountain News,* shed its inhibitions, too, in a different way. It surprised the populace of Cheyenne that Sunday morning with battalions of newsboys imported from Denver and fluttering copies of the alien paper on every block within a half mile of the Industrial Club.

As the Thomas Flyer approached the jumbled, jubilant carnival that Cheyenne had become, Montague Roberts was well aware that he was nearing the end of his stint. For a only a few minutes more, he remained in the epicenter of the transportable holiday. But he was tired, after twenty-six days of managing the fate of the car and extricating it from mud, snow, ditches, and the occasional swamp. He was tired of not knowing quite where he was going, and of heading north, east, and south on local roads in order to go west ultimately. He was tired of well-meaning guides who didn't have any idea where they were. Mostly, though, Roberts was looking forward to a different kind of challenge: driving in the French Grand Prix race in May. "I sail for Paris the 15th of May, to race in the Grand Prix," he said with undisguised excitement, "and as I will drive the only American car, you may look for a surprise from me."

The Grand Prix was the pinnacle of the world for a racing driver in 1908. It was certainly where Roberts wanted to be. The Grand Prix had prestige and history—two whole years of it in the young world of automobile racing. The New York-to-Paris Race, on the other hand, was a one-of-a-kind event, unsanctioned by the powers who guided the careers of drivers and uncertain in terms of its influence. Understandably, Monty Roberts was dreaming of glory in the Grand Prix, and of the chance to be the champion of racing for 1908.

Had Monty Roberts stayed with the scuffed and muddy Thomas Flyer, though, and driven through to Paris, he'd have been the champion of the entire automobile age. What Lindbergh was to a later, aviation era, Montague Roberts could have been to the revolution of his own times. Instead, the Thomas Flyer that sped toward Cheyenne was about to lose its hero.

"You may just say for me," Roberts had told someone at breakfast early that morning, "that the man who will take this car at Cheyenne will take her through to Paris a winner."

"That man," he continued, "is neither Brinker nor Mathewson, but George Schuster, who knows as much as any of them and has been with the car from the start. This is official." George Schuster had every reason to believe it. The next time they stopped, he would lose Monty Roberts as a teammate, but he would have the car. And it would have him.

Over the last stretch leading to Cheyenne, the Thomas crossed the same trail trod by other pioneers for fifty years or even more. It hadn't been graded or paved in all that time. As though to illustrate that point, Roberts met no traffic on the route, except for a single prairie schooner, lumbering over the ruts left by its many predecessors. Within two miles of Cheyenne, the Thomas attracted its first escort, a herd of fifty cowboys, whooping and shouting it along and swinging their lariats overhead, as though it were a reluctant calf. A few cars eventually fell into the procession, too. When the Thomas was within a mile of downtown Cheyenne, every bell, horn, siren, and whistle sounded throughout the city. Startled bystanders put down their newspapers, picked up their toddlers, looked toward the east, and started up a shout that lasted until well after Roberts and his cowboy postriders thundered by. Buckwalter was turning his camera all the while. "A majority of those pictures," predicted one observer, "will represent merely a sea of heads, swept by a storm of waving hats, with a maelstrom to indicate the position of the American car. Pity 'tis the camera couldn't catch the cheers."

At the Industrial Club Building, Monty Roberts slowed the Flyer down, crawling forward over the last few feet in deference to the pedestrians still jumping out of the way. With the car nosing into its space at the curb, he leaned forward and set the handbrake with one long, graceful pull, stopping the car and ending his 2,052 miles in the New York-to-Paris Race. He was still in some blurry moment of his own when Katherine Mackenzie, holder of the *Denver Post* silver cup for the most beautiful woman in Wyoming, swooped down upon him with a bouquet of roses. "Roberts was upset," according to the reporter covering the day for the *New York Times*. "With a great effort he arose from his seat, removed his heavy fur cap and goggles and modestly bowed to the young lady and the assembled crowds, blushing like a schoolboy."

The time was 1:15 in the afternoon. Roberts, Schuster, and Miller ducked away to sleep away the rest of the day. Linn Mathewson climbed into the driver's seat of the car and took it to a nearby garage. Floyd Clymer happened along, by no coincidence, and soon convinced Mathewson to let him sell Thomas cars in Berthoud. He also talked himself into a ride in the Flyer, and so the trip was an utter success for the "Kid Dealer."

At dinnertime, the Industrial Club was lined in electric lights—red, white, and blue—the likes of which had never been seen in Cheyenne before. Mrs. Christine Myers, regarded as the city's best cook, was called in to prepare a special turkey dinner for the eighty-five people who attended the banquet for the Thomas team, while the fashionable young men of the city, who couldn't necessarily afford the five-dollar cost for a seat, fought for the chance to wait on the tables—and thus, to be there. After dinner, a haze of blue smoke hung over the room, rising from the many Havana cigars that had been saved for a special occasion.

Among those in Cheyenne for the banquet and the change in drivers the next day was Harry S. Houpt, the New York Thomas dealer who had not only helped put the Flyer in the race but Monty Roberts in the Flyer. Edward Morse, manager of the Thomas factory, was also present and puffing away at the Industrial Club.

When Monty Roberts was called on to speak, the ovation almost shook the chandeliers out of the ceiling. For several long minutes, he had to stand still at the head table and let it continue—possibly the hardest part of the whole trip. He probably would have rather been shoveling. "I hope the car will be able to keep the lead that it has," he said near the beginning of his remarks. Roberts was undoubtedly speaking for Morse's benefit as he continued. "It all depends on the mechanics," he said. "Driving the car is a cinch, and I want to thank Mr. Miller and Mr. Schuster for keeping the Thomas up so well." Having done the best he could to correct the crooked pitch of celebrity worship, he slipped from team business into anecdotes, which he loved and so did the audience. Among his stories of the trip was one that had occurred only days before:

I have never been west before and I have always wanted to see a cowboy. They kept telling me I would see them when I got west and it seemed to me I had been out west for weeks when a few days ago a man rode up behind us on horseback, whooping and yelling.

We carry guns on the car, and I was just thinking of getting one of them out when he came up alongside of the car and I saw he had a little bouquet in his hand.

He had on a pair of those fuzzy pants, too, and then I knew he must be one of the cowboys I had been wanting to see. He leaned over in his saddle so far that I thought he would surely fall out and handed me the bouquet, which had a little American flag fastened to it. "Go to it, old man, and good luck to you," says he, "and plant that flag in Paris."

That's the spirit we have met all along the route.

All of Roberts's memories of the trip weren't quite so rosy. There was the treachery of the other drivers, in Roberts's view, and the many barbs directed his way. There was the wind cutting into his face like knives and the times when he couldn't move his fingers on the steering wheel, for the cold. There were also the many nights without sleep, devoted to moving the car through deep snow, and, worse yet, fighting or listening to fights all the while to determine how to best proceed. That fell away, though, once Roberts was finally finished and that spirit, the kind he'd found all along the way, was what he took with him as he unbuckled the straps that held his personal suitcases on the car. That spirit and the echo of the cheers.

There had never been any reason for Montague Roberts to start the New York-to-Paris Race; the idea was absurd from the very beginning. But to most observers, millions of them, there was no reason for him to leave the race, either. The Thomas without Roberts seemed absurd. Within days, though, Roberts would be on a train, not in a car. For the first time in a long time, he would be heading out without a care in the world, and he would be heading east.

Early Monday morning, Linn Mathewson and Ed Morse conferred about routes and strategies for the next leg of the trip. Harold Brinker was involved, too, since the Alaskan part of the route was fast approaching and that brought in a new set of complications—even aside from the mountains and the ice and the polar bears and the chance of drowning in the ocean while still sitting in the car.

The Thomas Flyer, making good progress, was likely to reach San Francisco in time to catch a coastal ferry for Seattle, where it would be loaded April 1 onto the *Santa Clara,* the ship scheduled to take all of the racecars to the Alaskan port of Valdez. The other cars, lagging by at least four days and as many as thirteen, were less certain to catch the *Santa Clara*—and that presented a problem. Not only weren't there many suitable cargo ships sailing to Valdez, perhaps two or three in the course of a month, but later arrivals in Alaska would probably be doomed by the weather, as the snow there melted into mud such as even Iowa never saw. Several of the lagging cars had applied to the race committee in Paris for permission to ship the cars by train, in order to make the scheduled sailing, but no allowances were forthcoming. That tangle of rulings and sailings, and its effect on the other racers, was an important topic for Morse, Brinker, and Mathewson. The pressure to make the April 1 sailing from Seattle would preoccupy all of the racers.

At eight o'clock the next morning, the Thomas Flyer was sitting outside of the Inter-Ocean Hotel, surrounded as usual by a throng of excited fans. It was ready to go, although little had been done to it since it arrived the day before. Some people in the crowd were saying that the presence of the round-the-world racer was even more compelling than Cheyenne's last big thrill, seeing President Theodore Roosevelt arrive in the city on horseback, galloping in for the sheer joy of it. That was in 1903 and it was still a fond memory. But the Thomas Flyer enveloped the city as nothing and no one else ever had. It was a car just like any other car, if a little dirtier, but it had an aura. People crowded around it and found a place on it for their initials, because that particular Flyer— metal and leather, rubber and wood—was going somewhere. And who didn't want to do that, in one way or another?

Eight o'clock came and went, though, and the Flyer wasn't going any- where. Hansen was ready. Mathewson was ready. Miller was ready. But George Schuster was not. In fact, he had refused to continue the trip. There was a heated argument with Morse at the hotel regarding that very point.

Captain Hansen, standing in front of the hotel with the car, wasn't aware of what was happening upstairs. Neither were the fans assembled for the send-off. At first, the captain coolly signed autographs and posed for pictures, looking every bit the Arctic hero. As time dragged by, and the novelty of his presence wore off, he tried harder to keep the crowd engaged. He told jokes. Then he made a broad comedy of flirting with Katherine Mackenzie, who was on the scene, determined to charm her way into a ride in the Thomas. At least, it appeared to be just a comedy; Hansen had no doubt taken note of the young woman regarded as the belle of Wyoming. He clowned around some more and then, at about nine, Morse sent word to move the car back to the garage. Upstairs, Hansen finally found out what was going on. Schuster had disappeared.

Chapter Fourteen

On Strike

Car	Miles	Place	Team
Thomas Flyer (U.S.)	2052	Cheyenne, Wyoming	Mathewson, Schuster, Miller, Hansen
Züst (Ita.)	1539	Omaha, Nebraska	Sirtori, Scarfoglio, Haaga, Ruland
De Dion (Fra.)	1313	Tama, Iowa	St. Chaffray, Autran, Lascares
Protos (Ger.)	1118	Rochelle, Illinois	Koeppen, Snyder
Moto-Bloc (Fra.)	1101	DeKalb, Illinois	Godard, Hue, Livier

George Schuster was one of twenty-one children born to Casper Schuster, a blacksmith who moved to Buffalo from Germany in the mid-1800s. Casper had three wives over the course of his long life, the second of whom, Barbara Neuman Schuster, was George's mother. George spent his early years in the city, but the family later moved to a farm, where Casper started a sideline, making wagons. There were a lot of workers—that is, children—helping out in the smithy, but George was one of the best and left with at least some of his father's expertise in metalworking.

In 1890, when George was seventeen, the bicycle craze was sweeping America, as well as most other places. Before the young smithy knew it, he was in the midst of a world that was awaiting new men, both in the sport and the expansive industry behind it. In cycling, Schuster found competition that was open, unlike that of the more clubby sports popular up to the 1890s. In baseball, rowing, or even track, participation was largely predicated on whom one knew. Bicycle racing required no connections; it was boxing without punches. A fellow fresh off the farm could enter and win—and Schuster did. In 1896, he was even crowned city champion in Buffalo. By then, he was making his living in the bicycle business. "I worked for the Clinton, Electric City and Globe Cycle companies and became known as one of the best 'wheel truers' in Buffalo," he boasted.

With no formal training or education, Schuster managed to find a place in two of the most advanced industries of his day, as he parlayed his knowledge of blacksmithing into a role in bicycling, which led him to a place in the automobile business. At Globe Cycle, Schuster worked for Dai Lewis, and when the Welshman started selling Ramblers, Schuster started fixing them. Thousands of men all over the United States and in Europe were following the same route, building the automobile industry on top of more traditional skills. Only a few were innovators, at the forefront of change, but the rest at least had a place in the business that was showing the way to everyone else, and that was just where they wanted to be. It was where George Schuster wanted to be.

In 1902, E. R. Thomas took possession of some of Globe's manufacturing facilities for his new automaking company, and Schuster went along. Newly married, he started as a metalworker at the first Thomas factory, not even the size of a whole city block then, to craft radiators onto chassis. In those days of 1902–3, ten years before the assembly line seized hold of the automobile industry, cars were constructed in place, one part at a time, by expert mechanics. At first glance, a car factory back then looked like a repair garage does today.

Schuster took intense pride in his work. The best bicycle wheel–truer in Buffalo became, by turns, the best radiator solderer, chassis inspector, motor-tuner, and test-driver. He had the workingman's conceit in believing that his results spoke for him. He didn't see why he needed to be dazzling or impressive, when his work was. And that was all right, so long as he wasn't ambitious for anything other than his next promotion on the factory floor.

In 1905, when Schuster was thirty-two, the Thomas Motor Car Company expanded into a new factory, two blocks wide and four long. George Schuster was rarely there, though. Having been named chief troubleshooter, he spent much of his time on the road, or on the water, solving problems with Thomas cars as far away as Puerto Rico. Although there was no specific warranty on cars, as there typically is today, luxury manufacturers sent experts out to fix stubborn problems whenever they occurred—and wherever the customer lived. Schuster's job was to remedy what was wrong with the car, or the chauffeur, and not to leave until everything was running perfectly. Sometimes he devoted weeks to a single problem.

On occasion, Schuster drove a Thomas car in an endurance test for the factory, such as the time in 1907 when he made it to Erie, Pennsylvania, and back to Buffalo without once downshifting from high gear. In the days before automatic transmissions, when shifting was a fairly rigorous exercise, that was an eye-catching feat. Schuster also delivered cars or demonstrated them to prospective customers, though the factory preferred to send someone like Monty Roberts on most such visits, a person who could lend something to an occasion other than mere work, however well rendered.

When E. C. Morse called Schuster in Rhode Island on February 11 and asked him to serve as Roberts's mechanic on the New York-to-Paris car, there was a terse moment of negotiation. The race itself didn't offer any pay for the participants. Though two prizes of $1,000 had been offered privately to the winning team, such monies would be split at least three or four ways among the team members. No one could expect to make a great deal of money racing overland to Paris—except George Schuster. At his insistence, he received a bonus of $50 per month, doubling his regular salary. He also exacted a guarantee of employment with the Thomas Motor Car Company for the rest of his life.

Schuster and Roberts made an extraordinary team, of course: Roberts, the effortless one, and Schuster, the diligent. One of their closest competitors, Bourcier St. Chaffray, took note of that fact at just about the time that Roberts left the team and was receiving praise around the world for the gaping lead opened up by the Thomas:

Besides Roberts, the Thomas has a man full of resources. He is a good man. His name is Schuster . . . the mechanic of the Thomas car. When the car has stopped at some place in the middle of a field or a road for repairs to the tires or chains, one finds on the ground the visiting card of Schuster. It is a large place of oval shape, where the back of said Schuster is portrayed in the grass as well as on the snow. At once and in any condition of mud, the brave mechanic takes the opportunity to go under his car and to survey everything. He also takes the wheel and Roberts gets a rest.

St. Chaffray had good help on the De Dion, but no one like Schuster. Monty Roberts knew it as well as St. Chaffray did and never made the mistake of overlooking George Schuster. He included him in every discussion of the Flyer's success and sought out his opinion on matters pertinent to the race. But all along, Roberts had been unique. He saw something in Schuster that was easy to overlook; if it was star quality, it was of a low and steadily burning type. Others only saw a face in the background.

Even to the least sensitive observers, Schuster had proven himself indispensable to the progress of the Thomas Flyer. Without him, the car could barely hope to succeed. And that was his point, exactly. If he was crucial to the running of the car, then why was a brat like Linn Mathewson taking over? The soft burning star exploded in Cheyenne.

After Schuster disappeared from the hotel, Monty Roberts and Harry Houpt ventured into E. C. Morse's hotel room, to defend the frustrated mechanic. Morse only said that he couldn't drop Mathewson from the roster of drivers. And he couldn't drop Brinker, either. Both drivers meant something in the west, one as a socialite and one as a racing man. There was nowhere that Schuster represented such things, and certainly not in the west. He was a backstage sort.

Sales mattered most to Morse—and everyone else who wanted to stay in the automobile business. He was prepared to send the car out with Miller as mechanic, leaving Schuster behind. Once Schuster came to his senses, he could catch up to the car by train, if he wanted. Morse wouldn't stop him. To that, Roberts stated very simply that the car could not hope to win without George Schuster onboard. It probably wouldn't finish, either. Miller was an excellent mechanic, but he didn't have Schuster's intensity.

Houpt, listening to the discussion, was awaiting an opening. He regarded the conflict as an opportunity to ensure Roberts another stint as driver. While the others talked, he was quietly scheming. If Harold Brinker, almost as respected a driver as Monty Roberts, was in charge of the car when it reached Europe, he would naturally expect to finish the race. Houpt formulated another plan, though. He wanted his man Roberts to meet the car somewhere in Russia or Europe in midsummer and take it to the finish line in Paris.

Under direct pressure from Roberts, and the more subtle influence of Houpt, Morse had a change of heart. He decided to assign Schuster to drive the car through Alaska and Siberia—nowhere, in terms of Thomas sales. If the Thomas failed up there for some reason, it would only be Schuster at the wheel. But in the event that the car did make it through, he insisted that Roberts take over the driving when the car drew near to Europe. Roberts gave his promise, and Harry Houpt nodded gently in the background.

Linn Mathewson wasn't affected and didn't care, since he was leaving the car in Ogden, anyway, but Harold Brinker was sorely disappointed when he heard that his leg of the trip would end at San Francisco. He had no say in the matter, though. If he demurred, Schuster would gladly take over even earlier. Brinker accepted what he could get. The only person left to tell was George Schuster, who was still AWOL.

No one knew where Schuster had gone, but when he reappeared at the hotel, he received the offer with very few words. He did insist that he would be regarded as the captain of the Thomas team, even when Mathewson and Brinker were driving. Morse agreed, so that the car could finally leave, but Mathewson and Brinker never did.

At eleven o'clock, the Thomas was once again removed from the garage and parked in front of the Hotel Inter-Ocean. While Roberts stood to the back and watched, Mathewson climbed into the driver's seat. Schuster took his seat, Hansen climbed in. Roberts stepped forward and shook Mathewson's hand. Charles Van Loan was supposed to take the last of the four places, George Miller having ceded his place to the reporter. Miller would ride in one of the pilot cars that accompanied the Thomas out of Cheyenne. By that point, though, Van Loan had already made the mistake of standing close to Katherine Mackenzie.

Van Loan was as aggressive a reporter as there was in the west, a very happily married man, too, but nothing could make him immune to the belle of Wyoming. He trudged back and found a seat in one of the pilot cars lined up to follow the Thomas. Miss Mackenzie took her place in the Thomas, Van Loan having first bundled her up in a long coat, a fur hat, a veil, and goggles. "Oh dear," she wrote for a newspaper the next day, "riding in that big Thomas isn't a bit like studying in the convent.

"Everything was so unexpected and all at once I was in the Thomas and a-going, headed for Paris, before I really knew it. The wind cut like everything and my face got hot and stung," Mackenzie wrote. "I don't very often think 'Gee!' but I guess I thought it several times on that ride. Sometimes I thought 'Whiz-z-z' along with it. One time was when we made a sharp curve onto a small bridge and I thought sure we were going off into a ravine.

"Mr. Mathewson is a nice man," Miss Mackenzie noted, "but he is all business. He don't pay any attention to anything but business." Neither, of course, did Schuster. But they weren't the only men in the car. "I wasn't a bit afraid," she continued. "I knew I could stay with the machine as long as the others, no matter how fast we went. And then there was Captain Hansen right at my side; I knew he wouldn't let anything hurt me. He is so gallant. He kissed my hand when I left the car. I guess he did it so that he could distinguish himself in the moving pictures Mr. Buckwalter was making at the time."

In Katherine Mackenzie—lively, intrepid, and connected as if by an invisible wire to any camera lens within focusing distance—Captain Hansen found his perfect match. They parted company in Laramie, though, about fifty-seven miles from Cheyenne. That was as close to Paris as Miss Mackenzie was to get that day.

On the same morning, March 9, the Züst finally started out from Omaha, with new springs, courtesy of the Union Pacific railroad. For the first time, the Italian car was making progress in a steady way, with no snowdrifts, mudslides, ditches, breakdowns, or Indianans. No hazards at all. Scarfoglio pronounced the day "beautiful" and the road "magnificent."

Anyone else would have enjoyed the respite, emptying the mind and filling the eyes with the clean lines of the Nebraska countryside, fields

of brown meeting the sky of light blue. Another person might understandably have swooned with joy at the sight of every curious steer
standing in the sun to greet the car with a moo. Or seized the chance to
admire Nebraska's many streams, burgeoning but not dangerous, as
they made their way to the Platte River. Practically everything in Nebraska made its way to the Platte, which ran like an aorta across the
middle of the state. The New York-to-Paris Race did, too, generally following the river west. For the Züst team, making good time in dry
weather, it was no great challenge to log miles in Nebraska.

That left the occupants of the car with the greatest hazard of them all:
too much time to think. Antonio Scarfoglio wrote:

> Ordinarily we are quite taciturn on the car. We do not feel any need for
> speech or exchanging ideas. Each day's journey is like a great parenthe-
> sis across which the brain of each of us rides alone. We have one single
> point of contact, one common sentiment, one common need—to push
> forward. For the rest we remain almost estranged and indifferent to
> each other. Each of us lives upon his reveries and illusions; each thinks
> his own thoughts. Scarcely half a dozen words are exchanged in a day
> and then they are words which belong to the journey and to the car.
> Sometimes Haaga sings to himself of his own country. Not so Sirtori; he
> steers without uttering a word for hour after hour, like an automaton.
>
> But to-day I have felt more lonely than ever before, for the immen-
> sity and grandeur around us are painful to the eyes and the heart. Hith-
> erto I did not suppose that this was possible. I am convinced of it to-day.
> And the others are not happy, particularly Haaga, who pictures his
> home on the horizon, and his wife coming to meet him across the grass
> with open arms.

The irony was that the sense of depression in the Züst was countered
with the utmost excitement on the part of nearly everyone they passed.
Only the year before, a group of prominent farmers in Nebraska had
made a pledge to boycott the business of any person even seen driving
an automobile. No such prejudice was in evidence toward the New
York-to-Paris cars. In some towns, the whole population turned out to

greet the Züst. The total might be only fifty or seventy-five people, but in the fine spring weather, not one person missed the chance to see the Züst cutting a new line around the world, including a slash across Nebraska.

In the small city of Columbus, a former pioneer named Max Gottberg was waiting most anxiously of all for the arrival of the Züst. Gottberg had arrived in Columbus from Arkansas in 1881, with his mother and two sisters. They immediately started farming an eighty-acre tract that his mother had purchased. "Men without enough money to buy good school clothes for their children," Gottberg recalled of his fellow pioneers, "talked about forming huge irrigation companies, coal-boring syndicates, oil-drilling enterprises, and always the agitation for another railroad branch somewhere." Apparently Gottberg had done some of that kind of talking himself. By the time it faded, he was firmly ensconced in the machine age, running the first steam-powered thresher in the area and then, after a visit to the St. Louis World's Fair in 1903, driving one of the first three cars in the county. Gottberg was soon fixing cars, too, and even as the New York-to-Paris racers approached, he was in the process of building a big new garage, with a salesroom on the side.

Like others operating cars in rural Nebraska, including the New York-to-Paris racers, Gottberg generally ordered gasoline in fifty-gallon drums, which were delivered to the train station. Around Columbus, though, there was one other option, known only to the locals: Park Miller, the milk man, had in his wagon a five-gallon cream jug filled with gasoline, which he sold at the going rate of nine cents a gallon. Park let it be known that he was more than willing to make detours to rescue stranded automobilists.

Antonio Scarfoglio should have been cheered by his arrival in Columbus, a prosperous town like many others along the route, with three-story brick buildings lining the main street. In the 1880s, an eastern investor had agitated to move the U.S. capital to Columbus, arguing that it would be safe from attack since it sat exactly in the middle of the United States, east to west. He went so far as to reserve lots for the White House and Capitol.

To Antonio Scarfoglio, however, the center of the United States would have meant only one thing: that from that point on, more of America's wretched roads were behind him than in front of him. It also meant that he was unquestionably moving through the west, with all that that implied to people throughout the world. There were some noticeable signs even in the quiet of Nebraska that the wilderness was not entirely tamed. Newspapers in Nebraska still carried advertisements from fur traders. "Wolf—" exclaimed one. "Kill the brute! Skin him properly and ship his skin . . . There's money in it."

Scarfoglio had already seen a few cowboys in Omaha, and he'd seen Indians, too, in an encampment. "Thirty or forty miserable, terra-cotta coloured men," he observed. "They wear long, long English frockcoats and gloves of unspeakable filthiness. Civilization and spirits have reduced them to this abject state. Only the women retain some of the Indian tradition and manner. . . . The men salute with a short wave of the hand; they read the papers and know what and who we are. But the women, in whose hearts remains an unconquerable and instinctive fear of all that is new, are frightened at the sight of this machine driven by white men."

Pioneers were still around, too, in large numbers. Max Gottberg was one, of course. In Columbus, he volunteered to act as a guide for the Züst, instantly hopping into the backseat when his offer was accepted. Aware that the New York-to-Paris excitement would increase auto sales, he returned to Columbus from his stint as a guide and hired an extra force of construction workers to rush completion of his new garage. Gottberg's instinct was correct. The race generated a wave of new automobile sales and he would be there to meet them, that spring and for the following thirty-six years—just as soon as he hung the "Ford Motor" sign outside his new building.

Ever since Buffalo, Emilio Sirtori had made up time lost to repairs by driving around the clock. He was remarkable that way, refusing to admit to the need for sleep. Sirtori had a stony inner reserve, along with a sense of frustration at the mishaps the car continually encountered. About them, he could do nothing. About running thirty-six hours at a clip, though, he could. There was desperation even in his posture at the wheel; he crouched over it, as though he were pushing the car, rather than steering it. In view of the deprivations on the Züst, the lack of sleep, basic exercise, and occasional silence, it was no wonder that Haaga was seeing mirages and Scarfoglio was giving in to his natural tilt toward gloom. Meanwhile, Sirtori drove on and occasionally tried to wiggle his fingers, just to see if he could. Following the crooked curve of the Platte, they were still three days behind the Thomas.

Katherine Mackenzie reported that she once heard Linn Mathewson and Harold Brinker agree that "they were going to drive like a— a— a— like everything." Mathewson did make a strong run to Laramie on his first day behind the wheel, while all the pilot cars tried to keep up. In one of them, Van Loan sat next to an irresistibly callow photographer from the Bronx, assigned to shoot pictures of the Thomas for the *New York Times.* Over the route from Cheyenne to Laramie, Van Loan helpfully pointed out places of interest for the new man, making sure he didn't miss the Little Big Horn battlefield where Custer made his last stand, and the very cave in which Jesse James had killed twenty-three sheriffs. The young pup believed every word. Van Loan's stint as a tour guide was the talk of the banquet held for the racers that night, an informal dinner for fifty at Laramie's Thornburgh Hotel. Mathewson was cheered, Captain Hansen spoke, and then Van Loan stood up and in a serious moment, he asked the assembly to drink a toast to the health of George Schuster and George Miller, the machinists for the Thomas Flyer. Immediately a shout of approval rang out in the dining room.

Schuster couldn't hear it and neither could Miller. They were across town at the Lovejoy Garage, where they had dismantled the Flyer in order to overhaul it. "We intended to do this work in Cheyenne," Schuster told someone who sought him out there, "but we found that there was no place in the capital city where the work could be done satisfactorily." Anyway, he had been blind with rage back in Cheyenne and that would have made the wrenches hard to find. After the civil war there, Schuster redoubled his efforts to find problems on the Thomas before they caused breakdowns, not because he was devoted to Linn Mathewson, which he wasn't, but because he considered the car to be his—his car to take to Paris.

Mathewson didn't see it that way, nor did he seem to miss Schuster and Miller at the banquet in Laramie. To him they were employees, if not servants. "Owing to the bad roads on the other side of Rawlins," he wrote from Laramie, "I thought best to have the car thoroughly over-hauled here, and Mechanics Schuster and Miller . . . will spend all night on the job in order to send the American car westward at an early hour to-morrow morning."

If Mathewson took Schuster and Miller for granted, he was openly critical of Captain Hansen. As the team continued west from Laramie on the way to Rawlins, halfway across Wyoming, the Thomas met swirling snowdrifts. When the car ascended higher country, Mathewson took action, as he noted, "I decided to ship all excess baggage on to Rawlins, and the car was stripped of all unnecessary weight, the only exception being the fated Capt. Hansen, who may be a good man for Siberia, but here it is a case of 'everybody works but Hansen,' he sits around all day."

Mathewson's remarks about Hansen weren't just muttered over a beer; they were printed in an article on the front page of the *New York Times,* giving rise to a notion that hadn't occurred before to any close observer of the race. St. Chaffray might have been right.

While Hansen was with the leading Thomas in Wyoming, however, St. Chaffray was still in Iowa. Even at a standstill, awaiting parts for the De Dion, he was managing to stay ahead of the two lagging cars, Koeppen's Protos and Godard's Moto-Bloc.

The race was best described by the number of states separating the cars, rather than the number of days. Lieutenant Koeppen in the Protos and Baron Godard in the Moto-Bloc were just entering Iowa, for example, when Sirtori and Scarfoglio were starting across Nebraska from Omaha: a one-state difference. At the same time, Mathewson and Schuster were heading out of Cheyenne: two states in the lead.

As Lieutenant Koeppen soon noticed, German Americans were much more prominent in Iowa than in any of the states to the east. The *Des*

Moines Register, the largest general-circulation newspaper in the state, went so far as to run a headline about his car in German: *Die Protos Maschine Durch Dreck und Koth.* No translation was even provided.*

German-Americans celebrated Hans Koeppen. At the banquet held for him in Cedar Rapids, one young reporter was so excited that he forgot to write anything for his paper. Koeppen made a speech that night—according to the account filed by one of the older reporters—in which he promised to complete the trip to Paris even if it took him five years. His resolve, so spirited and impressive, satisfied something deep within the audience and brought forth a long ovation. After the party, though, Koeppen left by train for Dubuque, a city in northern Iowa, to visit relatives. He told his new teammate, O. W. Snyder, that he would meet the car in some other Iowa town farther west. Such diversions did not break any race rules, as long as the car itself was duly presented in the checkpoint towns, but Sirtori, driving the Züst until his hands were numb, didn't take any train trips. Neither did St. Chaffray or Godard. Lieutenant Koeppen was different.

Koeppen's occasional sidetracks only showed that he was new to everything he'd taken on when he left his comfortable life in Germany and joined the New York-to-Paris Automobile Race. The other team captains were racers of one stripe or another. He was an army officer. The others had been thinking about the race, if not preparing for it, for months before the start. Koeppen entered within a week and a half of hearing of it. Almost two thousand miles along, he was still just a personable young fellow from Berlin; whether or not he would assume the many madnesses of an automobile racer had yet to be determined.

Across Iowa Koeppen and Snyder jockeyed with the two French cars for position, the exact order at any one time depending less on driving skill than on the deepness of the mud and the gravity of the mechanical problems that hounded each of the three cars. Race fans and editors around the world had started to ignore the lagging cars, especially since the Thomas and Züst were shaping up as worthy adversaries at the front of the pack. As long as the other cars were around, however, decorating

---

*The sentence means "The Protos Car Through Dirt and Mire."

the cornfields and barnyards, Iowans had something to talk about—and there was nothing that Iowans liked more than that. Except maybe their mud, which they defended heartily when it came under attack.

"These automobilists should remember," said a person in Council Bluffs, "that this Iowa mud is very productive, and that, after all, the corn crop is more important than the international endurance race."

Reporters tended to cheer the race, but editorialists were paid to sneer.

"Someone ought to start an automobile race from Denison to the moon," suggested an editorial in Denison. "It would be a great means of advertising the city and people would just go silly over all who started in the race—and with just as much reason as in the New York to Paris race over an impossible route."

"It's debatable whether a good driving team [of horses] could not have come out winner in the automobile race," noted a wiscacre in Waterloo. A writer in Boone tried to be a little more helpful, in a detached sort of way: "The machines should have been equipped with runners, like a sled, or fins, like a fish." Then it would not be a car race, though, it would be a sled race, or a fish race, and if either one of those had had the contagious success of the New York-to-Paris Automobile Race, the twentieth century might have turned out quite differently.

The editor of the Marshalltown newspaper caught the idea best of all, though. "The New York to Paris endurance test," observed the paper, "was won by the Iowa people who waited on the streets for days to see the cars go by." Some of them waited for weeks, though, if they wanted to see any of the laggards: St. Chaffray, Koeppen, or Godard.

Sirtori and the Züst team made it to Wyoming on March 12, after a two-day stop in Paxton, Nebraska, to await a replacement for a shaft that broke in two after the car fell into a mudhole in Ogallala. That same Ogallala mudhole had captured the Thomas, too, but without damage to the undercarriage. Owing to the delay, the Italians were no longer two days behind the Thomas. They arrived in Cheyenne four days behind, almost to the minute.

The city took pride in its own broad-minded generosity, demonstrated by the fact the reception for the foreigners was practically identical to the one accorded the Yankees. Only two things were different.

Mr. Hartman, the manager of the electric company, fussed with the blue electric lights in front of the Industrial Club and arranged somehow to make them look green, so that the Italians would be welcomed by their own national colors of red, white, and green. And the Kid Dealer, Floyd Clymer, stayed home in Berthoud; remarkably enough, he didn't want a Züst dealership. Mrs. Myers, though, was in the kitchen at the Industrial Club all afternoon, whipping up yet another turkey dinner with all the trimmings.

Remaining in Cheyenne overnight for the banquet, Arthur Ruland assured everyone he met that the Züst would catch up to the Thomas and that a four-day lead in such a long race was nothing, absolutely nothing. Sirtori, on the other hand, was telling people that the Züst was already in the lead, since the Thomas had disqualified itself long before, as far as he was concerned, by accepting so much assistance in Indiana. Antonio Scarfoglio spoke almost incessantly, despite the fact that few people in Cheyenne could understand Italian. They were polite enough to listen, anyway. "His language and modulation were very beautiful," recalled one resident. Henry Haaga was perhaps the most addled of the four race-dizzy men who tumbled out of the Züst into Cheyenne. He kept saying that as soon as the race was over, he was going to move to Cheyenne. That is how homesick poor Henry Haaga felt.

Chapter Fifteen

Rockies

Car	Miles	Place	Team
Thomas Flyer (U.S.)	2390	Granger, Wyoming	Mathewson, Schuster, Miller, Hansen
Züst (Ita.)	2052	Cheyenne	Scarfoglio, Sirtori, Haaga, Ruland
De Dion (Fra.)	1516	Missouri Valley, Iowa	St. Chaffray, Autran, Lascares
Protos (Ger.)	1332	Marshalltown, Iowa	Koeppen, Snyder

I n Kendallville, Indiana, Sheriff Edward Stanley finally grew tired of reading in the national press that Indiana was populated by bandits and cranks, at least where foreign automobilists were concerned. There was no choice but to find the missing Moto-Bloc parts.

Without warning, the sheriff arrived in Wawaka with a posse of twenty-seven men, including three deputies. Breaking up into teams, they set out to search every single house, barn, and business in the whole town. A boy named Clyde Zimmerman was standing within earshot when one of the deputies gruffly told a homeowner that "it would go bad for the thief" if the search teams had to find the stash on their own. Clyde, in the parlance of the detective, cracked wide open. He led Sheriff Stanley's men to a pile of sawdust behind a mill, claiming that he had seen two men lingering there the day before. Digging just where Clyde pointed, the deputies found Livier's movie camera, along with many other Moto-Bloc souvenirs. The sheriff took Clyde Zimmerman into custody as a suspect and notified the French consul in Chicago, who passed the news of the recovery on to Charles Godard.

Driving through eastern Iowa, Baron Godard was feeling fine. That wasn't an unusual state of affairs. Godard was always optimistic, probably he was damned by it. But the Moto-Bloc was doing well, too—and that was rare. It had been overhauled, if not renovated, during its stop in Clinton, and according to Godard, it was running better than it had since the day the race began in New York. "I expect that I will be able to fly along from now on," he predicted. Making eighty miles a day, he had his sights pinned on the leaders, one thousand miles ahead.

Reaching Cedar Rapids in easy fashion, Godard declared with his old insouciance that he would be out of Iowa in three days. It had taken the Thomas two days longer than that to get through. Consistent progress of that sort could bring the Moto-Bloc to the front of the pack, though, which is just what Godard was planning. With that, he left Cedar Rapids, hoping to reach Tama, fifty miles west. He didn't realize, though, that in Iowa, there was nothing so simple as going west in order to get west. Where automobiles were concerned, Iowa in 1908 was a maze.

In the New York-to-Paris Race, the first cars through a particular town typically drew energetic volunteer pilots, anxious to guide out-of-towners through scrambled roads, or over open fields, to the next stop. The laggards didn't receive quite such personalized service, in part because of the assumption that the runners-up could follow the leaders. Of course, when a car was weeks behind, as in the case of the Moto-Bloc, there was not much of a trail left to follow. To help with navigation, paid pilots could be hired at any time, but Godard was fretting about how much money he'd already spent. When he left Cedar Rapids on a stormy Sunday morning, he set off with only a set of handwritten directions. They had been free for the asking.

But they didn't mean much later, when the Moto-Bloc was stranded in confusion, surrounded on all sides by cornfields, with unmarked roads crisscrossing them. The maze closed in, making the same sense from any direction. When it began to rain in the afternoon, Godard was still driving, but he wasn't getting anywhere. Within minutes, the winds picked up and the skies tore open in a full-fledged storm, forcing him to pull over to the side of the road. With no top for the car, Godard and his two teammates, Livier and Hue, could only sit under oilskins. Where their slickers didn't quite cover them, they could feel the icy rain seep through each successive layer of clothing until their skin was soaked and raw. Godard glumly arranged the oilskins over the dashboard, knowing perfectly well that whatever the rain was doing to him, it was doing to every square inch of land before him.

Each of the men in the Moto-Bloc looked up when they heard the sound of an approaching car. When it drew near, the other driver stopped and shouted through the rain to ask if they were the French motorists. Godard nodded forlornly, but perked up when the stranger, wasting no time, told him how to get back on the route to Tama again.

After midnight, when Godard arrived in Tama, the rain was still coming down and it had yet to stop the next morning.

All of the New York-to-Paris racers had been caught in the peculiarly sticky "gumbo" mud of Iowa. The Protos, only a few hours ahead of the Moto-Bloc, was faring surprisingly well, though. An automobilist named Maurice Hutchinson, whom Lieutenant Koeppen hired as a guide, reported that the big, heavy Protos "fairly plows into the roads." He added with a touch of awe that it "rides with the same ponderous solidity as a threshing engine." It was not the sort of endorsement that the Protos sales department could use on a brochure, but it did explain why the German car was making progress, slowly but steadily, across Iowa.

The Moto-Bloc was a fairly heavy car, too, but it had a worse time than the Protos, caught by mud up to the hubs in many places. As the team struggled on through the gumbo into western Iowa, the reports Godard filed from the road grew shorter and shorter, rather like the diary entries of a shipwrecked explorer. "We have expected the roads to improve every day," he wrote on March 16, "but they seem to grow worse instead. We are hopeful we may some day come out of it all and run once more on solid ground."

As Godard approached the town of Jefferson, he heard the courthouse bell ring out joyfully to announce his arrival. People flocked to the main street, but he didn't stop to greet them. With decent traction in town, his Moto-Bloc "tore on through with scarcely diminished speed, and with the fading out of its volleyed exhausts in the distance."

Things were different in the town of Carroll in the next county. Those few who awaited the car there saw it pulled in by a team of horses—like an old farm implement, not a modern French racer. The Moto-Bloc had already been boosted out of many a ditch by Iowa farm horses, but this time it needed a full-scale rescue. The car had serious mechanical trouble, although Godard would not divulge exactly what was wrong. He only said that he would have it sent by rail to Omaha to be fixed, and then return it to the mud puddles of Carroll County to continue the race again.

Godard soon thought better of that idea. He decided to ship the Moto-Bloc all the way to San Francisco by railroad. He still wouldn't say what was wrong with his car.

At the time, the leading cars were in Wyoming. It was perfectly apparent that the train offered the only chance for the Moto-Bloc to be on the West Coast in time to join the other cars for the trip to Alaska. Of course, it was entirely against the rules to use the train, but Godard could not pause to consider that nuance. He had to get out of Iowa or risk losing his mind.

In Council Bluffs, on the western edge of Iowa, a small gaggle of people was waiting to see the Moto-Bloc, "ignominiously riding a freight train," as one of them put it, on the overcast morning of Thursday, March 19.

During the stopover, the car sat high up on a flatbed car in the rail yard—as though it were on a stage or a pedestal or even a funeral pyre. It was no longer adored, but "exhibited to the rude gaze of an unfeeling public," in the description of the *Council Bluffs Nonpareil*. Fairly rude and indifferent itself, the *Nonpareil* continually referred to Godard as "Vuitton," the advertisement for "Vuitton Bags and Suitcases" still being displayed on the trunks attached to each running board.

Square and solid, Charles Godard stood guard on one side of the car, while it awaited a connection to another train. Livier and Hue were stationed on the other side, all three Frenchmen looking dark, disappointed, and slightly dangerous. Just as the gloom of the moment settled completely down from the gray clouds to the cinder pavement, a newspaper photographer scurried out of the crowd and started to set up his tripod on that pavement, as though he meant to take a picture of the Moto-Bloc. Of course, the car had been photographed thousands of times over the previous six weeks, but that was different. That was when it was in the race.

"Hi, hi," Godard shouted, not as a greeting, but as an attack. He suddenly exploded in anger, running at the man and his camera. "No photograph," he repeated several times, before reverting to his own language and spitting out a long string of words in French. Someone standing nearby came forward to translate. "He says the car is in privacy now," said the interpreter. "If it was on the ground, it wouldn't make any difference. He says you shan't take a picture of it." The photographer said nothing but continued to prepare his camera for the picture. Godard kept yelling at him. "He don't want a picture taken of the car," warned the interpreter. The photographer went about his business, focusing the lens on the stranded auto. As if that wasn't irritating enough for the Frenchmen, the photographer talked to himself all the while in little nothings: "There now," he said. "I've got it, that's fine, couldn't be better." Arthur Hue joined Godard in shouting and gesticulating, while Maurice Livier scrambled around the end of the flatbed car to join them. He was holding a pickaxe and raised it over his shoulder.

"He says he will fix your machine," the interpreter told the photographer as quickly as he could.

A stream of railroad workers left what they were doing in the train yard and came over to shout words of encouragement to the photographer. Outnumbered, Godard, Hue, and Livier turned away. On Godard's order, they scrambled to grab hold of a tarpaulin that was crumpled at the base of the Moto-Bloc, struggling to stretch it out over the car to block it from view. Just as they were set to raise it, they heard the click of the camera. It might have been the report of a rifle, for the effect it had on them.

The Moto-Bloc was out of the race, all hope dying on a dreary day in the rail yards, when the crowds stopped cheering. A kind of a spell was broken that day and people were themselves again, feasting upon failure.

"By rail to San Francisco is not a bad idea if getting there is the ultimate purpose," sneered the *Nonpareil,* commenting on Godard, the Moto-Bloc, and the whole New York-to-Paris idea. Watching the train leave for the west with his car as freight, like a load of so many potatoes, Godard laid the blame on the roads of New York State, the mud of Iowa, and the people of Indiana. He had had more than his share of bad luck—but only in proportion to his tendency to believe himself somehow or other above luck. Charles Godard had once been indomitable, even in the Gobi Desert. That was before he decided to drive to Paris from New York in an automobile.

The De Dion, with Bourcier St. Chaffray at the wheel, received no siren salute when it arrived in Omaha, March 15, but that was only prudent, since it snuck into town at three o'clock in the morning.

If anything, Bourcier St. Chaffray was overrested from his three unintended holidays in Iowa, and he drove with a new rapacity as he entered Nebraska. "The beginning of the Far West is charming," St. Chaffray wrote the following morning from Omaha. "It gives us an opportunity to recommence life and to realize the dreams of every man in a younger country. We had a shave and appeared to be young boys." The De Dion seemed to share his mood and made good time on its first day out.

Between the towns of North Bend and Rogers, the cool night was split open by firecrackers set off by boys waiting for the De Dion. Cars full of college students were waiting along the way, too, with well-rehearsed cheers. "Ko-la-la! Hip, hip, hurrah! De Dion, De Dion, De Dion!" rang out from dozens of bellowing voices, just as the French car passed. Unfortunately, St. Chaffray's first guide was less robust. As soon as the night quieted down, he dozed off.

St. Chaffray didn't know that the man was asleep; he assumed he had just stopped talking because the car was on the right road. Into the moonlight, the De Dion sped merrily farther and farther off course. A few hours later, at 11:30 P.M., it was stopped in front of Park Miller's house in Columbus, on course again and looking for gas. Before waking up Miller, St. Chaffray broke out dinner and had a midnight lunch with Autran and Lascares, under the stars and accompanied by a decent red wine.

St. Chaffray was back to his old exuberance, with nothing to complain about and plenty to remark upon. To a reporter who found him in front of the milkman's house, he declared that driving on Nebraska's firm roads on such a starry night was a delight. Where the mud was bad, he'd found that he couldn't even force the farmers to accept money for towing the De Dion out.

The next day, Lieutenant Koeppen was finally nearing Nebraska, too. He and Snyder had made a clean dash of sixty-seven miles on the way out of Iowa and toward Omaha, even sparing time for a lunch break at a restaurant in the town of Missouri Valley, near the border. While they were eating, Gottlieb Storz, the owner of Omaha's biggest brewery, was in his mansion on West Farnam Street—Omaha's version of Park Avenue. Heavyset and more than sixty years old, he was in an even bigger hurry than the Germans in the Protos, bustling around the paneled rooms of his brand-new Elizabethan home, giving orders to the servants.

Koeppen and Snyder finished their lunch in Missouri Valley and set off again. They were driving though Council Bluffs, just across the Missouri River from Omaha, when they noticed a massive touring car coming toward them. Every passing auto caught Koeppen's attention in that raw March weather, but the approaching car had an air of importance and dignity—except for the hefty man in the passenger seat who was waving frantically. Once both cars had stopped, Gottlieb Storz hopped out of the passenger seat and greeted Koeppen warmly in a spill of German and then, with a little impatience, took him to the back of the car, which held "a supercargo of mineral water, buttermilk and shredded wheat biscuits," all of it in the form of a gift for the Protos. Koeppen tried to explain that there might not be room for so much food in the Protos, but Storz would have none of that. The food was perfectly good, he said. Other cars from Omaha pulled up, including one containing Fred Metz—Storz's prime competitor in the brewing business. There was a growing traffic jam, under a veritable cloud of cheerful German banter. Fortunately for Koeppen and his chances of reaching Paris, the Union Pacific sirens broke up the crowd, signaling the approach of the German car into Omaha and also ensuring it.

In Omaha, the mounted guard of the Landwehr Verein German Club was waiting to lead the Protos through the city, with the club's rank and file in full uniform marching on foot or arrayed on the Storz Brewing company truck.

Koeppen, smack in the middle of Storz's well-organized melee, was also parading into another sort of uproar in Omaha automobile circles. He arrived on the same day that the city reacted to the news that the mayor of Cincinnati, Ohio, had issued an order forbidding females from operating automobiles. The very afternoon that Koeppen arrived, the Amalgamated Order of Female Chauffeurs had called an emergency meeting "to take such action as was deemed necessary." In Omaha, though, their privileges were safe. "I am for anything the women want and the chauffeuses need not be alarmed," said Mayor James Charles Dahlman in a hurried response to the Cincinnati action. "If the mayor of Cincinnati, duke of Duluth, marquis of Kansas City or any other public servant makes such a fool order, the chauffeuses may come to Omaha and run their automobiles—if they can dodge the holes in the pavements."

It was in Nebraska that Hans Koeppen joined the ranks of the automobilists, male and female, sparing time at every stop to take a driving lesson from Snyder. He ought to have learned before, but there hadn't been time during the crowded hours leading up to his departure from Berlin. Over the first sixteen hundred miles of the race, the conditions were too demanding for a beginner. Anyway, neither Maas nor Knape would have been inclined to teach him anything. And Koeppen, for his part, considered that his place was in command of the team, not operating the machinery. Chicago had changed his mind about that.

Driving a car in 1908 was not a simple task. Trying to handle a brute as overloaded as the Protos was especially difficult. On the positive side, there was not much traffic on most American roads then, but on the negative side, there were a great many ditches. For the New York-to-Paris racers, there were also bridgeless streams to ford, or even worse, narrow bridges to cross, with only inches to spare on either side of the track. Those things required an expert driver. Nebraska was Koeppen's only chance to become one, with fairly good roads, mostly clear weather, and O. W. Snyder willing and even anxious to have another driver in the car.

St. Chaffray, who had taken to driving through the night, was remarkably contented considering that he was twelve hundred miles behind the Thomas Flyer, seven hundred behind the Italian Züst, and only a precious few ahead of the Protos. Suddenly a form leapt into the road to chase the car, and St. Chaffray realized that it was a dog, barking and wagging his tail. The dog ran hard and had no problem gaining a lead on the De Dion—but then he had a couple of advantages, knowing the road and being able to see in the dark. Then the dog started to dart in front of the car. St. Chaffray jerked the wheel to avoid it, and the De Dion dropped heavily into a ditch. With help from a farmer and a few horses, it wasn't stuck for long. And St. Chaffray emerged as happy as before, telling the farmer that the people of Nebraska were "so good that he would rather run into the ditch than kill one of their dogs." Back on the road once more, he was expansive with his own good fortune— the feeling almost every driver knows, when free of restraints and moving fast.

At five o'clock in the morning on the sixteenth, St. Chaffray arrived in the city of Grand Island. He'd gone almost 160 miles since leaving Omaha twenty-five hours before, but just as he drove the huge De Dion into the outskirts of the city, it coasted to a stop, making a terrible grating noise. A knuckle joint had cracked, disabling the driveshaft. Three days would be lost in Grand Island, locating a replacement, having it shipped in by train, and installing it.

Even as St. Chaffray was passing the time, being entertained elegantly, if quietly, by Grand Island's society leaders, a report that Koeppen was about to arrive crossed the mayor's desk. He ordered the waterworks station to sound the prearranged signal on its steam whistle and within a half hour, four thousand people were standing around the Hart Garage, where the Protos was due to stop. John Hart, who was inside overseeing repairs on the De Dion, made several frantic phone calls, including one to the mayor. He then hung up the telephone, went outside, and told everyone to go home: the German wasn't coming that day. It was a false alarm. Hart didn't add that the whole thing had been a prank brought off by a teenager with access to the telegram wire. They could read about that in the paper later.

At breakfast time on March 19, St. Chaffray left Grand Island without fanfare, starting west again.

At lunchtime, Max Gottberg arrived in town, driving a pilot car followed by the Protos. Koeppen was only four hours behind St. Chaffray—the closest he'd come to third place since leaving Manhattan behind. His only problem was getting through Grand Island.

"No car in the New York to Paris race received such a rousing welcome as did the German car Protos and party, which was escorted into the city 'midst pandemonium," exclaimed the editor of a local paper. Only after luncheon for fifty and a couple of selections by the Leiderkranz Choir was Koeppen allowed to leave again for Paris. It was about an hour's delay, one that some of the other racers would have avoided—Sirtori probably wouldn't even have gotten out of the car under the same circumstances. Koeppen, however, was an ambassador of sorts and he didn't shirk many German societies along the American leg of the race route. His tact cost him, though. Within three days, he was running a full twenty-four hours behind St. Chaffray, the widening gap due in part to the sense of occasion he brought to every Nebraska town along the way. Scarfoglio had grown to disdain the same outpouring by the Italian-Americans of upstate New York. Koeppen sat beaming at every banquet thrown in his honor as though it were the first, and he lost twenty hours in three days.

In strict truth, the De Dion was not the first New York-to-Paris car into Cheyenne on Friday, March 20. The Moto-Bloc had gone through on a freight train that morning, accompanied by the quiet clapping of the wheels. But St. Chaffray arrived in the afternoon, announced by the boom of his own engine. He was just in time for his banquet at the Industrial Club. Mrs. Myers, having long since been called into the kitchen, created a dinner that was authentically French, even to the consommé course and the salad's place after the main entrée. After the meal, Bourcier St. Chaffray made "one of the wittiest speeches heard at the Industrial Club for a long time." Although it may be hard to judge much from that statement, speeches at industrial clubs being so rarely renowned for their wit, people who were there said that the roof almost lifted up with all the laughter.

It was a high night for fun in Cheyenne. Over at the New Atlas Theater, Harry Buckwalter was running the movie he'd taken during the Thomas's run through Cheyenne twelve days before. It was not only among the finest movies he'd ever shot, in his own opinion, it was the very first motion picture of any sort to depict Cheyenne. As Buckwalter introduced the show, which was bound to be a hit, he made a point of mentioning that he was donating all of his profits to the Denver-Cheyenne good roads movement, a cause that had become close to his heart, or some other part of his anatomy, after he swerved and skidded his way from Denver to Cheyenne in a car.

The beauty queen Katherine Mackenzie was, of course, one of those in attendance at the moving picture show. After she and all of the other local stars of the show had been introduced to the audience, the movie began. As the lights went down, the entertainers on the Atlas's regular bill crept out from backstage to watch: the "Three Broadway Girls," the Devan Brothers, who were tumblers with an acrobatic dog, and Marquis and Lynn, who played violins "in positions you have never seen them manipulated in before." All of them, except the acrobatic dog, wanted a look at the race and the moving pictures.

Some of those who had been in Cheyenne for the arrival of the Thomas Flyer grumbled that the movie would show nothing more than a sea of heads. In fact, Buckwalter did a great job of capturing action, including the arrival of the car, the cowboys buzzing around the car on their horses, the welcome extended to Monty Roberts, the procession of cars leaving the city, and the very steep inclines that were flattened out by the powerful car. One report, the nearest thing to a movie review that there was in 1908, concluded that "the action is so realistic that it is difficult to realize that it is merely pictured."

"The painful anxiety of some quite well known Cheyennese to get into the picture is betrayed," the review also noted.

Buckwalter's movie was already playing on theater circuits in the east and far west. He reported that it was drawing especially big crowds in Chicago.

Lieutenant Hans Koeppen was due to arrive in Cheyenne the day after St. Chaffray did. Residents could discern that fact either by reading the local papers or by seeing Mrs. Myers in the kitchen at the Industrial Club, working on fleischbruche, kartoffelschnitzel, and wein-

waffein. The Protos was anything but ignored in Cheyenne. After Lieutenant Koeppen made his way through the crowds—as large for him as
for Monty Roberts—he gave a sort of news conference at the Inter-
Ocean. "I have not unlimited money for expenses as have the other contestants," he said, "and I must proceed with caution. But the Protos is a
grand car and her condition is the same as when she left the factory. She
will go far and farness is better than fastness in so long a race." Such
comments had been well polished over the course of the route. They
served to explain in one dignified statement why he was last, whether he
minded that he was last, and whether he was still serious about the race.
He was. But after all, he had to say something when people in
Cheyenne pointed out that the Thomas Flyer was already through
Wyoming—and Utah and all of Nevada.

At the wheel of the Thomas, Linn Mathewson had made fairly
good time through Wyoming, though in most places, there was no road,
only the treeless wilderness of high country.

Wyoming's open space belongs to the wind, which blows almost constantly in spring months. But it was water that presented the greatest
challenge. Over long stretches, the snow was still lying in drifts; with
sunny days on the mountains, the spring runoff carved out gullies too
deep to cross in a car. On the plain, new streams were as profuse as cap-
illaries. Whenever the Thomas came to one of them, Mathewson or
Schuster or some other member of the crew who was feeling lucky
would have to decide on a detour, to the right or to the left. If a bridge
couldn't be found—or made—a car would have to ford the water. The
line of the race route, which looked perfectly straight leading west from
Laramie on a map, would be a drunken scribble if it were to show the
actual route of a car finding its way through central and western
Wyoming in March of 1908.

The official race route dictated that the cars parallel the Union Pacific
railroad, which ran through southern Wyoming. The terrain of the state
along that sector was inconsistent but could be summed up as steadily
rising flatlands, interrupted by well-defined clusters of mountains, poking up almost like islands on plains of brown and green. To avoid the

worst of the mountain terrain, both the rail line and the New York-to-Paris course started out due west from Cheyenne and skirted south of the Laramie Mountains, a long range that sat on a north-south line. Turning north, the route passed between the Laramie range to the east and the Medicine Bow Mountains to the west, with a stop in the city of Laramie along the way. About sixty miles to the north, it then headed west, skipping past the Medicine Bow Mountains, which then lay just to the south of the route. For almost three hundred miles after that, the route ran through largely empty territory: grazing lands and near desert, marked occasionally by oil-drilling or coal-mining operations.

At a town called Carter, in the southwest corner of the state, the terrain changes again, dramatically. Over the final fifty miles of a westward journey, the mountains rise again, in the form of the steep Uinta range, long, dark gray masses that enclose the Bear River Valley. For the New York-to-Paris racers, the small city of Evanston was the goal, perched at the western edge of the Uintas, and only a few miles from the border with Utah. Thirty years before, the Union Pacific had found a way through the peaks, with the help of expert surveyors and thousands of day laborers. Very few autos, though, and not even many wagons for that matter, attempted the ten-thousand-foot climb in 1908, when each yard was another challenge. But there was a shortcut and it beckoned to the New York-to-Paris racers.

"Learning that the wagon roads between Carter and Evanston were impassable because of ten feet of snow," Linn Mathewson wrote, "I at once made arrangements with the Union Pacific officials who very kindly allowed us to use the railroad right of way between Carter and Evanston, a distance of forty odd miles. This saved many days' work getting through snowdrifts and especially when we passed through the tunnel through Aspen ridge, more than one mile long, thus cutting off the worst mountain climb of the trip. The roads over the divide, which is 9,000 feet above the sea level, are in such condition that a saddle horse could not get through, and in order to use them it would be necessary to build a road several miles long."

The Union Pacific designated the Thomas as a "special train," for scheduling purposes, and sent a man named Brown to guide it along. He arrived clanking with lanterns and other equipment. The Union Pacific didn't do anything by half measures, especially where equipment was concerned. The railroad had a certain addiction to equipment. To make room for Brown and his matériel, Captain Hansen and George Miller went ahead to Ogden by passenger train. Mathewson and Schuster would take the car through.

Mr. Brown's first question was how long the car would need the rails. Schuster thought about it long and hard. He wanted to give the car plenty of time, but he didn't want to scare the railroad man off by asking for too much of a window. Finally, he estimated four hours. Brown made arrangements to keep all other traffic off the busy line for four hours. With the tires bumping along on the ties on either side of the two rails, the Thomas headed out on the only good road through the mountains.

"We had gone only a few miles when our rear right tire blew out," Schuster wrote. "Replacing this and pumping it up took a good half-hour." That half hour ate into the Thomas's clearance on the rails. Two more flats put it, as Schuster explained, "hopelessly behind schedule. A fast passenger train was due in a few minutes and we were miles short of the switch on which we were supposed to turn off." He and Mathewson were certain that they would be overrun by the train, and smashed into little bits to adorn the mountains for miles all around. Mr. Brown the railroad man wasn't concerned. He set a series of red lanterns alongside the tracks in such a way as to warn the coming train. The engineer read the signal and did indeed slow the train, but he still bore down on Mathewson and Schuster, who were able to pull off the rails onto the siding, just as the locomotive passed.

Red lanterns were all right for trains coming from behind, but not for oncoming traffic. Once the Thomas entered the Aspen Ridge tunnel, it had to pass through smoothly, before an expected freight train met it head-on. Schuster was already gripped by that thought as the Thomas approached the tunnel. When it suffered another flat within sight of the entrance, he had his doubts that there was time to fix it and still get through. A half hour later, though, they disappeared into the mountain, making a break for the other end.

Almost immediately, Mathewson made a discovery: wooden railroad ties aren't used inside of tunnels, or at least, they weren't used inside the Aspen tunnel. With no fear of erosion, the rails were set right into the stone. The smooth road nearly paralyzed him—he couldn't steer by feel. The dim light shed by the gas headlamps on the front of the car was no help. From where he sat, it just made for dancing shadows that confused him all the more. And with ditches of running water on either side of the railbed, there was good reason to worry about making a wrong move. After a rushed discussion, Schuster pinned himself to the front of the car, peering ahead and swinging his arms to direct Mathewson. Tense and exhausted, they emerged from the tunnel, visibly relieved. Brown, on the other hand, was almost bored by the whole interlude, calmly hopping out at the first siding to wait for a maintenance crew to come and pick him up. With that, the Thomas was no longer a special train. After spending the night in Evanston, Mathewson and Schuster had to find a road again, in deepening snow.

George Miller and Captain Hansen were waiting in Ogden, about fifty-five miles away (as the crow flies). Hearing that his teammates were stuck in a snowbank on the Utah side of the mountains, Miller boarded a passenger train going east. When he spotted Mathewson and Schuster, shoveling their way along, he leapt off the train like a bandit and rolled into the snow. As soon as they dug him out, he helped to dig the Thomas out.

After twenty-five hours of sheer struggle, Linn Mathewson finally pulled the Flyer into Ogden. He had done his job beautifully, no one could argue with that. "I have nothing but praise for Schuster and Miller, the two boys who have made the trip with me," he said after arriving. But he was the boy; Schuster and Miller were each older than he and even if the word was meant affectionately, the phrasing was not. They didn't make the trip with him; they were with the car. He took a weeklong ride with them. That sort of thing may seem inconsequential, but it was Schuster who had sacrificed himself to the journey whenever someone had to. He was the one who walked ten miles in the dark to find gasoline, no mundane task in the snowy foothills of the Rockies, and who walked in front of the car, up to his knees in mud, to show the way in a gully they couldn't avoid. It was always Schuster, in fact, who found a way. That was easy enough to forget, after the car was safe.

Pioneer Tracks

TUESDAY, MARCH 18, 6 A.M.: LATEST OFFICIAL STANDINGS

Car	Miles	Place	Team
Thomas Flyer (U.S.)	2718	Cobre, Nevada	Brinker, Schuster, Miller, Hansen
Züst (Ita.)	2390	Granger, Wyoming	Sirtori, Scarfoglio, Haaga, Ruland
De Dion (Fra.)	1690	Grand Island, Nebraska	St. Chaffray, Autran, Lascares
Protos (Ger.)	1467	Omaha, Nebraska	Koeppen, Snyder

The Italians started out from Cheyenne a full week before St. Chaffray and Lieutenant Koeppen arrived there. Intent on catching the Americans, they were still at it late into the night the first day out of Cheyenne, poking slowly across a spongy plain by following a guide who went ahead on foot. Sometimes the man disappeared in the dark, but his torch could always be spotted, blurred only by the oily smoke trailing behind it. Whenever the car slipped in the mud, Scarfoglio, Haaga, and Ruland had to get out and push: three mud hogs coaxing the hippo along. At about midnight, the guide returned to the car for good, too cold, wet, tired, and plain dirty to continue. The mud caked all over his legs weighed as much as a couple of bricks. He barely uttered a word as he flopped into the seat next to Ruland, afraid that the others would pounce on anything he said and talk him into continuing. He couldn't.

Sirtori drove ahead anyway, certain that he could feel his way along, but within a few hundred yards, the car ground to a stop in the blank wilderness. Even the engine died. Everyone in the car sat perfectly still, listening to the silence for a clue. As they waited, the Züst began to tip slightly to one side. That was the clue. The car was suspended in a bog. Numb with cold and exhausted after almost twenty hours on the road—most of it without a road—Sirtori and Ruland built a camp on a patch of dry land, while the guide stood nearby, holding the torch again. Haaga fretted over the car. Scarfoglio just wanted to escape the only way he knew how, lying down on the ground and making a pillow out of his arms.

Sirtori was kneeling by the campfire, trying to turn tinned meat into dinner, and Scarfoglio was drifting off to sleep when Haaga suddenly shouted through the dark that they'd better come back to the car.

It was sinking. "At 2 o'clock the front springs had vanished," Scarfoglio wrote. "At 2:30 the petrol tank behind was submerged; at 3 o'clock the engine rested on the mud." A half hour later, the engine was gone. The windshield poked out of the surface like a hand, waving good-bye.

Help had to be found before the car vanished entirely. Sirtori and Scarfoglio set off in search of a town, a farm, or a house. At times, they walked single file, holding on to one another by the waist; at times, they found themselves tumbling down steep hills, cut and bruised because of it. Scarfoglio was tired to the point of delirium. He couldn't feel his legs. When he could no longer tell if time was passing, he came to the conclusion that he had died a little while before. Then the lights of Medicine Bow came into view, a beacon from the land of the living. Without much delay, a team of strong horses was brought out to salvage the Züst, which revived after a thorough rinsing in Medicine Bow.

In open country, the Italians generally followed the telegraph wires, which followed the railroad tracks. Towns dotted the route: eighty or one hundred miles apart, a full day's travel in a car at that time of year.

Over long stretches, the only signs of civilization were isolated shacks occupied by telegraph operators or railroad signalers. At one telegraph shack, otherwise surrounded by nothing but hundreds of miles of brown earth, they were intrigued to find a neat little house sitting right next door. Since the operator, an elderly man, lived in the shack, they couldn't imagine who lived next door—who else would choose to live in such a lonely spot. They learned that a Japanese man lived in the house with five grown sons who rarely left his side. Sirtori badgered the operator, asking him how six people could possibly support themselves, without hardly leaving the house, but the old man only shrugged. He had been interested in his neighbors at first, he said, but not anymore.

They hadn't spoken to each other in years. The Japanese man would only smile when Scarfoglio asked him how he made a living and why he lived in that desolate spot. At that, the Italians shrugged too, climbed back into the Züst, and drove away from the two shanties, sitting right next to each other, or so it seemed at first glance.

Stopping at a ranch in a tiny outpost called Wamsutter, the Züst team was greeted by cowboys, dressed in sheepskins and bandanas whipping in the wind. Though most of the west was as civilized by 1908 as a Boston suburb, with amateur basketball leagues, advertising agencies, and candy shops, the rangelands were not. In Wamsutter, at least, the ranches were in a continual state of war. At lunch, which was served in a shed, the Italians eyed their cowboy hosts, each one sitting with his gun next to his plate, a bridle hanging handy over his shoulder. At any moment of the day or night, they were ready for battle.

Farther on, the Züst stopped in front of a railroad post perched on the banks of a creek. As usual, Scarfoglio had to see who was inside. Scarfoglio, the man who complained of loneliness even when he was in the midst of a cheering crowd, couldn't help being fascinated with the isolated signal-keepers he met along the way, people who were "sick with solitude," at least according to him.

The woman who lived in the railroad cabin had been installed there long before, solely to tend the signal lamp on the bridge spanning the creek. Every six months, a train stopped with her supplies, her mail, her tobacco. Other than that, she was completely cut off. "She spoke nervously," Scarfoglio said later, "laughing with every word, interrupting herself, losing the thread of each sentence, picking it up again, and asking us the most ingenuous and puerile things."

"Do the ladies in town still wear green?" she inquired, "and black feathers?—and velvet?—and tailor-mades?" But they just didn't know.

Sirtori always wanted to go fast, pressing on even after the sun went down, in order to reach the next big town. But in the dimming light, he was oblivious to nearly everything that might lay between his car and the Arc de Triomphe. He should have known better. In the desert part of the state, the plain was gashed by hundreds of ravines, carved out by streams long dry—*arroyos,* in the parlance of the west. Each of the New York-to-Paris racers grappled with them, driving miles in one direction or the other to find some shallow point at which a car might cross.

As Sirtori persevered in the twilight, an arroyo lay across his path a few miles ahead, as quiet and as dangerous as an iceberg to a ship sailing onward in the dark. It was no mere ditch, but a jagged 150-foot drop. As the Züst drew nearer and nearer, Sirtori was feeling nothing but quite pleased with the car's speed. And also with his own stamina. He was only two and a half days behind the Thomas, gaining ground and fixed on the moment when he could pass the Americans. He went a little faster.

The wheels of the Züst bounced along gamely over rocks and ruts, even as the ravine loomed. Scarfoglio was bumping along beside Sirtori in the front, thinking about clean white sheets and a bed to sleep in. The others were in the back. In a single split second, Sirtori saw the shadow of the arroyo and filled with panic. He took his hands off the wheel as though it were suddenly redhot and pulled on the handbrake with all of his might. With the rear wheels locked, the huge car spun around, with the back end cutting a wide arc in the dirt. Scarfoglio, Haaga, and Ruland were all flung out and rolled like crumbs on the ground. Only a second later, Sirtori himself dove out of the car. It was a brave last second, though. The Züst skidded and shook until it was backward to the ravine, stopping with the rear wheels jutting out in midair. The frame rested on the lip of the ravine.

If Sirtori hadn't remained in the driver's seat to the last second, applying the brakes with all of his heft, the car would have tumbled into a wreck at the bottom of the ravine. If he'd remained in it another second, though, he might have added just enough weight to push it over. His timing saved the car, along with his life. Perhaps by then, the two were indistinguishable.

Sirtori couldn't speak at first; his heart was beating almost into his throat. The other men gingerly approached the car, after calming down and congratulating themselves on being alive. Because the Züst was resting on loose gravel, it might still collapse into the ravine at any moment. Anchoring themselves with ropes, in case the car slid away, they used boards, boulders, and all the time in the world to pull the Züst out of the air and back onto firm ground. In conversations all over the world about the near wreck, Sirtori was hailed for his quick thinking. And then cursed for insisting on driving through the dark.

Sirtori wasn't one bit chastened. He settled into the driver's seat in the Züst, once it had all four tires on the ground, and leaned his bulky body forward into the wheel just as before. He continued to drive as though the finish line were around the next bend, peering into the twilight and telling himself that he could still see, that his eyes had grown used to the dark. In fact, they stung from the cold, but he squinted ahead by the hour and by the day, looking for the road, and the image of the Thomas Flyer.

By the time the Italians arrived at the Uinta Mountains, four days after Mathewson and Schuster, the Union Pacific Railroad was prepared for them. The Züst team duly sent a telegram to the district manager of the railroad requesting the same right-of-way that had been accorded to the Americans. The response came by wire, too. Company officials had held discussions, and round-the-world racecars would no longer be allowed to use the tracks, including the mile-long tunnel through Aspen Ridge.

Sirtori's eyes finally went dull, when he read the telegram from the district manager of the Union Pacific.

Apparently, the jangling of the Thomas's tire chains had damaged the railbed, spraying gravel in all directions. Some people believed that explanation and some didn't. It was true that the Union Pacific had opened its shops in Omaha to the foreign cars and had saved the day for two of them. The Aspen Ridge tunnel had been a boon for the Thomas, though. Without it, and the clear path of the tracks, the Züst was going to have to cross over the mountains, and not straight through them.

Emilio Sirtori stood in a field in Spring Valley, bundled against the wind in a fleece-lined coat and lace-up boots that reached to his knees. His thoughts were fixed on the Uinta range, lying to the west. The Bear River Valley led through about half the range, but after that, the car would have to wend its own way through the peaks. Wyoming had made Sirtori into a westerner, at least in appearance. Rather thickset for a cowboy, he nonetheless looked as though he had become part of the spare March scenery. Like a cowboy, bent and crooked from long hours in the saddle, he stood stiffly, his frame suited after so many weeks only to sitting in the driver's seat of the Züst. Moving his eyes over the mountains, he was trying to get used to the fact that they were going to be taller for the foreign cars than they had been for the Thomas.

Sirtori had already learned that in a world filled with loyal American race fans, snowdrifts could seem lower for some cars than for others. Why couldn't mountains be taller? He turned away from the view in Spring Valley and returned to the Züst, where his teammates were already getting ready to follow the wagon road. They had plenty of time to prepare. The Züst was out of gas and the nearest supply was in Evanston, thirty-five miles to the west. Of course, fuel could be shipped in by train. In 1908, the train could do anything. It was the automobile that was awkward and unwieldy.

Ogden, Utah, was the goal, on the other side of the Uinta range. A neat city and a Union Pacific one, just like Omaha, it was nestled in green country dividing the Rocky Mountains from the deserts to the west. According to local motorists, the trip out of the mountains into the open was practically child's play, little more than a glide downhill over perfectly good roads. Almost a week before, however, when the Thomas Flyer had arrived, those same fine roads had been packed with snow and the men arrived exhausted.

"Schuster reeled like a man stunned with a blow," wrote a reporter who greeted them. "Miller talked almost incoherently. Mathewson, nervous and red-eyed, surveyed the machine as if loath to leave it." They had to be helped to the Reed Hotel, Ogden's gray granite landmark.

Harold Brinker had been waiting in Ogden to take the wheel, and Captain Hansen was on hand, ready to take his place in the car once again. Charles Van Loan was hanging around the hotel, too.

Just before the Thomas finally arrived, Van Loan had grown bored, which reporters are apt to do when their story is a hundred miles away. Just to pass the time, he undertook a minute study of Captain Hans Hansen.

Mathewson and Van Loan had decided somewhere back in the eastern part of Wyoming that they didn't much like Captain Hansen. Van Loan's new assignment was to determine exactly why not. He started with the medals jangling from Hansen's uniform. Van Loan told everyone that they were cigar wrappers.

Captain Hansen, for his part, wasn't bored at all by Ogden. On Sunday night, about ten hours after the Thomas arrived, he received a note in a flowing hand:

My Dear Captain:

I have seen your manly figure and classic brow around the hotel for a couple of days. I feel that I must meet you and hear the music of your voice before you leave on your dangerous journey around the world. Won't you please call at my room in the hotel at 8 o'clock this evening.

Signed,
One who admires you

The note included a room number. At eight o'clock exactly, Hansen knocked on the door.

"Who is there?" asked a feminine voice.

"It is I," Hansen replied in a deep tone. With that, he heard the sounds of struggle inside the room, of chairs tipping over and objects thrown to the floor. "Let me at him," a man inside was saying. "I'll teach him to come around here." Another piece of furniture fell over.

"Oh dear, don't shoot. Don't kill him," cried the female voice.

It was no female, though, but Linn Mathewson, doing his best imitation. Van Loan was there, too, playing the role of the jealous husband and stomping across the floor to open the door. To his utter delight, the hall was completely empty in both directions. Van Loan and Mathewson grabbed their hats and gave chase, scouting around until they found Hansen burrowed away in the garage with the Thomas. "There's a wild-eyed man back at the hotel," Mathewson told him, "looking for you and saying that he'll fill you full of lead if he finds you!"

The next morning, Harold Brinker took his place in the driver's seat of the Thomas, as the team prepared to leave. George Schuster and George Miller were revived and fresh, after resting for almost twenty-four hours straight. Only Captain Hansen was groggy and stiff, having slept all night in the car.

Brinker, who was more straightforward than Mathewson, was just happy to be part of the race. He didn't seem concerned that Schuster insisted on making all the decisions; he only wanted to drive and make good time. He figured that offered him the best chance at keeping his seat past San Francisco.

Originally, the route called for the racers to cross due west across northern Nevada and go through Reno on the way to San Francisco. Late snows, however, in the Sierra Nevada Mountains near Reno forced race officials to make a switch and send the cars southwest through Nevada toward Southern California. Brinker was happy to think that he wasn't likely to meet with much snow, as the course started out from Ogden by drifting north around Salt Lake and into the desert.

With the car overhauled and the crew well rested, Brinker had a fairly easy drive over his first three days at the wheel. The route in Utah, over hardpacked sand, was easy. The only inconvenience that he felt was worth mentioning was that he almost starved to death. The provisions onboard the Thomas and its pilot car didn't last long, and the men were half-crazed with hunger when they finally reached a restaurant and ordered food at the end of the first day. Food, in the accepted sense, wasn't what they received, however. "When it was placed before us," Brinker wrote of the meal, "we were unable to take it, hungry as we were. We decided it would be best to push on to the next point. When we arrived at Montello [Utah], every man on the car was ready to eat almost anything."

In that, Brinker may have been a little expansive. The only meal available in Montello was salt mackerel and tea. They decided to push on again. In Cobre, Nevada, two days out of Ogden, Brinker finally found edible food.

Nevada was in the midst of a mining boom in March 1908. Of course, there had been gold and silver strikes before, making millionaires of wily prospectors, but the new flowering was modern in every respect. It was dominated by corporations, making gold factories out of mountainsides. Day laborers manned the mines and occasionally rebelled against the corporations, leading to some of the deadliest strikes in America's business history. Just days before the Thomas Flyer arrived in Nevada, the U.S. Army finally left, having been on guard at the mines for months.

Using stock-issuing corporations to stake new mines only expanded the overall sense of speculation, allowing people to make money either by discovering a gold mine or just by taking a flyer on one. Brokers all over the country grouped the mining companies according to the boomtowns of Nevada, so a person in Minneapolis or Hartford with spare cash for stock would choose from among the Comstocks, Goldfields, Tonapahs, or Bullfrogs.

The whole state was money mad. Four days before the Thomas Flyer arrived in Nevada, twenty students at the University of Nevada abruptly quit school and boarded trains for mining country. Someone had to be getting rich; more than $20 million in gold and silver was being extracted annually from Nevada, a state of only forty-two thousand residents.

As of 1908, stagecoach lines were still in operation between cities in Nevada, but the automobile was starting to have an effect, as a three-day mule ride to a distant camp became a four-hour car ride. One editorialist in Salt Lake City even boasted that "the greatest triumphs ever wrought by automobiles have been in the deserts of Nevada. . . . Many a stamp* is now ringing in southern Nevada in camps that, except for the automobile, would still be as silent as they were for ten thousand years prior to the advent of the automobile."

Goldfield already counted forty autos on its streets, which was not bad for an isolated city of eight thousand. Not one of the cars had been there two years previously. That is because none of the people were there. Goldfield didn't so much grow, as pop, like corn, into a sprawling city, with tall buildings, telephone service, and a luxury hotel. There

---

*A machine used for crushing ore

were mansions for the goldstrike millionaires, but there were also mud huts, looking rather prehistoric, for the newcomers.

Fortunately, there were a lot of cars in Tonopah, too, a slightly more established boomtown near Goldfield. Brinker was seventy-five miles outside of Tonopah when he gunned the engine just a little too hard trying to get up a sandy bank and stripped the transmission. The Flyer sat inert in the sand, its radiator grille still festooned with cards, flags, pennants, ribbons, and other tokens of good luck jammed there by wellwishers along the way. But without a transmission, it was just another dead beast in the desert. Fortunately, there was a ranch nearby, but unfortunately, there was no machine shop or Thomas parts depot in the middle of the desert. It fell to Schuster to decide what to do. He rented a horse from the rancher, took a revolver for protection, and made his way alone to Tonopah.

Arriving at 5 A.M. a day later, Schuster found out where the local Thomas dealer lived and woke him up. The other teams would not have had the luxury of consulting a Züst, a De Dion, or a Protos dealership in such a small town, but the advantage was short-lived. The dealer didn't stock the transmission parts Schuster needed. And so, without missing a beat, the dealer sent his mechanics out to take them from other Thomas Flyers in town, whether the owners were home or not.

No city could do much more than that, but Goldfield tried, as it awaited the Flyer the next day. Schools were let out, business leaders bickered over who would ride in the welcome car, and the hotel planned a dinner that would be extravagant by the standards of either New York or Paris. The members of the Goldfield Hunt and Country Club—something of an extravagance itself in a place without foxes or golf—planned to challenge the Thomas to a short race through the desert. Saloons in town were ringing with a song written especially for the Thomas. The chorus ran:

> Yankee Boy, 'round the world you are racing;
> The Yankee car the others are chasing.
> Now your car is riding—riding very nice
> But up north you'll hit some ice.

> If you had waited awhile,
> You could have crossed the Strait;
> But now you'll have to take your car across as freight
> If you win the race,
> You'll fill our hearts with joy,
> For we are cheering for our good old Yankee Boy.

If Schuster heard the song, it would have hit home—the race he was running was indeed with the weather in Alaska, just as the song implied. By the time the Thomas approached Goldfield, it was a good five hundred miles ahead of the Italians and a thousand ahead of St. Chaffray. Lieutenant Koeppen, running behind the Frenchmen, was no concern at all. None of them were, actually. What worried Schuster was the chance of reaching San Francisco in time to sail on March 26 for Valdez, Alaska.

If the men of the Thomas team missed the boat on the twenty-sixth, they would have to wait a week for another. That would reduce the odds of getting across Alaska, due to melting snows, and across the Bering Strait, due to lack of ice. In fact, there were a great many questions swirling around those Pacific sailings. Various race officials were encouraging the cars to skip the Alaska leg of the trip, since the bad weather across the country had put all of the cars so far behind the original projections for a sailing in early March. Some said that the Thomas should wait in San Francisco for the other cars before sailing. Schuster wasn't inclined to speculation or debate; he was supposed to get to San Francisco in time to go to Alaska, and that was what he intended to do.

At the wheel of the Thomas Flyer, Harold Brinker pulled into Goldfield at about 8 A.M. At 11:30, he was on his way out, on Schuster's order. Everyone in town was disappointed, but it was hardest on the schoolchildren; with the holiday over early, they had to go back to school in the afternoon.

From Goldfield, Brinker continued south, still driving away from San Francisco—and the mountains that lined most of the California-Nevada border. He crossed the border at Death Valley, that sandy, salty, and alkaline basin that is the lowest point on the continent, as much as

280 feet below sea level. Death Valley wasn't particularly treacherous in March, nor was it especially empty, as the Thomas passed many camps, alive with men and mules, digging valuable borax out of the soil. With every passing day, the basin grew hotter, though, and that did not bode well for the teams following the Thomas by a week or even more.

The Thomas Flyer was in California, heading for Los Angeles, on the day that the Italians finally arrived in Utah. It hadn't been easy crossing Aspen Ridge, pressing the car to a height of eleven thousand feet, sometimes on a track never intended for a vehicle as wide as a European touring car. According to Scarfoglio, one side of the car would often be scraping the mountainside while the wheels on the other side were following the line of the drop-off.

"We saw Ogden in the distance," Scarfoglio wrote March 21, "and its houses scattered in the plain seemed like seeds on a field, encircled by the mountains. Then suddenly, the Great Salt Lake appeared before us and gleamed like a peerless sapphire."

"I give you the news, with pleasure," Emilio Sirtori wrote very pointedly in a letter that day, "that the auto Züst got to Ogden at 4:30 to-day, without special aid."

The car, according to Sirtori, "swam through creeks and jumped through snowdrifts, and took all the chances of such a hard trip for the men as well as for the car." He wanted compensation, in the form of some penalty for the Thomas, which had used "special aid," in the form of rail tracks and tunnels. To Sirtori, it had become an American race, and the Thomas had an advantage, however unintended and perhaps unsolicited.

And so, after just twenty hours of rest, Sirtori set off to vanquish the Thomas in the only way he knew, by driving all the more intently toward it. Setting off from Ogden, the Züst team was about eight hundred miles, or six days, behind the Flyer: even farther behind than it had been the week before. An Italian band regaled the Züst as it rolled out of Ogden for the west, never to return.

Near a railroad outpost called Kelton in northern Utah, there was a telegraph operator who lived alone at his station and had precious few people to talk to, day in and year out: another of those solitary figures who kept the west connected by rail or telegraph. But he refused to be lonely sitting at his telegraph key, peppering the line with messages, filing reports on the temperature, or speculating on problems unlikely to occur; picking over the answers; and following up on stray points just to coax a response. He was never far from the key, making a general nuisance of himself, one that all the other stationmasters understood perfectly. He was fighting the great battle of humankind, all day, every day—he was staving off solitude. On March 23, 1908, though, a miracle came. Something happened at his station near Kelton, Utah. Telegraph operators up and down the line took their heads off their hands when they read his messages that day.

The Züst broke in Kelton. It didn't just break down, it fell into pieces. Easing over a railroad track, the frame cracked, just as it had in Nebraska. The steel brace welded on then had held strong, shifting all of the strain to the rest of the frame. In Kelton, it gave way, and so did Emilio Sirtori. He and the others abandoned the car in the empty, dusty expanse and walked a few hundred yards to the telegraph operator's shack, descending upon him and overwhelming him with the boldness and the noise of people in the flesh. Over the wire, every word had the same inflection, or lack thereof, and the same pale blue color of the ink in his pen.

While Arthur Ruland tried to work out a way to ship the car back to Ogden by rail, Sirtori sat in the corner, smoking cigarettes and cursing. He told the others that he was through with the New York-to-Paris Race. Scarfoglio shouted at him in Italian, while Henry Haaga tried to reason with him more gently in a combination of Italian, English, and German.

Ruland poured over schedules and sent a blaze of messages, with the help of the stationmaster. They ignored the emotional scene surrounding Sirtori as best they could, scribbling messages back and forth to each other, some to be sent, some just coming in through the wire. As Ruland rifled through the messages that piled up, he suddenly froze. One of the messages was from New York, advising him to return for his own sake.

Ruland had been away for six weeks, taking a full share in the Züst team, with all of its troubles. He didn't share in the glory, when it occurred, and was never listed as a member of the team. Ruland didn't forget that he was a sales manager, working the race like a prospect and figuring, like a sales manager, that his reward would come in the form of increased business. Six weeks was a little bit too long to leave his wife, though, who was said to have started sharing their apartment in Staten Island with another man. When she and her new friend traveled, according to investigations by the man's wife, they pretended to be brother and sister. Ruland held the message in his hands and said nothing. Sirtori, in his corner, was still cursing away whatever it was the other two were trying to say. And the stationmaster finally knew what it was like to have people around.

Chapter Seventeen

California Postcard

Car	Miles	Place	Team
Thomas Flyer (U.S.)	3451	Mojave, California	Brinker, Schuster, Miller, Hansen
Züst (Ita.)	2616	Kelton, Utah	Sirtori, Scarfoglio, Haaga
De Dion (Fra.)	2226	Rawlins, Wyoming	St. Chaffray, Autran, Lascares
Protos (Ger.)	2109	Laramie, Wyoming	Koeppen, Snyder

The Western Motor Car Company, the Thomas dealership in Los Angeles, took out half-page advertisements in the Sunday paper during the New York-to-Paris Race to trumpet the progress of the Flyer. Anyone who wanted to know even more about it could stop in at the dealership, where an elaborate display in the window showed the progress of all of the cars, using models set up on a map.

Los Angeles had only about a hundred thousand residents in 1908, putting it 102nd in population among U.S. metropolitan areas, far behind huge cities such as Evansville, Indiana; New Bedford, Massachusetts; and Allegheny, Pennsylvania, all of which were in the top fifty. Greater Los Angeles, however, had a way of laying claim to rich people from all the other towns in America. Beverly Hills was incorporated in 1908, giving them one place to live. And in March of the same year, just as the New York-to-Paris racers were due to arrive, Madame Ida Hancock unveiled plans for a new mansion on the corner of Wilshire Boulevard and Vermont Avenue, giving the upper classes the chance to follow her to the outskirts, and an area that would soon be named "Hancock Park."

Madame Hancock was plain "Ida" in the 1860s, when her husband inherited fifty-five hundred acres in West Los Angeles. It was just a lot of scrubby land then, but the Hancocks would grow rich with it, dealing smartly in the city's first two great products: oil and real estate. With only a little exaggeration, it can be said that everyone in Los Angeles in 1908 was dealing in real estate, if only in respect to the value of their own homes. Real estate prices were to Angelenos what sports scores were to people in other cities. Avidly reported and endlessly discussed, they were part of an equation that was already serving the region well. Every snippet of publicity that reached the rest of the country about Los Angeles's climate, its clean air, and its outdoor lifestyle brought a new wave of arrivals. No city matched Los Angeles in those days for boosting itself.

The city's leaders, looking at the original route of the round-the-world race, were baffled by the implication that the city of Los Angeles wasn't on the way to Paris from New York. Despite the fact that the route quite obviously ran straight west across the northern part of the United States, they nonetheless couldn't understand why LA wasn't included. And then it snowed—not in LA, but in the Sierra Nevada Mountains in northern Nevada. No sooner was the race route changed, to loop south of the Sierra Nevadas, than Earle C. Anthony, owner of the Western Motor Car Company, started working the problem.

Anthony, twenty-eight, was already the dean of LA's automobile dealers, selling a range of high-priced cars. He would remain at the forefront for decades, helping to change the American landscape along the way. It was Anthony who gave the world its first gasoline station in 1904, with a couple of curbside pumps he called "the Red and White Filling Station." A little later, he went to France and brought home the first three neon signs ever to glow over the U.S. roadside. And still later, in 1925, he started radio station KFI in Los Angeles, one of the nation's earliest broadcast stations. He wanted it as a medium for automobile advertising. When Anthony heard about the change in the route of the New York-to-Paris Race—the greatest publicity beacon that automobiling had ever known—he immediately contacted Edward L. Thomas.

E. L. Thomas was E. R. Thomas's son and a vice president of the Thomas Motor Car Company. Lanky and trim, with a reddish moustache and a freckled face, Thomas was no older than Anthony. He happened to be on the West Coast in March, visiting Thomas dealerships and preparing to meet the Thomas Flyer team in San Francisco. The point that interested Anthony was that the race committee was allowing the contestants to choose for themselves whether to drive straight up central California toward San Francisco or to cut across to the ocean— through LA—and use the coast road north.

The central route was risky, encompassing rugged mountains in the early going. The coast road, though longer in miles, was pristine, probably the finest long-distance highway in the whole country.

Earle Anthony, of course, wanted the Flyer to use the LA route. He was an authority on road conditions—having sent out many of his own well-publicized automobile expeditions—but his real area of expertise was the world of wealthy, slightly bored people, in particular the ones who moved to LA wanting nothing more than to live in the right place and drive the right car. With the famous Flyer in town, Anthony envisioned a sales boom for Thomas cars. He had no trouble convincing E. L. that the Flyer should take the long way, the easy and predictable way, and pass through LA.

No sooner did the race committee officially change the route to run south in Nevada than Anthony had the Thomas's new Los Angeles plan settled and ready for publication in the *Los Angeles Times*. He and E. L. would drive out well in advance to meet Brinker and Schuster in Daggett, near Barstow, about eighty miles due east of LA. As soon as the New York-to-Paris racecar arrived, they would all go to LA, where they would be escorted by a car carrying Mayor Arthur C. Harper, a former banker, and Allan Hancock, Ida's son.

Leaving nothing to chance, E. L. and Anthony arrived in Daggett on Friday, March 20, two days early, and took rooms at a hotel. With temperatures soaring, the desert town was described as "hot as a furnace," but Anthony and E. L. stayed busy. The first task they gave themselves was to buy supplies for the Thomas Flyer and its crew. The purchases were delivered to the hotel, where they were piled in crates and boxes on one side of the small lobby. When the right motor oil couldn't be located, though, E. L. rashly decided to go all the way back to LA to fetch some. Anthony talked him out of it and finally found high-grade oil that could be delivered by train.

The Thomas was reported to be safely through Death Valley and in California—and on Sunday, March 22, the city of Los Angeles was waiting to greet it. "Thomas Flyer, America's Winner," began Western Motor Car's banner ad in the paper that morning, "Will be in Los Angeles Today. See it in our garage today, and other Thomas Flyers just like it, which we can deliver at once. $4,500, F.O.B. Los Angeles." The many articles that appeared that day about the car didn't fail to cite, with a glow of gratitude, E. L. Thomas's ability to change the route of the race to include Los Angeles.

Hundreds of automobilists drove out along the course, found a place to picnic, and waited for the excitement. Mayor and Mrs. Harper were in the front of the throng, sitting in Allan Hancock's car. The *Los Angeles Times* had a photographer waiting nearby.

That afternoon, the Thomas arrived in Mojave, an isolated desert town where no one was expecting the racer. That may have been a relief to the team, after starting the day in the rather antic little city of Goldfield. At the Mojave telegraph office, Schuster found a series of frantic telegrams from E. L. asking, advising, and finally ordering him to make his way immediately to Daggett, en route to Los Angeles. The same messages had been sent at intervals during the afternoon to all of the likely California towns where E. L. might hope to intercept his racer. George Schuster read the telegrams and then took stock. Daggett was still fifty-five miles to the south. San Francisco was in the exact opposite direction—and just where LA was situated didn't seem to matter much to George Schuster, at all.

Schuster had to be in San Francisco on March 23, in time to load the car on a train for Seattle. (The use of the train was allowed once cars reached the official debarkation point at San Francisco.) In Seattle, a freighter was due to leave for Alaska on March 25. That connection would deliver the Flyer to Alaska on March 30. If the team members missed the train, though, and so the freighter from Seattle, they would have to wait until April 1 for the next Alaska-bound ship, arriving April 6—the loss of a whole week.

Standing in the Mojave telegram office, Schuster was acutely aware that he had only two days to make the trip to San Francisco and load the car on the train. The Los Angeles route offered better roads but would almost certainly take longer than two days.

With that, Schuster ignored E. L.'s telegrams. After consulting briefly with Harold Brinker, he gave the order to turn north. The Thomas Flyer had no use for Southern Cal.

The Mojave telegraph office notified the *Los Angeles Times,* which informed E. L. Thomas and Earle Anthony, and later all of LA, that the Flyer had flown, "without the sanction of the owner." Hundreds of cars waiting for the Thomas on the roadsides east of Los Angeles peeled away, unceremoniously. E. L. boarded a train to chase the Flyer north to Bakersfield, still hoping to convince Schuster to turn back. Perhaps he just didn't want to set foot in Los Angeles for a while.

George Schuster couldn't worry about E. L.'s hurt feelings; he had only one concern, the car. The Cheyenne agreement had put him—not E. L.—in charge. His decision to ignore Los Angeles was the first test of that agreement. Schuster couldn't worry about that, either.

The terrain between Mojave and Bakersfield was stony and steep, with "heavy mountain roads," as Schuster called them. Eventually, the Sierra Nevada Mountains would tail off toward the coast, dividing the dry desert to the south and the green San Joaquin Valley to the north.

Bakersfield, tucked at the northern edge of the mountains, was fairly rugged in another way, with more than its share of outlaws and murder cases. One of the more colorful was George Sontag, an infamous train robber. In 1892, he stopped a Southern Pacific train near Bakersfield, robbing it of $1,200 and two sacks of Peruvian money. He then rode ahead to the next station in a buggy and calmly boarded the same train as a passenger. That was his escape. It worked, too, but when he was having breakfast the next day at a restaurant in the town of Visalia, about fifty miles north of Bakersfield, he was recognized and arrested without incident. There were much more dangerous outlaws in the area during the years leading up to 1908, when the racers passed through. Bakersfield was booming as never before, recognized as the capital of the oil industry in California, but that didn't make it any less wild.

By the time Brinker, Schuster, Miller, and Captain Hansen pulled into Bakersfield at 12:40 A.M., they had been on the road for almost eighteen hours. But they had logged 382 miles—the best single day's run of the whole race. The next best was 219 miles, which Monty Roberts had made in a single day in Ohio.

Brinker's smooth record through the badlands on the way to Bakersfield pleased George Schuster. And Brinker, too. He was still hoping that if the car made good time with him at the wheel, he would be asked to continue as the Thomas driver through the rest of the race.

In Bakersfield, the hotel dining room reopened after midnight, just for the Thomas team. Captain Hansen revived first and proposed a toast to his daughter, Lydia, on the occasion of her birthday. With Mathewson and Van Loan far away in Denver, Captain Hansen was among friends again, fellows who understood him—either that or ones who didn't make the mistake of even trying to understand him. Perhaps because San Francisco was practically in sight, George Schuster was in a rare, talkative mood, relating the recent adventures of the road for the Bakersfield residents who crowded into the dining room, despite the late hour. "Although we had many trying experiences in the east," Schuster reflected, "of which everybody has read by this time, we had no difficulty with the machine and the big car is now in just as good shape as when we started.

"We never know how far or where we are going," Schuster said brightly of the rest of the race. "We just turn her loose and let her go." That wasn't quite true, but with one quick, easy run through the San Joaquin Valley, the Thomas team would be in San Francisco, just in time to catch the train to Seattle.

Early the next morning, when Schuster came down from his room, a clerk handed him a telegram from E. L. Thomas, instructing him to wait in Bakersfield. E. L. was on his way and wanted to see him— "badly." In response, Schuster hurried through breakfast and the team left even earlier than planned. He had to be San Francisco, three hundred miles away, by the next day, and he didn't want to get caught up with E. L. or anyone else.

With flat terrain and clear weather, Brinker was cruising along at 40 mph, and even higher speeds when the conditions allowed it. Schuster sat tensely beside him in the passenger seat, determined that the car keep up that rate. Following the directions of a local guide, however, they repeatedly found themselves on narrowing roads that ended up in sheep corrals and private courtyards. For his own protection, the guide was suddenly put out of the car at one such ranch.

After finding the route again, Schuster still had hopes of catching the train in San Francisco. But then the Thomas Flyer, stalwart through the worst conditions of eleven states, had a minor breakdown on the smooth roads of Fresno County, two hundred miles short of San Francisco. It was only an hour's delay, but Schuster knew that the race-within-the-race was over. They wouldn't make the train.

The Thomas Flyer arrived in San Francisco the next day, March 24, preceded by a brass band and followed by hundreds of automobiles, all of them Thomas cars, or it seemed at first glance. The city still showed scars from the Great Earthquake and Fire two years before, with some city blocks empty except for rubble and ash, but its lively pace had been restored and a garland of new buildings made San Francisco the most modern city in the nation. It was a fitting backdrop for the celebration of the success of the first leg of the New York-to-Paris Race.

"It was distinctly the hour of the automobile in San Francisco," wrote W. H. B. Fowler, one of the *Chronicle's* star reporters. "Never before in the history of the city has there been such a demonstration of automobile enthusiasts. It seemed as if every motor car in the city desired to take some part in the parade." During the excitement over the arrival of the Thomas, E. P. Brinegar, the manager of the Thomas dealership in San Francisco, was overheard commenting on the American leg of the New York-to-Paris Race. "As a people, we are ashamed to show the foreigners the kind of roads that we use," he admitted, before making a deft rotation in his logic. "One thing is certain: our bad roads are entirely responsible for the perfection of the American car."

After parking the car at Brinegar's dealership on Golden Gate Avenue, Brinker was said to be "jovial," and Schuster, in his relief, had become a veritable raconteur, telling dramatic stories from the trip. Normally, he'd have been under the car, checking something and trying not to listen, while someone else unwound. Schuster even published an article under his own byline in the *San Francisco Examiner.* "The trip across the continent has been a hard one," he wrote, "and we are glad to have a chance to lay off for a day or two and take things easy before we start on the next stage of our journey, which is the trip through Alaska. I have been on the car since it left New York and although we have had many pleasant experiences, there has been a lot of hard work, and we need a rest."

E. L. Thomas finally caught up to Schuster in San Francisco. Whatever was said about bypassing Los Angeles (and the fact that the Flyer missed the train, anyway, as Earle Anthony, for one, predicted it would), Schuster soon put the boss's son to work, helping to outfit the car for the Alaska journey. Schuster was also overseeing carpenters, who were building special storage compartments onto the back of the Flyer. He turned down E. L.'s suggestion to build sleeping compartments, as well. Hotels and camping tents were altogether more practical.

On the day that the Thomas Flyer arrived in San Francisco, it was nine hundred miles ahead of its nearest competitor, the Italian Züst. While the team members basked in the glory of that accomplishment, they weren't, as a matter of fact, sure where they were supposed to go next. The route specified Alaska, of course, but many experts close to the race committee in Paris strongly advised that the cars cross the Pacific by boat. At its best, Alaska presented problems for an automobile, but so late in the season, it would be an impossibility. Snow trails would be melting and so would rivers, which were useful as highways when they were frozen. For more than a day, telegrams from Europe, New York, and Alaska joined the debate, without any definite result. "There is a delightful haziness," observed W. H. B. Fowler, "about the arrangements, and just who is to settle the issue."

Not everyone thought it delightful, but the decision finally came on March 26, directly from the race committee in Paris. With the intention of making the trip "as hard as possible without being entirely unfeasible," the committee told Schuster to proceed to Alaska. Schuster made preparations to ship the car to Seattle.

The next day, George Sontag, the train robber, was released from Folsom Penitentiary, having been in jail since 1892. When he arrived in

San Francisco by train, two friends came to pick him up in a car. Sontag had never seen an automobile before. He backed up and turned away, as though looking for his own century again. Shaking his head, he refused to get near the car, and certainly not inside it. Someone had to send for a buggy.

The Flyer had already been loaded onto a freighter leaving for Seattle. After a two-day trip there, it would transfer to a cargo ship headed for Valdez, Alaska, a journey of six days. Up to the very last minute in San Francisco, Harold Brinker begged Schuster for the chance to continue with the car, as an extra hand, if not as driver. In fact, Brinker had handled the car perfectly, and he had always been careful to defer to Schuster. But George Schuster would not hear of taking Brinker along. It was finally his car, his race, and his big chance.

Chapter Eighteen

Death in the Desert

Car	Miles	Place	Team
Thomas Flyer (U.S.)	3832	San Francisco, California	Brinker, Schuster, Miller, Hansen
Züst (Ita.)	2718	Cobre, Nevada	Sirtori, Scarfoglio, Haaga
De Dion (Fra.)	2536	Ogden, Utah	St. Chaffray, Autran, Lascares
Protos (Ger.)	2325	Thayer, Wyoming	Koeppen, Snyder

The city of Los Angeles managed to recover from its disappointment over Schuster's decision to bypass Southern California. People in the city simply turned to the Züst, learning all about it and rooting for it heart and soul. It wasn't quite the outcome that Earle C. Anthony, the Thomas dealer, had envisioned.

Unfortunately, the Italian car was still two states away in Utah. After the Züst broke down, or disintegrated, in Kelton, two railroads had come to its rescue. The Southern Pacific line sent a special train to haul the broken carcass back to Ogden, and the Union Pacific machine shops stayed open all night to repair it. As a result, a mishap that should have caused a week's delay was set right in only two days. Emilio Sirtori emerged from his hotel room in Ogden and began to show a glimmer of interest in the old Züst again. At the same time, word arrived in Ogden that the Thomas team had missed the train to Seattle and would not be able to sail for Alaska until April 1, fully a week away. Without further comment, Sirtori returned to his place in the driver's seat of the Züst. The only subject he wanted to talk about, almost incessantly, was reaching San Francisco in time to catch a fast train to Seattle and make the April 1 sailing alongside the Thomas.

On the day that the Thomas Flyer left San Francisco, bound for Seattle, the Italians were in Nevada and making good time. Eastern Nevada is rippled with mountain ranges, but they run in a north-south direction, and so the car, following the same line, didn't have to do much climbing. Even as the Züst sailed through the rust-colored terrain, Scarfoglio was dividing his attention between the scenery and the keyboard on his portable Oliver typewriter. "The road is fair and is not hard on our pneumatic tires," he wrote. "The road is quite level, and our car, the Züst, is running at a fast gait," he continued, thinking for a while and then adding, "but it is a run without life and without enjoyment." That was a satisfying thought, and so he explored it further: "The air that is coaxing our faces is mild, but there is nothing to put one in good humor—not a tree, not a man, not a telegraph pole." The route through Nevada was undoubtedly desolate. Yet the eastern United States had affected Scarfoglio the same dismal way. And it was veritably jammed with trees, men, and telegraph poles.

After enjoying a hurried celebration in the town of Goldfield, which had unearthed thousands of Italian flags somewhere in its young attics, the Züst team continued toward California, becoming lost for most of a day in Death Valley. With no chance of reaching San Francisco in time to meet the Thomas in Seattle, the Italians surfaced unexpectedly in Daggett. That could mean only one thing, as telegrams flew over the wires: they were on the road to LA.

Anticipating that California's coastal road would be gentle on the car—not to say the occupants—Sirtori, Scarfoglio, and Haaga were indeed headed for the city of Los Angeles. They were accustomed to exuberant welcomes, but nothing prepared them for a party the way Los Angeles threw one. En route from San Bernardino, the three men in the Züst were almost continually pelted with oranges and flowers, all in the name of adoration, of course. Forgetting about the Thomas entirely, the city "went fairly wild over the Italians," wrote the correspondent for the New York Times. "The crew was almost mobbed. . . . They were hugged, cheered, almost drowned with champagne, and pulled and hauled about till they broke away and sought refuge at their hotel."

The response was like that given later in the century to movie stars and rock singers. In 1908, hysteria and hero worship were not yet woven into everyday life, though. Emilio Sirtori, for one, didn't know what to do with it. "He smiles sadly when complimented and seems bored," wrote a Los Angelan during Sirtori's visit. "He hates to talk about himself, but becomes eloquent about his car." He was also eloquent about the Aspen Tunnel in Wyoming. "We lost three days by going over the pass," Sirtori exclaimed to bystanders. "They [the Union Pacific officials] let the Thomas go through the tunnel. It took them [the Thomas racers] only six hours, and it only seemed fair that the Züst should follow, but they would not let us through." He was perfectly correct on principle, but in point of fact, the Züst didn't lose much time by going overland; with the help of a smart guide, Sirtori had actually managed it in a day.

The Züst remained in Los Angeles for only a few hours, but it was a celebration that included the city once and for all in the New York-to-Paris Race. The Züst team, heading north, was glad to be out of LA's peculiar storm of joy, and especially away from the raining oranges, but the drive to San Francisco proved to be even more dangerous, in a way. After seven weeks of persevering through snowdrifts, quicksand, and fast-running creeks, the Züst team was up against towns that Scarfoglio perceived as "lost in a wealth of flowers."

Scarfoglio's antecedent, Odysseus, had the same problem on the Island of the Lotus-eaters. In California, the islands were the towns. "We pass as quickly as possible," Scarfoglio wrote, "so as not to yield to the desire—delicious as they are—to put on our brakes and dismount beside one of these gardens, near one of these white-robed women who send us smiles and kisses on the tips of their fingers, and to finish here our race and our lives."

Sirtori and Scarfoglio each commented later on how much California reminded them of Italy at its finest. They weren't the first to make that discovery. When the Züst team arrived in San Francisco on April 4, they were greeted by tens of thousands of Italian Americans, including a personal escort by the president of the Bank of Italy (an institution that would later grow into the Bank of America, under the leadership of A. P. Giannini). According to close observers, San Francisco gave the Züst an even larger demonstration than it gave the American car, the Thomas Flyer.

On hearing that Charles Godard was also in town and that his Moto-

Bloc had been officially disqualified for resorting to the train in Iowa, Sirtori exploded. He contended that it was the Thomas Flyer that should be under scrutiny. "She is disqualified a half a dozen times," Sirtori fumed, claiming that all of the foreign teams were disgruntled about the injustices surrounding the American car. "Why, in one place in the Rocky Mountains," he insisted, "the Thomas reneged on a terrific hill, that took us six days to climb, by taking the railroad tunnel."

Every time he told the story, Aspen Ridge cost him another three days.

The sailing schedules on the Pacific coast didn't favor the Züst. By a good five days, the Italians had already missed the train that might have put them with the Thomas on the April 1 sailing from Seattle to Alaska. By less than a day, more to the point, they missed the steamer that would have at least put them in Seattle in time for the April 8 sailing. They even missed the train that would have allowed them a slightly later start from San Francisco. The best connection that Sirtori, Scarfoglio, and Haaga could make was a steamship leaving from Seattle on April 16—a twelve-day lag from the time they arrived in San Francisco. To make sure they didn't miss even that sailing, they booked passage on a coastal freighter leaving San Francisco for Seattle on April 10. That gave them six days to enjoy themselves in San Francisco.

When the Züst was leaving Ogden, Utah, for the second time (ten days before its triumphal arrival in San Francisco), Bourcier St. Chaffray was just arriving in the town of Evanston, in the southwest corner of Wyoming. He was leaving the Uinta Mountains behind, having visited nearly all of them, thanks to a guide who insisted on taking the De Dion along the summits, following the range north almost as far as it reached. Only then did the guide realize that following the summits wasn't a feasible way to cross the Uinta range. The car had to turn around. St. Chaffray later noted that the only competent pilot he had through the mountains was a dog, a long-haired mongrel who invariably chose the best path. Unfortunately, he wasn't available for the whole trip.

St. Chaffray wasn't sorry to leave Wyoming, even though he had learned a few new things there. "When small rivers were crossed at a speed of thirty miles an hour the water came up high on the car for a second, but we rushed through," he explained. "When a speed of only ten miles an hour was observed, the car sank in the mud." It might have been a metaphor, embracing the whole reason that some men chose to race around the world in the first place. Back in Wyoming, however, in places where the water was too deep to shoot, the Frenchmen built bridges, as many as five in one day. Unlike the Americans and Italians, who made a practice of dismantling any bridges they constructed along the way, the French left theirs standing, an act of sportsmanship intended to help the German Protos, which was still trailing by a few days.

As St. Chaffray prepared to leave Evanston, he hired a guide to help him find his way out of the Rockies and into Ogden, which had become a major stop for the New York-to-Paris racers: an oasis with a very good hotel.

Ogden was well known as a railroad hub, and that made it a hobo hub, too. Unemployed men clung to the railroads in those days, and in surprisingly large numbers, hopping the cars or just following the tracks on foot. The west had more than its share of hobos, representing the dismal side of its maverick image. Not only were rootless people pouring into the region every year, many of the businesses in that relatively young region went bust. That left legions of men roaming around the rails, constantly in search of a community where the law would leave them alone. "The entire road [railroad] between Omaha and Oakland is lined with hoboes," stated a 1908 report, "and they make life a weary burden for brakemen who eject them, and are only driven from one train to invade another."

On March 26, just as St. Chaffray and his team were breaking out of the Uinta peaks, a group of hoboes in central Utah, utterly disorganized except that they all wanted to get to Ogden, took over a train headed from Nevada. It was an act of desert piracy, as the tramps seized charge of the whole train. By the time the police caught up with it, though, all of the culprits had hopped off and disappeared.

Two hoboes turned up later in the day near Evanston, probably renegades from the hijacking. They stood for a long time on the tracks of the Union Pacific, about three miles outside of town, enjoying an unusual picture. A huge car—the De Dion—was jammed into a mudhole and four men—St. Chaffray, Autran, Lascares, and the guide—were trying one idea after another to extricate it. Jacks, tackle, levers, and a great deal of slush flew around the car, without any effect. So did a lot of cursing, as the Frenchmen pushed against bodywork or pulled on ropes to set the car free. St. Chaffray, thinking that he could establish some rapport with the hoboes, approached them and offered good pay for their help. It turned out that they were fellow Europeans, Hungarian by birth. In any case, they refused, explaining that they wanted the money—but not enough to work for it. Then they went about helping themselves to a spare axle that had been laid aside on the ground.

It isn't easy to help oneself to a spare axle, which weighs more than a hundred pounds, but between the two of them, they seemed likely to manage. What is harder to understand is why they wanted it, unless they knew of a pawnshop in the immediate vicinity that specialized in luxury French automobile parts. "Lascares, our companion on the trip since Chicago," wrote Bourcier St. Chaffray, "had a clear view of the situation, and saw the movement of the tramps. He took out his revolver."

At gunpoint, the hoboes not only decided to leave the spare axle alone, but to help pull the De Dion out of the mudhole. "With six men on the rope," reported the *Ogden Standard,* "and the engine throbbing and driving the wheels with great speed, the car was slowly dragged from the hole." (The paper got a little carried away; there being only six men present, five must have been pulling on the rope while one operated the car.) St. Chaffray admitted that the two hoboes had been good, clever workmen and paid them before going on his way.

"Without news without money," was the extent of the telegram St. Chaffray sent from Ogden to the De Dion factory in Toulon, France. More of both were headed his way, courtesy of the marquis. For the time being, through the rest of Utah and Nevada, St. Chaffray made much better progress than any of his rivals had. In Tonopah, he and his team struck local residents as a "jolly" trio. Tonopah may have been only four years old, but the editor of the local paper was a little older than that, and he was not fooled by their bravado. After the Frenchmen left, he mulled over one of the comments they'd been fond of repeating:

They say that the race proper starts from Valdez, Alaska and that the real test will come when the Siberia troubles are met.

The writer is not familiar with the rules governing the race, but it would seem folly to start from New York when the real race starts away up in frozen Alaska. Probably if the Frenchman were in the lead the race would have a very much different aspect and the real starting place would be New York.

While St. Chaffray was in Tonopah, he and the team were invited via telegraph to be the guests of honor at a ball in nearby Goldfield. They didn't know what to expect, but the invitation was accepted. "The mere matter of racing is always subject to social amenities," St. Chaffray observed in his return wire. He didn't regret his decision, later reporting that he had rarely been in such sumptuous surroundings, even in Paris. Having fairly flown through Nevada, the French team then crossed into California.

In Death Valley, the De Dion stopped. The valley, well named, had killed bigger beasts, and it had no trouble with a car, especially one that was lost on the wrong road. Stuck in sand up to the top of the wheels, the De Dion could only move in one direction: down. With Lascares temporarily blind from the sun and the blowing sand, St. Chaffray and Autran set off in search of help. Following the sound of bells, they walked for miles searching for the source. Later, they learned that the chimes were made by the wind, clapping against the sand, and reverberating through the ears of desperate men. The sound kept them walking, though, until they came on a one-man camp. That was something of a miracle, and so was the fact that the occupant agreed to ride his burro to a telegraph station and send a message to the town of Rhyolite for help.

When word of the stranded car reached Rhyolite, a major windstorm was just whipping up and no one seemed to want to go out into the desert for the sake of three automobilists. Finally, a teamster named Frank Hartigan volunteered for the job, setting off in a horse-drawn wagon, either for the promise of pay or for the chance to help the stranded foreigners.

An hour later, his horses came plodding back to their barn in Rhyolite. Hartigan wasn't in the wagon. His friends immediately set off in search of him and found his body by the side of the road. His neck had been broken, apparently from a fall. No one would ever know for sure. The horses may have become frightened by the storm and bolted. He may even have been blown off-balance by the wind. Whatever happened, Frank Hartigan's death was the first one associated with the New York-to-Paris Race. Although another teamster took his place in rescuing the De Dion, the car lost a full day. In retrospect, that was not much to lose.

Bourcier St. Chaffray was keenly aware that he was still not very far behind Sirtori in the Züst. On the day that the French car finally pried loose of Death Valley, the Italians were whipping up the coast toward San Francisco, hoping to catch an early steamer for Valdez. St. Chaffray was determined to catch up and put his De Dion on the same steamer. He had no time to waste on Los Angeles or the fine road up the coast; he had to hope for the best on the central route.

By the time St. Chaffray rolled into Bakersfield at 10:30 on Friday night, April 3, having been driving for most of fourteen hours, he was perfectly happy to obey the city's new ordinance, enforcing a 10 mph speed limit for cars. There comes a time, after all, when a driver is too tired to speed.

The rush was over, anyway. Somewhere between Bakersfield and Fresno, St. Chaffray came by the information that the De Dion couldn't ship out of San Francisco until the tenth, when the Züst was leaving, too. With that, he slowed down to a sensible pace. St. Chaffray knew that he could easily make San Francisco by then, and so he did, inspiring another celebration in the city when he arrived on the seventh. Unlike Emilio Sirtori, the French racing men didn't gripe about the Thomas car. They had only one complaint—that they'd lost the trunk containing their dinner clothes and so they couldn't go out on the town the very first night.

George Schuster, in his new role as the captain of the Flyer and its newspaper coverage, never failed to point out that he was the only member of the Thomas team who had been with the car ever since it had left New York. That clarification would not have been necessary on the Züst; Emilio Sirtori, Antonio Scarfoglio, and Henry Haaga had all been on the car since New York. The same was true of St. Chaffray and Autran on the De Dion. For all of them, one lifetime of their journey had ended. They could look back on the trip across the United States and see how wrong they had been about so many things, at the beginning and all along the way. It had been a race full of mistakes, and by the time they reached San Francisco, they could see that perseverance had been the only remedy for all of them.

The respite in San Francisco was as sweet as the eye of a hurricane, if just as temporary. While the Italian team and the French one prepared for the next stage of the race, mostly by dining out and going to musical shows, they could content themselves with a long lead over the Germans in the Protos, still picking their way through the Rocky Mountains. But then, the Thomas Flyer was already nearing Alaska.

Chapter Nineteen

Sharp Turns

Car	Miles	Place	Team
Thomas Flyer (U.S.)	6036	Valdez, Alaska	Schuster, Miller, Hansen, MacAdam
Züst (Ita.)	4090	San Francisco, Calif.	Sirtori, Scarfoglio, Haaga
De Dion (Fra.)	4090	San Francisco, Calif.	St. Chaffray, Autran, Lascares
Protos (Ger.)	2616	Kelton, Utah	Koeppen, Snyder

F ewer than twenty thousand people lived in all of Alaska in 1908, most of them miners and prospectors left over, like glints in a pan, after the glory days of the Yukon Gold Rush had receded. There were more bears than people, but then, Alaska had an abundance of practically everything the natural world had to offer. In addition to gold, coal, copper, and timber, it had snow—enough to upholster Alaska's craggy terrain every winter. One might think that the snow would isolate Alaskans and keep them buried in their houses, but quite the opposite was true at the turn of the century. Alaska's most sociable residents came alive in the wintertime, when highways formed in the hard-frozen top layer of snow, making travel easy and fairly cheap.

Dogsleds were the favorite mode of transportation, but horse-drawn sleighs were also used; in fact, the Fairbanks-Valdez stagecoach line was a fleet of open sleighs that operated only in the winter. A visitor to Alaska described the traffic on the trail: "Sleds are pulled by single men, by two- and three-men tandems, by dog teams ranging from the lone twenty-pound native dog to a dozen immense 'huskies,' and by horses, mules and cattle, arranged single, double, tandem and in teams of four. The loads vary from the 200-pound outfit of the individual miner who is going to Fairbanks to work to the two- or three-ton load piled high on a four-horse bobsled."

The port of Valdez, situated at the end of a gentle inlet, was founded as a beachhead for newly arriving goldminers in 1898. In its first year, it was just a tent city. Ten years later, when the steamer carrying the Thomas Flyer sailed into the bay, Valdez was a jumble of clapboard buildings, with fifteen hundred people, two hospitals, a dozen lawyers, electric lights, running water, and a telephone system. It even had its own slogan, "Gateway to an Empire," referring to its position as a conduit into Alaska's vast territory.

To the south, Valdez watched over the water, its only practical route to the outside world. To the north, skirting a wall of white mountains, it peered up the Valdez-Fairbanks Trail, 285 miles long, which connected it to the interior of the "empire." When the trail was paved in snow, it was safe, smooth, and breathtakingly beautiful. During the short days of winter, the light glimmered through air so clear that it created new depths in the golds of the morning, the bright blues of the afternoon, and the regal reds and dark indigos of early evening. The Alaska Mountain range started out in the distance but didn't stay there, almost hitting travelers on the trail in the eye, at first in the form of canyons of black slate nine hundred feet high, with only a narrow ribbon of blue sky showing at the top. To cross the mountains from the south, the trail climbed from 256 feet above sea level to 2,714 feet in the span of four miles.

Over the soft sounds of the sleigh ride, winter travelers on the Valdez-Fairbanks Trail could hear the gurgle of an insistent stream or the crunch of footfall from a wild animal running in the woods. That, of course, would not be possible in a noisy automobile.

Every ten miles or so, the Valdez-Fairbanks Trail left nature entirely behind, in favor of sheer comfort, as offered by its network of roadhouses. They were by no means primitive and not necessarily even rustic. One offered—in addition to accommodations for a hundred people, stables for forty horses and a heated kennel—a mini-mall of sorts, complete with a jewelry store and watch repairman. Mrs. Ed Wood promised good meals with fresh meat at her roadhouse, while another proprietor competed purely on price: "I am a bachelor," he boasted, "and do not need to make a profit for the maintenance of a wife and children." None of the roadhouses sold gasoline in bulk, since no cars existed in the interior of Alaska, but arrangements had already been made by the Standard Oil Company to make special shipments of fuel to Alaska, just for the racecars.

In warm weather, the world of the Valdez-Fairbanks Trail literally melted away. Most of the roadhouses closed, as only a few intrepid travelers found it worthwhile to push through the rough terrain left by the melted snow and the wilderness that was unleashed after winter temperatures lifted. One of the many questions facing George Schuster as he watched Valdez come into view was which conditions he would find on the trail: the glistening snowtrack or the primordial slop. The ship carrying the Thomas team was already two days late, due to coastal storms, and that couldn't help the situation.

On the day that the ship was finally to dock in Valdez, the Italian Züst and French De Dion were still in San Francisco, awaiting the next steamer to Seattle. Meanwhile, the Protos was only just arriving in Ogden, Utah.

The German car was fourteen hundred miles behind the runners-up, and thirty-four hundred miles behind the leading car, but that wasn't even the worst of it. For one thing, it had already been in Ogden twice before. The first time was in late March, when it broke a shaft in Rock Springs, Wyoming. The Union Pacific fetched it and then returned it to Rock Springs after it was fixed, a loss of four days. With the car working, Koeppen and Snyder crossed the Uintas and arrived in Evanston utterly exhausted. Koeppen could only mumble that he was relieved to be on the verge of leaving Wyoming behind. In fact, Wyoming had been no worse to the Protos than had New York, Ohio, Indiana, Illinois, and Iowa. Nebraska was the only state for which the Protos might grow nostalgic.

At Evanston, the car was in good shape, but Lieutenant Koeppen wasn't. He was practically out of money. He was also sick with what he described as a "mountain fever" and left on a train for Salt Lake City, Utah's banking center. While he was there, he arranged through his own savings account in Berlin for a new infusion of credit and, more to the point, cash. Before leaving Evanston, he told Snyder to take the car through to Ogden, a rather blithe order considering that each of the other New York-to-Paris racers had met with disaster along that same stretch. All alone, Snyder set out, an act of some bravery in itself. Encountering drier roads than the others, he covered the entire seventy-mile run very easily in a single day.

Lieutenant Koeppen met the Protos and its driver in Ogden the next day, April 3. Rejecting the opportunity to have the car overhauled in anticipation of the lonely desert run ahead, he made plans to leave again as soon as possible. While in Ogden, Koeppen admitted that he was eighteen days behind the Americans in the Thomas Flyer, but he made his usual gentle assurance that his team would finish first in the end. Snyder was less sunny, crisply making note of the fact that he had driven practically every mile of the trip since leaving Chicago. Even so, it was Koeppen who had Snyder's sympathies. "Mein Gott, it is no race," he exclaimed, "but an expense endurance test."

Lieutenant Koeppen was much more anxious about the progress of the car than he let on. On Friday morning, as the Protos prepared to leave Ogden, he read reports on the progress of the others and calculated that he had exactly five days to put his car in Seattle in time to sail with them. That didn't seem likely. Just before breakfast, Koeppen decided that he would go ahead by train to the Nevada border, possibly to inquire about using the original route to San Francisco, due west over the Sierra Nevada Mountains, where the worst of the snow had melted. That was one advantage of trailing the other cars by two weeks. In any case, Koeppen had been in the car with Snyder for a long time, and he decided he ought to go ahead by train. Snyder, riding with a hired guide named C. O. Wheat, was to meet him that night in a railroad depot called Tacoma, Nevada, not far over the Utah-Nevada border.

Tacoma consisted of about one hundred people, a few wooden houses, and a cluster of railroad warehouses, which sprang to life a couple of times a day when the Central Nevada trains stopped. It wasn't the sort of place that could hide news, or anything else. When Lieutenant Koeppen, attaché of the German Imperial Army, arrived late on Friday and asked at the station where he could find the German car that was entered in the New York-to-Paris Race, no one had to start a search. There was no German racecar in Tacoma. Koeppen strode quickly into town and began making more inquiries, but he couldn't find anyone who had heard of his car. Lieutenant Koeppen, according to a local report, "was in a peck of trouble and worriment about his machine."

As they described it in Tacoma, "he started the wires to working immediately and kept them hot." Even with the telegraph at its busiest, though, Koeppen couldn't find his car. Every telegram came back with a variation of the same message: "No German car here." Somewhere in the parched desert that clamped down over northwest Utah, his car was lost, stranded, or wrecked. The next day, Saturday, Koeppen hitched a ride on a wagon to the larger town of Montello, about twenty miles away. For a while, it seemed that there was nothing he could do but wait for the sound of the car to break the dull quiet of the desert town.

At noon, Koeppen grew tired of waiting. Under the circumstances, two hours of inactivity was about all he could take. He decided that if he could get to Lucin, about forty miles to the east over the Utah border, he could rent a team of horses and trace the route of his car. It was a flawed plan—the car might have been lost to the west of Lucin, after all. But Koeppen was compelled to act: to do something, even when there was nothing right to do. That is always a dangerous juncture. He rushed into it.

Unfortunately, there would not be another train to Lucin for more than a day. Lieutenant Koeppen could have chosen another town, one farther north, where the train service was regular, but something told him that Lucin was the place. "He then got possession of a handcar," marveled the *Ogden Standard* a few days later, "and with no one to accompany him but his own dear self, made a hair-splitting run to Lucin."

Three or four people from Montello gathered in the railroad yards to watch Koeppen leave. They were no match for the quarter million who had watched the New York-to-Paris racers leave Times Square two months before, but they did see an aspect of the race that was even more essential to the competition. Forcing the handcar forward by working the shaft up and down, Koeppen could only lift his head momentarily and smile, as people wished him good luck. In a few minutes, he disappeared into the blur of blowing sand at the horizon, but by that time, there was no one left to watch him go. He was alone even before he was out of earshot.

Working a handcar is a brutal chore. Hard enough when two people seesaw the heavy shaft up and down, it is especially grueling when a single person has to power the machine, keeping the pressure on the upward stroke as well as the downward one. With momentum, the shaft grows lighter, but then that momentum is unforgiving, and it vanishes if the operator eases up, even for a minute. In any case, Koeppen couldn't dally; if a train caught up to him, he would have to yank the handcar off the track. For more than four hours, he powered the handcar toward Lucin, in a hurry all the while to find his car. The New York-to-Paris Race was composed almost entirely of personal sacrifice—but no single effort made by the others quite matched Koeppen's marathon to Lucin.

The truly agonizing moment of the trip still awaited him, though; on arriving, he was told that Lucin didn't have any horses for hire. It was a town with one railroad track and a few dozen people, none of whom needed to go anywhere that the train wouldn't take them. Koeppen had no choice but to join them, taking a train to Ogden—which he could have done quite easily from Montello, in the first place.

On Saturday night, Koeppen arrived in Ogden for the fourth time. That was three times too many, the idea of the New York-to-Paris Race being to forge continually west and not to keep circling back to Ogden, Utah.

Koeppen was back at the Reed Hotel, but he was still without his car. Positioning himself in the lobby, he made it his business to speak with anyone who had been traveling in the region of northern Utah. Eventually, he struck up a conversation with a telephone lineman who had heard something in his travels about a car being "stranded on the rocks of Blue Creek Road," in the hamlet of Blue Creek, about fifty miles northwest of Ogden. The main industry of Blue Creek, and indeed of that road, was the Blue Creek Ranch, a cattle operation with a telephone in the office.

Koeppen called the ranch and asked if a man named O. W. Snyder was there. His back was undoubtedly still aching from his dash in the handcar when, a moment later, Snyder came to the phone, sounding hale and cheerful. Unlike Koeppen, he didn't seem to have a care in the world. In an ominously well-measured tone, Koeppen asked him why a

227

cable hadn't been sent to Tacoma, Nevada, or to Ogden, Utah, or anywhere else, reporting the car's position. Snyder replied that the Protos had broken down on Friday and that he had been repairing it: something about the differential. It was ready, though, he added quickly. The rest of the conversation determined the location of the car, but it didn't really accomplish much more than that. There may have been an element of protest in Snyder's failure to communicate. He was weary of driving and resented doing so while Koeppen took the trains. At first, Koeppen planned to go back to Tacoma, Nevada, to await Snyder and the Protos once again, but he thought better of it and set off to meet the car personally in Blue Creek. On Monday, April 6, the Protos was making progress west again.

On Tuesday, April 7, the car was on a train car headed back to Ogden.

The engine had two cracked cylinders. Without major repairs, it was as good as dead. Snyder stayed with the car, but Koeppen was still going west, sitting on an express train to Seattle. He intended to pick up a set of spare parts with which to repair the Protos. There was nothing else to do, except of course to quit.

St. Chaffray arrived in San Francisco that same day, April 7, and started sorting through invitations to dine, along with the names of tailors who might supply him with a new set of evening clothes. Antonio Scarfoglio was also in San Francisco with the Züst team and had just been handed a bundle of letters from his loved ones at home. Homesick, he sat alone in his hotel room, reading the letters with tears streaming down his face. Baron Godard, for the record, was arrested in San Francisco that afternoon, charged with going 50 mph in a 10 mph district. When he was caught, he was riding with a car full of new friends on one of the avenues near the ocean. Godard no longer cared very much what happened in Alaska, but the others—St. Chaffray, Autran, Lascares, Sirtori, Scarfoglio, Haaga, and even Koeppen—were all going about their days, wherever they were, whatever they were doing, with one eye out for news from Valdez.

On Wednesday, the eighth, the Thomas Flyer was driven slowly off a ramp onto Alaskan soil. "Ours was the first car ever seen there,"

Schuster reported, "and the inhabitants welcomed us with a band and parade." Schuster might not have been aware of it, but the welcoming committee consisted of the entire population of Valdez, with only the patients in the hospitals excepted. Few of the Alaskans had ever set eyes on a car before.

The grand parade into town couldn't include the Flyer. Deep snow trapped it near the dock and so it was temporarily parked in a warehouse there. The people of Valdez were more interested in the men than in the car, anyway. "All of the autoists are large athletic young men," noted the *Valdez Prospector,* "who look able to tackle a football game or a cinnamon bear."

Schuster wasted no time in accepting an invitation from a local man named Dan Kennedy to inspect the Valdez-Fairbanks Trail in a single-horse sleigh. The weather was warm, according to George MacAdam, the *New York Times* reporter who had joined the team in Seattle, and the early spring thaw was making the streets slushy, wherever there weren't giant mounds of snow. The expedition went as far as the first roadhouse and as soon as it returned to Valdez, Schuster sent a long telegram to the race committee, suggesting that the only way to cross Alaska in a car would be to dismantle it and ship the parts by dogsled. It was just too late in the season, as the *Prospector* explained:

> If the crust was firm enough everywhere to hold up the car there would be little trouble, but it would certainly break through and sink to the axles in hard snow, from which it would have to be lifted because it could not be pulled straight out. That would mean that the car would have to wait for the snow to melt in the summer as its weight is too much for anything but a strong derrick to lift.
>
> The story that the car is too wide for the trail is unfounded. Its track is fifty-six inches—the same as the stages and other big sleds on the trail.

The race committee finally surrendered the dream of Alaska, directing the Thomas team to return to Seattle. Schuster was glad to comply, loading the Flyer onto a southbound steamer on April 10, after only two days in Valdez. The De Dion and Züst teams left San Francisco for

Seattle on the same day, and all of them were still uncertain as to where they would go from there. That afternoon, Hans Koeppen arrived in Ogden for the fifth time, stepping off a train from Seattle with spare parts in tow. He and Snyder had to rebuild the cylinder block of their car or find someone who would.

Not only couldn't Lieutenant Koeppen find an engine specialist to help him, he also lost the services of O. W. Snyder, who suddenly quit the race. Snyder said that he was sick, but Koeppen thought there was something else and he was right. Snyder believed, along with most others, that the Protos was already out of the race, hopelessly behind and badly broken. He wanted to go home. He wanted to be free of the Protos, of the bad roads and the oberlieutenant who seemed to be stubborn about everything except his own attendance on the car.

As the situation disintegrated in Ogden, Hans Koeppen was alone in his room at the Reed Hotel. It wasn't the first time that he had been left behind in the New York-to-Paris Race—not only by his competitors, but by his teammates. He'd survived in Chicago, after all, after Maas and Knape abandoned him. But in Ogden, Koeppen was already running two weeks behind the other cars. And he was about to miss the boat, quite literally.

On Monday, April 13, with Schuster and his Thomas team still at sea, not even halfway back from Valdez, the French and Italian teams arrived in Seattle. It was the first time since Cedar Rapids that more than one New York-to-Paris racecar had arrived in a city at the same time, and they were greeted with citywide festivities. Through it all, Bourcier St. Chaffray was making very public plans to drive his De Dion across Alaska by a different route from the one that had stymied Schuster. He kept talking about Dawson, which is on the eastern border of Alaska, near Canada, and using it as a launching point. In the evening, the Italian American Society sponsored a banquet for the racers at the Butler Hotel, extending invitations very graciously to the Frenchmen as well. St. Chaffray, called upon to speak, announced his firm intention to cross Alaska, because, as he said emphatically, there is no word in French for "impossible." (He momentarily overlooked the word *impossible*.)

Suddenly, in the midst of the dinner, a telegram arrived from *Le*

Matin in Paris, addressed to the racing men. St. Chaffray read it aloud in French and then translated it into English and Italian. The message confirmed that the route had been changed, and it advised the racers to leave as soon as possible for Vladivostok, the Russian port just north of Korea. With that, reported the *Seattle Times,* "There ensued a scene of excitement in the lobby of the Butler that almost beggars description." St. Chaffray was on one side of the room, swearing intently, when the paper's reporter interrupted him. "It is an honor for any one of us to be able to say that we at least tried to cross Alaska," St. Chaffray said, "which is part of the route of the race as originally planned by myself. I have said there is no French word like 'impossible,' and I meant it as far as trying to cross Alaska is concerned." St. Chaffray then excused himself to crowd with all the others at the telegraph desk, making plans to sail for Russia.

That night in Ogden, Koeppen was oblivious to the upheaval, sleeping soundly. He received the news in the morning. "My first walk was as always to the post office," he wrote, "and my first message was from the *New York Times,* saying that the route was about to be changed to start in Vladivostok, and that all drivers would go there. The Thomas was returning to Seattle.

"I calculated the time and the steamer schedules," Koeppen continued. "The situation was almost impossible. The Protos was not ready. I could only keep from completely falling out of the race, but it was impossible without the train."

The same morning, Lieutenant Koeppen received a flurry of telegrams from St. Chaffray, personally informing him of *Le Matin's* decision on the Vladivostok route. Because St. Chaffray had been responsible for plotting the original route, including Alaska, he felt obliged to oversee the adoption of the revised plan. In addition, he was considered the field official of the race, although that role had always been ill-defined. It was still ill-defined, except to Lieutenant Koeppen, who may have suddenly recollected all those makeshift bridges that the sympathetic Frenchman had left intact in Wyoming for the trailing Germans. By telegram, Koeppen informed St. Chaffray that the only way he could hope to transverse Siberia during its short summer was to cross the

Pacific immediately. To do that, he had to use the train—an expediency expressly forbidden by the race committee in general and the *New York Times* in particular. Koeppen finished writing his message, handed it to the telegraph operator, and awaited a reply. He needed a miracle, or least a favor.

"St. Chaffray wrote," recalled Lieutenant Koeppen, " 'I am the leader of this race, appointed by *Le Matin*. What the *New York Times* says is nonsense. Let your car come by railroad.' I was still worried about the infraction, but St. Chaffray sent one more telegram, 'Don't worry.' "

And so, in a matter of a few more hours, Koeppen finally had his car moving smoothly—on the back of a train bound for the coast. He knew that the use of a train would probably disqualify the Protos in the end, as it had the Moto-Bloc in Iowa. He had once taken a stronger stand than anyone on that very point. But he had to keep a kind of promise with the Kaiser. He had to drive the Protos into Paris.

St. Chaffray didn't realize just how bad Koeppen's situation was, and neither did anyone else in Seattle. When the Protos passed through Pocatello, Idaho, on a flatcar, a few people straggled down to take a look. "It is a big machine," noted one of them, "but in its present condition, looks like a pile of scrap iron."

The new plan called for the New York-to-Paris cars to sail to Vladivostok and drive to Paris from there. Because the Thomas Flyer had been out in front, however, investigating Alaskan conditions, it was still out at sea, barely halfway to Seattle. Only the French and Italian teams were in Seattle and ready to sail.

And they did sail, booking passage on the *Aki Maru* out of Seattle at dawn on April 14. Emilio Sirtori missed the ship, arriving at the pier without his luggage and telling Scarfoglio that he couldn't possibly continue in the race. The nervous strain combined with physical exhaustion had completely ruined his health, so he said. With that, he promised to meet the car in Vladivostok. He changed his mind several more times during the course of the rushed conversation, but shouted to Scarfoglio as the *Aki Maru* pulled away from the dock that he would drive again in Vladivostok.

Two days after the Züst and De Dion teams left, a pair of motorists overturned while speeding in the small town of Castle Rock, south of Seattle near the Oregon border. They told authorities that they were the French entrants in the New York-to-Paris Race, on their way north to Seattle. For good measure, they complained about road conditions. The speeding charge was dropped, amid the rash of good wishes extended by the sheriff.

The "New York-to-Paris" defense had fooled many policemen, but for fakers across the country, time was running out as the racers left American soil. Koeppen gathered his broken Protos off the train, loaded it onboard a ship called the *Glenlogan,* and on April 19 sailed alone for Vladivostok. The Thomas arrived from Alaska in time to board the *Glenlogan,* too, but since the Americans did not yet have their Russian visas in order, Schuster had no choice but to watch it leave. After a scramble, he found another ship. On April 21, the Thomas Flyer was loaded onto a steamer called the *Shawmut,* bound for Japan, where the team could make arrangements for travel in Russia.

The first car to arrive on the Pacific coast was the last to leave. As Schuster watched the American coast recede, he was a full week behind the race's new leaders, and two days behind a car that didn't even have a driver. Or an engine.

Chapter Twenty

The Japanese
Countryside

Car	Miles	Place	Team
Züst (Ita.)	11,410	Biva Lake, Japan	Sirtori, Scarfoglio, Haaga
De Dion (Fra.)	11,410	Biva Lake, Japan	St. Chaffray, Autran, Lascares
Thomas Flyer (U.S.)	11,300	Kobe, Japan	Schuster, Miller, Hansen, MacAdam
Protos (Ger.)	11,000 (est.)	*en route on the Pacific*	Koeppen

The lively stream of news regarding the New York-to-Paris Race naturally petered out while the racers were on the Pacific, relaxing on their respective steamships. Without "Marconis," the radio sets that were still rare in 1908, ships couldn't send radio messages, and so the wide Pacific inserted a three-week intermission into the round-the-world show. The New York and Paris newspapers were not without their headlines, though.

The Duc de Chaulnes was dead. His marriage to Theodora Shonts had occurred only three days after the race started and their honeymoon coincided with the first eight weeks of the race. Having returned from the wedding trip, the duc and duchess were living in a suite at a Paris hotel, in no hurry to find a home of their own. In the middle of the night on April 23, the duc awoke from a deep sleep and clutched his wife in a convulsion. Even as she wrested herself free, he died, the result of a morphine overdose.

For the cars on the route to Paris, the race action began again May 2 when the *Aki Maru* docked in Yokohama, Japan's most modern city as of 1908. While St. Chaffray waited, gazing up at the ship with Autran and Lascares, the De Dion was hoisted out of the hold, tight inside a wooden crate, and deposited on the dock. Scarfoglio and Haaga were standing around nearby, awaiting the appearance of the Züst, the next car to drift out of the air and onto the dock.

235

Yokohama shares a well-protected bay on the eastern coast of Japan with the much larger city of Tokyo, less than thirty miles away. It was nothing more than a modest fishing village when Commodore Perry decided it should be developed as a port in 1859. Under foreign influence, it grew into Japan's most efficient shipping center, with a long line of bustling, Western-style buildings along the waterfront boulevard, called the Bund. A visitor interested in Japanese culture might well cringe to see the clunky buildings lining the Bund, but longtime residents from Europe and America pointed them out with pride.

Since Tokyo Bay is in the central part of the long, thin main island of Japan, the De Dion and Züst teams faced a choice: they could either take a boat around the island, a journey of about 550 miles, or they could drive to the western coast, where they could leave for Russia from the port of Tsuruga. They chose to drive, in order to save time.

Saving time wasn't, however, a Japanese priority in 1908. Patience was the national virtue, and the society it sculpted stood in direct contrast to the wonders that impatience had inspired in the industrialized West.

Japan was more industrious than industrialized in 1908. Burgeoning from a 50 percent increase in the population since 1870, it struggled to keep every last person employed in some form. Visitors who took glee in uniquely Japanese sights such as bamboo houses, cherry tree glades, and bell shrines couldn't help noticing another hallmark of the landscape, the way that even simple jobs were shared among a handful of people. "Why fifteen servants in a house which we would run with six or eight?" wrote the American writer Julian Street on his first visit. "Why men and women drawing heavy carts that might so much better be drawn by horses or propelled by gasolene? . . . Why this waste of labour everywhere? . . . Must work be spread thin in order to provide a task and a living for everyone?" That was precisely the policy as implemented by the government. Overpopulation was no disgrace in Japan, but unemployment—that was unthinkable.

Before leaving Yokohama for Japan's western shore, the two racing teams were obligated to obtain a special permit allowing for travel by foreigners. "In order to obtain this permit," Antonio Scarfoglio wrote, "there have been necessary, I believe, at least one hundred different signatures, twenty schemes, thirty journeys, numerous yen, and eight days' time."

It only seemed like eight days. The two teams were actually in Yokohama five days, awaiting permission to proceed. Bourcier St. Chaffray probably didn't even notice. During the delay, he existed in a dark, smoldering state of panic. He had been expecting to be greeted in Japan by a new infusion of money, in the form of a letter of credit extended by the De Dion factory. The longer he waited for it, the more anxious he became. Finally, he received a message from the factory blandly informing him that the marquis was withdrawing the car. France was out of the New York-to-Paris Race.

The marquis had simply decided that the new route through southern Siberia was too similar to the course followed in 1907's Peking-to-Paris Race, in which the De Dions had been also-rans. He must have been tired of spending money on the effort. He may also have had some inkling that the race committee was going to compensate the Thomas Flyer a number of days for its detour to Alaska. From the Marquis de Dion's point of view, continuing in the race would mean a large expenditure on a car that was already losing to the Thomas, over a course that held no romance, to him at least—and in territory practically devoid of newspaper photographers and luxury-car customers, the two species that automakers such as the Marquis de Dion liked best.

From St. Chaffray's point of view, the situation looked much different. The word *impossible* had suddenly entered the French language. With his usual abundance of energy, he plotted ways to push it right back out again. "The three brave Frenchmen were wandering through Yokohama," Scarfoglio wrote, "worried, hungry but steadfast. They will go on living by selling postcards, fortune-telling or anything, but will drive on to Paris or die in the attempt."

The editors of the *New York Times* were just as aware as the Marquis de Dion that the race had lost some of its appeal—its madness—by forgoing the Alaska trip and the dash across the Bering Strait. "Motoring across the east coast of Japan," the paper offered hopefully, "may not be the easiest going in the world." Fortunately for the paper, it wasn't.

As the crow flies, the distance from Yokohama across the island to the port of Tsuruga was only about two hundred miles, but the route on the ground was at least three times that, winding through innumerable rice fields and one mountain range. To prepare, and to impress the locals, Henry Haaga took to driving the Züst up and down the Bund, hitting fifty or even fifty-five, and setting new landspeed records for Japan with practically every pass. It was a good chance to clear the carburetor; he wouldn't get the Züst to much more than 25 mph on the inland roads.

On May 6, as the Züst team was preparing to leave Yokohama, Scarfoglio was surprised to see Bourcier St. Chaffray bustling around the De Dion, flush with money and ready to join the expedition west. Someone on the French team had succeeded in arranging credit. It might have been St. Chaffray, who was capable of almost any miracle with a blank telegram form in his hands. It might have been Lascares, the Chicago lawyer, or Monsieur Autran, who was rumored to have a comfortable fortune of his own, back in France. Someone, somewhere came through and the De Dion was on its way again. For the first time since they were skirting the Erie Canal, the two cars were traveling together. A translator was accompanying them.

No one had ever attempted to cross Japan in an auto before—Japanese roads weren't even constructed for horses, let alone cars. Carts were typically pulled by humans, and a double-yoke wagon or carriage would be too wide for most thoroughfares. A huge European touring car was preposterous. Height was a problem, too. A vehicle as large as a Züst or a De Dion would barely squeeze through the typical Japanese village, where narrow streets were turned into veritable tunnels by low overhangs, often leaving a main street that was not more than eight feet wide or six feet high.

The weather that May in central Japan was hot and sunny, leaving the vegetation, as Scarfoglio reported, "magnificently in flower." He hated it. "A thick heavy perfume, consisting of all of the perfumes exhaled from all the dying blossoms, circulates in the air and beats into our faces like the wind, penetrates through the nostrils to the brain, and gradually becomes unbearable," he wrote. He also found the "swarm of houses and men" across eastern Japan disconcerting after traveling through so much vast, empty space in America. Most of the Japanese found his car no less dizzying. Very few people in the hinterlands had ever seen a car before. People crowded around both the Züst and the De Dion whenever they stopped, reaching out to touch them and then scorching their hands on the hoods.

On the second day of the trip, the cars had to climb over Mount Fuji, Japan's tallest mountain. From a distance, Fuji looks smooth and symmetrical, inspiring philosophers to compare it to every kind of sleek abstraction of thought and emotion. Up close, it was a very real mountain, with heartless inclines; jagged, tilting angles; and a tendency to set warm days on fire. As a volcano, even one that had been dormant for two hundred years, Mount Fuji knew something about heat.

The route over the mountain was only eight miles in length and at the foot, someone, perhaps Henry Haaga, suggested that they could probably drive the cars all the way up. The guide laughed uncontrollably at that, while the others looked on and wondered why.

In short time, they found out. The road was so steep, with its poor traction and narrow track, that the engines could barely have supplied enough power under the best of conditions. Overheating on a hot day, they were no match for Fujiyama. The men spent at least half of their time outside of the cars, pushing. Before long, they knew without being told that the cars were about to fade; they saw it in the gradient of the mountain and heard it in the whir of the engines. Silently, they would jump out and take their places behind each car, stripped to the waist, and on the verge of overheating themselves.

The path presented its own problems, twisting almost constantly. Vehicles more than ten feet long couldn't make turns of ninety degrees and more on such a narrow path. Crossing America, the New York-to-Paris racers had been stopped by many substances—mud, water, and snow—but never before by geometry itself. Help was never far away on Fuji, though. No sooner did a crew of local laborers gather than they picked up each car at the back and straightened it out on the path. Eventually, the teams hired laborers—coolies—to accompany the cars, pushing them on the way up mountains, and holding them back with ropes on the way down.

In many towns, the huddled forms pushing the cars or pulling them with ropes were women. The status of women in Japan in 1908 was rather shocking for visitors from the West, who couldn't help noticing that the females did the dirtiest and most grueling work, while the males took the easier jobs. To an outsider, it looked like slavery.

Life on the road in Japan left Antonio Scarfoglio longing for his care-free days in Wyoming, battling the Uinta Mountains. "We were for twenty-four hours continuously ascending mountains," he wrote of Japan, "not like the toilsome yet friendly slopes of the Rockies, but only goat tracks covered with stones."

"The Züst and De Dion," chimed in Bourcier St. Chaffray, "have struggled through mountain gorges and over roads which were only wide enough to allow the wheels of the cars to pass between the mountain torrents on one side and the rice fields on the other."

Even as Scarfoglio and Haaga sweated and strained to thread the Züst through the mountain maze, they saved their sympathy for St. Chaffray, Lascares, and Autran, who were laboring just as doggedly over the De Dion. The Frenchmen couldn't even be certain why they were exerting themselves—to what end. The De Dion car had already been pulled from the race by the manufacturer. Whether or not the sheer insistence of the three teammates could keep it in the race was a question hanging in the air over every step, along with grunts that questioned the folly of the predicament even more plaintively.

Sympathy can be an exacting luxury, however. While Scarfoglio and Haaga were out in the isolation of rural Japan, feeling sorry for the Frenchmen, officials at the Züst factory were preparing to pull their entry, too.

The French and Italian teams were en route across Japan when the race committee in Paris handed down a decision. The Thomas Flyer was given an allowance of fifteen days, in recognition of the time it lost during the detour to Alaska. In other words, the De Dion and Züst cars could beat the Thomas Flyer into Paris by two weeks and still lose to the American car.

At the same time, the race committee ruled that the German Protos would be penalized fifteen days for resorting to the train from Ogden,

Utah, to Seattle, Washington. Privately, the Americans were disappointed that the Protos hadn't been disqualified entirely, but the committee concluded that there had been some honest confusion about the rules on shipping the car. In any case, Koeppen's prospects for winning—never exactly robust—were fatally handicapped. He could beat either the Züst or the De Dion to Paris by two weeks and still lose to them. And as to Schuster in the Thomas, Koeppen could beat him by nearly a month and still lose.

Lieutenant Koeppen, still somewhere on the Pacific with his broken car, had once said that he would humbly accept disqualification in view of the dire measures he'd taken in Utah. But as time went on, hope replaced humility, as it often will. And Koeppen nursed it along, denying more and more vehemently that he had done anything wrong in shipping his car, and leaning heavily on the fact that St. Chaffray had, after all, condoned the action.

During the trip across Japan, Scarfoglio and Haaga weren't aware that the Züst factory had lost interest in them. And St. Chaffray and his team were certain that they would take the De Dion to Paris somehow—by selling postcards and telling fortunes, if necessary. The two teams battled forward as though the finish line was around the next bend.

Most of the time, they did, anyway. Arriving in a small town called Chimena, about a half day's travel away from Tsuruga, the cars stopped to take on water and to light the headlamps, since the sun was starting to go down. "A great crowd gathered round us," Scarfoglio reported, "while the rapid operations of taking in water were being completed, and some charming looking mousmés came to offer to the guide the delights of their tea-house."

According to a European play about Japan that was popular during the Victorian era, a *mousmé* was a maiden, barely into her teens. Scarfoglio already disapproved of the role relegated to females throughout Japan and he didn't much like the idea of *mousmés*, whether the ones in Chimena were adolescent prostitutes or merely girls forced into otherwise amusing total strangers. "The guide sang their praises with vivacity, making a long speech in order to convince us," he wrote. "St. Chaffray, who has a decided taste for the Japanese race, was attracted; Autran did not intervene; I cut the discussion short by saying that to-morrow at two o'clock a steamer left Tsuruga for Vladivostok, and that we must embark in the morning. This would render it necessary for us to travel all through the night, but it must be done. So we departed. I was regarded with disdain by the mousmés, with melancholy resignation by St. Chaffray, with anger by the guide and with stupefaction by the village."

It was just as well Scarfoglio spoke; the last jaunt overnight included another mountain. By the time St. Chaffray reached Tsuruga, the port in western Japan, he was utterly exhausted. It even showed in his voice, which drooped over the very wires that carried his telegraph messages around the world to New York. His ebullience was gone, at least temporarily. "Our wheels were pulling themselves along between the rocks," he wrote of the end of the journey in Japan, "but they rolled and rolled until we reached this place. We will be glad to embark for Vladivostok." It had taken the two teams five days to cover two hundred miles in Japan.

Lieutenant Koeppen was onboard the *Glenlogan,* sailing directly to Vladivostok. Thanks to the close relationship between Germany and Russia, his visa requirements were easy to meet and so he could skip Japan. George Schuster and his team were Americans, though, and they needed authorization to set foot on Russian soil. Their trip to Japan was necessary only as an opportunity to meet with Russian consular officials and arrange for Russian visas.

Relations between Japan and the United States were actually much worse than those between Russia and the United States. In both Japan and the United States, a war for control of the Pacific was expected imminently. The two nations gave vent to interminable discussions on the topic and then bided more time by regularly waving their fleets at one other. The show of strength naturally led to an escalating battle of suspicion, especially along Japan's eastern coast and America's western one. The four men on the Thomas team had been well inculcated into the hostilities, having spent time shooting the breeze with the sailors on three different U.S. steamships over the previous few weeks. Thus educated, they arrived in Japan, as George MacAdam wrote, "full of prejudice."

The Americans landed only briefly in Yokohama, where they stopped for tea at the busiest European hotel and overheard people all around them informing one another that the Thomas was finally across the Pacific and making bets that one of the other cars would arrive in Paris first. With that, the American team went back out onto the Pacific, but only long enough to sail 220 miles south and east along the coast to the city of Kobe, where the Flyer was unloaded.

Kobe was almost directly across the island from Tsuruga, with fewer mountains in the way than there were on the route from Yokohama. The total distance to Tsuruga was only ninety miles and yet, when Schuster asked around Kobe in search of a qualified guide, he received some rather disturbing news. No one knew the way across the island. And there were no route maps.

The train crossed the island, and that was all that anyone needed to know. Finally, Schuster met a man named Mancini, a ship broker who owned two automobiles, accounting for one-third of Kobe's grand total of six cars.

Mancini certainly didn't take his cars on long trips. A person wouldn't try to drive a car into a scene in a woodblock print or painted on a screen. It was just about as practical to try to drive one onto roads that were built hundreds of years before for foot traffic. But Mancini was still an extraordinary adventurer, inasmuch as he was willing to help Schuster drive to Kyoto, the ancient capital about one-third of the way across the island. "I don't know the road all the way to Kyoto," he admitted, "but I can easily find it by inquiring of the natives along the way. I don't believe you'll find anyone who knows the entire road from Kyoto to Tsuruga. The best that you can expect is to get an interpreter who can inquire from village to village."

Bridges presented the biggest problem as Schuster drove west, officially taking the wheel for the first time. Most of Japan's many bridges were built of bamboo, and the very sturdiest were designed to carry two thousand pounds, in the form of a horse and a load. When the Thomas Flyer first came to a bridge that didn't look as though it was strong enough to hold a forty-five-hundred-pound car, George Miller walked out halfway and tested the construction. "A single man jumping upon the bridge proved it as springy," MacAdam wrote, "as the best advertised mattress in the back of America's magazines." But like an old boxspring, it emitted a chorus of creaks and groans with every touch. By the time the examination was through and Miller was finished trampolining, there was a long line of carts jammed behind the Flyer, waiting to cross. Schuster decided to back up and go twenty miles out of his way to another crossing. But backing up wasn't easy; almost nothing was, by car, in rural Japan. The path leading to the bridge was so narrow that the Thomas had nowhere to go, except forward, and nowhere at all to turn around.

For most of an hour, Captain Hansen and Mr. Mancini paraded up and down the line, exhorting the carts to back up and make room. Eventually, all of them did and Schuster could inch along in reverse until he reached a wide spot in which to turn the car around. Patience was the only option.

The next day, en route through rolling hillsides, George Schuster did something he'd never done before. The Flyer was making progress in a valley that encompassed the town of Otsu. Speeding along on an unusually good road, Schuster suddenly stopped the car, despite the fact that it wasn't about to fall off a cliff, hit an ox, fall apart, or break some local law. The car wasn't stuck, but for just about the only time in the race, George Schuster was, as he noted:

> At the farther end of the valley between high mountains, over which hung heavy clouds which seemed almost to touch the trees on the mountain tops, was Lake Biwa—a sheet of water twenty miles in length and several miles in width. The sun shining through rifts in the clouds enhanced the beauty of this scene, and a rainbow was formed over the lake, the ends touching either shore.
>
> We were on a race around the world, but this scene was well worth a short pause.

A little while later Schuster stopped again, this time more rudely. He was facing yet another uncertain-looking bamboo bridge, an unusually long one over a muddy creek. All of the men got out of the Thomas and jumped up and down on the bridge. "It tumbled suspiciously," as MacAdam put it. George Miller wasn't sure. He shuffled and skidded down the bank to the water's edge and then waded into the middle of the slow-flowing creek, looking up at the bridge and running his eyes over the construction. "Well," he called up, "perhaps you can make it." That was enough of a certificate for Schuster.

Miller, MacAdam, Captain Hansen, and the translator, Mr. Ito, walked across the long expanse, each man carrying a few heavy items. Then they turned to watch Schuster. He was all alone in the Thomas, partly in the interest of lightening it and partly in the interest of reducing the casualties, should the bamboo break and fling the car into the water twenty feet below. Once Schuster started, he had to keep going, as quickly as possible. The bridge might accommodate a rolling weight, but not necessarily the strain of a stationary one. The spans shook and trembled as the wheels turned steadily over them, and the cross girders groaned. Occasionally some piece of bamboo or a joint would crack, making all eyes on shore grow wider, but Schuster couldn't worry about it or send Miller down for another look. He had already made his decision. In a matter of seconds, or years, the front wheels were on the other side of the creek, and then the back ones were, as well. With the Thomas on land once more, Schuster shouted "All aboard for Paris," and the others returned the call, scrambling into the car again.

That night, the Thomas team stopped in a town only twenty-five miles from Tsuruga. The journey through Japan was nearly over—or it seemed to be. The next morning Schuster found out that the road to Tsuruga simply wasn't wide enough to accommodate the Thomas Flyer. And that was that. The only other route was eighty miles long and included the chance to climb one of the steepest mountains in the region. He had no choice.

Climbing the mountain was not so bad, with the help of forty or fifty peasant laborers. MacAdam marveled that in all such predicaments, the Japanese worked as though each one of them "had a wager on the American car reaching Paris first." Because the Thomas Flyer had a special gear arrangement, quite unusual for the time, that kept the car from slipping backward, the job of pushing it uphill was taxing but not dangerous. On the way down the same mountain, though, the brute strength and dug-in heels of all of the laborers on the ropes couldn't keep the Thomas from breaking loose.

As the mountain pulled the car away from the workers, Schuster kept his head, as though he had been expecting just such a thing to happen. He probably was. With sensitive steering and the best possible use of the brakes and gearing, he managed to keep the car from breaking entirely out of control and perhaps dragging a great many of the human anchors crashing down the hill with it. It lunged for the bottom of the hill, but still had a driver at the wheel.

Crossing Japan had not taken as long as a trip across Alaska might have. The last-minute addition to the New York-to-Paris Race had, however, tested the cars against a region entirely unprepared for the automobile.

By traveling through the hinterlands, as few foreign travelers did, the New York-to-Paris racers saw a Japan beyond the capital of Tokyo or the hybrid port cities. On the American team, all stains of prejudice were washed away. "Never was a people's courtesy put to a greater strain," MacAdam reflected, looking back on the trip through Japan, "a big, snorting, strange machine, filled with strange people, crowding the natives out of their narrow village streets into doorways and alleys, blocking their highways, disrupting traffic, frightening horses and bullocks, splashing wayside groups with mud. All this—and the Japanese continued to smile and shout a hearty 'Banzai!' after the fleeting intruder." ("Banzai" is a cheer that means "May you live ten thousand years.")

By the time the Thomas team arrived in Tsuruga, the Frenchmen and Italians were already on the water, heading to the Asian mainland. It was a miserable crossing, as Scarfoglio said, full of "quarrelling with the Chinese stewards and with the German cooking." But all of that was nothing, because then they reached Vladivostok.

Chapter Twenty-one

Second Start

Car	Miles	Place	Team
Züst (Ita.)	11,800	Vladivostok, Russia	Sirtori, Scarfoglio, Haaga
Protos (Ger.)	11,800	Vladivostok, Russia	Koeppen, Fuchs, Neuberger
Thomas Flyer (U.S.)	11,500	Tsuruga, Japan	Schuster, Miller, Hansen, MacAdam

Hans Koeppen was the first of the New York-to-Paris racers to reach Vladivostok, disembarking from the *Glenlogan* on May 12. He had never been to Russia before, and certainly not to Vladivostok, but he was undaunted by the raw atmosphere that greeted him at the port, going about his business with the confidence of a man well rested and slightly impatient. No sooner was he was off the ship than he arranged for the Protos to be unloaded. It would only barely roll, with a couple of the tires flat, but that was just as well, because it couldn't go any farther than a government warehouse until it was cleared for entry. Koeppen left it behind temporarily, hiring a horse-drawn cab to take him into town.

After twenty-three days at sea, Lieutenant Koeppen's appearance had changed. He had an untrimmed beard, and his hair was long, too, drooping onto his neck, just where it had always been shaved short. It hadn't taken him long to forget how to dress, either. He wore leather coveralls, intended for blizzards, something of an overcompensation for Vladivostok in late spring. A little unusual-looking, ill-prepared for Asia, and grimly determined, Hans Koeppen was not very different from the city he faced: Vladivostok, Russia's stab at the Pacific.

The route into Vladivostok took Koeppen along a strand of seawater, interrupted by a Russian Orthodox church indicating that the ocean-front, for the time being at least, had been claimed. The city was built along the tip of a peninsula that helped define two bays, Amur and Un-suri. It was bracketed by jagged hills and, like San Francisco, had to

248

fight its way into them whenever it grew. Koeppen could see the hills in the distance as he drew into the center of the city, but at closer range, he was more fascinated by the mix of people on the street: Russian officers in white uniforms; Chinese merchants in their stalls and shops; soldiers of all grades; Korean workmen; Japanese sailors; European businessmen. On the main street, Svyetlánskaya, he passed a statue of Admiral Nevélski, the Russian explorer who discovered Amur Bay in 1838. It was inscribed with the words of Nicholas I, the czar at the time: Где разъ поднятъ русскй флаг, он уже опускаться не долженъ. Koeppen couldn't read Russian, and so he rode on, trying to make sense of something else in the perplexing city.

Not too coincidentally, Vladivostok was just about the same age as Yokohama. Yokohama's redevelopment started in 1859; Vladivostok was founded one year later. The fact that the Pacific represented the richest opportunity in world trade had seeped through the many layers of the Russian imperial court, just as it managed to do in Japan, where the royalty was even more isolated. The same news never quite reached the imperial family in China, historically the greatest trading nation of them all. In the late 1800s, China was drifting politically, and other countries, including the United States, Germany, and Britain, had already split it up into economic zones: colonies without settlers, but with myriad opportunities for foreigners to grow rich. To stake its claim in China, Russia built Vladivostok on a spit of its own territory just north of Korea, and due east of China. To back up that claim, it started work in 1891 on the Trans-Siberian Railway, designed to connect Moscow with the new frontier to the east. Vladivostok was to be the last stop and it was in the thick of the Far East's roiling politics.

As part of the overall plan, Russia took economic control of Manchuria, the fertile section of northern China that seemed to bulge right into Siberia, at least from the Russian point of view. The Russians were benevolent overseers in Manchuria, concentrating their energies on building up the city of Harbin as a central capital, completing the Trans-Siberian Railway via a shortcut across the bulge, and establishing a huge naval base at the city of Port Arthur on the Pacific.

Japan, intent on being one of the Pacific's invaders, rather than one of the invaded, built up its military and attacked Russia for control of Manchuria in 1904. The initial assault on Port Arthur, the start of the Russo-Japanese War, was regarded as firm evidence of Japan's overestimation of its military power. To the shock of most people in the West, however, Russia suffered one loss after another in the ensuing war. According to the peace treaty brokered in 1905 by Theodore Roosevelt, Russia was forced to cede to Japan southern Manchuria as well as its gleaming gem in the Pacific, Port Arthur (now in Chinese control and called *Lü-shon*).

After the war, many of Russia's battalions retreated to Vladivostok, which took on a new importance as a military base. As the soldiers filed past the statue of Admiral Nevélski on Svyetlánskaya Street, they probably tried not to glance at the inscription: "Where once the Russian flag has been unfurled, it must never be lowered."

When the New York-to-Paris Race arrived in Asia only three years later, Vladivostok was still filling up with Russian soldiers, living in rows of barracks hastily arranged between the hills. The soldiers might have given the city a martial atmosphere, except that whenever they were in town, which was often, they acted as though they were on furlough, rather than on patrol. To bolster the city's merchant population, Vladivostok had been designated a free port. One way or another, it boasted 120,000 residents, most of them drawn by some sense of Russia's future or their own. Very few had actually been born in Vladivostok, still an outpost city in an unsettled region.

Lieutenant Koeppen was staying at the Hotel d'Allemagne, the German Hotel, which was regarded as the best in the city. And in Vladivostok, where even the flophouses were expensive, it took courage to check in to the Hotel d'Allemagne. "Living is extremely dear," wrote Karl Baedeker, the famed travel writer, in his notes on Vladivostok. He wasn't being philosophical. Koeppen had been warned, though, and he alighted from the cab in front of the hotel on Pekinskaya Avenue, intent only on getting some sort of a good room for his money.

"In my already somewhat aggressive leather suit, with my face, framed by a huge beard, wind-burned from the weather and sea, I probably looked somewhat wild," Koeppen admitted, "when I hastily stepped inside the Hotel d'Allemagne and two well-dressed men stopped me with a question:

" 'Did you come in on the *Glenlogan*?'

" 'That's right. I come even from it.'

"The two colleagues examined me," Koeppen continued, "obviously without knowing what to do next. 'Do you expect someone with the ship?' I asked, hoping to allay their uncertainty, but otherwise unsuspecting.

" 'Yes, we expect Ober-lieutenant Koeppen. We are the two drivers who are to continue with him on his trip to Paris.' "

"Well Good Day, Gentlemen! I'm the man you're looking for," Koeppen said. The two men looked for a Prussian officer somewhere within the Neanderthal they saw before them.

"I believe they took it for a bad joke," Koeppen reflected, "and stood with doubting expressions until they were amiably assured that I am real. With that, they welcomed me with salutes and signs of respect, but all the time, with something in their good German souls doubting I was the man they had seen before in pictures. Only later, after I had seen to my grooming again, and the handsome sailor beard fell to the shears of the local barber, did they look on me with favor."

The first of Koeppen's new teammates was Casper Neuberger, a burly man with a full, smooth face and black, slicked-back hair. He was from Bavaria and spoke with a country twang. His colleague was Robert Fuchs, agile and fair, with an urbane moustache, turned up at the ends. Fuchs was from Berlin and spoke in the clipped pace of the big city. Both men were senior mechanics with the Protos factory. On meeting them, Koeppen was delighted to see that help had arrived, but he was still a bit uncertain. Describing their demeanors as "unimpressive and simple," he wasn't convinced that they would be any more reliable than his previous teammates. For the time being, though, he had his own work to do.

On the first evening in Vladivostok, Lieutenant Koeppen was already busy, reading through a bag of mail that Fuchs and Neuberger had brought him, writing a new installment of his narrative for the *Berlin Am Mittag* newspaper, and trying hard to stop thinking about how much he was paying for two microscopic rooms at the Hotel d'Allemagne.

The next morning, Koeppen, newly shaved and looking crisp, paid visits to most of the local Russian officials, looking for advice, favors, and letters of introduction to other officials along the route. The governor of Russia's Maritime Province greeted him in a palatial government building—built of granite brought in from the west, as opposed to wood, the only local building material. The governor made it clear that he admired Germans, as most Russians did then, and he promised to supply a guide so that the Protos would get off to a good start. But even so, he made it clear that he didn't hold out any hope that Koeppen could make an automobile trip to the west. In the first place, he said that the country was "perfectly roadless." But that wasn't the worst. "In this season," he added, "with the thaw and the continuous rain, it is also perfectly groundless."

Koeppen had already noticed the rain, which was remarkable in that it only stopped a few times a day, to let a gray streak of sunlight warm the puddles. By day, Koeppen wandered around the city, good neighborhoods and very bad, even poking his head into opium dens, to wonder at the blurry line between living and death there. He spent his evenings with a German couple named Eichwede, who lived in Vladivostok because the husband represented a shipping line.

"Fuchs and Neuberger," Koeppen noted, "had turned with hot hunger to the job of preparing the car for the second start [from Vladivostok to Paris]. Since there was time, they took everything apart, including the motor, in order to test every individual part for fitness and durability. . . . Always dedicated, they were busy in their workshop from daybreak until late at night." The workshop was lent to the team by a local retailer called Kunst & Albers.

Plunked down in the middle of one of the world's most exotic cities, Koeppen behaved just as he had in the blowing snowdrifts of Indiana, the mud of Iowa, and the mountains of Utah. He made friends and wandered around, while someone else bore down on the work at hand.

Hans Koeppen made his contribution, though, invisible as it may have been at such moments. He *was* the Protos. Whenever the car was in hopeless shape, which was often, he saw it through. Oberlieutenant Koeppen had an inexhaustible supply of hope. And so he sat, puffing on a pipe and chatting with Mrs. Eichwede, while Fuchs was in a garage, helping Neuberger to rebuild the car. In either place, the people sometimes fell silent, but the sound of the rain never did.

In terms of the race, Lieutenant Koeppen had Vladivostok to himself for two days. On May 15, a ship called the *Longmoon* docked and Antonio Scarfoglio came bustling down the gangplank with Henry Haaga, followed a short time later by Bourcier St. Chaffray, Monsieur Autran, and Emanuel Lascares.

No sooner did Scarfoglio set eyes on Vladivostok than he was pining for Japan, the very country that had made him pine for Wyoming. Even the soldiers, whom he had considered rude and menacing in Japan, garnered new respect once he was in Vladivostok—a city that was little more than an immense barrack, in his view, teeming with gold- and silver-trimmed uniforms. "One remembers," Scarfoglio noted, "that at Tokio the officers are not so brilliantly dressed, and do not walk along the streets arm in arm with ladies."

Vladivostok might have made Scarfoglio long for East Utica, too. He found himself in a nation so dependent on German influence that the colloquial word for the world outside of Russia was "Germania." Scarfoglio wrote:

> The Italian plant does not give any fruit here, neither does the English, the French, the American, or the Japanese. The only one that flourishes is the terrible German race, traces of which I have seen in the sand of every country. It has intruded itself, its language, its beer, and its customs everywhere. . . . At Vladivostok everything is German: the principal bank, the principal firms, the steamers, business, the semi-official language. In this town at the end of a continent and on the shore of an unknown sea, where the Germans have managed to become the gods and protectors of the country, they are absolutely insufferable.

More than ever, Scarfoglio felt as though he were in a foreign country. And likewise, more than ever, Hans Koeppen was at home.

Bourcier St. Chaffray didn't have time to record his own impressions of Vladivostok. As soon as he left the ship and checked in to the Hotel d'Allemagne, he was met with a sheaf of telegrams. The Marquis de Dion was still adamant that the team was out of the race, but St. Chaffray had expected that. The latest news was far worse.

The marquis knew how St. Chaffray felt about the race and how devoted he was to the idea of finishing for the sake of France. The marquis couldn't counter all of that, or battle what made St. Chaffray who he was. And so he didn't bother with words, at all. He simply sold the car. By the time the *Longmoon* tied up in Vladivostok, the factory had already taken payment for it from a Chinese gentleman. His representatives had papers giving them possession and they took the big gray De Dion away before St. Chaffray could even bid it some sort of good-bye.

De Dion cars were rare items in the Far East, but even so, it is hard to envy the new owner. He bought a car that had been bounced around and beaten up by the American continent, absorbing ten years' worth of normal wear in its three-month trip from New York on the way to Paris. For the first time, though, that wasn't St. Chaffray's problem. Sadly, he told Autran and Lascares that there was no more for them to do, that having reached Vladivostok, they had to make plans to leave. As to St. Chaffray, though, he intended to stay.

At the Hotel d'Allemagne, Antonio Scarfoglio and Henry Haaga were reunited with Emilio Sirtori. At first sight, they could see that he was restored to his robust, and somewhat fleshy, self. The nervous strain that had debilitated him in Seattle was all gone. He was back to fighting form, but his fight was not to be with the tracts of Siberia. Even as he met his teammates, he had in hand a whole series of telegrams from Milan, delivering orders that he return immediately to the factory.

The Züst factory was no more enthusiastic about the completion of the New York-to-Paris Race than was the Marquis de Dion. Each considered that the American car, with its two-week allowance, was unbeatable and, anyway, the expenses in Asia would be terrific and the chance of publicity scant. Quitting was a rather obvious business decision.

But the New York-to-Paris Race was supposed to be sport. Six teams had been asked to master three continents, thousands of technical problems, hundreds of geographical ones, and a different meteorological danger, nearly every day. With wits and as many tools as would fit in the trunks, the men in the cars were supposed to skip over time and advance the automobile age. The race was a sporting challenge, one of the greatest of all time. But in Vladivostok, it was reduced to pure business.

Two kinds of men started the race, sportsmen and hired professionals. Charles Godard, Auguste Pons, and Bourcier St. Chaffray—the Frenchmen—were all sports, and they dominated the atmosphere of the early part of the race. The Germans—Koeppen, Maas, and Knape—were amateurs, too. The Americans, on the other hand, were all on the payroll, even Monty Roberts, who seemed to be above the fray but took orders from E. R. Thomas, just as Schuster and Miller did. The Italian car was a mix; Antonio Scarfoglio, the grandest of amateurs, complaining but unstoppable, rode with Emilio Sirtori and Henry Haaga, both factory men.

By the time the Züst and the De Dion arrived in Vladivostok, amateur sportsmen were going out of style. Koeppen may have been one of them, but he had gone begging to the Protos factory to send a couple of good, reliable pros. They arrived in the form of Fuchs and Neuberger. The Thomas Flyer, which was due to arrive within days, was led by the working man, George Schuster. His assistant was George Miller, another factory mechanic. Captain Hansen was an amateur, though George MacAdam, the fourth man in the car, didn't count either way: he was a reporter. Both the Protos and the Thomas were part of the real world, because they were part of a grander factory structure, bolstered by company men.

That left the Züst. While the company executives in Milan weren't as decisive as the Marquis de Dion—few people were—they did anticipate that recalling Emilio Sirtori would inevitably lead to the withdrawal of the car. They didn't think they were betraying anyone on the team. Sirtori's own communications from Utah and California and especially from Seattle had told them how hopeless and unfair the race had become. They thought he would be delighted to come home.

It was only logical to think that a man who had quit the race three times—three that were reported—would be relieved to be out of the thing. But on the contrary, Sirtori pelted Milano with telegrams insisting that he be allowed to continue driving. Confusion reigned, as it always did when Sirtori was roused to emotion. No one in Milan knew quite what to do. The Züst contingent in New York City, including Arthur Ruland, still struggling to replace Benz with Züst in the American marketplace, rallied for Sirtori.

While the Italians were pleading with one another over thousands of miles of telegraph wires, Bourcier St. Chaffray was meeting with businessmen in Vladivostok and filling the telegraph wires with a thick hail of his own messages. Autran tried to find out what he was doing, but St. Chaffray wouldn't say. After months in league with Monsieur Autran, he suddenly seemed to have nothing left in common with his old compatriot.

On the afternoon of May 18, the SS *Mongolia* docked in Vladivostok and the Thomas Flyer was unloaded. Schuster drove it gingerly through the streets to the Grand Hotel, where lodgings were said to be less impressive than the Hotel d'Allemagne, but then, less German, too. Captain Hansen sat next to Schuster, translating the Russian street signs on the way to the Grand Hotel, and as they pulled up at the entrance, he told them to take a good look at the railway station, just across the street. It was not only the point that defined the city, but one end of the railroad line leading to Moscow.

After Schuster parked the Flyer in front of the hotel, the residents of Vladivostok gathered to inspect it. They had only caught glimpses of the Protos, which was buried in the Kunst & Albers shop. The De Dion had already been swept away to Peking. The big Züst was the only other car that Vladivostok had really had the chance to examine. All through late afternoon, Captain Hansen stood outside the hotel with the Thomas, utterly in his glory, as he chattered away in Russian, Chinese, or any one of a handful of dialects heard in the air of Vladivostok. After a sort of free ride across the American west with the Flyer, his responsibilities were about to grow steeper, as the team's chief guide and translator in Siberian Russia. But for the moment, Captain Hansen was relaxing in his beloved banter, the language he knew best of all.

The consensus was that the Thomas was the "trimmest car in the race." Over at Kunst & Albers, though, Koeppen was doggedly taking weight off of the Protos, formerly regarded as the heavyweight of the race. He not only removed all of the equipment intended for polar exploration, but also shipped nearly all of his spare parts ahead by train, with the result, as he later wrote, "that we never again saw most of them." In any case, the Protos was altogether quite a different car than it had been in the United States.

By agreement, the race was to begin again with all of the remaining cars evenly matched on a sort of second starting line — none was to make a midnight flit and speed out of Vladivostok ahead of the others. Once the Thomas Flyer had arrived safely, Wednesday, May 20, was chosen as the date for the new start.

With only one day to spare, George Schuster turned his attention to preparations, the most pressing of which was securing a supply of gasoline. Without special arrangements, there was no gasoline to be had in Siberia. The race committee had arranged for fuel on the original race route, through Alaska and northeast Siberia, but that didn't help much on the new course through southern Siberia. Lieutenant Koeppen had made purchases during his first few days in Vladivostok and had arranged for barrels to be shipped ahead. Schuster tried to do the same thing on his only full day in the city and came back to the hotel empty-handed. All of the gas was spoken for.

At the hotel, Schuster was handed a message from Bourcier St. Chaffray, asking the American driver to come to his room in the Hotel d'Allemagne. George MacAdam tagged along. Sirtori, Scarfoglio, and Haaga of the Züst were already there, finding places to sit or lean in the small hotel room.

"There is no petrol," St. Chaffray said dramatically. "There are no means of getting any. What there was is in my possession, and I offer it to the car which will agree to take me onboard."

The next-nearest supply, as St. Chaffray pointed out, was in Yokohama.

The members of the Italian team were infuriated by the whole idea of using blackmail to obtain a place in one of the cars, and they left the room almost immediately, shouting at St. Chaffray all the while. St. Chaffray was unperturbed. "He stated," MacAdam said, "that he could get a seat on the German machine, but the Thomas was sure to beat the Protos into Paris and he wished to be on the first car to arrive. He further said that it would not look well for a Frenchman to ride on a German machine."

George Schuster replied that he would think about the proposition for a day and quietly left St. Chaffray's room. As soon as he and MacAdam were alone, he let his fury fly and swore that he would rather stay in Vladivostok for the rest of his life than let St. Chaffray bully his way onto the Flyer. He just wasn't ready to say so to St. Chaffray.

On hearing of the struggle over the gasoline, Lieutenant Koeppen agreed to delay the start of the race, and then Schuster went to work, using his fluent German to good effect. First, he roamed down to the docks to beg or buy extra gas off the handful of boats that ran on it. Then he went to Kunst & Albers, which, like any good department store, always had something extra in the storeroom. It was able to sell Schuster a quantity of gasoline. The next morning, St. Chaffray knocked on Schuster's door, expecting to make arrangements for the balance of the trip. Instead, Schuster said in as few words as possible that he had all the gas he needed. St. Chaffray started to say something more, but he couldn't think of anything. Schuster shut the door and ended the argument his way, without any words at all.

With that, St. Chaffray's plan collapsed. It may have been dastardly, but so was pulling his car from the race and selling it to someone in another country. St. Chaffray was still burning to be in the race, and that is something the others ought to have understood. They felt the same way. The logical place for him was on the Züst. It was going to be in need of a first-string driver, if Emilio Sirtori were really called back to Italy. Had St. Chaffray been a little less aggressive, and just waited around Vladivostok, he might have gotten his ride. But he made enemies before anything could happen in his favor.

On the evening of May 21, Bourcier St. Chaffray quietly transferred

the rights to all of his gasoline to the Züst team. With a small pile of be-
longings and souvenirs from the trip, he boarded the Trans-Siberian
Railway at the station across from Schuster's hotel. The New York-to-
Paris Race had been born in his mind, but that didn't mean anything in
Vladivostok. He boarded the train and somewhere along the way, his
boots dried off. That's when he knew that he really was out of the New
York-to-Paris Automobile Race.

Chapter Twenty-two

Sportsmanship

Car	Miles	Place	Team
Protos (Ger.)	12,004	Lisi, Russia	Koeppen, Fuchs, Neuberger
Thomas Flyer (U.S.)	11,944	Pogranitchnaya, Russia	Schuster, Miller, Hansen, MacAdam
Züst (Ita.)	11,800	Vladivostok, Russia	Scarfoglio, Haaga

The morning air in Vladivostok on May 22, 1908, was warm and free of rain. But that was only the air.

The sky was still full of the same teary clouds that had bored everyone in town for weeks. And the ground was still soggy from recent rains: soggy, that is, where it hadn't surrendered entirely to puddles. A couple of dozen people took advantage of the temporary respite, gathering for the start of the second leg of the New York-to-Paris Race. Most of them were native Germans, who watched closely as Neuberger and Fuchs drove up in the Protos. Lieutenant Koeppen sat in the back with Captain Appelgren, the attaché recommended by the governor-general. Oddly, the spectators made no sound louder than a mumble at their first sight of the car. They only seemed confused.

The light gray body of the Protos was scuffed and dented in places, like a suitcase that had traveled the world. If possible, it looked even more worn than it really was, due to the hundreds of signatures left on the body, the canvas, the trunks, and the interior. In the rushed excitement of an encounter with a New York-to-Paris car, anyone who wasn't yanking a tidbit from the car seemed be scrawling something upon it. Schoolchildren in Rochester, couples in Omaha, soldiers in Wyoming— all kinds of people put a name on the car. It was a form of reverse souvenir, another way of stealing a moment that actually belonged to someone else. In Chicago, where the Protos stopped for three days, one person had taken the whole thing to the limit, painting "CHICAGO" in

261

bold white letters across the hood of the German car. Not only did that forge a satisfying connection with the race, it told every other city in the world a little something about the superiority of Chicago. Just how it did that may not be clear to anyone who doesn't paint names on cars, but the lettering remained on the Protos hood through the rest of the journey across the United States and then over the Pacific to Vladivostok.

In Vladivostok, the Germans who turned out to see the second start of the race took a good look at the Protos after it came to a stop in a square near the center of town. Not many of them knew anything at all about cars, but the Protos did look German, mostly because of the German flag fluttering off the back, next to a Russian one. Cheers caught in the throats of even the most ardent Germans, though, because the car said "Chicago" right across the front. The vandal back in Chicago would have burst with pride to know that even on Russia's frontier, people knew what Chicago was: Chicago was American. But the flag was German. And so the car was greeted not by cheers, but confused murmurs.

While the onlookers tried to decide what to do next, George Schuster was still at the Grand Hotel, seeing to the last preparations for the start across Asia. He intended to join Koeppen in the square momentarily, despite orders from Buffalo to ignore the Protos and treat it as a nonentry.

Back in Buffalo, the Thomas factory was preparing a formal protest against the very presence of the Protos in the race, in light of its train ride through the American northwest. As the Thomas managers quite correctly pointed out, the Thomas had incurred seventeen hundred miles' worth of wear and tear that the Protos avoided. Nonetheless, for both Schuster and Koeppen, Vladivostok represented a chance at a new start. The first part of the race had probably cast the finish, just as the Marquis de Dion had calculated. Yet the fact that the Thomas team was set to win didn't take any pressure off Schuster. He still had something to prove, as a driver and captain, and that left him with a unique viewpoint: if Hans Koeppen didn't have a place in the race, then Schuster wouldn't really have one, either. He needed a competitor, someone to beat, just as Monty had beaten all the rest.

After Schuster double-checked his supply of parts, tools, lubricants, and, most important, his list of train stations and checkpoints, he was ready to go, except for one thing.

On the docks back in San Francisco, just as Schuster was about to board the boat for Seattle with his car, a woman carrying a child had rushed up to him. Stuffing a small, folded American flag into his hand, she said, "Wear this and you'll always have good luck." Inside the flag was an infant's slipper. The entrants in the New York-to-Paris Race had been barraged with just such flotsam throughout the journey across America. Scarfoglio had received more handkerchiefs than he could count. Monty Roberts collected flags by the dozen. Koeppen had received a giant pretzel. But surprisingly enough, the baby slipper meant something to George Schuster. In the first place, he described the donor as "very pretty." Until an unassuming fellow like George Schuster becomes the driver of a famous racing car, very pretty women don't normally rush around trying to get near them. By doing so, the young mother in San Francisco demonstrated his brand-new status as well as anyone could. Perhaps because Schuster was a family man, the baby shoe affected him, too, reminding him of his own toddler and his wife back in Buffalo. Just as the Thomas Flyer was ready to leave the hotel courtyard in Vladivostok—and just after a senior army official told Schuster that a car trip across Russia was plainly impossible—he carefully refolded the slipper into the flag and then put it into the inside pocket of his overcoat. Mere mechanics didn't need luck. But racecar drivers live and die upon it.

Schuster climbed into the car, while Miller settled into the passenger seat next to him. Captain Hansen and the reporter, George MacAdam, were in the back. When everyone was ready, Schuster revved the engine and then let out the clutch—and the engine kept revving. "[I] started the Thomas only to find the clutch slipping so badly that the car could barely crawl from the court of the Grand Hotel to the street," Schuster recounted. With that, he refrained from any impulse he might have had to throw the baby slipper to the ground and stomp it into the mud. Instead, he sent word to the Protos about his stroke of misfortune and asked Koeppen to delay the start for an hour or two.

Koeppen had already done his share of waiting, though. He gave the word to Neuberger to go. With the break in the weather, the driving wasn't bad, at least not in town, and a few hundred yards of decent conditions straight ahead were a greater temptation than Hans Koeppen could bear.

The good highway didn't last long. "I was extremely surprised," Koeppen wrote later, "immediately after leaving the city to find bottomless roads." The car fell into its first brook after only a mile and a half. There were others awaiting it, but so near to Vladivostok, the delay was brief. Passersby fetched planks and a temporary bridge was constructed to ease the Protos out of the water.

The road was generally narrow, with thick forests on either side and branches overhanging in places. Though the terrain was steadily rising and steep in places, the greatest danger was posed by the lurking presence of bogs—deep, wide, muddy holes. Avoiding the puddles generally meant avoiding the bogs, but when the rains returned at midday, the puddles that betrayed the bogs disappeared into a roadbed completely covered with water. The Protos would fall into bogs with a sickening jolt, and only occasionally get out under its own power. Anxious to make headway against the absurd distance ahead, Koeppen found instead that, for him, the legendary scope of Siberia was no more vast than the quarter acre surrounding the latest boghole. As he grew intimately familiar with each tree and rivulet of water in the vicinity, a thicket there or a patch of straw there, they were Siberia to him.

"The stops became ever more numerous," Lt. Koeppen lamented. "The strength of our engine was not sufficient to pull the car out of the bogholes, of which there were many." Normally, the four men could work the car out, drenching themselves with mud in the process, but only about twenty miles out of Vladivostok on a relatively broad stretch of the road, the back of the car slid into the most stubborn bog of them all.

Koeppen walked around the car, ignoring the mud that clutched at his boots, seeming to want them as well as his car. The Protos was on a level section, which might have come as a relief, except that water stayed trapped on flat land and the back of the Protos was submerged up to the top of the wheels. There wasn't any traction at all. To be free of the bog, the car would have to be lifted up or dragged lifelessly out. Four men couldn't possibly accomplish that, even if they had no choice but to try. Anyway, as the hours went by, their best efforts were making the situation worse.

"After a while," Koeppen wrote, "we heard the rumble of an engine. It was the Thomas team, with its sturdy machine."

Approaching in the Flyer, Schuster likewise heard the engine of the Protos, revving and whining to release every last gust of its horsepower. As he came upon it, he assessed the predicament instantly. "With the churning of the wheels," he noted, "it was sinking deeper." It occurred to him that he could stop and help, but that sort of thing hadn't been done in the New York-to-Paris Race since the guileless days of the Hudson River Valley. Schuster started to drive around the foundering car.

"Let's help them," Captain Hansen suddenly blurted out.

Schuster slowed the car. By the time he stopped, he had changed his mind about helping. He never explained why. "In comradely fashion," Koeppen marveled, "he helped us to get rolling again." With a rope tied between the cars, the two teams joined together, everyone but the drivers standing side by side to push. The Protos gave out a raspy rumble, but the Thomas was even noisier, pulling the towrope tight and then roaring louder as it inched forward and took the other car along. Miller kept his eye on the rope; he had seen it strain many times before, but it never looked quite so delicate before, pulled out to the width of a whisker, or so it seemed, in an Olympic tug-of-war between the Thomas's finest car and Siberia's best mud. MacAdam backed up as the struggle reached its peak and took photographs of the effort. Finally, the Protos surged out, and once its wheels found traction again, it kicked up onto firm ground and thanked the men behind it with an extra spray of mud.

Lieutenant Koeppen thanked them with the slightly frothier spray from a bottle of champagne that had somehow made it past every round of weight-cutting in the Protos luggage compartment. Once the wine had been poured and finished, the crews separated again, into their respective cars and their respective sides of the competition. Koeppen watched the Thomas Flyer speed away down the flat, wide road. "It has now the lead," he was thinking to himself.

In late afternoon, Schuster struck a boghole and it was the Thomas Flyer's turn to sink helplessly into the mud. Koeppen never came along to return the day's favor, though. He had taken another route and with afternoon turning dark early, Captain Hansen volunteered to walk ahead to look for help.

Hansen had grown more serious since starting west again—Siberia being generally devoid of flirtatious women and dance halls. He proved that he knew the dominant languages of the land, although he actually didn't know his way overland quite as handily as he had implied. With the Thomas Flyer stuck in the mud, though, Schuster entrusted Captain Hansen to find help. For Schuster, it was quite a concession, since he usually didn't trust anyone else with crucial jobs. Hansen came through, returning only a short time later with forty soldiers who made quick work of pulling the American car free. The soldiers were attached to a post only a few miles ahead and they invited the crew to spend the night in the safety of the post house. In fact, they not only made it an invitation, but a strong piece of advice.

While engineers and builders were constructing the great Trans-Siberian Railway in the mid-1890s, the Russian army was building a string of small fortresses, spaced at intervals of about ten miles. For the nomads in the vicinity, the coming of the railway to Russia's wild east spelled the end of a traditional way of life just as the completion of transcontinental rails in the United States and Canada closed an era of freedom for Indians in the Wild West. In each case, the disruption was not only the result of the railroad line itself, which was harsh enough as it slashed across formerly open spaces; it also came from the settlement that inevitably followed the rails, bringing new practicality to agriculture, lumbering, and mining in places once considered remote. Russian princes, consulting maps in their Moscow palaces, talked with giddy excitement about the possibilities of exploiting Siberia and harnessing it. But they were six thousand miles away.

The nomads of Russia's southeast frontier, which included lower Siberia and upper Manchuria, knew better about the land, if not its future. They were known as the Chunguse and they were descended, however loosely, from those Huns whose antics had inspired the construction of the Great Wall to protect China in about 220 B.C. The Huns later turned toward Europe and controlled much of it, along with central Asia, in the A.D. 300–400 era. Attila was their most famous leader. The secret weapon of Attila's Huns, and the Chunguse who followed from them, was the horse. They rode small mounts, sticking like glue even as they wheeled them around, starting, stopping, and turning with precision.

The talk of the Trans-Siberian Railway in 1908 was the uprising of Chunguse marauders and robbers: two separate but related entities. The marauders collected in armies of hundreds to stage surprise attacks on villages and towns, pillaging under an aura of protest against development. The robbers operated in smaller groups and they were a violent lot, without politics or remorse. In a village called Manchesuria, used as a Chunguse winter refuge, the spring thaw revealed thirty dead bodies, left like litter in the snow over the preceding months. All had been murdered. The Russian military constantly played hide-and-seek with Chunguse robbers. Local Chinese authorities in Manchuria made examples of any who were captured, using cleverly engineered devices for public torture. One was a bamboo cage, in which the thief would be tied in such a way that he had only two choices. One was to remain in a crouching position and suffer agonizing back pain. The other was to stand up straight and strangle himself. The device may have amused the passing townsfolk, but the deterrent value was lost since the captive's comrades would be long gone, galloping through open country, by the time the noose was innocently dropped around the poor man's neck.

Hansen, who knew all about the robbers, was assuredly brave to walk through the fading light by himself to the army post. That night in the small dining room, he served as interpreter while the soldiers regaled the Thomas Flyer team with the latest Chunguse stories, which went up and down the railway tracks even quicker than the trains. Schuster was more interested to know if the soldiers had heard anything of the German car, but there was no news.

○ ○ ○

In changing the route after the frustrations in Alaska, the race organizers were relieved to think that by May the snow would be melted in southern Siberia. What it left, however, was water and mud. Schuster had driven through wetlands before, but never a thousand miles of it. He knew that it looked impossible. It felt impossible, too, but he kept on going. Within a few days, just before leaving a town called Nikolsk, he took a long look at the railway track, leading almost due west.

The engineers who planned the Trans-Siberian Railway knew all about the spring weather and specified that on floodplains the tracks be constructed on a fifteen-foot embankment. Schuster gazed at that embankment, keeping the rails above the muds, and then turned to the old road and set off west. "With the crew wading ahead to pilot," MacAdam reported, "the car proceeded for some fifteen miles at little better than a snail's pace.

"Then the rear wheels sank out of sight in the water," MacAdam continued, "and the hubs became imbedded in the mud beneath. We discovered we were in the middle of a swollen stream, and thirty feet from either bank."

Schuster climbed up on the back of the seat and looked around. His sight had been trained for so long on Miller's back, with his concentration on the shifting balance of the car, that it took his eyes a minute to adjust. The land was either a shallow pond or a deep puddle, but water covered it nearly as far as the eye could see. A few leafless trees stood in the water, which was chilly, although the air temperature was warm in a cheerless way. And the rain was still coming down.

Captain Hansen started to wade away to find help, but he hadn't drifted out of sight of the car before he noticed that Chinese peasant farmers were approaching from almost every direction. They had never seen a car before—and still couldn't see one, with the Thomas up to the middle of the hood in muddy water. Those who were willing were hired to pull the car out of the stream and they remained with the car for another five miles, until someone spotted a wagon splashing its way along from the opposite direction. Hansen spoke to the driver for a minute and then paused before translating for Schuster. "He says," Hansen reported, "that the road ahead is even worse."

Schuster pondered that possibility, cursed it, and then announced that the car would have to go back to Nikolsk—back over all of the waterlogged mileage it had managed to cover during the previous two days. Late at night, the team arrived in Nikolsk, the car and each of the men neatly covered in a glaze of mud. While Schuster dried water from his hair at the post house, the officers excitedly told Hansen that they knew where the German car was; it had left that morning on the railway tracks.

Koeppen had arrived in Nikolsk a short time before, after devoting two days to covering about eighty-five miles. He heard that the Thomas had been in Nikolsk overnight and had just left to continue the overland trip. "We saw the uselessness of this start," Koeppen wrote, "and took a shot at applying for permission to use the railway embankment." Taking refuge at the local German Club, Lieutenant Koeppen passed the time pleasantly until finally, late in the night, he received permission to use the rails. "Completely glad," as he wrote, the team set off across town to take advantage of the offer.

The Protos took hungrily to the tracks, bouncing along with the rightside wheels on the outside of the rail and the leftside ones aiming down the middle. Driving a car on the Russian rails took unceasing concentration and brute strength to keep the car on its narrow line. The problem wasn't with the leftside wheels, there was plenty of room for them in the middle. But where the rightside wheels were concerned, the railroad ties didn't overhang the rails by much, leaving only small room for error. The car could get stuck or even turn over if they slipped off. At the same time, if the wheels were allowed to drift too near to the rail, the tires would be slashed to ribbons by the pins and latches that connected lengths of the track.

The strain was so great that Fuchs and Neuberger traded the driver's seat every ten or fifteen minutes. Meanwhile, the others in the car worried about the onset of locomotives. There were train schedules to follow, of course, but even so, there were near misses, too.

The news that Koeppen was in the lead—a solid lead of at least a day—hit Schuster hard. The Thomas Flyer had been out in front since Times Square. Beating Koeppen in the race, over which the four-week allowance still loomed, wasn't as nearly as important to Schuster as just beating him to Paris. He devoted a day in Nikolsk to preparing the Flyer for the tracks, and the next day, he set out with a resolve to catch up.

For the moment, it didn't look much like an automobile race. A view from up high would have shown a land of mud and slush blanketed with trees, rising and falling over low mountain ranges, with two gray cars, like toys in a track, one out in front of the other on the Trans-Siberian.

On May 28, the Thomas reached the lively town of Pogranitchnaya, having just missed being smashed to bits by a freight train that afternoon. Schuster learned to his dismay that Koeppen was still sixty miles ahead. Meanwhile MacAdam had even worse tidings. Three Chunguse spies had been captured in Pogranitchnaya the week before. They told officials, as MacAdam recounted, "that they had heard of the projected trip of the rich automobilists through the country, and believed a good ransom could be secured by their capture. Added to the other difficulties we are experiencing, this indeed makes a pleasing prospect." MacAdam's account was sent by courier to Nikolsk and telegraphed there; remarkably, it appeared in the *New York Times* on May 29, only one day after it was written.

Almost a week later, no one in New York or Paris had heard anything from either the German or the American car. It was cause for concern, especially since no one so far away could do anything to contact either car.

The Italian team was still in Vladivostok, in disarray. On May 28, Emilio Sirtori reluctantly obeyed orders from the factory and boarded a ship bound for Italy. After months of longing to be finished with the daily miseries of the New York-to-Paris Race, he finally was. Scarfoglio remembered him standing on deck, as the ship left the dock, crying his eyes out. "We," Scarfoglio wrote, referring to himself and Haaga, "the car and the journey had entered into his life like a wedge and become part of his existence, one of its necessary constituent elements. Now that he is leaving us he can scarcely contain his grief."

Scarfoglio and Haaga were left behind in Vladivostok, the last of the New York-to-Paris entrants to remain. The city terrified them, with its rare mix of nationalities—rare because it seemed to include every strain except Italians. After considerable effort, they found one Italian man, a pianist who had arrived there with an orchestra popular with the Russian officers during the war with Japan. With that war over, the officers didn't need to be cheered up quite so often and the orchestra was no longer in demand, leaving the pianist stranded. Fortunately, movies had just recently arrived in Vladivostok and he found work in the local picture house, playing accompaniments.

Haaga ought to have been able to make friends with someone in town, but he and Scarfoglio were frenzied by the specter of danger all around them. "We sleep together in one room," Scarfoglio wrote in a dispatch, "always go out together arm-in-arm, eat together at the same table, owing to an instinctive fear that one may be snatched away and leave the other alone." Oddly enough, the fear that drove them to a state of panic was not that of being kidnapped and thrown into a slave galley or a snake pit or whatever image they had conjured up during all those long walks and meals together—it was the fear of being the one *not* kidnapped, and of being all alone in Vladivostok.

Scarfoglio insisted in his memoir that he and Haaga were awaiting fuel contracts, but in fact, they needed money. By remaining in Vladivostok after Sirtori left, they hoped to force the Züst factory to reestablish its support. Scarfoglio wrote daily articles for his father's paper, describing the situation with all the melodrama at his command, which was considerable, each line imbued with the general hope that he wouldn't be cracked over the head and left to die in an opium-laced alley before the Züst officials made up their minds. On June 1, they did. But they knew a little bit about forcing others to tough decisions, too. The factory would assume half of the expenses for the remainder of the trip; the other half would be underwritten by a Russian nobleman, Baron Edward Scheinvogel, who would meet the team in Irkutsk and drive the car the rest of the way to Paris.

Sharing the car with a Russian was not at all what Scarfoglio had in mind. He liked Italians—except in American banquet halls when they were giving speeches about Christopher Columbus—and didn't think that he and Haaga needed the deadweight of a baron in order to complete the trip. The factory left him no room to reject the new plan, though, except inasmuch as he could always quit and follow Sirtori home.

The Züst finally left Vladivostok on June 5, two weeks after the other two cars. On leaving, Scarfoglio had been warned with great attention to detail about the Chunguse robbers, "who go about in bands of 20,000—so we were told," Scarfoglio wrote, and also about the wild animals, "Manchurian tigers, as numerous as mosquitoes or sands of the sea, tigers that have been made voracious by two years of famine." Scarfoglio could afford to be jovial about good, honest mankillers. Once the car left the shadows of Vladivostok, he wasn't afraid of a thing.

Chapter Twenty-three

Wild East

THURSDAY, JUNE 5, 6 A.M.: LATEST OFFICIAL STANDINGS

Car	Miles	Place	Team
Protos (Ger.)	12,995	near Chailar, Manchuria	Koeppen, Fuchs, Neuberger
Thomas Flyer (U.S.)	12,506	near Zizikar, Manchuria	Schuster, Miller, Hansen, MacAdam
Züst (Ita.)	11,800	Vladivostok, Russia	Scarfoglio, Haaga

On June 5, the *New York Times* finally heard from MacAdam. According to his report, Schuster had abandoned the train tracks almost a week before. The possibility of being obliterated at any moment by a locomotive gave the mud a new appeal. Schuster felt certain he could triumph over the bad roads with the unyielding perseverance for which he was known.

Later the same day, he was back on the train tracks.

To the west of Pogranitchnaya, the Thomas crossed into Manchuria on the Chinese Eastern Railway (the continuation of the Trans-Siberian in the Russian-dominated province). The sun was out and the temperature summery, or so it seemed when the car was moving. Whenever the Thomas wasn't supplying a breeze, the air was just plain hot. In a particularly desolate spot, on a plain shadowed by distant mountains, the mixture of throbbing, rattling, and rasping noises made by the car was suddenly split open with a cracking sound. There was no voice to it, only a terrible clap in the air.

Schuster immediately stopped the car, jumping out with Miller to examine the undercarriage. They discovered that the transmission casing had broken open. Oil was leaking out, splashing on the ties and dripping into the gravel below. They also found the cause: a driving pinion had detached, losing a half-dozen teeth as it cut through the transmission case.

The men started to talk about the setback and the need for a new

274

case, but Schuster interrupted them sharply. The car was still on the tracks. And, as he pointed out, so were the trains. The four of them lifted the car, one wheel at a time, over the rails and then eased it down the embankment. Freeing itself from their hands, it coasted a little way and then came to a rest at the edge of a field. The field was somewhere to the west of Pogranitchnaya, 8,570 miles from the nearest Thomas dealership.

Schuster assigned himself the task of setting out on foot over the tracks, toward the town of Pogranitchnaya. MacAdam tagged along, trying to keep up in the blazing sun. After a fifteen-mile hike, they arrived in early afternoon, and Schuster lost no time in going to see the Russian railway officials to tell them what had happened. No one in the office could understand anything he said in English, German, or the small smattering of what he regarded as Russian words. He calmly left the station. He had no reason to stand in front of a desk in Siberia, or the edge of Manchuria, or wherever it was that he was, sputtering to no avail.

Paris *Matin* had a man on the scene, a small and pudgy, very bald man named Felix Neuville, who was in eastern Russia to report on the race and, above all, to help the racers negotiate Russia's cavernous bureaucracy. Monsieur Neuville had already been helpful to Scarfoglio, giving him advice on fuel back in Vladivostok. It was a tribute to his glossy diplomatic skills that each of the racers considered him a special ally. Neuville spoke all of the languages of the region, had the backing of an important French newspaper, and could sort out the many layers lurking within a Russian business conversation. In addition, he wore very presentable three-piece suits, rather than the coveralls favored by the racing men. Schuster had only left Monsieur Neuville in Pogranitchnaya that morning and so he had no trouble locating him again. Together, they went back to speak to the railway officials.

MacAdam's assignment, meanwhile, was to buy a supply of food to take back to the car. It wasn't easy. The only fresh food that the Americans could choke down in Russia were hard-boiled eggs. Even the bread, which seemed to be made of unmilled grain, was barely edible. Prepared food was out of the question; it made foreigners sick.

MacAdam, poking around town looking for imported canned food,

275

ended up at a general store. Just inside the door, he found himself frozen in fascination with the skin of a large tiger that had been shot only fifty miles away. Of course, tigers don't normally attack people and MacAdam probably knew that. He probably also knew that such statements are typically written by people in the safety of offices, not those about to go sleep in the open air of tiger country. When he finished his shopping, the railway officials arranged for two Chinese laborers to give him a ride in a handcar back to the Flyer. Hansen and Miller were happy to see MacAdam and, of course, his crates of food. Trying to think of everything, as Schuster might expect them to do, they sent nearly every piece of excess baggage back with the handcar, instructing the workers to ship it all on to the next large city, Harbin.

Settling in to their new home, MacAdam, Hansen, and Miller made a tent out of pieces of canvas and rubber coats stretched around a framework of old railway timber. They made kitchen utensils out of tomato cans and copper wire. After that, there was nothing at all to do.

"The night was melancholy," MacAdam wrote, "and the only noise was the frog chorus. Songs failed to relieve the loneliness."

Because of the fear of Chunguse bandits, one man had to keep watch at all times. MacAdam drew the first overnight watch, despite having been on the road most of the day. He sat down and looked around. The empty night was cheered by very little—except for all the raincoat arms sticking up off the sides of the tent, waving around in the breeze. The campfire offered the only conversation. MacAdam was staring into it, growing drowsy, when he heard footsteps approaching. Whoever it was, they were bearing down ferociously, not sneaking up. MacAdam scrambled to his feet, ready to face a gang of bandits, "but," as he wrote later, "the visitors were two soldiers sent by the commandant of the Pogranitchnaya garrison with a hundred rounds of ammunition each and fixed bayonets. They were accompanied by three watchdogs."

The soldiers hadn't had any trouble finding the autoists, thanks to the campfire. And, they explained as they stamped it out with their boots, neither would the Chunguse bandits.

The only wonder was that the bandits would need a light. Everyone else already seemed to know about the stranded Americans in the New

276

York-to-Paris Race. The next day, each train that went by carried an audience, just waiting to catch sight of the Thomas Flyer. Entertainment
on the Trans-Siberian Railway being what it was, the sight of three haggard men with a broken car and a tent patched together out of raincoats
made for a magnificent diversion. The windows of the passengers cars
were filled to the very edges with faces.

Behind one of the windows on one of the trains sat George Schuster.
Having walked east to Pogranitchnaya, he had boarded a morning train
with Felix Neuville and was heading west to Harbin, the biggest city in
northern Manchuria—another three hundred miles away. In planning
for emergencies, Schuster had sent a selection of parts to Harbin weeks
before. He wasn't at all sure they had arrived or that he would be able to
locate them if they had. In either case, Neuville would be able to help.

The city of Harbin was a Russian creation. Built up from a village for
the sake of the railway, it had burgeoned since the Russo-Japanese War.
In the American west, the charm of frontier towns was that they were in
a rush to prosper, but often didn't appear prosperous. Russia, on the
contrary, wanted Harbin to look like a great city even before it was one,
and so Schuster was greeted by a place only eight years old, but already
stretching itself out over wide avenues lined with huge granite buildings. Rich merchants and railway officials made their homes in mansions along the Súngari River.

In Harbin, Schuster and Neuville tracked down the crate of Thomas
parts and Schuster selected what he needed to repair the Flyer. Still
worried—always worried, in fact—he cabled the Thomas factory in
Buffalo to send a whole new transmission. Even as an express shipment,
it would not arrive for at least two and a half weeks, and maybe more,
depending on the Russian post office. Schuster would intercept it farther along on the trip, but for the time being, he had everything he
needed to make the Thomas Flyer roadworthy, or railworthy, again.

After a day in Harbin, he returned to Pogranitchnaya. During all the
time Schuster spent in railway cars or staring at the ceiling in hotels, he
thought very little about the Thomas. The questions surrounding it were
settled in his mind even before he took his first step toward Pogranitchnaya. Again and again, his thoughts returned to the Protos and how, with

every hour, Hans Koeppen was pulling farther away. Schuster was surrounded by the biggest part of the world, the blended border of Siberian Russia and northern China, but Koeppen's progress was all that he could think about. Everything else would be the same the next day or in a hundred years. Koeppen alone seemed to be moving.

Storms descended on the Flyer campsite, deluging the three men on guard there with hail and rain in frigid temperatures. The men were cold and wet—and thanks to whoever it was who thought of sending the excess baggage on to Harbin, they remained that way for most of the next three days. As soon as Schuster arrived with the parts, he and Miller repaired the Thomas and it could finally move again, five days after it had rolled to a stop.

Koeppen had indeed been taking good advantage of Schuster's problems, making fast time, as Neuberger and Fuchs perfected the technique of driving a car on a railway track. Visually, their efforts made for a grotesque cartoon of the transition between the rail age and the automobile one. But the Germans had strong stomachs, and the Protos logged steady progress during the first week in June.

Crossing the eastern part of Manchuria, the team passed teams of laborers, employed on railroad repair work, as Koeppen described:

These Chinese or Korean workers were fun. They were exceptionally interested in our machine, since they had never in their lives seen a vehicle without either a smokestack or horses. With smiles, they regarded the car from all sides, examining the engine with the hood open, tapping it, pointing here and there and even crawling underneath the car in order to regard the secret of self-propulsion from the ground.

Grinning at it and then at us, they stuck out their thumbs, jerked them up and at the same time, said the word, "Cho."

We hear this strange call often on our trip. When we pass a poor Chinese village, the inhabitants come out with their thumbs forward—the indication of their greatest applause. They might have held our automobile for an attractive toy, for its mechanism was inexplicable for them, with all its humming and rumbling, however, it didn't frighten them in the least; quite the opposite, it seemed to heighten their delight.

These pig-tailed men may have been from the lowest working class, but they were intelligent and confident, a fact I learned from a coolie who learned to speak and write German from a book. He also taught himself English, using a manual. He said that he wanted to go to Hamburg to get a job as a waiter.

In Manchuria, the train stations were typically made of wood and decorated with apes or dragons. At each one of them, Koeppen asked for news of the American car, already three days behind. He was focused on reaching the large city of Tchita, another five hundred miles east. Tchita (or "Chita," as it is sometimes spelled in English) had special importance for Koeppen and Schuster. The Trans-Siberian Railway had offered a special prize equivalent to $1,000 to the car reaching it first.

When the prize was announced, just before the racers left Vladivostok, the railway administration hadn't realized that the cars would end up stealing onto its very track. That favor was prize enough for any entrant. Or it should have been. One night at about nine o'clock, Koeppen pushed his team to remain on the rails, despite the rather pressing fact that the Protos had lost its headlights somewhere in the Rocky Mountains—and the even more pressing fact that a train from Sandawodi was due to come along at eleven o'clock. The car had only a short distance to travel to the next station, though, and Koeppen was certain it would arrive there in less than two hours.

It didn't. Fuchs was driving; he and Neuberger were in the front, concentrating on the tracks. For all their exertions, the Protos was emitting a painfully slow rhythm of ker-thunks, instead of the patta-patta-patta beat it made during the day.

The guide in the car over that span was a second lieutenant from the Russian army, who nervously and almost incessantly lit matches to check his watch. Visibly trembling, he finally announced to the others that it was eleven o'clock. The news didn't make Lieutenant Koeppen uncomfortable. He was certain that luck would be on his side. And it was. Miles up ahead, the Sandawodi train had suffered a slight derailment involving the wheels on one car, forcing it to stop for a half hour. "It happened," Koeppen observed, "we did not have a crash."

279

"The Second-Lieutenant," he added, with the satisfaction of a first lieutenant, "stood more fears in two hours on that daring railway ride, than he had in all the rest of his life."

News of the adventurous trip reached up and down the Trans-Siberian line. The next morning, Koeppen was handed a telegram from the railway company, expressly forbidding him from using the tracks ever again.

No sooner had George Schuster repaired the Thomas Flyer transmission, hundreds of miles to the east, than he received the same message. He immediately contacted Felix Neuville, who had remained in Harbin. At Schuster's specific request, but on behalf of Koeppen as well, Monsieur Neuville made an appointment to see the commander of the First Russian Army, General Horwath.

If the New York-to-Paris Race had been a mere endurance contest, the cars would have simply waited for his answer. But Schuster was certainly not going to stop while Koeppen kept going. And Koeppen was not going to stop and let Schuster gain so much as a yard.

In fact, Koeppen was not certain what Schuster was doing, but he was hungry to open up his lead over the American car and so he set out as quickly as possible over the land route, at least to the next station. He still had a way to go when the sun went down, disappearing behind the very hills he was trying to cross.

With Neuberger at the wheel, the Protos climbed a fairly steep grade and came to a ravine, seventy-five feet deep and about fifteen wide. Neuberger could see that there was a wooden bridge across the gap, and he slowed as he allowed the weight of the car to settle onto it. Halfway across, he heard a sharp sound and he decided to stop. Inexplicably, he pressed his foot down on the accelerator, though, instead of the brake. It was unlike Neuberger to make such a mistake, but with a raspy roar, the Protos lunged forward to the other side of the ravine, momentarily out of control. It came to a stop as soon as Neuberger sorted his feet out on the pedals.

Neuberger got out to check the car and then called the others to see what he had discovered. They climbed out to join him. "The bridge had disappeared," Koeppen reported. "It was all tumbled away, including the support and struts." None of the four men could be induced to get back into the car. They left it where it was and groped their way in the dark until they reached the station, still wondering who or what had pressed down on Neuberger's foot, the one that hit the gas pedal.

The next morning, General Horwath proved to be immune to Monsieur Neuville's winning ways. In fact, he barely let Neuville into the conversation, as he complained in no uncertain terms that the cars, especially the German one, had caused serious delays on the Trans-Siberian. The mail train, he pointed out, had once been held up for a whole hour. Adherence to schedules was not a trait normally associated with the Russian civil service, at least not by American and European travelers, but the Trans-Siberian existed to set new standards in many respects—including punctuality. General Horwath was not inclined to be casual about it, nor about the danger to the cars and to the trains. Neuville tried to veer off into a discussion of the international publicity given to the railway because of the race. He didn't get very far. Then he focused on a more specific topic: the interest of Grand Duke Serge Mikhailovich in the race.

Serge Mikhailovich was a member of the Romanov family, which had ruled Russia for almost three hundred years. At thirty-nine, he exerted lofty influence in Moscow, being the general of the artillery, the chairman of the Russian Theatrical Society—and the cousin of Czar Nicholas II. His name was bandied about in whispers, as well. Though married, he had recently purchased a lavish country house for Matilda Kshesinskaya, prima ballerina of the Mariinsky Theater.

In addition to everything else, Grand Duke Serge Mikhailovich was a member of the Russian committee overseeing the New York-to-Paris Race. Moreover, he happened to be on a train headed east from Moscow, on a trip to inspect military installations in and around Vladivostok. General Horwath knew all of that, even as Neuville reminded him. In his view, the grand duke was more likely to blame him for forsaking the train than the foreign automobilists. And so the prohibition remained. For days, Koeppen and Schuster persevered over roads that hadn't been maintained since the Trans-Siberian started running. Even where the mud wasn't a hazard, rocks, trees, and ditches marred the way.

At Kasanscho, one of the stations leading up to Harbin, an official took Lieutenant Koeppen aside to tell him the latest gossip. Grand Duke Serge Mikhailovich was approaching and had already given orders that the train on which he was riding stop immediately whenever one of the New York-to-Paris cars was spotted. He wanted to see the cars for himself. Koeppen casually asked when the grand duke's train was due in Harbin.

Koeppen had to cross paths with Serge Mikhailovich in order to plead his case and it wasn't likely to happen with the Protos muddling through some dank forest, out of sight of the rails. He decided to be in Harbin to meet the train. On the morning when the grand duke's train was due, though, the Protos was stopped in a small village, more than fifteen miles from the city, in need of a small repair.

With the chance of seeing the grand duke slipping away, Koeppen appealed to the village mayor, who borrowed two horses so that they could ride together into the city. Just before he left, Koeppen told Fuchs and Neuberger to follow, as soon as the car was fixed. It was a typical Koeppen shuffle, leaving others to toil, but part of being single-minded is being selfish-minded, too. And so he rode off and left the broken car behind. When the grand duke's train pulled into the station, Lieutenant Koeppen was on hand and in his army uniform. Naturally, he was brought forward to be introduced. General Horwath was also there to meet the nobleman.

In person, Serge Mikhailovich was polite and not especially imperious. A slender man, he wore an army tunic and sported a fashionably pointed beard. On meeting Koeppen, he expressed surprise at finding one of the New York-to-Paris contestants in Harbin and enthusiastically accepted Koeppen's offer to show him the car. With that, the express train was no longer on a schedule. It pulled onto a siding, and the grand duke took to a horse to retrace Koeppen's route. General Horwath, invited to go along too, took advantage of the chance to show off his own intense interest in the New York-to-Paris racers.

Before long, the royal party found the Protos stuck in a swamp and up to the hubs in dirty water. Serge Mikhailovich cried out, shocked to see the massive car lying helpless in the muck, like a fallen tree.

Inwardly, Koeppen was delighted. He couldn't have planned a better tableau. Assuring the grand duke that such situations were a daily occurrence, he wished aloud that General Horwath had been able to permit the racers to use the tracks. Serge Mikhailovich immediately turned to the general and sternly gave him permission to let the cars return to the rails.

"After photographs and a very friendly leave-taking," Koeppen recorded, "the Grand Duke continued his journey. Now we were luckily again on the railway embankment."

A grand duke's power in such matters was absolute, but not unreasoned. According to the new rules, each automobile had to make room for a railroad official with portable telegraph equipment, so that positions could be reported regularly.

MacAdam described one of the other frustrations. "The railroad," he wrote, "insists on holding the car at various stations until the stretch ahead to the next station is entirely clear. There are many delays in consequence, and faster progress is impossible."

By the time George Schuster reached Harbin, he was six full days behind Koeppen. It was hard to make up time, under the circumstances. Koeppen felt just as constrained by the new rules and he resorted to the tracks less and less frequently past Harbin, in the western part of Manchuria.

To the west of Harbin, the land flattened out into gently rolling hills and dried almost into a desert. Low grasses covered the hills, and altogether the land was fine for motoring. In addition to Fuchs and Neuberger, the Protos carried Rittmeister von Albrecht, the cheerful young railroad man assigned to the car, along with a local guide.

With about 250 miles to go before reaching Tchita, the Protos crossed out of Manchuria and into a corner of northern Mongolia. Officially, China controlled the territory, but the Russian army manned posts there, just as it did along the rest of the railway. With no particular hazards to worry about, Lieutenant Koeppen was relaxing in his place in the backseat, contemplating the fact that his car was striking over the exact same routes taken in Mongolia's days of great empire as far back as the early 1200s. Looking around at the empty landscape, it was a little hard to imagine Mongolia mustering a force capable of taking over a tiny hamlet, let alone all of Asia and a good chunk of Europe. But they had gathered just such an army, and on the very tracts that surrounded Koeppen and his team.

Fuchs was at the wheel when the car arrived at a fast-running stream in the Mongolian steppes. Koeppen waded into the water to test the depth. He returned and told Fuchs to take a long head start, gain as much speed as possible, and muscle the car across. Fuchs did just as he was told. The car backed up on the brown earth, accelerated with a bit of thunder, and then struck the water with a clumsy slap. Water splashed for yards all around and it was hard to tell what was happening underneath the cascade, until in a moment, the radiator of the Protos emerged and the front wheels clung to a beachhead on the other side.

After that the car didn't move. It couldn't. A spring had snapped and with the full weight of the car bearing down, there was no way for the rear axle to move.

The Protos was about eleven miles from the railway tracks, leading west to the next station at Jakechi. Rittmeister von Albrecht volunteered to go for help, with the local guide, who estimated that they would be back at about five o'clock in the afternoon. After they left, Koeppen, Neuberger, and Fuchs were passing the time, trading ideas on extricating the car, when they each looked up, hearing the faint clanking of bells. A caravan of Russian families slowly approached, arrayed on horseback and in carriages. They were colorful, in a scruffy way, identifying themselves only as immigrants in the region. Koeppen took note of the fact that the men were drunk, but he didn't hold that against them—as long as the horses were sober, he was willing to be broadminded.

He was also willing to pay ten rubles for the use of the horses in pulling the Protos out of the water. Despite the fact that Koeppen couldn't speak Russian and they couldn't understand German, a deal was struck. The horses, however, were not the towering draft horses of New York or Iowa. They were the compact little horses popular on the steppes. Try as they would, they couldn't budge a five-thousand-pound waterlogged automobile out of the stream.

The Russian men became angry, first directing their vitriol at the horses and then at the Germans, from whom they demanded more money. As they became more vehement, Koeppen stepped forward and threatened them with a real fight. That didn't intimidate the men, who were glistening with courage—and reeling with every step. The women in the party, however, had seen enough. They insisted that the men take the ropes off the horses and with only a little more shouting, they did. The horses were returned to harness and the caravan clanked its way back over the steppes, until it was a sound as soft as the hills, just the way it had arrived.

At six o'clock, Koeppen began to worry that Rittmeister von Albrecht had gotten lost. At eight o'clock, he was certain of it. "I decided to go out on my own and see if I could find him," Koeppen wrote later, but it was only a matter of time before he himself was lost. "After about half-an-hour, the skies started to cloud over and I had to rely strictly on my instincts for orientation," he explained. The landscape was hilly and monotonous, though, and the skies were cloudy and just as featureless. Koeppen's instinct for orientation disappeared when the moon did. He relied rather heavily on his feeling that the railroad line was off to his right. Whenever he felt that he might be going in the wrong direction, he turned right.

At midnight, Koeppen was lost and he knew it—a cold admission to make to oneself. He knew that he should have reached the tracks long before. He also knew that he was terribly thirsty. "As I continued on," he wrote, "I saw a light in the distance. I was overjoyed because, while such a little light might be just an illusion, I found I could still see it from the next hill. Then, from the next-closest hill, I was startled and just stood still. The light disappeared. I began to believe that some evil ghost had put it in front of me and then jumped to the next hill to fool me. But no matter how hard I looked in each direction, the light was gone. I was overcome with hopelessness. I thought about the car, and

285

both my drivers, and the object of our journey—and about my parents in Berlin. The blackest visions overcame me.

"The conditions of being thirsty and tired were having a negative effect on my mind and I could not get rid of the visions and illusions I had about my parents," he continued. Koeppen kept marching, in what he hoped was the direction of Jakechi or the train tracks, or anything indicating human habitation. Eventually, he saw a group of riders silhouetted against the sky. Realizing that they had to be the Cossack rescuers Rittmeister von Albrecht had summoned, he started to call to them. On hearing him, they galloped over.

The riders weren't Cossacks, though. They were six Chunguse horsemen, stocky in build, wearing layers of brown clothing: smocks, vests, capelets, and hoods. They were also heavily armed, as Koeppen could see immediately. He had to assume that they were bandits, and he used bits of Russian and Chinese, along with all of the hand movements he could think of, to indicate that he was a peace-loving wanderer who was lost. Bypassing the fact that they were studying him intently, without seeming to listen to whatever he was saying, he gestured in several different directions and asked for help in finding Jakechi.

"They sort of understood me," Koeppen wrote, "understood what my circumstances were. They made it known to me that they could show me the way, but first they wanted money. Because I was in a bind, I agreed to let them take me [to Jakechi]. Then their demeanor changed and the situation became critical. They gathered around me. I was very careful not to turn my back. I had a few thousand ruble with me and they would have had a field-day with me, had they known."

The bandits, no longer listening to anything that Koeppen said, took small steps toward him. They were trying to encircle him, but he kept backing away or skipping sideways. There were, however, six of them, and the odds were in their favor. It was 2 A.M. in a vacant section of a nearly empty land. The closest people were miles away. The Chunguse could do anything they liked. They knew it and Koeppen certainly did, too.

"With no time to hesitate," he wrote, "I jumped backward, pulled out my revolver and fired several shots into the air, fully resolved to put the next bullets into one of the bandits. It was all a surprise to them: the revolver under my coat and the sudden shots I got off." The bandits scrambled onto their horses, despite the fact that they each had rifles of their own. They left in a hurry, apparently uninterested in losing two or three men in order to rob just one.

Had they known how much money Koeppen was carrying, they might have reconsidered the equation.

Koeppen reloaded his gun and kept walking. Two hours later, he saw a red light in the distance and ran toward it, afraid it would disappear. He didn't stop running until he opened the door of Jakechi station. Entering it, he said later, was one of the happiest moments of his life.

The night manager came out to look. He had never known the sight of Jakechi station to fill anyone with so much joy. He greeted Lieutenant Koeppen and brought him tea, and little by little the people in town straightened out the mess that Koeppen and the Protos had fallen into. In the early morning, a detachment of soldiers returned with Koeppen to the car and dragged it out of the stream. After returning to the station, the Protos crew was sitting around a breakfast table when someone spotted another detachment of soldiers riding through town, with Rittmeister von Albrecht among them.

Von Albrecht had been so lost that he ended up at the next post house down the line. Led into Jakechi station, he could only sit in a wooden chair, drinking vodka, smoking cigarettes, and swearing that he would never ride in an automobile again as long as he lived.

During the morning, the stationmaster asked Koeppen for a favor. His sister wanted to ride in the car. And so, when the Protos had been repaired and was ready to leave, she took a place in the back, perched between Koeppen and von Albrecht. She rode along for hours, on the route of Genghis Khan, until they let her off at another station to return home by train.

Chapter Twenty-four

Blue Water

Car	Miles	Place	Team
Protos (Ger.)	13,672	Missawoia, Russia	Koeppen, Fuchs, Neuberger
Thomas Flyer (U.S.)	13,672	Missawoia, Russia	Schuster, Miller, Hansen, MacAdam
Züst (Ita.)	12,337	Harbin, Manchuria	Scarfoglio, Haaga

T he sun was on its way down on the evening of June 14, gathering the last colors of the day over the rivers and ornate churches of Tchita, when the Protos approached from a height to the east. Hans Koeppen appreciated the beauty of the place, along with its romantic history, but he was taking in more than that as he gazed down on Tchita. "The prize was ours," he reflected later.

Winning the $1,000 bonus for reaching Tchita before any of other entrants was Koeppen's first turn at good news since the beginning of the New York-to-Paris Race. For seventeen weeks and four days, his name had been linked with nothing but disappointment and disaster. As of June 14, that changed, and headlines in New York, Paris, and Berlin affirmed that he had finally worked out the mysteries of racing a car around the world. He had the prize to show for it.

Tchita was a pretty city of seventy-three thousand, with a museum devoted to the gold mining, as well as the gold smuggling, for which the region was known. A hundred years earlier in its history, before it gained the amenities of a self-respecting city, it was regarded as a suitable substitute for death, and the czars banished political enemies there. One group of ninety-six high-ranking officials, called the Decembrists (because they staged an unsuccessful coup in December 1825), were sent to Tchita to live out their days. The story of the Decembrists became legendary when the wives of more than a dozen of them gave up lives of luxury to move to Tchita, voluntarily, to be near their husbands; one of the women had lived in a palace in St. Petersburg, where she trod on marble floors that had once been in Nero's forum in Rome. In Tchita, she took up a new life as a peasant, in a hut with a dirt floor.

As Tchita developed, it became the capital of the mountainous Trans-Baikal region, which became a repository for many thousands of political exiles, keeping pace with the revolutionary fervor back in Moscow and St. Petersburg. To reduce any sense of community or camaraderie, political and criminal prisoners were regularly shifted from one work camp to another, marching in lines that were a common backdrop for the road life of the region.

Rittmeister von Albrecht, who had ridden in the Protos most of the way since Vladivostok, left the team in Tchita, where his sister lived. He described the atmosphere in the car as he had known it. "Lieut. Koeppen has displayed the most wonderful vitality on the run," he said in an interview, "and pushed the car to the limit. The Protos stopped at night only long enough for the crew to get three or four hours sleep and was then off again."

In pushing the Protos to remain on the road eighteen or twenty hours each day, Koeppen could rely on Casper Neuberger and Robert Fuchs. They alternated the driving, while he saved his vitality—and mulled over contingencies for the next leg of the trip.

The Thomas car included more men, four altogether, but all of the driving was handled by George Schuster. He also made the decisions and oversaw the maintenance on the car: he was the sole driver, the chief mechanic, and the captain. In each capacity, he struggled through Manchuria and Mongolia to close the gap against Koeppen's team. It wasn't easy.

On the night of the fourteenth, when the Protos arrived in Tchita, Schuster was running three days behind. The next morning, while Koeppen was scribbling a few last telegrams on his way out of Tchita, Schuster pressed forward toward the city, logging one hundred fifty miles in his best day since Vladivostok. He had another three hundred miles to go as he approached the small town of Sryetensk, along the placid Shilka River. As the Thomas made progress on the road, Schuster spotted a caravan different from any he'd seen before, one that told him for certain that he'd crossed over the border into Siberian Russia. "We passed a party of shackled convicts," he wrote, "marching toward Stretensk [Sryetensk] under the guard of a company of soldiers."

Sryetensk had started as a prison camp at the end of the eighteenth century. That was not an unusual provenance for a Siberian town, but it had developed industrially since then and was home to a surprisingly large factory for the manufacture of soap. An army camp of sixty-eight hundred Cossack soldiers also contributed to the local livelihood. An English traveler who passed through in 1900 was ill-impressed, though, describing Sryetensk as "a few old barns stuck anyhow on a humpy wilderness of dust."

Still, Sryetensk looked impossibly big and complicated to the families of the farmers and woodsmen in the district, a great many of whom were in the streets that night. They were milling around and waiting anxiously for a performance by a traveling circus that had arrived that day. The animals, conjurers, and acrobats were waiting, too, in tents along the river, ready to start the performance at the appointed time. The evening was quiet in Sryetensk, except for the chatter of people, with children asking their parents about the circus and gaggles of men pretending they weren't very interested in it, anyway. More kept arriving in anticipation of an exciting show. And they received nothing less, as the unmuffled engine of the Thomas blasted a fanfare that scattered people from the streets even before they set eyes on the car.

In fact, the people of Sryetensk had never set eyes on any car before. Suddenly, one swooped into their midst and when Schuster stopped the Thomas Flyer in the middle of town, it was as though each person there had been slapped by the sight or the sound of it. They reacted differently as people do to a slap, approaching with animation or diffidence, confusion or plain curiosity. The car was a sensation and the street was even more crowded than before. Miller immediately started some minor work on the engine; Captain Hansen asked around for lodging; the people of Sryetensk jammed around the Thomas; and the owner of the circus walked slowly around in the background, tacking up notices that the circus was postponed.

Two days later, Schuster drove over the rise to the east of Tchita and saw the city lying below, but by that time, he was as downcast by the sight as Koeppen had been joyous. Schuster had made up time, but he was still two days behind the German car. No one could fault him for the breakdown near Pogranitchnaya, which cost five days. But the fact remained that the Thomas Flyer, which had never known anything but good news and glory across America, had made the long drop into second place.

During the trip across America, Schuster had watched from the mechanic's seat while others received the credit for the good showing of the car. All the while, he was certain that he could do as well or better behind the wheel and completely in charge, but after three weeks, he wasn't. He wasn't doing better at all and the car was losing.

"The Thomas car in the New York to Paris race arrived here at midnight yesterday," MacAdam wrote in his dispatch from Tchita. "The crew of the car staggered into the hotel, mud covered, hollow-eyed, with drawn faces and completely worn out."

At least Tchita had a hotel, possibly even a decent one. According to Schuster, the roads of Siberia were about the same as those in America, but the accommodations were abysmal—nothing like those downtown hotels in which Monty Roberts could order a thick steak and all the trimmings, even after midnight. And while mealy food and vermin-infested quarters may be regarded as the stuff of manly adventure for a couple of days, they wore on Schuster week after week. The food was not any better for the Germans, but Fuchs and Neuberger were alternating behind the wheel; they weren't pushing themselves to the brink of their limits, as Schuster was, driving every mile of the race himself. With each new day in second place, he could only think of one solution. He had to work even harder.

Schuster saw much more of Tchita than he ever intended, having to wait for six hours for a supply of gasoline that should have been awaiting him at the train station. When he finally left at noon, he was angry and impatient and started a fifty-four-hour run, with only the briefest of stops. Most of them were for rest or for ferry crossings. One was for the sake of a young colt that abandoned his mother to follow the Thomas Flyer. In view of the fact that a Thomas car can't feed a colt, no matter how affectionate he feels toward it, Schuster stopped the car. The four men wrangled the little horse into a makeshift halter and then dragged him back to his mother. He stayed behind, but didn't seem happy about it, in contradiction to all of the other horses and farm animals—and people—who stampeded away at the sight of the car.

During the fifty-four-hour dash from Tchita, Schuster began to give in to exhaustion. The team stopped for lunch at a rustic inn, ordering the same thing they'd had for breakfast that morning and for practically every other meal ordered on the road: hard-boiled eggs, black bread (of which they could only eat the crusts), and tea. Schuster fell asleep twice in the midst of the meal, still holding his food in his hands. A short time later, though, he climbed back in the car, Miller cranked the engine over, and they continued to the west. Schuster gave the road everything he had and on June 19, he arrived in the twin towns of Verkhne-Udinsk, only to learn that he hadn't gained so much as a moment.

"Proud birds were making noise above our heads," Koeppen wrote that same evening, 110 miles ahead, "and wild mountainous scenery seemed to be tumbling down into the water. . . . Before us like in a fairy tale was the mighty Lake Baikal."

Baikal, one of the natural wonders of the world, is the deepest and oldest lake in the world. It is also the cleanest, with water so clear that putting it into even a sanitized glass beaker immediately contaminates it. Much of southern Siberia's topography may be a confusion of overflow, runoff, and swampland, but if so, then Lake Baikal is the redemption of it all, fed by more than three hundred rivers and streams emanating from every direction, bringing pure water to a deep blue bowl.

Among the many people to regard Lake Baikal as the most beautiful place on earth were the ancient Mongols, who called it the "Holy Sea." For centuries, biblical scholars believed that Baikal was the site of the Garden of Eden, and expeditions regularly combed the vicinity for evidence of Adam and Eve. "Like in a real ocean," Koeppen said of his first view of Lake Baikal, "the waves were huge on its broad surface. Far in the background, from high mountains and snow-covered peaks, the sun was just going down and musical streams of light danced on the white and green water-caps, which we observed with speechless amazement from the forest. We just watched this natural wonder in awe."

As a sight to behold, Lake Baikal was hypnotic. As an auto route, it was much less attractive, offering a shoreline jammed with mountains and constantly interrupted by rivers. And yet it had to be reckoned with: the fourth-largest lake in the world in terms of surface area, it lay right in the path of the New York-to-Paris Automobile Race. In shape, Baikal is more or less like a crescent, or a sliver of the moon: 387 miles long and about 50 miles wide. It leans back only slightly from a true north-south line.

When Koeppen first saw Lake Baikal, he was standing just to the east of it, on one of the mountains adjacent to the Selenga River, the biggest of the rivers feeding into the lake. The mouth of the Selenga is located about eighty miles from the southern tip. Even as the sun disappeared behind the mountains across the lake, Koeppen had yet to make a thousand-foot descent to the water. He decided to forgo it until morning, staying in the nearby village of Bojarski.

For once, Koeppen had plenty of time. His plan was to make his way down to the Selenga River, follow the railroad tracks alongside it to the lakeside town of Missawoia, and board the ferry there for the other side of the lake. Monsieur Neuville had advised the teams to use the Missawoia ferry. Driving around the south tip of the lake was out of the question. The terrain was too rugged, a crush of cliffs and mountains.

The Circum-Baikal Railroad, which did curve around the south end of the lake, had been the last section of the Trans-Siberian to open and it was a masterpiece of construction engineering: a line that had to be threaded through forty tunnels and over almost as many bridges. Before the Circum-Baikal was completed in 1903, whole trains were actually loaded onto ships and ferried across the lake, between Missawoia on the east shore and the town of Baikal on the west. The ferries, specially manufactured in England, doubled as icebreakers in the winter. For almost ten years, ferrying the trains was preferred to building a railroad around the wilds of Lake Baikal.

To catch the westbound ferry with time to spare, Koeppen awoke at dawn, with Neuberger and Fuchs. The road leading down to the Selenga was badly neglected and would have been treacherous at night. Even in daylight, the car leaned around saplings sprouting in the roadbed and inched around curves intended for horsecarts. The team arrived in Missawoia early, though, ready to cross on the 8 A.M. ferry.

"Those were our intentions," Koeppen wrote and it would have seemed that nothing could stop them. "As it turned out," he continued, "there was no such thing as that ferry."

The ferry had moved its eastern base about twenty miles south to the town of Tanchoi. That happened back when the Circum-Baikal Railroad opened in 1903. Koeppen's information, courtesy of Monsieur Neuville, was so outdated that it brought hilarity to some of the fishermen relaxing in the sun on the dock. It also brought a bombardment of questions from a state policeman who thought that there was something suspect about a group of Germans in a great hurry to get through Missawoia— in an automobile.

The route to Tanchoi called for the Protos to cross a series of rivers, only some of which had bridges. If the water proved to be shallow, the Protos drove across. If it was slow-moving, Koeppen arranged for a barge to carry it across. But the river at the prosperous lakeside village of Michiha was neither shallow nor slow; it was five feet of water, all in a rush for the lake, and Koeppen had no choice but to request permission to use the railroad bridge, sending a telegram to the Circum-Baikal's district manager in the city of Irkutsk, on the other side of the lake. "The first thing in the morning," he wrote, "we still didn't get a reply to our telegram and after many hours of waiting, still no answer and on the fourth and fifth telegrams, valuable time passed and we were wondering what we should do. In spite of being surrounded with wonderful scenery, with train and telegraph service at hand, we were helpless."

Losing an hour of travel time irked Hans Koeppen. Losing one day after another was infuriating. Trapped in Michiha, he was miserable. And yet, it was Koeppen's particular style of misery. Out of all of the four million square miles of Siberia, he was stranded in a pretty village with all of the amenities of a resort. Other people got stuck in wastelands.

"There was nothing left for us," Koeppen reflected in Michiha, "but to balance our anger with the people against the beautiful nature that surrounded us. We kept ourselves busy by mountain-climbing along the shoreline, taking note of wonderful trees and plants all around us. In the afternoon, we refreshed ourselves in the sunshine with a swim in the lake."

One hundred miles to the east, the sun made for scorching temperatures as Schuster drove the Thomas Flyer through the mountains leading to Lake Baikal. The road twisted into curves and climbed steep inclines, but at least it was dry and Schuster could make good time.

For centuries, the region had been occupied by the Buryats, whose existence revolved around the animals they raised: reindeer, sheep, horses, goats, camels, and cattle. Until the advent of the Trans-Siberian, the Buryats had been isolated in their huge chunk of Siberia, and their way of life had changed very little through the centuries. Compared with the Manchurians or even the Mongols, they weren't very sophisticated; as many travelers pointed out, visiting Buryat territory in the Trans-Baikal was distinctly a step back in time: a hundred years, or five hundred, or a thousand. The herds didn't keep track of the years; the Buryats didn't, either. Their villages were made up of unpainted wooden buildings, brightened by white windows and shutters. Some of the villages were enclosed for the sake of grazing animals, with gates at either end leading to the main thoroughfare.

"Villagers frequently run into their houses," MacAdam reported, "but then gather at the windows and doors to watch us pass." At one village, though, the greeting was more aggressive. The gate was slammed shut and it stayed that way no matter how much Schuster honked the horn and shouted. That only succeeded in summoning dozens of curious locals. When Captain Hansen got out to make inquiries, the gatekeeper appeared out of the confusion and said that he was under direct orders to keep the gate shut and, what is more, to detain the automobilists. Hansen started to ask why and then he heard Schuster shouting from the car that they didn't have time to argue. Hansen pushed past the gatekeeper and started tugging at the wooden gate, which looked flimsy enough to crumble in his hands. But it didn't. The gatekeeper, for his part, started tugging at Hansen.

Schuster leapt from the car with the vigor of a man finally faced with the personification of a month's worth of frustrations on the road in Asia. Joining the fracas, he wrestled the gatekeeper away from the entry. The villagers had been fascinated with the car until the start of the fight, which proved even more entertaining. MacAdam, meanwhile, crept around the scuffle and slipped through the rails of the fence. From the other side, the gate opened with a quick shove and as soon as George Miller saw the doors swing open, he jumped into the driver's seat, put the Thomas in gear, and punched it through. He only barely slowed down as MacAdam scrambled in. Hansen and Schuster weren't far behind.

By the time the sun went down, the Thomas was on the heights overlooking the Selenga, not far from the spot where Koeppen had stopped for the night exactly two days before. Schuster didn't have the luxury of a choice, though. He ignored warnings about the condition of the road and started down, trying to steer around the ruts and the fallen trees without drifting off the side and down a cliff. At all costs, he kept the car moving. It was worth risking disaster to reach Missawoia in time for the 8 A.M. ferry.

A couple of towns south in Michiha, Lieutenant Koeppen had devoted the whole day to waiting for clearance to use the railroad bridge. As of early evening, when word finally came through from Irkutsk, he had been waiting for thirty-six hours. He tore open the telegram, lest he waste another couple of seconds on Michiha. Permission was denied.

More telegrams followed, and the regional manager finally made a concession: Koeppen could load the car onto a railroad car leaving Michiha for the short journey (on the Circum-Baikal rail) to Tanchoi. It wasn't the most generous offer ever proffered, since trains are made for carrying freight, after all, but with clearances from his office, it would at least see the Protos through to Tanchoi. Koeppen immediately set out to put his car on a train, but soon learned something new about Michiha: the loading facilities at the village station wouldn't accommodate a three-ton automobile. At that point, it was time for Koeppen to leave the charming but hopeless village of Michiha.

For more than twenty hours, George Schuster had been driving the

Thomas with less and less feeling in his arms. Steering it was heavy work, even on decent roads and straightaways, but to handle it with pinpoint accuracy on an overgrown path, dizzied by ruts, was more akin to grappling than driving in the normal sense. The brute strength required made his arms numb on the inside, while the bitter cold of the night did the same from the outside. At dawn, he had his reward and the car rolled into the fishing village of Missawoia. Everyone was asleep, even with the roar of the Thomas shaking the timbers, and most of the streets were deserted. The only soul to be seen was a boy in ragged clothing, a young tramp. Hansen asked for help and the boy climbed nimbly into the car as though he had been riding in the things all his life, guiding Schuster as far as the freight yard, where, as MacAdam wrote in the bluntness of the moment, "we discovered that the freight steamer was a myth."

The freight yard at Missawoia encompassed the train station and the fairly important juncture of the Trans-Siberian Railway, leading to the east (and ending at Vladivostok), and the newer Circum-Baikal line, heading south around the lake. As the sun came up, the station was busy with stevedores, engineers, and a few hollow-eyed passengers. Suddenly Schuster caught sight of a familiar face.

Over on the Circum-Baikal track, Lieutenant Koeppen was standing very straight, considering the hour, watching Neuberger and Fuchs secure the Protos on a flatcar. A few minutes before, they had driven it up a sturdy iron ramp, with help from a half-dozen Russian railroad workers. Schuster drove the Thomas across the yard.

The two cars hadn't been so close since the Thomas pulled the Protos out of the bog hole near Vladivostok. After 1,872 miles through Asia, they were sitting in the same train yard—for all intents and purpose, drawing yet a new starting line. The four men practically spilled out of the Thomas as soon as it stopped. Koeppen gave a friendly greeting, even while Schuster pelted him with questions. The oberlieutenant explained that the only way to get across the lake was on the ferry—from Tanchoi. And the only way to get to Tanchoi was on the railroad—from Missawoia. He, Fuchs, and Neuberger had driven back and forth to Michiha for nothing, but at least they had gotten the Protos back to Missawoia in time to load it on the dawn train, which would put it safely on the morning ferry.

Schuster couldn't load the Thomas Flyer on the same train, because it was leaving in four minutes. Koeppen hopped up onto the flatcar and stood next to his car as the train began to leave. "I'll wait for you in Irkutsk," he promised.

Chapter Twenty-five
Flash Flood

Car	Miles	Place	Team
Protos (Ger.)	13,672	*in transit on Lake Baikal, Russia*	Koeppen, Fuchs, Neuberger
Thomas Flyer (U.S.)	13,672	Missawoia, Russia	Schuster, Miller, Hansen, MacAdam
Züst (Ita.)	12,337	Harbin, Manchuria	Scarfoglio, Haaga

A new starting line was drawn by the encounter in the gray light of the Missawoia freight yard, but Antonio Scarfoglio and Henry Haaga were nowhere near it. They were still four hundred fifty miles to the east. And yet, they and the Züst were still in the race. After leaving Vladivostok, with an interpreter tucked into the back with the baggage, they had discovered all of the same mud and most of the bog holes that had captured the Protos and Thomas Flyer almost three weeks before. Driving all day and most of each night, they took pride in the fact that they were making better time than Schuster had over the same distance. Not long before midnight, a well-meaning Russian called out to them to stop, but Scarfoglio had the interpreter reply that they couldn't pause for an instant, that "the Americans were still ahead of us by too many days."

As Scarfoglio drove along through Russia's wilderness, he disdained the Americans and the Germans for resorting to the train tracks. His consolation for trailing the others was that he and Haaga had run an honest race throughout, being the only ones who had kept to the road. After receiving a hearty welcome from the soldiers in Nikolsk, Scarfoglio and Haaga set off gamely to the northwest. That same stretch had changed Schuster's mind about the ethics of rail travel, and conditions there had only deteriorated since the Thomas made its desperate U-turn. The water was even deeper, because the Ussuri River had finally broken past its banks and through the dikes that were supposed to control it. The Züst was forced to inch its way along in well over two feet of water. "We navigate, as it were, in the midst of a flooded plain," Scarfoglio explained. "The water reaches up to our springs and it is necessary to proceed at a walking pace so as not to give the magneto a bath. And the perils are increased by the fact that the road is absolutely invisible beneath the flood."

With one man walking ahead through the chilly water, testing for holes, the Züst kept moving, but not fast enough to reach a town before midnight, not when the rain was still falling and the water still rising. "At two o'clock," Scarfoglio wrote, "the rain ceases and a great reddish moon breaks through the clouds. As far as the eye can reach a vast waveless ocean extends. It is opaque and calm, inhabited by a strange population of skeleton trees. . . ." When the water crept to within an inch of the magneto, at about three-thirty in the morning, Haaga stopped the engine. He removed both the magneto and the carburetor in an effort to keep them dry.

The bloated bodies of drowned animals collected around the car, pushed into dead herds by the breeze. And the water was still rising. It lapped over the fenders, the hood, and even up to the boxes and suitcases. The interpreter felt a panic rising with equal insistence in his heart. He wanted to leave and escape to some village where he would be safe and warm, but when he put his leg in the water, he was poked hard in the thigh by the horn of a dead bull. With a nervous jump, he retreated to the car, even as the water kept moving in a tide, higher and higher, to cover the seats. All three men moved to the storage box at the very back of the Züst and perched there, watching the waterline nibble at the dashboard.

The interpreter was shaking with terror, not so much of drowning or of dying, but of something he'd never even thought about before, of sitting on a storage box in the back of an Italian luxury car in a Siberian flood, trapped by a herd of dead animals and two foreign autoists casually chatting about the irony of having no water in Death Valley and too much of it in the Ussuri Valley. It was the unknown and it was everywhere. The interpreter was bawling.

His choking sobs were the only sound to be heard any distance from the car, as the floodplain continued to swell, showing every sign of becoming a true lake. Scarfoglio realized that the time had come to make another plan.

The men prepared to swim away in three different directions to look for help, stripping off most of their clothes, so that they wouldn't be weighed down. The dark water, seeming to lead nowhere under a dull night sky, offered the only exit. It wasn't an appealing one, with only dead animals and broken tree branches beckoning them into the murk. Having decided to go, they agreed on a specific time: if the water didn't start to recede by that specific time, then they would dive in.

When the specific time arrived, they agreed to give the water another chance, postponing the call to abandon car. Another "solemn moment," as Scarfoglio called it, came and went. The men found another reason to remain on the car. Finally, at about five o'clock in the morning, the water stopped rising. It didn't move at all for a long and well-studied moment. Then it started to recede.

Once the engine was dry, with the parts bolted on again, Haaga turned the crank and the Züst started up. The world made sense again, the car taking the men through a few inches of water to the village of Grodekovo, where most of the populace had been up all night, awaiting them and worrying.

"They regard us as raving madmen," Scarfoglio wrote, not without pride.

After nearly drowning on the open road, Scarfoglio and Haaga felt differently about the railroad track and they began to use it, even though it meant taking a train official along as a passenger. When they finally left the tracks behind, the team had a remarkably easy trip through Manchuria. "We have been racing as if on a real motor track," Scarfoglio beamed. "Richly violet in color, beautiful irises cover the marvelous landscape. It is like traveling on polished crystal." He delighted in the pagoda architecture of Manchuria, the Buddhist shrines by the roadside, and the way that Chinese culture was at once ancient and intent on constant improvement. Among the very few annoyances, for a man normally buffeted by them, was that people warned him at every turn about the Chunguse bandits. He only scoffed in reply, complaining that he had

303

yet to see a horde of twenty thousand coming for him, out for blood and intent on throwing him in a pit with a floor of knife blades.

Though he roundly deserved to, Scarfoglio never did meet a bandit.

Almost one thousand miles to the east, Lieutenant Koeppen had a calm ferry ride across Lake Baikal on the morning of June 21. The lake was known for its sudden storms, and an old saying held that "it is only upon Baikal in autumn that a man learns to pray from his heart." But in that particular late June, Koeppen was more inspired than intimidated, marveling at the mountain panorama that surrounded the water, every glance giving too much for any one eyeful. That the mountains and the lake were exaggerated in size was something one might get used to, but that the colors were just as large, and exaggerated too, whether somber or bright, kept even regular riders on deck. After two hours, the Protos was on dry land again, on its way to the city of Irkutsk, forty-four miles up the Angara, which is the only river to flow out of the lake.

Irkutsk was founded in 1652—only nine years after Lake Baikal was discovered by European Russians. From the first, it was distinctly a European outpost, with the strong presence of Roman Catholic, Greek Orthodox, and Lutheran churches. It was growing fast as of 1908, having more than doubled in population since 1897. With just over a hundred thousand residents, Irkutsk was by far the biggest city that the New York-to-Paris entrants had seen since starting across the Asian mainland. A gateway to the Siberian east, it enjoyed an enticing split personality, with an aspiring sense of society at the core and a rapacious frontier hunger on the fringe.

Lieutenant Koeppen arrived in Irkutsk on Sunday afternoon, June 21, with a long list of errands. He planned to stay over at least one night, but the next day he had to decide whether to wait for George Schuster, as promised—or not. "It was a crucial choice," Koeppen wrote, "because his more powerful machine was able to take the lead we had away from us." He seemed already to have made up his mind.

"From this point on, the real race was beginning," he told himself.

Chapter Twenty-six

Out in Front

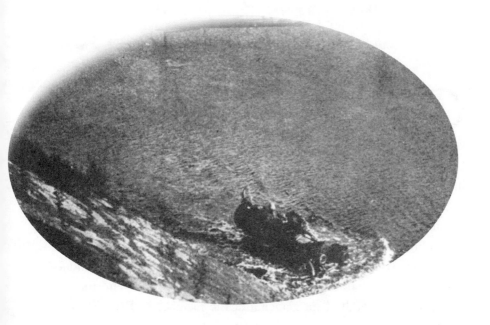

Car	Miles	Place	Team
Thomas Flyer (U.S.)	15,208	Omsk, Russia	Schuster, Miller, Hansen, MacAdam
Protos (Ger.)	14,974	Kainsk, Russia	Koeppen, Fuchs, Neuberger
Züst (Ita.)	13,220	near Tchita, Russia	Scarfoglio, Haaga

O n any hot afternoon in June, the best place to be in Irkutsk was under a shady tree along the Angara River, and from that very perspective, a long line of fashionably dressed picnickers waved straw hats and handkerchiefs as the Thomas Flyer left the city on June 21. The American car was already more than a half day behind the Protos, since Lieutenant Koeppen had given in to the urge to skip town and leave his competitors far behind.

The new starting line wasn't to be in Irkutsk, after all. It had indeed been drawn at the train station in Missawoia. As George Schuster sped away from Irkutsk, he kept glancing at the picnickers along the riverbank, people who were carefree, clean, and well fed—none of which Schuster had been in months. He started to think about Cazenovia Park, where Buffalonians would go to ease themselves through just such a summer Sunday. He couldn't deny that he was tempted to stop the car and reenter the world of Sunday afternoons again. All of the men in the Thomas Flyer were quiet, seeing the picnickers wave and then return to their little tables or their blankets.

The Thomas and the Protos, with its fifty-mile lead, were about a third of the way across Russia. Before them lay the Ob River and its myriad tributaries, the decisive north-south line of the Ural Mountains, and the hilly farmland of European Russia. But before all of that, the cars had to cross the plains of western Siberia. The word most commonly attached to those plains by travelers was "endless." What western

Siberia offered in such rare abundance was monotony, one thousand miles of it. For a land traveler, the grasslands barely changed in either terrain or texture for weeks on end. That was a long time to be trapped with the same thoughts and responses to the exact same sights, like some piece of machinery caught but still moving.

Western Siberia started to prey on both teams, as the Germans grew depressed and heartsick, despite being in the lead. The Americans were more irritable than morose, perhaps because they were in second place.

George Schuster, behind the wheel, was delighted by one aspect of the region: he was finally on a road with signposts. They were not much more than thickset poles painted in black-and-white stripes, but whenever Schuster saw one, he knew he was on the right road to Moscow. The posts were fifty years old or more, remnants of the legendary Tea Route. What the signs meant to him was that he didn't have to rely entirely on Captain Hansen for directions anymore. Hansen had chosen a wrong turn on the way to Tchita that cost the team four hours. Schuster had never been certain about him after that.

Hansen, for his part, wasn't too certain about Schuster, either. He and MacAdam watched Schuster persevere day after day on the very brink of exhaustion. And they were tired of it. According to MacAdam's assessment, Schuster's heroics were Hans Koeppen's greatest asset:

On the Thomas car George Schuster, who took charge of the auto at San Francisco, has been driving exclusively on the journey through Asia. The strain of the actual work at the wheel and the vigilance necessary to escape danger, combined with the lack of rest and good food, has so worn upon him that he falls asleep whenever possible, often at the banks of rivers while waiting for the ferries. The strain, taken in connection with the number of narrow escapes the Thomas crew has had, has apparently affected even Schuster's strong nerves.

In the "grim silence of the Thomas," as MacAdam described it, the thinking was that Schuster was so tired, "he has been afraid to get the speed out of the Thomas that would put it on even terms with the Germans." Driving late into the stretched-out days of Siberian summer, everyone in the Thomas was hoping to catch Koeppen, but on all other points they disagreed. Making a good run two days out of Irkutsk on the way to a city called Kansk, Schuster felt as though he were on the verge of collapse. As soon as he could, he pulled up at a village to find lodging. The others protested. With good weather and decent roads, the thing to do was press on, so they said, but Schuster replied that he had to sleep. Someone else could have taken over the driving for a while, but Schuster said no. He just needed a little sleep.

The next day, the Thomas team learned that Koeppen had opened up his lead and the Protos was fully twenty-four hours ahead. Schuster couldn't do much more than he was already doing, but with renewed intensity, he threw himself into the driving, edging the speed up as far as he could. There was no advantage to going too fast and causing a skid or an accident, especially in the empty plains of the Irkutsk region.

Practically any mishap would cost half a day, just to locate help. Schuster was caught between the inclination to speed up and the determination not to skid, but the more he thought about the latter—the more he thought about his driving at all—the slower the car seemed to go. He was too tired to drive without thinking, the way he always had before. Finally, he was too tired to drive at all.

"In the evening," MacAdam wrote, "weariness for the first time compelled Schuster to give up the wheel, and Miller had his chance to show what he could do. The good Thomas car immediately took on new life, proving that despite all the troubles it had met with in its journey across America and Asia, it still had its old vitality."

There was jubilation in the backseat. "Capt. Hansen and *The Times* correspondent," wrote MacAdam, speaking of himself in the third person, "felt that they were really in an automobile race, and the weariness of the grind lifted."

Schuster's situation was not quite so simple. "Half an hour later," MacAdam wrote, "the fascination of driving proved too much for Schuster, and he again took the wheel. Soon the car was lagging, as it had been, and the prospect of catching the Protos grew dimmer."

Schuster's valiant and pathetic, utterly stubborn insistence on driving didn't do much to restore pleasantness to the Thomas team. Conditions couldn't have been much worse, except that it was just then that the car arrived in mosquito country. "The air was thick with mosquitoes and gnats," Schuster wrote. "Even with our faces and arms covered with netting, they seemed able to get inside of that and torment us." They went straight for eyes, ears, noses, and even mouths.

Chasing the Protos toward the city of Kansk, the Thomas generally had little trouble with the road on the smooth plain. In a small village next to a river, the Flyer was loaded without much trouble onto a ferry—little more than a small barge, actually, guided by ropes. Once the car was loaded, a few onlookers from the village hopped aboard, just for the privilege of riding across the river with the car. A few more followed and by the time the ferry finally pushed off, half of the population (by one estimate) was crowded onto the ferry with the New York-to-Paris racer. It was a proud moment for almost everyone, until midway across the water, the whole thing sank into a yard and a half of water. With no less enthusiasm, the villagers swam to shore, fetched ropes, and pulled the car to dry land.

Further to the west by about a day, the commandant of a local road-house stood in his main room, vociferously refusing to give the members of the Thomas team a place to sleep, when the place started to crowd with local residents who wanted a look at the quartet of automobilists. Hansen started to argue with the commander, but it was Schuster who solved the whole problem by falling sound asleep on a bench, even as the argument raged. With the issue suddenly settled, Hansen stopped arguing, looked around, and let barely another minute pass before starting in on the story of the race, telling it like an old-time minstrel, "to the villagers, who sat with wide-open eyes listening intently and hardly knowing whether to believe all the wonders he related." He had the same effect on people who listened to his stories in Paris and Manhattan.

The conflicts within the team didn't go away as easily. In a small city in the midst of the plains, the team finally disintegrated. The strains of the previous few weeks had escalated and became unbearable. With Schuster's hearty approval, Captain Hansen decided to take the train to his home in Tomsk, four hundred fifty miles west, to visit his wife and daughter. MacAdam also dropped out temporarily, noting that the jarring of the road had been no easier on his intestines than it had been on the Thomas's transmission. He needed to recuperate. Both men promised to connect with the car farther along, but by then, Schuster didn't much care whether they did or not.

Oddly enough, once Hansen and MacAdam were out of the car, Schuster changed his mind about the driving. He decided to alternate with Miller. They even rigged up a seat belt so that one could sleep, while the other drove. Schuster had decided to keep the car moving night and day until he caught up to Koeppen—and on reaching the large city of Tomsk, he knew he was getting close. Tomsk, about the same size as Irkutsk, was home to the only university in Siberia, along with its oldest public library. The city was burnished with something of a cosmopolitan air, which contrasted sharply with the pale of oblivion that clapped around most of the towns and villages in Siberia. Hansen and MacAdam were waiting in Tomsk to rejoin the Flyer, and they met Schuster with the exciting news that the Protos was only a few hours ahead.

Koeppen was taking the same Tea Route west to Moscow as Schuster, and he had been enjoying the same fairly smooth ride, but the battering of the railroad ties earlier in the trip had taken a toll on the Protos. The differential gear had wobbled loose, making it practically impossible to handle the car. Miraculously, Neuberger managed to secure the gear again with pins that he fashioned on the roadside, but it eventually wriggled free of them. Five times, the pins fell out, and five times Neuberger crafted new ones into place. "We crept dejectedly and carefully on to Kainsk," Koeppen wrote, "when, 60 versts [about 40 miles] from there, in the small village of Kolnokowo, our interpreter, Mr. Konnenberg, who was sitting backward, drew our attention to an object in the distance, which seemed to be advancing fast. We turned and as if on command, the words escaped our lips: 'The Americans!'"

"To keep our car running was no small effort," Koeppen lamented. "To see our competitors getting closer and closer was a situation that rubbed our nerves almost too far. But now they were nearly with us. Nervously, Neuberger sped up, in order not to let them get ahead."

Neuberger couldn't push the car too much, in case the differential fell apart again. But he stayed ahead of the Thomas for a good fifteen minutes.

Schuster was steadily catching up, driving the Thomas faster than any vehicle had ever gone before on the Tea Route. That included the ailing Protos. "Finally," MacAdam wrote, "the American machine poked its nose right up against the German's gasoline tank."

Neuberger had no choice but to pull over and let Schuster pass. Koeppen later said that the differential loosened again at that moment and forced the decision to end the drag race on the Tea Route. In any case, it was over. "As the Thomas flew by," MacAdam wrote, "a great shout burst involuntarily from the throats of the four men in unison. The Germans responded with the best of feeling, waving their hats and cheering."

Koeppen didn't remember his response in quite the same way. In fact, he barely remembered it at all.

"I was at a loss whether or not to answer. I wanted to do nothing," he wrote. "We smiled and probably nodded. In reality, for us, crying was closer. . . ."

Koeppen couldn't expect to get all the way to Paris with rudimentary pins holding the differential gear together. As a matter of fact, he couldn't even get to the major city of Omsk, which was five thousand miles closer. On the way there, the rear axle failed completely and the Protos had to be towed by horses all the way back to Kainsk. Neuberger and Fuchs devoted a day to making the best repair they could, while Koeppen ordered a new rear axle, specifying delivery to Omsk. He felt certain that the car could make it to Omsk and meet the part there.

The Protos had other mechanical problems, as well, though, and it needed other spare parts. Instead of waiting around, Koeppen decided to take the train ahead, past Omsk to a city called Ekaterinburg, in order to look for the parts he had shipped there from Vladivostok. "Our chances appeared to be zero," Koeppen wrote. That being the case, leaving was the only productive move he could think of. As he departed Kainsk on the train, he was aware that the Thomas Flyer had taken a one-day lead that was likely to grow.

Neuberger and Fuchs stayed behind with the car and managed to get it operating again, but not as a racer. It moved more like a person just off crutches, very carefully and deliberately. Everything depended on nursing it along as far as Omsk—where a new axle might or might not be waiting by the time the car arrived.

On June 30, when Schuster arrived in Omsk, he was gliding along three days ahead of Koeppen. He immediately set out to locate the transmission that had been sent with such care—and expense—from Buffalo. But it wasn't at the train station. In fact, it was nowhere to be found.

Omsk, a city populated largely by Moslem Tartars, was centered around the headquarters of the Fourth Siberian Army. As the biggest city in Siberia, it had a certain swirl. At least, MacAdam thought so after he came upon an English-language newspaper, the first one he'd seen in more than two months, and caught up with the American headlines. William Howard Taft had received the Republican nomination for president. William Jennings Bryan, hero of the state convention in Nebraska (among many others), was on the verge of the Democratic nomination. For the time being, Theodore Roosevelt was still the president of the United States, but after almost two full terms, he had opted not to stand again. Unfortunately, the paper didn't contain the only news that really interested the Americans in the New York-to-Paris Race: the location of Lieutenant Koeppen and the German Protos.

Because no one had heard anything from the Protos in a while, the conviction took hold, on the Thomas team at least, that Koeppen had found a way to sneak into the lead and was miles or even days ahead. Anxiety woke Schuster up at 4 A.M. and prodded him to depart from Omsk. He had been desperate for so long that even his most intrinsic characteristic, the chill of his rational mind, was going into unchartered territory, just as the car itself was. The roads were generally good ahead, but there were still hazards, including a mile-wide swamp on the far side of the Irtish River, thirty miles west of Omsk.

As the ferrymen explained while they were taking the Thomas Flyer across the river, the road beyond was elevated well above the swamp, but rain had made it soft and slick. Road workers had placed a thick layer of straw, almost like matting, over the surface to provide traction for wagon traffic. Whether it would support a ton-and-a-half automobile, though, no one could say. The ferrymen were doubtful. Schuster went ahead, determined that slow and careful driving would see the Flyer across. He was almost right. The car was just about to leave the swamp when the straw caved in under one of the rear wheels. The Flyer abruptly slipped toward the edge of the road and it was heading into the murk. Schuster wouldn't let it go, fighting the pull of the swamp with the power of the Thomas six-cylinder engine. "As I tried to force the car through," Schuster wrote, "there came a *crack, crack* of stripped gears."

Forty people—men, women, and even little children—answered the call for help, hauling the Thomas out of the swamp and into the yard of a blacksmith shop in the nearby village of Marianovka. Dressed in caftans and leggings, belted tunics and bright scarves, they would have made a colorful picture postcard of tradition on the steppes, except that the rite in which they were engaged was the brand-new one of dragging a six-cylinder roadster out of a pond. The Thomas Flyer was no joke, though. It retained its dignity, even while it was being inched home by kids and grandmothers and everyone in between. It may have been a wounded soldier, but the Flyer was still a soldier, with its sturdy posture and an array of tools and necessities hanging from every hook. Schuster and Miller started their examination by throwing buckets of water at the undercarriage to wash the mud off. Then they took a look underneath. "We found several teeth of the driving pinion broken off and many others badly worn," Schuster explained.

Before an hour was up, Schuster was on the road again, but he wasn't going toward Paris. He was headed east, back to Omsk, and there was no engine in his ears. He was sitting glumly in a horse-drawn *telega* wagon, listening to the oversized wheels groan and grind their way slowly over the road.

The only object of Schuster's mission was the spare transmission, but once in Omsk, he still couldn't locate it. He sent telegrams to every freight office and stationmaster who could possibly have seen the hefty package, handled it, or received it erroneously. No one knew anything about it.

The only working Thomas Flyer transmission in the Eastern Hemisphere was lost. Schuster couldn't order another one from Buffalo, and he couldn't return to Marianovka without a replacement. For more than a day, he badgered railroad officials, all the while certain that his own chances were down to zero. Every time he felt that way, he sent more telegrams. Then, finally, he heard some encouraging news. The Germans were still behind.

The Protos had only just arrived in Omsk. It hadn't been secretly in the lead, after all—it had been limping along for the past three days on the road from Kainsk. Neuberger and Fuchs had finally succeeded in bringing it in.

The postal service in Omsk worked much better for the Protos than it had for the Flyer. Neuberger picked up the spare rear axle that Koeppen had ordered, putting an end to the nagging problems with the differential once and for all. The German car was in a position to start again, leaving Schuster to riding in *telegas*. Its superiority didn't last long, though.

In Ekaterinburg, Lieutenant Koeppen learned by telegram that the Protos wasn't going to leave Omsk after all, not at any time in the near future. Mechanically, it still had problems, some of them left over from the trip across America and the dubious repairs made by the earlier drivers, but Koeppen had lived with that sort of thing for most of the previous five months. There was something even more troubling. "Neuberger became ill with malaria," Koeppen wrote, "and Fuchs had an intestinal fever. The strain that was put on us in the last few days since Irkutsk, since we didn't get much sleep and we were hungry, the onslaught of the mosquitoes—and we also suffered from depression, which must have contributed to their being sick."

Lieutenant Koeppen had no choice but to wait in Ekaterinburg for them to recuperate.

Schuster was waiting for news of his lost transmission in Omsk. On the evening of July 3, for all of the hurry and rush that had surrounded both cars since Vladivostok, no engines roared and neither car was budging. On July 4, though, the American team had a little holiday—not in honor of Thomas Jefferson and 1776, but because of a more immediate patriot, George Miller, who fixed the Thomas Flyer running gear, using a few homemade rods in place of the missing teeth. Schuster heard the news when a horseman, just arriving from Marianovka, dropped off a note at his hotel. As fast as the fastest *telega* would go, he returned to the blacksmith shop.

At the same time, Koeppen's stay in Ekaterinburg dragged on and turned into, of all things, a vacation, complete with sightseeing. The town, as he learned, was named after Catherine ("Katerin") the Great, and it had a certain dash, as a center for trade in precious stones. Koeppen even visited the nearby town of Tjumen, through which more than one million exiles had passed on their way to various destinations in Siberia. In the story of the effort to populate Siberia, Tjumen was a shadowy version of Ellis Island. One day, Koeppen visited a horse market on the outskirts of Ekaterinburg, where Tartar and Kirgise plainsmen sold horses that they had gathered from the wild. "I watched as one farmer bought a Kirgesan horse and tied it to the end of his wagon," Koeppen reflected, "but the horse reared and threw itself down and broke its halter. It refused to be parted from his herd. It took about two hours to make it take one step."

While Koeppen was watching the horses, Schuster was on the road in the repaired Flyer, heading fast toward Ekaterinburg. "My patience was tested as the Thomas passed through on July 7," Koeppen wrote. He and Schuster met at the hotel where Koeppen was staying.

There was no animosity or resentment of past actions, such as Koeppen's quick exit from Irkutsk after promising to wait. On the contrary, by that point, Schuster was more comfortable with Koeppen than with the people riding in his own car. Koeppen was a nice fellow, much too polite to show that his patience was nearly broken by Schuster's appearance in Ekaterinburg. The two of them had dinner together, conversing amiably in German. "If the Protos arrives in Paris a week after you, it will be no disgrace," Koeppen remarked, "considering what we have gone through."

The cars were still only days apart, despite the Protos's problems, and by all estimates they were only a few weeks from Paris. The Thomas Flyer still had the advantage of its asterisk, its one-month allowance over the Protos. Technically, it could win the race, even if the Protos arrived in Paris twenty-nine days earlier. In that sense, the Flyer's position looked good. But the race had been honed, in the reality of the road, to Koeppen versus Schuster. All talk aside, each of them had to be ready to win, and likewise, ready to lose.

On that very point, the Thomas factory was trying to contact Schuster, but the telegram from Buffalo somehow missed him at the hotel in Ekaterinburg. While Schuster was listening to Koeppen's tale of temporary repairs on the Protos axle, he was still thinking about the Flyer's transmission. The whole car was no stronger than its ersatz gearing and those substitute teeth that Miller had fashioned at the smithy. Taking Koeppen's tale of woe as a warning, Schuster assigned Captain Hansen to go by rail as far as Moscow in search of the lost transmission, telling him to stop at nearly every station along the way to make inquiries. Schuster also contacted Monsieur Neuville and hired him to do the same on a more southerly branch of the railroad.

Without Captain Hansen, the car did not have a translator, but Schuster was certain that his German would suffice as the car drew nearer to Europe and the pronounced German influence in Russia grew stronger. Bidding good-bye to Hans Koeppen—and fervently hoping he didn't see him again until Paris—Schuster left Ekaterinburg with the abbreviated team he called the "Three Georges," himself, George Miller, and George MacAdam.

The next day, back in Omsk, Casper Neuberger felt well enough to set out in the Protos. Robert Fuchs decided that he was ready, too. They made a few more repairs on the car and then, heroically, climbed into the car with all of its discomforts and quirks and pulled out onto the road west again. Neither Neuberger nor Fuchs had to do it, after all. Many men in perfect health had turned away from the road west over the course of the New York-to-Paris Race. Three days later, though, they picked up Lieutenant Koeppen and his new translator in Ekaterinburg. Then they set off across the Ural Mountains for Moscow, nine hundred miles away, hoping to reach one of the major cities along the way each day: Perm, capital of the mountain region; Kasan, a trading city famous for leather; and Nizhni Novgorod, an industrial city rich in eight hundred years of history.

Schuster, a day ahead on the same route, was relieved to discover that the Urals look much worse on a map than in real life. Although they form a distinct border between Asia and Europe within Russia, they are actually more like hills than mountains. And the route to Perm offered one of the easiest crossings, with wide, well-graded roads, steep in places but never unmanageable. Veering north to Perm, however, meant leaving the route of the Trans-Siberian Railway, which led right to Moscow. Perm was on a parallel line, leading to St. Petersburg. Both Schuster and Koeppen intended to veer right back south after leaving Perm and pick up the main track again well before Kasan. For at least a few days, though, they would be separated from the railroad that had become a veritable lifeline.

The mountains may have been kind to Schuster, but the weather was not. He was no sooner back in farmland east of the Urals than it started to storm. MacAdam and Miller argued for stopping, but Schuster shouted them down. "As long as the wheels will turn, I'm going to drive this car," he insisted.

"Both men and machine were in bad shape," Schuster admitted. "The gears growled as we rolled along in low. Lack of sleep, irregular meals, and strange food made us irritable. I had not heard from my family since Seattle, but a letter from Miller's fiancée, Miss Margaret Reilly, caught up with us. She said the Buffalo newspapers were writing about me but rarely mentioning him. Miller, usually a placid fellow, complained, 'You are getting all the credit.' "

Schuster knew it, even without seeing the papers. He was an expert on the subject of celebrity as it related to the New York-to-Paris Race, having been in Miller's place during the drive across America. But he had learned early on how the race worked, and he'd staked out his territory. The Thomas Flyer wasn't just his car, it was his turn in the limelight. Nonetheless, he told Miller he'd try to make amends somehow. He wouldn't even have made the offer for anyone but Miller.

Perm was a town of myriad government offices and one good hotel, but even so, Schuster had no intention of staying over. Arriving at midday, he immediately stopped at the telegraph office to pick up his messages, one of which was from Monsieur Neuville. The transmission had been found, which was good, but it was in Kasan, which was very bad. If Schuster had chosen the standard route, he would have run smack into it, on his way through Kasan. As it was, there was no direct train service between Kasan and Perm, and so the transmission was as far from reach as ever. Schuster sent a reply to Monsieur Neuville, telling him to remain in Kasan guarding that spare. Schuster wasn't yet sure where he could intercept it. The whole situation was a fiasco of the type he'd seen too often, demanding that he find the way to turn the world from its stubborn course, mechanically, strategically, diplomatically, or all of them at once. Somehow, he was expected to find a way. He turned to the second telegram. It was from the Thomas factory in Buffalo—from E. R. Thomas, himself, in fact. Schuster read it only once:

"Do you want us to send Montague Roberts to help you when you get on the good roads of Europe?"

Chapter Twenty-seven

The Favor of the Czar

Car	Miles	Place	Team
Protos (Ger.)	18,468	Moscow	Koeppen, Fuchs, Neuberger
Thomas Flyer (U.S.)	17,849	Kasan, Russia	Schuster, Miller, MacAdam
Züst (Ita.)	15,185	Atchinsk, Russia	Scarfoglio, Haaga

Schuster stopped the Thomas Flyer in front of the telegraph office at Obansk, twenty miles to the west of Perm. The operator, who understood German, helped him send a reply to E. R. Thomas: "July 9: Arrived today. Expect to reach Paris on July 24. Schuster."

Schuster was so mad he could have "eaten nails," as he put it. E. R. perceived as much, when he was finished reading all twelve words in the telegram. To Schuster, the suggestion that he was good enough to take the car through the bogs of Siberia but not through the capitals of Europe epitomized the course of his career. It was also the very reason he kept driving on toward Paris, with nerves he could barely feel and limbs he could hardly move. Having sent his telegram, Schuster took a drink of cognac from a bottle he carried on the car and got on with the race.

Even with Miller's repair, the Flyer only drove reliably in the low gears. That was a constant concern, but Schuster was heartened by the fact that he was running at least a day ahead of Koeppen. And the roads were getting better the farther west he drove in Russia. The countryside was more thickly populated, too, and the people less retiring.

To MacAdam, it came as a relief to be among the European Russians— "People," as he described it, "whose faces indicated that they took just a little more than a passing interest in life." That was supposed to be a reflection on the Siberians he'd come to know. MacAdam would get his comeuppance, though, for slighting Asiatic Russians; before too long, he would find out what his friends, the European Russians, thought of automobilists.

MacAdam wasn't the only one taking note of the different types of Russians. Even Hans Koeppen, normally loath to make disparaging generalizations, commented on the difference between Russians on either side of the Ural Mountains. Koeppen, however, was more sympathetic to the outlying tribes, observing that Tartars seemed "more rational and more intelligent" than their neighbors closer to Moscow. Perhaps he meant by that they didn't throw rocks, an area in which the Americans were gaining extensive personal experience. In the region of Perm, the Thomas Flyer was regularly pelted by villagers and passing caravans. The caravans were made up of thirty or forty horse-drawn vehicles, driven by people who had never set eyes on an automobile before. Even after the Thomas went by, though, a great many of the wagonmasters were still without their first glimpse of a car, the majority being either drunk or asleep or both.

"The women were better behaved than the men, so far as vodka is concerned," MacAdam wrote, "but they were much worse in disposition, as we were soon to learn. They would shake their fists menacingly at us and then, with a terrible scowl on their faces, would point to the open fields, indicating that we should take to the fields." In one village, the adults actually stood back and encouraged the children to throw rocks at the Thomas; the more industrious of their neighbors had already spread broken glass on the road under a layer of sweet hay. For people who had never seen an automobile, they seemed to know instinctively how to make a wreck of one.

Life was undoubtedly complicated in western Russia in the early 1900s. When the Thomas blew out a tire in the middle of one town, the people on the street screamed and ran for cover. The first thought was that it was a bomb planted by a terrorist. The more anxious that residents became, though, the more that there was to be anxious about. In one of the larger towns, a gaggle of citizens had gathered to look at the Flyer on the street, when a Cossack came along and beat them back with a type of whip called a knout. Men, women, and children were attacked with equal brutality, beaten right back into the buildings, simply because he didn't like the way they were standing. And as long as he felt that way, it was the law.

As the Thomas Flyer left Obansk, a storm broke, drenching roads that were already soggy. As the rain beat down, Miller spoke up and once again argued against continuing in the rain. It wasn't that he hated getting wet, it wasn't even that he dreaded the thought of the car getting stuck in the mud. The week before, he had patched the running gear of the Flyer together with his own two hands, doing work in a village smithy that would have been challenging in the Thomas factory back in Buffalo. He'd done a brilliant job, but not a perfect one and he knew that better than anyone. Shouting through raindrops that made him sputter when they hit him in the face, he told Schuster that they had to stop the car—the road was full of potholes that were slippery in the rain. Pulling out of them put a terrible strain on the transmission.

Schuster was too tired to raise his voice, replying that the best thing to do was to keep going and maintain the lead over the Koeppen. As soon as the car reached the city of Kasan, they could install the new transmission and put the whole problem of the gearing behind them. The more stops they made, Schuster pointed out, the longer it would take to get to Kasan. Miller barely spoke again, even as the car mustered its way through the worst of the mud. The next day, the sky cleared and finally gave the land, and the automobilists on it, a chance to dry. The road itself stayed messy, though, and the mire was especially thick on a lopsided stretch running up a hill about fifteen miles from the small city of Viatka.

Viatka was on the Trans-Siberian's northern line, the one that ran parallel to the main line to Moscow. Schuster was planning to turn south at Viatka and rejoin the main line at Kasan, the biggest city in the region. All he had to do was reach Kasan. With the Thomas Flyer repaired there, it would be a relatively straight shot to Moscow and then on to St. Petersburg, another five hundred miles beyond that. St. Petersburg was a designated stop in the race. It was also home to the Imperial Automobile Club, which was offering a $1,000 award for the New York-to-Paris team that reached the city first. In Schuster's view, he would practically have that prize as soon as he reached Kasan. It would be his first honor as the Thomas driver.

The Flyer doggedly extricated itself from one pothole after another on the road to Viatka, but in the middle of the steepest part of the crooked road, it finally stopped cold, caught in mud up to the hubs. Schuster gave the engine more gas, expecting the car to pull through just as it always had before, but instead, two chilling snaps emanated from the undercarriage. A luckless moment passed as the engine whirred and the car stayed perfectly still—exactly like the men in the passenger seats—and then it was confirmed: the transmission was failing again.

Within a short time, a team of horses had pulled the Flyer out of the pothole. Schuster managed to engage what was left of the gearing, at least long enough to bring the car into Viatka. By then, though, five more teeth had broken off of the gears and the car was shot.

The Thomas could not go to the new transmission in Kasan. The transmission would have to be brought to the Flyer in Viatka, despite the fact that there was no direct train service between the two cities— and despite the fact that it weighed hundreds of pounds. Someone would have to make a dash to Kasan, retrieve the part, and arrange to haul it back to Viatka. "Suppose you go," Schuster said to George Miller, "You can be a hero. MacAdam can go along and write the story."

Miller turned him down. "Schus," he said, "You had better do it. You can at least talk German." Schuster was exhausted, and he wouldn't have minded the rest, but without a translator—without Captain Hansen— his knowledge of German was at least occasionally a valuable asset. The trip would entail four days: two at best to reach Kasan in a horse-drawn wagon, and at least two to bring the transmission back.

With Schuster gone, Miller and MacAdam settled into village life in Viatka. Fortunately, it was a relaxed and friendly place, in its own peculiar way. Their neighbors arrived in shifts every day to watch them eat. The truly curious could have watched them sleep, as well, since they both resorted to a loft in a local barn, forsaking the inn after losing track of the number of different insect species to be found in their beds there.

323

○ ○ ○

To the east, Koeppen was also waiting out a breakdown on the road from Perm to Viatka. One of the Protos's springs broke, a serious problem but unfortunately nothing new. In fact Koeppen was keeping track and it was something like the eighteenth spring to break since Vladivostok. Neuberger and Fuchs busied themselves making the repair, while Koeppen stood back in the afternoon sun, joined by villagers who arrived to have a look at the car. With the weather quite warm, he had his translator, Mr. Reiski, ask one of the children to bring them milk from the village. Communications having thus been opened, Reiski continued to chat with the people standing around.

"Just listen to what this farmer said," Reiski reported to Koeppen.

"What?"

"He said, 'Ahead, not even five versts [three miles], the Americans are stuck.' "

Neuberger and Fuchs stopped what they were doing. "The Americans?" Fuchs said.

"The car is in undrivable condition," Reiski relayed, "parked at one of the farmhouses."

Koeppen had assumed that Schuster was four or five days ahead, maybe even as far as Moscow.

Twenty minutes later, the spring was fixed and the Protos was speeding ahead toward Viatka. Neuberger and Fuchs were talking excitedly about spotting the Thomas. Koeppen was in the backseat, shrouding his high hopes in the conviction that the farmer was mistaken, that it was some other car. Not that there were any other cars in the region, but Koeppen had convinced himself that someone must have come out from Moscow. He didn't want to believe that he was really about to pass the Thomas, in case a grave disappointment was in store.

The sun made it a hot afternoon. Bees and other bugs moved a lot faster than anyone else, and made the only noise to be heard, too. In Viatka, Miller and MacAdam were in the farmyard, vaguely tinkering with the Thomas Flyer when they heard the Protos approaching. They walked over to the side of the road to look. As soon as the German car pulled to a stop, Koeppen bounded out. "He greeted us cordially and commiserated with us on our predicament," MacAdam recalled. Miller enjoyed a good laugh with Neuberger; what else was there for two ace mechanics to do in the middle of a filthy byre?

"It was very bad luck," Koeppen thought as his car pulled away. "But it turned into very good luck for us. That's the way it is in life and sports. We probably deserved this piece of luck because of all our previous mishaps." The Protos turned south toward Kasan, passing horse-drawn *telegas* and a countryside dotted with peasant farmhouses; they were generally not much more than wooden huts, like log cabins, unpainted but well kept just the same. Inside one of them, along the road to Kasan, George Schuster was sipping a cup of tea with a family. He was on his way back from Kasan, but his wagon horses needed rest, and so he had a break, too. Sitting with the cup in both hands, he heard the rasping motor of the Protos approaching from the distance and knew just what it was. It was that he was no longer in the lead.

"Automobile! Automobile!" cried a neighbor woman, just outside the window. All of the family members emptied from the house and joined the farmworkers and others, hurrying to the roadside. Schuster was left all alone in the hut, with its own dim silence.

"I was too tired to go out and wave," he wrote later. Viatka was a disaster for Schuster, costing five days altogether and giving the Protos a lead of two days.

Koeppen knew he had a chance and he rushed forward on smooth roads, enjoying scenery worthy of a light opera on the route to the rich, old city of Nizhni Novgorod, the last major stop before Moscow. "We drove past mountains and forests, through fields and orchards; we passed through small, beautifully situated cities and villages," he marveled, "and frequently saw the grey walls of a castle or monastery. Again and again, the Volga River appeared, with its bright, mirror-sharp reflection below us." Koeppen was on the lookout for a Protos car that had been sent from the dealership in Moscow to meet him. He didn't find the car, but in Nizhni Novgorod, he did meet two men sent by the dealership to escort him into Moscow. As they traded stories and solidified plans at breakfast, over a table full of European-style delicacies, a festive atmosphere attached itself to the Protos team.

At nine o'clock that night, July 18, Moscow came into sight and Koeppen could barely contain himself. The car was already sagging on two broken front springs and a flat tire, but Koeppen gave the order to keep going. At nine thirty he pulled up to the Hotel Billo, where hundreds of people were waiting to see the Protos—the first car ever to cross Russia. "Externally, we had a rather sad appearance," Koeppen admitted, "but internally, we were ecstatic, surrounded by good friends and rescued from the Siberian morass and the miserable streets of eastern Russia . . . Moscow belonged to us!"

Koeppen delayed for a day and a half in Moscow, so that the dealership could refit the car with a lightweight body and install new springs. Many of the tools were also left behind. From Moscow through to Paris, the roads would be as good as any in the world: well engineered and paved with macadam or some other hard surface. The reduction in weight was a defensive measure, intended to lessen the strain on the car and so the chance of a major breakdown on the last stretch of the trip. While the car was being refitted, Koeppen took full advantage of the layover in Moscow. He didn't want to rest, though; he wanted to take a walking tour of the Kremlin, the towered citadel that was only a historical site then and not used by the government as it is today. He also wanted to see any reminder of Napoleon's conquest of Moscow in 1812. There wasn't much to see, most of the city having burned down while the French had charge of it, but Koeppen was thrilled just to stand on the actual hill from which Napoleon had first seen Moscow. On July 19, he left the city with Neuberger and Fuchs and a new translator, Dr. Donalies, a scholar who had come from Germany for the honor of riding in the car.

By express train, the ride from Moscow to St. Petersburg took twelve hours. A sportsman had recently completed the trip in an auto in only nine hours, or an average of 55 mph. Koeppen couldn't make that kind of time, though, not with his car occasionally requiring minor repairs. For good measure, the springs broke again—twice, in fact, making it at least two times since Vladivostok that they had snapped. Nonetheless, the driving was a pleasure. On long stretches, the road was a veritable enclosed highway, with very few intersections or—as Koeppen looked at it—opportunities to make a wrong turn. The houses on either side of the road were set far back, leaving wide lawns that were taken over by children and dogs, romping on the grass.

Two days after leaving Moscow, the Protos arrived in the swank suburb of Zareskoje Selo, on the outskirts of St. Petersburg. A whole procession of automobiles from the city was waiting there to fall into line behind the Germans, saluting them with hats held high and horns honking without stop. Koeppen responded with the beaming smile of a man who is a hailed a hero—and for the very first time, deserves it. The Protos, with a less pronounced sense of occasion, stalled in the middle of the parade, the result of dirt in the gasoline line. When the cars started forward again, they swept a cloud of fine dust up into the air. The haze was so thick that Koeppen couldn't even see the czar's summer palace, though he drove right by it. That didn't matter. He was more interested in the fact that by reaching St. Petersburg first, he won the $1,000 prize offered by the Imperial Automobile Club.

St. Petersburg, the capital of Nicholas II's Russia, was the embodiment of the wealth and splendor of czarist rule, as European in its spirit as Moscow was adamantly Russian. St. Petersburg also had its industrial side and was home to Russia's biggest arms factory. It certainly had its discontent, too, which erupted into violence that nearly resulted in the overthrow of the czar in 1905. That discontent didn't go away, of course, and the next revolution, in 1917, would succeed in deposing the czar. But Koeppen saw none of the brooding inequities of St. Petersburg society. He was there in its last heyday, welcomed into a glittering imperial circle. There may not have been a more rarified place to be in the world than in the embrace of that doomed aristocracy.

"While our car found room in the garage of the Imperial Automobile Club, and was taken care of," Koeppen wrote, "we got a rapturous welcome from the president and numerous members of the club. After the Tchita prize, now the second prize was ours. As a complete surprise, we learned that His Majesty the Czar contributed a special medal for whichever car was the first to reach St. Petersburg. And, the honorary president of the Imperial Automobile Club, Grand Duke Michael Alexandrovitch, the younger brother of the czar, contributed a huge golden cup, as a prize for the car that reached Paris first. We had already earned the Czar's medal."

While the *New York Times* was trying to keep up with the many details of the lionization of Hans Koeppen in St. Petersburg, the paper couldn't even locate George Schuster. Day after day, the editors speculated on the master strategy that was apparently keeping him from the road to Moscow. One report suggested that he was bypassing Moscow in order to go straight to St. Petersburg for the sake of the prize money. There was nothing quite so cunning at work, though.

Schuster kept getting lost—due, as MacAdam put it, to the Russians' inability to understand hand signals. The Thomas crew's inability to understand Russian might have been a factor, too.

Schuster had made a mistake in banishing Captain Hansen to Moscow. While Hansen's charm undoubtedly grew thin after the first sixteen or seventeen weeks of an automobile trip, he could speak Russian. As a result of just one of the wrong turns that the Thomas took because of the communication problem, Schuster lost fifteen hours.

"Once, the car sank up to its hubs in a mudhole," MacAdam reported, "and the crew had to walk to the nearest village to get aid to extricate it. The men who could be convinced to come out to help were mostly drunk, and the crew had great difficulty in directing them in sign language to build a corduroy road (using logs for traction) over which the Thomas could pass." Three hours were lost, while Schuster, Miller, and MacAdam took turns improvising the hand signals to explain traction and road construction and what corduroy was.

When Schuster bumped into Nizhni Novgorod at 2 A.M. on July 20, he was finally on the right track. A local automobilist, the first that the Thomas team had seen since leaving Japan, volunteered to escort the Flyer into Moscow. By the time Schuster arrived there, the Thomas was ailing again, in need of a day's worth of repair to the driveshaft. Though the welcome from Moscow's auto enthusiasts was warm, Schuster was ill at ease, having heard that Koeppen had left St. Petersburg the same day. That gave Koeppen a three-day lead, with only about a week's worth of driving left, assuming that all went well on the final leg to Paris.

On leaving St. Petersburg, Koeppen headed southwest, toward the coast of the Baltic Sea.

In 1908, the map of the Baltic coast was simpler than it is today. Russia and Germany were the only countries on it. The Protos, setting off early in the morning, went through regions that are now the separate nations of Estonia, Latvia, and Lithuania. If there was an extra measure of anxiety in the pace, it stemmed from the fact that the next border was the one with Germany, which also encompassed what is now northern Poland. Koeppen intended to reach the frontier of his homeland before nightfall.

In the border town of Eydtkuhnen, thousands of people were waiting to welcome Lieutenant Koeppen and the Protos. "On German soil," he acknowledged to himself, "which we wished for, over a long, long time." He was already awed by the mixture of frenzy and peace he felt at being back, when he spotted a group of officers from various posts in the region. Representing the army, they had traveled to Eydtkuhnen in order to salute him. Nothing of the sort had ever happened to him before.

The next day, Koeppen set out in what became a triumphal tour of his country. He had not realized before just how avidly his trip had been followed, or how much it meant to Germany. He had been counted out entirely on the American leg of the race. Completing his own round-the-world journey in his homeland, he showed that the greater part of heroics lay in simply refusing to quit.

The return of the first of the New York-to-Paris racers to Europe was overwhelming to all those who had thought the trip impossible—and even more so to those few who had believed right along that the automobile could indeed conquer the world.

"To travel and to travel—there is a difference," Koeppen said in trying to explain the race. "A person who travels in a luxury train from one main city to another, getting off every now and then to enjoy the sights and to study the make-up of the great capitals, may make himself better acquainted with them, but he will not get the close feeling with the land and with the people who do not breathe city air and are not corrupted by another culture. In other words, when you travel from city to city, you don't get the flavor of the lives and the soul of the land." Many of the people who turned out to honor the Protos were not as impressed by how far it had gone—more than twenty thousand miles, counting ocean travel—as by how near to them it had brought the most distant places.

They cheered for the car, but in Germany, they also cheered for Hans Koeppen, the young German whose story was well known throughout the world, starting with the string of debacles that crippled his car early on, and how he been abandoned by teammates on two different occasions. Those who knew Koeppen couldn't quite understand why he put himself in the way of so much trouble. He wasn't a typical, hard-bitten adventurer. He had been fortunate in his upbringing, adored by his parents, and he was already marked for advancement in the army. It had never been difficult to be Hans Koeppen, not until January 26 when for some reason he climbed into a Protos car and started a journey that he could not quit. With that, he had to face his worst problems alone. But no longer.

They crowded around him in Eydtkuhnen, in Gumbinnen, Insterburg, and Wehlau. "The closer we got to Berlin, the more public our journey became to those around us," Koeppen wrote. At ten o'clock, on July 24, he met a convoy of fifty cars from the German Imperial Automobile Club in a town called Muencheborg, thirty-two miles from the capital. Many hundreds of club members wanted to be part of the escort, but only the fifty finest vehicles were chosen for the honor guard.

At midday, Oberlieutenant Koeppen arrived in Berlin, a city that had turned itself inside out in anticipation of his arrival. By the hundreds of thousands, Berliners left their homes and businesses to stand on the streets and await a glimpse of the handsome oberlieutenant. According to the newspapers, it was the biggest and most excited crowd that Berlin had ever seen. "There must have been as many people waiting for us," Koeppen marveled, "as waited for the soldiers to return from France in 1870." He may have been right, the crowd was estimated at more than a million. All along the route of the homecoming, people in the windows or along the street threw flowers and waved flags and handkerchiefs. The noise was deafening, as people shouted jubilantly and tried to catch Koeppen's attention. All that he heard in the happy din were the high-pitched voices of the children, which pleased him because it seemed to him that the whole day was a holiday for the young, who responded so easily to the car and its feat.

Along Unter den Linden, and then in the central business district on the Friedrichstrasse, the Protos crept slowly ahead, as fast as the police could clear the street before it. At noon, the car arrived at the Ullstein Publishing House Building, from which it had departed six months before. That winter day had been cold and gray, but when the car arrived back in the same place, it was in the sun.

Just as before, the front of the building was draped in the flags of Germany, France, and the United States. Lieutenant Koeppen was climbing down from the backseat, when he paused, suddenly aware that one other aspect of the day was exactly the same as in January when he left. The Maennerchor Society was there again, but they were singing a song of welcome, not farewell. The moment they finished, the crowd pressed around the car from the street and a detachment of revelers scooped Lieutenant Koeppen up, carrying him into the publishing house on their shoulders.

The turmoil of the streets was too much for Koeppen's parents; his mother had stayed home, while his father was waiting for him inside the Ullstein Building. The formal lobby, with a grandiose staircase curving up to the second floor, was filled with other invited guests, including a whole detachment of officers in dress uniform from the General Staff of the Army. Koeppen's superior officers were there, too, basking in the honor that the lieutenant had brought to them and the army. A ceremony was in order and Koeppen was guided to a place on the steps, beside the Ullsteins and several government officials. Franz Ullstein, one of the brothers who had helped to sponsor the trip, made a speech that began, "On the 26th of January, Oberlieutenant Koeppen started a very heroic journey towards the west from this house. And after six months, he returned to us from the east and accomplished the journey that was his. . . ." Ullstein went on and others spoke, too, with words of praise for the young man who regarded the impossible only as a place to start.

At the culmination of the short ceremony, Lieutenant Koeppen was called upon to say something. It was his perfect moment and no one could take it away from him. His name was on the lips of practically everyone in Berlin, and even the Kaiser was said to be boasting about his feat.

Koeppen looked around at the room, lit with crystal chandeliers that made a sparkle out of every glint of silver on the army uniforms he saw, that picked up the white of his father's hair and the shine on the faces of the well-dressed men and women who had been standing in the sun too long, awaiting his arrival.

"I don't deserve credit for the car's good showing," Koeppen began, in contradiction to all that was going on around him and all that he had been for so long. In fact, there was a new note of vigor in his voice, a tone that even his father had never detected before.

"The great dash across Russia, you see, was due entirely to the devotion and skill of my drivers, Casper Neuberger and Robert Fuchs."

Chapter Twenty-eight

New York to Paris

Car	Miles	Place	Team
Protos (Ger.)	20,497	Brunswick, Germany	Koeppen, Fuchs, Neuberger
Thomas Flyer (U.S.)	19,937	Eydtkuhnyn, Russia	Schuster, Miller, Hansen, MacAdam
Züst (Ita.)	16,208	Omsk, Russia	Scarfoglio, Haaga

While Lieutenant Koeppen was in Berlin, word flashed through the city that Schuster was on the Russian-German border and charging fast. That would put the Americans only two days behind and give them time to catch up. Unfortunately for them, it wasn't true. Schuster and his team were still in Russia, at least a day away from the border and three days from Berlin. The only real news out of the Thomas Flyer was that Captain Hansen had rejoined the car in Moscow, rounding out the team to four again.

In St. Petersburg, the Thomas was accorded an enthusiastic escort into the city from Zareskoje Selo, with a luncheon banquet at the Imperial Automobile Club. There were no prizes, though—no records, no money, no royal baubles, and much more talk about the Protos than Schuster would have wanted to hear. The Thomas was the second of the racers to arrive in St. Petersburg, and there was little royal interest in that fact. In the evening, Ludwig Nobel, scion of the Swedish munitions (and prize-giving) family, hosted a dinner in honor of the members of the Thomas team. Ludwig had derived his own huge fortune from Russian oil, and the party at his house was as sumptuous as anything the royal family might have offered. Nonetheless, the fact remained that there was no imperial recognition of the Thomas team. While George Schuster of South Buffalo, New York, was no snob, he grew tired of Nobel's party very early in the evening: it didn't mean a thing.

As soon as it was over, or perhaps a minute before, Schuster gathered his crew and they left St. Petersburg for the long swing south and west around the Baltic Sea. Schuster was still in the race to reach Paris first and he kept the pace, "fighting sleep and fatigue," according to MacAdam, all along the way. He was no longer trying to log every mile himself; he and Miller alternated behind the wheel, keeping the car moving at least twenty-one hours out of every day.

Almost around the clock, the Flyer made progress through the Baltic farmland, a tribute to the man in the driver's seat, sitting bolt upright and staring straight ahead, and equally to the man in the passenger's seat of the roadster, strapped in at the waist, beaten by the air, tussled by the turns, and trying to sleep. Miller was in the driver's seat one night when Schuster suddenly reached over and turned the wheel, just as the Thomas was about to speed over an embankment. Even if it wasn't always clear who was driving and who was dozing, the car kept moving.

For the first time since the start in New York, the conditions of the route posed no problem, aside from the "monotony of magnificent roads," as MacAdam put it. The highways only improved after the Thomas crossed into German territory on July 25. So did morale in the car. The people in Germany were effusive in welcoming the Americans, and the landscape reflected a neat and prosperous way of life. Though Schuster learned that the Protos was still ahead by at least three days, he was intent on continuing to drive in swing shifts at the wheel, in order to catch up before the finish.

Late on the night of the twenty-fifth, the Flyer reached Königsberg (now called *Kaliningrad*), the capital of the German province of East Prussia. An old university town, as well as a river port, Königsberg was famous as the home of Immanuel Kant, the philosopher. It was a beautiful old city, in his day as well as in 1908, dotted with medieval buildings and fortifications that made it a popular destination for tourists. When Schuster arrived in Königsberg, however, he had no choice but to stop. The radiator on the Flyer had sprung a leak.

In the warm weather of July, running the car continuously with its faulty radiator, Schuster was lucky to reach Königsberg without the engine overheating. He had trouble examining the problem by the streetlight outside his hotel, but then, he didn't have to see much. He had entered the automobile business by crafting radiators. He knew even without looking that the radiator on the Thomas would have to be removed and taken to a machine shop to be welded. As Schuster left the car and walked slowly into the hotel, he wasn't mulling over the repair. He was thinking that he could no longer hope to catch Koeppen purely on the merits of driving. His only chance was that the Protos would suffer a breakdown, too, something even worse than a leaky radiator.

The next morning, Schuster and Miller pulled the radiator out of the Flyer and brought it to a local shop, where they set about patching it, finishing at midday. All the while, Schuster declined to telegraph a report to either Paris or New York—or Buffalo. For the time being, he had slipped into his own world, unable to concern himself with the location of the Protos, the relative progress of the Thomas, or outside comments on either subject.

"We have constantly lacked enough sleep," Schuster explained, "and often have had nothing to eat. If it had not been for the fresh air we inhaled all the time, probably none of us would have been able to stand the hardships." He climbed back into the Thomas in Königsberg and continued west. With nothing to spare, he was racing entirely on emotion, without cunning or calculation, driven only by the specter of winning and losing. It was enough to propel him over the next 340-mile stretch to the city of Berlin.

The Imperial Automobile Club in Berlin didn't receive any messages from the Thomas Flyer team—no one did. But Count Sierstorpf, the president of the club, did know the date on which the American car had reached Königsberg. Making calculations based on that bit of intelligence, he organized a long and boisterous convoy which traveled east on Sunday afternoon, July 26, in order to meet Schuster in the town of Muencheberg. The Thomas didn't make progress according to Count Sierstorpf's calculations, though. His formula had not provided for soldering time for a crumbling radiator. Over the course of six hours in Muencheberg, the joviality in the convoy slowly ebbed—but not the good intentions. Promising to remain ready to return at a moment's notice, the Berliners reluctantly headed home. Their spirits shot back up, though, as soon as they arrived back in Berlin on Sunday night.

There was news from Paris that night, but Schuster didn't hear it. He didn't stop to pick up any of the messages left waiting for him in cities and towns along the route. He just kept on driving along in ignorance, the last luxury of the desperate. It was on Monday morning that Schuster arrived in Berlin and learned the news: Hans Koeppen had arrived in Paris the night before. The race between Schuster and Koeppen was over.

At 6:15 on Sunday evening, the Protos had slowed down on the Boulevard Poissonniere, covering the last mile of its journey—8,280 miles since Vladivostok, 21,933 since Times Square. The car came to a stop, for good, in front of the offices of *Le Matin,* where a delegation of editors was waiting to congratulate Koeppen, Neuberger, and Fuchs. A cold buffet had been ordered for the reception. When it was over, Koeppen spent the rest of the evening sitting in the dining room of his hotel, the Regina, having a gourmet meal and holding court for the other guests, most of them Americans. The Regina was especially popular with Americans. The next day, Lieutenant Koeppen was invited to have breakfast with the German ambassador, Count Radolin.

Koeppen might not have noticed, but his greeting in Paris was distinctly tepid. A less generous soul, just in from Vladivostok by way of every bog in Siberia, would have taken one look at the cold buffet at the *Le Matin* offices and understood completely. Most would have thrown it plate by plate against the wall. And the buffet constituted the highlight of the welcome. One need hardly drive all the way around the world, after all, to come by an invitation to see one's own ambassador— and at breakfast. Fortunately, there were Americans on hand to giggle and fawn, and fill in the quiet that Paris held out for the racers.

On Monday morning, while Lieutenant Koeppen was having his breakfast with Count Radolin, George Schuster was having his breakfast with Count Sierstorpf at the Imperial Automobile Club in Berlin. Several people at the club congratulated Schuster on his good showing, even while consoling him on losing the race to Koeppen. Schuster thanked them all, without protesting. They didn't understand and he wasn't up to reminding them that according to rulings made by the race committee, the Protos would ultimately be docked two weeks for re-sorting to the train in the American west. At the same time, the Thomas would be allowed two weeks for attempting the trip to Alaska.

Schuster had a whole month in which to get to Paris and still win the New York-to-Paris Race. He had, however, lost his race: Vladivostok to Paris. It was the one he had chosen and even demanded, fought to the marrow and, in his own mind, fought alone. The only thing that he and Koeppen shared was a certain maniacal courage and for Koeppen, apparently that had been enough. He was in Paris.

At midday, the Thomas Flyer left Berlin, with Schuster, Miller, Hansen, and MacAdam onboard. They were in no rush to get to Paris. In fact, the new plan was a radical departure, as Schuster announced that they would thenceforth stop at night. Just like regular people, they would sleep in beds for eight hours at a time. That was the plan, but on the second day out of Berlin, the clutch shaft gave out, costing sixteen hours, even with a machine shop only three miles away. Back in the Trans-Baikal, a worn clutch shaft probably would have been worth at least a week's delay. Time itself, however, was worth more the closer that the Thomas drew to Paris. The loss of a full day made MacAdam pessimistic that they would ever reach the finish line. Schuster no longer cared about time. All he wanted to do was make Paris sometime soon, check in at *Le Matin,* and then find a hotel. He was looking forward to that. What he didn't much relish was the obligation to endure another tempered reception for the second car on the scene.

With a heavy fog settling in the next morning, the men in the Thomas should have been cheered up by a car full of women who arrived specifically to pilot the Thomas through western Germany. The women, however, couldn't resist a little fun and there was apparently nothing more fun than going too fast in a fog bank—especially with overloaded farm wagons dotting the road. "It was only by good luck that several collisions were narrowly avoided," MacAdam noted.

George Schuster was so exhausted in every way that he didn't look at all well. He probably wasn't. With one breakdown or setback after another, the plan to stay at hotels soon fell apart, a fact that certainly didn't disappoint the hotels. In Cologne, Schuster entered the fine old

Dom Hotel, followed by Miller, Captain Hansen, and MacAdam. They were about to enter the dining room for dinner, when the head waiter scurried over and, with a heroic burst of speed, caught them just before they set foot through the door. He quickly advised Schuster that the hotel had a canteen for servants around in the back. Schuster flew into a rage. The four of them were dressed like farmhands, smudged like coal stokers, and they limped like stevedores, but they were round-the-world racers. They expected to be treated in the best manner of the host country. Captain Hansen knew a lost cause when he saw one. He herded the team to another restaurant across the street.

Schuster crossed the Rhine on July 29, skirting through Belgium and finally entering France. He was still in a haze of despondency or exhaustion, probably both, and he didn't keep anyone on the race committee apprised of his progress. Entirely by his own choice, he was more isolated in France than he had been in Siberia. It was no longer a race to him, it was an obligation to bring the car in. He couldn't do it if he had to hear what the Thomas factory had to say.

On the evening of Thursday, July 30, the Flyer was in striking distance, following the signs for Paris. By that point, it wasn't much of a rarity on the road. It could have been any car, arriving back in town after a long ride in the country. For George Schuster, as for anyone else heading to Paris, there was not much more of the trip left. He took advantage of the good cobblestone road and accelerated to 60 mph. He'd lost his headlights somewhere along the way and wanted to reach the city before dark.

"Nobody knew our schedule," Schuster recalled, "but beginning at Meaux, 25 miles out, crowds began to cheer us. Bicyclists rode excitedly alongside. Summer evening diners in sidewalk cafes raised their glasses and shouted, 'Vive la voiture américaine.' " The same American flag that had hung from the back of the Flyer in the chill of Times Square the previous February was still fluttering behind it in the warmth of a summer night in Paris. It was not just any car, as it headed into Paris.

Word spread by telephone that the New York-to-Paris Thomas Flyer was coming and within minutes, the streets along the route filled with people, rushing downstairs or across sidestreets to catch sight of the

Americans before they passed, before the moment passed. The Parisians "cheered them to the echo from the moment they passed the city walls until their journey ended at the *Matin* office," marveled an American who was there. In the Place l'Opera, in front of the famous Café de la Paix restaurant, women in gowns and men in cutaways and top hats poured out onto the sidewalks to have a look at the battered car and spattered men, just in from New York.

Schuster was still a half-mile away from the *Le Matin* building, and anxious to nudge his car through the melee, but what all Paris was trying to tell him was that that didn't matter anymore. None of it mattered: Vladivostok and Valdez, San Francisco, Cheyenne and Viatka. Mojave. The race had a winner. Someone had taken an automobile from New York all the way to Paris—and it was George Schuster, the mechanic from Buffalo.

There was only one person in the city of Paris who wasn't intoxicated by the newly proven fact that an automobile could go anywhere. He was standing in the middle of the Place l'Opera and he happened to be a policeman. "You are under arrest," he thundered at Schuster.

The celebration wound down, at least in the vicinity of the car.

"You have no lights on your car," the policeman said. He didn't care where the Thomas had been, although a chorus of voices tried to tell him. He waved them away. That wasn't his concern. A car had to have a headlight to be on the streets of Paris at night, or else the driver was to be placed under arrest. Fortunately Paris was built on equal parts law and imagination. A man on a bicycle with a light on the front rode up to the car, hopped off, and deposited the whole bike into the seat between Schuster and Miller. The Thomas had a light. The policeman looked it all over and then stepped aside.

By the time the Flyer arrived at the *Le Matin* building, the crew had to struggle to get through the crowds and into the front door. Inside, the members of the New York-to-Paris Race Committee were waiting with the senior executives of the paper. Because they hadn't had any advance notice of the Flyer's arrival, they didn't even have a buffet on hand. But they did have champagne spilling into glasses. It wasn't a staid or well-planned celebration. Or perhaps there had been a plan, but it fell by the wayside, as Schuster, Miller, Hansen, and MacAdam were given toasts, cheers, hugs, handshakes, and kisses. There were also speeches and a buoyant consensus declaring "the performance the most remarkable ever undertaken in the history of sport." The New York-to-Paris Race became much more than just sport, though, once it was won. It took the limits off the automobile, for all time. If more needed to be said after the greeting extended by hundreds of thousands of Parisians, the editors of *Le Matin* formally declared the Thomas Flyer the official winner of the New York-to-Paris Race.

"Schuster is much broken nervously by the trip," observed an acquaintance, "but he is the happiest man in Paris to-night, nevertheless." The celebrations in Paris continued for days, and George Schuster had only to stand on a balcony to draw a crowd calling his name and still marveling at what he had done.

Chapter Twenty-nine

Young Men in the Morning

During the first few days of August, newspapers in the United States and Europe naturally ran editorials expressing admiration for George Schuster and the Thomas Flyer team. Some regarded the completion of the journey as a human triumph. Others regarded it purely as a mechanical achievement, the real dawning of the day of the automobile. While everyone else rose up to cheer, though, the editor of the *New York Evening Mail* seemed to tip back in his chair and think. Calculating that the Thomas had traveled on average 107 miles per day, he figured out that a team of relay runners covering 200 miles per day, as a YMCA relay team recently had, could have arrived in Paris a whole month earlier than the car—assuming, of course, that not too many of the relay runners froze to death or drowned along the way.

In any case, a relay race doesn't count as travel, since the same person wouldn't arrive in Paris as started in New York. Someone probably pointed that out to the *Evening Mail* editor, because the opinion piece went on to quote Henry David Thoreau on his theory that walking was actually quicker than taking the train, if the time to earn the money to pay for the ticket was factored in. On that basis, the *Evening Mail* was perfectly right. A slow-footed ant could have beaten the Thomas Flyer to Paris, if Schuster had had to earn the money in advance to pay for the car and all the expenses.

E. R. Thomas could speak to that, and he did, in the many interviews he gave in the aftermath of the victory. The race had cost nearly $100,000, but that didn't bother him. When he was reminded that Jefferson DeMont Thompson had promised $1,000 for the flag that went round-the-world, E. R. could barely answer fast enough, insisting that he wouldn't take $10,000 for it. In the aftermath of the race, the Thomas Motor Car Company was enjoying banner sales, thanks to the fame of the race-winning Flyer, "the most distinguished self-moving vehicle in the world," according to the *New York Times*.

o o o

In those first days of August, Hans Koeppen was back at his desk in the General Staff of the Army, and at his desk at home, too, weaving the story of his trip into a book, "my first and probably my last literary effort," as he called it. His publishers—the Ullstein brothers, of course—wanted the book to be out in time for Christmas, and so Koeppen was working diligently all through August. The book represented his only chance at recouping the savings he had sacrificed to the race. Overall, though, Koeppen's life had returned to normal. He became a popular figure in automobile circles, but he was not a celebrity in the modern sense. Outside of the theatrical profession, celebrities in Germany in 1908 tended to be scandal-ridden socialites. It wouldn't have suited Hans Koeppen to remain in the spotlight, and no one expected it of him.

In between parties of one sort or another in Paris, George Schuster managed to catch up on his rest. One of the most deluxe of the banquets thrown in his honor was hosted at the Grand Hotel by Bourcier St. Chaffray, who confided that ever since he withdrew from the race, he had been praying for the success of the Americans. No one reminded St. Chaffray that while he may have prayed for the Americans, he had ceded his gasoline rights in Vladivostok to the Italians.

George Miller remained with Schuster in Paris, but the war between the front seat and backseat ended for good not long after the Thomas's arrival, when MacAdam suddenly remembered crucial business elsewhere in Europe. Apparently he wanted to have his own city in which to sleep. Even Captain Hansen decided to move on, rather than stay and spend the week going to parties—an indication, in his case, of a very precarious mental state. Turning his back on Paris at its most flirtatious, a chance he might never have again, Captain Hansen boarded a train headed for Tomsk, back in the quiet of Siberia, to join his wife and daughter.

On August 5, Schuster and Miller were in the port city of Le Havre, boarding a transatlantic liner. In New York, the celebrations would start all over again. Having become accustomed to being hailed a hero, Schuster had time aboard ship to mull over a rumor that interested him far more than any further speeches. He had heard that the Thomas

Motor Car Company was going to give him a bonus of $10,000 for bringing in the Flyer a winner.

Schuster wasn't a company man by nature, and, likewise, the leaders of the company held out no particular affection for him. That was all right. He was a working man and a certain stiff distrust of the bosses sat easily with him. But for six months on the road, he had done his job, and then some. The most unfrothy of men, he had also endured six months of high praise and public posturing from company officials and others. He simply wanted to know how much of it was true, and a dollar amount seemed the best way to judge. As he looked out from the deck of the ship, he rolled figures around in his mind.

Aside from a few more parades and the matter of money, Schuster had nothing left to do, in relation to the race. As invitations poured in from cities requesting a chance to honor the Thomas and its driver, he could have remained on the road for another six months, if he wanted. On the contrary, though, Schuster bluntly told anyone who asked that he wouldn't repeat the New York-to-Paris Race for anything. He just wanted to go home. According to the *New York Times*, the departure of the Thomas team for New York on August 5 ended "the most interesting and exciting chapter thus far in the history of automobile contests." That showed how much they knew in New York. The race wasn't even over yet.

On August 5, the Züst was still dragging its way through western Siberia, a day or two from Ekaterinburg.

"Another sixty-five miles to-day, in spite of the rain and the very bad road," Antonio Scarfoglio wrote that night on his portable typewriter. "We should have continued traveling through the night, but Haaga was not very well, and we preferred to stop." The two men found a roadside inn of a type typical of small Siberian towns. Travelers slept on low benches in a communal room, sitting upright or in some generally vertical contortion.

The next morning, Henry Haaga was so ill that he couldn't stand up. He was running a high fever and suffering from what Scarfoglio diagnosed in a general way as colic. For four days, Haaga grew weaker and

345

more uncomfortable. He was the one in trouble, but Scarfoglio was the one who knew it, seeing his teammate "suffering the agony of fever in a primitive village, and I, alone, ignorant and compelled to watch his life ebbing away." Without delay, Scarfoglio sent for the nearest doctor, fifty miles away. Days passed before the medical man finally arrived.

The initial consultation did not go especially well, coming to an end when Scarfoglio grabbed the doctor by the collar and hurled him out the front door. He thought he was dealing with a poseur who knew less about medicine than he himself did. The doctor, for his part, thought that Scarfoglio was the one making Haaga sick. Remarkably enough, they communicated all of that and even had extended arguments on medical topics, despite the fact that Scarfoglio's knowledge of Russian ran to only five expressions:

> *Drasti gaspada*—How do you do?
> *Drasti*—Fine
> *Cu da*—Where are you coming from?
> *Su da*—Where are you headed?
> *Durac*—Idiot

The word for *idiot* was a recent addition to the list. "It was hurled at me by a Russian girl," he recalled, "to whom I had made a declaration in French, being persuaded that French was the language of love in all latitudes."

For a week, Scarfoglio tended Haaga alone, with occasional visits from the doctor. Between the two of them, they eventually revived the patient without killing each other. On August 12, Haaga could take a few steps outside, although he wasn't well enough to ride in the car, let alone drive it, until the eighteenth—the day that New York City welcomed Schuster and Miller home with a parade all the way up Broadway.

"We have been traveling for seven months," Scarfoglio wrote, "seven months during which half of the earth has passed under our wheels. In all that time we have only had one desire, one hope, one vision— Paris . . ."

The Züst's benefactor, Baron Scheinvogel, had ridden with the car for a short time after joining it in Manchuria, but early on, he had taken advantage of the looming temptation of the New York-to-Paris Race: the first train home. That couldn't have been a disappointment to Antonio Scarfoglio. The astute journalist, who seemed to observe every detail in a landscape and every nuance in a conversation, never once mentioned Scheinvogel in his many writings on the race.

Through most of August, Scarfoglio and Haaga, alone against the Russias, were still oblivious to the fact that the other two cars had long since reached Paris. It was only when they reached Moscow that they learned they were racing for third place. By that time, they weren't competing against other cars anyway.

At the start in New York, a voice in the crowd had labeled the Züst the "children's car," because while Emilio Sirtori looked manful enough at twenty-six, neither Scarfoglio nor Haaga was more than twenty-three, and they each looked even younger than that. Whoever yelled "children's car" probably forgot all about it even before the words were in the wind; it was the kind of morning to say everything that came to mind, and say it loud. Scarfoglio remembered "children's car," though, and never stopped wondering if it were true. But then he brooded over all sorts of things that he could easily have forgotten about instantly—if he were a little older.

St. Petersburg ignored the Züst. It might as well have been a dray wagon arriving in the city, for all the greeting it received. All of those aristocrats who had vied for the chance to do honor to the Protos, and even the Thomas, were nowhere to be seen. A pair of English tourists were the only ones who took note of the car. They were amused by the inscriptions and signatures—the graffiti—left all over the car body. They didn't take any note whatsoever of the drivers, who might have been marked by the trip, too, had anyone cared to ask.

St. Petersburg didn't stop Scarfoglio and Haaga and neither did two serious automobile accidents farther on in Europe. The moment the car entered France, Scarfoglio was overcome with joy. Very politely, he asked the first woman he saw—first explaining his situation and how he had been struggling for eight months to get to France all the way from New York City—if he could please kiss her. Granted permission, he did so, with abandon. In France, such an impulse did not necessarily make a man a *durac*. The next day, as the sun went down, the team, which included Baron Scheinvogel again, stopped in a town outside of Paris. None of them wanted to finish the journey at night, dirty, hungry, and impatient.

Scarfoglio's face still had cuts from the second of the accidents. "All barked and bruised," he wrote, "encrusted with the dust of all the roads of the worlds." He was describing the car, but he could have been speaking about himself. The following noon, when all were in better shape, the Züst would make its entrance into the city.

The editors of *Le Matin* spread the word and Parisians were waiting all along the route for the car to pass. The editors treated the team heroically. Berlin, for its part, had done the same the week before. It wasn't a case of pandemonium in either place, as when the Protos arrived in Berlin or the Thomas Flyer in Paris. But each city acknowledged the return of the Züst, many people treating Scarfoglio and Haaga as though they were "the moral victors." They may not have beaten the other cars in the race, but they certainly beat the course.

No one who started the New York-to-Paris Race realized how agonizing and exhausting it would be. The millions of people who followed the progress of the race probably never really understood that aspect of it, for all of the firsthand reporting from the course. They didn't have to, though, to understand what it meant to drive from New York to Paris. At some point in their lives, each one had started something big or small that turned out to be too much, too hard, and too frustrating at every turn. The real trial of any endeavor is how easy it is to buckle: to make up a lie to suit oneself and a plausible excuse to suit everyone else. That was the anguish of the New York-to-Paris Race, for all the world to see. In sheer hard work, it was the equal of any of the world's pioneering challenges, but what may have made it the cruelest of all, and also the most representative of the dramas of every life, was that it was far and away the easiest to quit. And that is what Scarfoglio and Haaga never did.

Staying in the race wasn't a case of survival, as in a trip to the North Pole or to the moon. Such feats were a matter of life and death. The New York-to-Paris Race was something else, something just as desperate and somewhat more familiar, at least for young men in the morning of their lives. The racers who finished continued for one reason: because they said they would when they started.

George Schuster would receive for his feat a grand total of $1,650. E. R. gave him a bonus of $1,000 and the rest came as a result of endorsements of automotive parts. Once the excitement was over, that ultimate souvenir, the flag that hung off the back of the Thomas, was apparently just a piece of cloth; E. R., who had turned down $10,000 for it right after the race, told Schuster to try to get Jefferson Thompson to make good on his offer of $1,000. Thompson, however, welched on the deal.

Schuster had wanted, just once, to be in the center of the action, to play in the big leagues and deal with the most powerful people—as an equal. The New York-to-Paris Race gave him that chance, but afterward he returned to his job at the Thomas factory, thoroughly convinced that he was not on an equal plane with such men. He was the one, after all, who had taken a car around the world.

The Men and the Cars

The New York-to-Paris Automobile Race not only inspired a great many people to purchase cars, in order to shatter their own limitations, it forced governments and civic groups to address the need for better highways. In the United States, the "Good Roads" movement was a direct outgrowth of the embarrassment of the conditions during the race, leading to a building frenzy that has yet to slow today.

The New York-to-Paris Race remained a touchstone among modern achievements in the twentieth century, until Lindbergh's flight across the Atlantic in 1927 usurped it, a more dramatic technological feat and one rendered in an age with a ferocious ability to create celebrities out of newsmakers and, what is more, legends out of celebrities. Things were quite different in 1908.

The winners of the New York-to-Paris Automobile Race were private citizens when they entered the race, Montague Roberts being the only one with at least some name recognition. In the years after the race, none of the entrants looked to prolong their fame. In fact, all returned willingly to the genial obscurity from which they'd sprung. **Antonio Scarfoglio,** after sometimes weeping openly in homesickness on the trip and claiming to feel "dead" because he wasn't with his loved ones in Italy, spent a few days in Paris and then accepted an invitation to go to London to show off the car. Within a week, he was already engaged in journalism again and his friends could see that he was back to full strength, protesting mournfully that he had gone all the way round the world in a motor car and it hadn't affected him even a little. He could barely even remember any of it, so he said. And he went on complaining—to the delight of those who loved him and wanted him to be happy. When he wasn't complaining, he was writing a 368-page book on the race, *Round the World in a Motor Car.* Scarfoglio remained a journalist and made a minor mark by founding Italy's first magazine devoted to a serious discussion of the cinema.

Hans Koeppen's book was published in autumn 1908. A bestseller in Germany, it more than succeeded in restoring his fortune. The following year, he was promoted to a captaincy, and a few months after that he was married. Koeppen fought in World War I and was fortunate to be included in the small proportion of junior officers on the German side to survive the war. He remained in the army, holding staff positions with the Luftwaffe before and during World War II. Koeppen retired with the rank of major-general in 1944 and died in 1948.

Montague Roberts raced cars for a few years after 1908 and even helped **Harry Houpt** start a new car company. It didn't last long. Though Monty was jailed rather frequently for breaking speed limits, he settled down to a quiet family life in New Jersey, where he had a long career as an engineer. He was always happy to reminisce about the race. Roberts died in 1957. **George Schuster** outlived all of the other major participants in the New York to Paris Race. After owning a Dodge dealership during the 1920s and 1930s, he rounded out his career as a machinist at a factory in western New York. During the 1960s, when he was in his nineties, he was brought back into the spotlight, with appearances on national television and the publication of a popular memoir of the race. George Schuster died at the age of 98 in 1973.

The Thomas Motor Car Company enjoyed a sales boom during the year after the New York-to-Paris Race, but in 1910, a new model intended to capitalize on the surging momentum disappointed buyers. In the teeming marketplace of the day, it did not take long for the company to collapse entirely. On March 17, 1913, the Thomas factory and all of its contents were auctioned off. Lot number 1829 was listed as the "Famous New York to Paris Racer."

Lot 1829 was purchased by the publisher of the *Buffalo Commercial* newspaper, who left it sitting in the yard of his country home in Elma, New York, for the better part of thirty years. Its provenance is a little disjointed from that point on. In the early 1960s, however, the famed car collector William Harrah of Reno emerged with the remnants of a Flyer thought to be the New York-to-Paris car. George Schuster was flown in as the guest of the prodigiously charming Mr. Harrah, and during the course of his visit, he vouched for the authenticity of the chassis. The Flyer was rebuilt in the Harrah shops and the resulting vehicle is splendid to behold. Even though more of it harkens from 1962 than 1908, it remains in the National Automobile Museum in Reno as a reminder of the heroic race. The Protos entry is displayed in the Deutsches Museum in Munich. It has long since been returned to its civilian garb, a dapper black car that no longer looks like either a prairie schooner or an army truck. But then, such vehicles are just relics. It was the men, not the cars, who triumphed over the New York-to-Paris Race.

Notes

Chapter One

HOLIDAY

Newsboys' banquet "Lincoln Day Feast for 300 Newsboys," *New York Herald,* Feb. 13, 1908.

Tailor killed "Shot Down in Street by Two Blackhanders," *New York Evening World,* Feb. 11, 1908.

Grande Redoute "White Permissible at the Pink Ball," *New York Herald,* Feb. 15, 1908.

Printer's suicide attempt "Bridge Jumper Brought Back from the Dead," *New York Telegram,* Feb. 13, 1908.

Umbrella sale Macy's adv., *New York Herald,* Feb. 13, 1908.

Temperatures in city "Weather," *New York World,* Feb. 13, 1908.

Cars ads and prices Broadway Mammoth Automobile Exchange ad, *New York World,* Feb. 14, 1908.

Description of Thomas building "They're Off in Race to Paris," *New York Times,* Feb. 13, 1908, p. 2.

Dockstader's Lincoln "Welcome to Town Overcomes Him," *New York Evening World,* Feb. 12, 1908.

By ten o'clock (Tribune *quote*) "Globe Circlers Off," *New York Tribune,* Feb. 13, 1908.

Starting line in Times Square "Diagram of Parking Spaces and Arrangements for Start," *New York Times,* Feb. 11, p. 2.

Size of crowd "Six Autos Off on 21,000 Mile Race to Paris," *New York Evening Mail,* Feb. 12, 1908.

The crowd was one of the worst (Globe *quote*) "Six Cars Leave Times Square," *New York Globe,* Feb. 12, 1908.

NOTES

Women spill into street "Globe Circlers Off," *New York Tribune,* Feb. 13, 1908.

Smell of gasoline "Globe Circlers Off," *New York Tribune,* Feb. 13, 1908.

Brass band "Six More Autos Off on Trip to Paris," *New York World,* Feb. 13, 1908.

Hoyt's background "Colgate Hoyt Dies in Oyster Bay Home," *New York Times,* Jan. 31, 1922, p. 12.

Aerial warfare joke "Aero Club at War Over How to Fly," *New York Times,* Oct. 31, 1908, p. 9.

Thompson and scooters "New Scooter Club for Long Island," *New York Times,* Mar. 9, 1908, p. 7.

Shonts party on grandstand "Six More Autos Off on Trip to Paris," *New York World,* Feb. 13, 1908.

De Chaulnes's debt "Sues de Chaulnes for a Tailor Bill," *New York Times,* Mar. 26, 1908, p. 7.

De Chaulnes's addiction "De Chaulnes Dead After Honeymoon," *New York Times,* Apr. 25, 1908, p. 1.

Send me a cake of ice (New York quote) "Vast Throng Sees Autoists Begin 22,000-Mile Journey," *New York World,* Feb. 12, 1908.

This stupendous undertaking (Baltimore quote) Editorial page, *New York Times,* Feb. 13, 1908, p. 8.

You think that automobile race (Denison [Iowa] quote) Untitled editorial, *Denison (Iowa) Bulletin,* Mar. 11, 1908, p. 5.

They pushed and shoved (Globe quote) "Six Cars Leave Times Square," *New York Globe,* Feb. 12, 1908.

As clear and distinct (entrant's quote) Antonio Scarfoglio, *Round the World in a Motor Car* (London: Grant Richards, 1909), p. 28.

Hoyt fires starting pistol "World's Racers Leave New York for Paris," *Motor Age,* Feb. 13, 1908, vol. 13, no. 7, p. 1.

Chapter Two

A RACE COURSE

What needs to be proved (Le Matin quote) "Paris-Peking Automobile," Paris *Le Matin,* Jan. 31, 1907, p. 1, reprinted in Allen Andrews, *Mad Motorists* (New York: Lippincott, 1965), p. 13.

De Dion's idea for race Griffith Borgeson, "The Automotive World of Albert De Dion," *Automobile Quarterly,* Fall 1977, vol. 15, no. 3, p. 280.

This is a real Jules Verne (De Dion quote) "Paris-Peking Automobile," Paris *Le Matin,* Jan. 31, 1907, p. 1, reprinted in Allen Andrews, *Mad Motorists* (New York: Lippincott, 1965), p. 15.

Round the world without a boat "Here to Paris by Auto," *New York Times,* Nov. 26, 1907, p. 4.

The loss of a machine (Amundsen quote) Roald Amundsen, letter, Nov. 30, 1907; "Feasible, Says Amundsen," *New York Times,* Dec. 1, 1907, p. 1.

The cars will have to (Mabley quote) "Plans for Auto Race New York to Paris," *New York Times,* Nov. 28, 1907, p. 2.

New York Times *becomes cosponsor* "Plans for Auto Race New York to Paris," *New York Times,* Nov. 28, 1907, p. 1.

Chapter Three

HEROES WANTED

This latest race (ACA member quote) "Auto Race to Start from Times Square," *New York Times,* Nov. 29, 1907, p. 2.

Everyone knows that it is a monster (Le Matin *quote)* "Auto Race to Start from Times Square," *New York Times,* Nov. 29, 1907, p. 2.

Standard Oil involvement "Non-Freezing Oil for the Auto Tour," *New York Times,* Dec. 4, 1907, p. 1.

Man can overcome (Levy quote) "Difficulties of the Tour," *New York Times,* Dec. 2, 1907, p. 1.

George Kennan, Siberia and the Exile System *(London: J. R. Osgood, McIlvaine, 1891); n.b. His nephew and namesake would build on that reputation, becoming a diplomatic expert on the Soviet Union starting in the 1930s and continuing in that capacity for more than seventy years.

De Windt's trips "Harry De Windt, Explorer, Is Dead," *New York Times,* Dec. 2, 1933, p. 13.

Two or three woebegone (de Windt quote) Harry de Windt, *From Paris to New York by Land* (New York: Warne & Co., 1904), p. 152.

Vermin was everywhere (de Windt quote) De Windt, *From Paris to New York,* pp. 27, 92.

Jailhouses for prisoners De Windt, *From Paris to New York,* pp. 17, 23, 29.

Patience, without which (de Windt quote) De Windt, *From Paris to New York,* pp. 13, 29.

I'll go the instant (Roberts quote) "Auto Racers May Start in February," *New York Times,* Dec. 2, 1907, p. 2.

Has automobiling come (driver's quote) "Autoist Has Trainer for Vanderbilt Race," *New York Times,* Sept. 20, 1905, p. 9.

Roberts's birthplace "M. H. Roberts, Auto Racer, Is Dead at 74," *Nutley (N.J.) Sun,* Sept. 26, 1957.

Roberts's army career "Auto Racers May Start in February," *New York Times,* Dec. 2, 1907, p. 2.

Trip to Deal "Racing Drivers Meet," *New York Times,* Oct. 18, 1940, p. 23.

Record-breaking debut Montague Roberts, "Automobile Racing Most Fascinating of Sports," *New York Times,* Oct. 18, 1908, p. AS3.

Franklin Roosevelt "M. H. Roberts, Auto Racer, Is Dead at 74," *Nutley (N.J.) Sun,* Sept. 26, 1957; "World Racer in '08 Tries His Car Again," *New York Times,* Mar. 24, 1953, p. 33.

Roberts's impression of estate "World Racer in '08 Tries His Car Again," *New York Times,* Mar. 24, 1953, p. 33.

On the latter (Roberts quote) Montague Roberts, "Automobile Racing Most Fascinating of Sports," *New York Times,* Oct. 18, 1908, p. AS3.

Twenty-four-hour race "Houpt Company Has Star Racing Team," *New York Times,* May 30, 1909, p. S4.

Houpt gives Roberts car "Briarcliff Race," *The World,* Feb. 9, 1908.

French teams in Alps "Auto Test in Alps for the Big Race," *New York Times,* Dec. 22, 1907, sec. 3, p. 3.

Chapter Four
RACE TO THE STARTING LINE

Hansen at World's Fair "Automobiles Pass Through Rochester," *Rochester Union and Advertiser,* Feb. 17, 1908, p. 11.

Hansen in Argentina "Autoists to Start on Trip Round the World," *New York World,* Feb. 9, 1908.

He is a remarkably (New York quote) "Bets He'll Reach Paris in 100 Days," *New York Times,* Jan. 14, 1908, p. 3.

He is a courageous gentleman (Pirelli quote) "Expects American to Win Auto Race," *New York Times,* Feb. 4, 1908, p. 2.

Koeppen's meeting with Herr de la Croix Hans Koeppen, *Um Welt de Auto* (Berlin: Ullstein, 1908), p. 9.

Conference with Ullsteins Koeppen, *Um Welt de Auto,* pp. 10–11.

Schedule for leaving Berlin Koeppen, *Um Welt de Auto,* p. 12.

Knape as boat racer "Autoists Here for Big Race," *New York Times,* Feb. 8, 1908, p. 1.

The men who are entered (Pirelli quote) "Expects American to Win Auto Race," *New York Times,* Feb. 4, 1908, p. 2.

Kaiser's interest in race "Emperor's Good Word," *New York Times,* Feb. 8, 1908, p. 2.

Chapter Five
TO DEFEND AMERICA AGAINST THE WORLD

The most beautiful song (Koeppen quote) Koeppen, *Um Welt de Auto,* p. 14.

My seventy-nine-year-old (Koeppen quote) Koeppen, *Um Welt de Auto,* p. 15.

Entrants seasick "Paris Racers Here to Start," *New York Times,* Feb. 9, 1908, pt. 2, p. 2.

Statler investment "E. R. Thomas Motor Company," in George S. May, ed., *Encyclopaedia of American Business History & Biography, Automobile Industry, 1896–1920* (New York: Facts on File, 1990), p. 441.

Arrival of foreign drivers "New York-to-Paris Auto Drivers Arrive on Liner," *New York Globe,* Feb. 8, 1908.

Import statistics "Big Duty on Cars," *South Bend Tribune,* Feb. 25, 1908, p. 4.

There will be little time (New York quote) "Paris Racers Here to Start," *New York Times,* Feb. 9, 1908, pt. 2, p. 2.

Boston customer for Flyer "Thomas Car Has Arrived at Cleveland," *Buffalo Evening Times,* Feb. 18, 1908, p. 1.

Thomas loaded on train "Paris Racers Here to Start," *New York Times,* Feb. 9, 1908, pt. 2, p. 1.

Gadski position in U.S. "Mme. Gadski Is Dead After Motor Crash," *New York Times,* Feb. 24, 1932, p. 21.

Godard greets boy "Paris Racers Try the Road," *New York Times,* Feb. 10, 1908, p. 1.

The Italian psychology (Scarfoglio quote) Scarfoglio, *Round the World,* pp. 24–25.

The date was February 11 (Schuster quote) George Schuster with Tom Mahoney, *The Longest Auto Race* (New York: John Day, 1966), p. 11.

Chapter Six

ONE DOWN IN NEW YORK

Captain Koeppen makes a dry (Lausanne quote) "Raid New York–Parigi," *La Tribuna* [Rome, Italy], in translation, Feb. 14, 1908.

Description of Sizaire-Naudin "Six Cars Leave Times Square Cheered by a Crowd of 50,000 Persons," *New York Globe,* Feb. 12, 1908.

Godard as stout and genial "American Car to the Front," *New York Times,* Feb. 13, 1908, pt. 2, p. 2.

Rifle hanging on Thomas "Immense Crowd Greets Autoists," *Poughkeepsie Daily Eagle,* Feb. 13, 1908.

Above the layer (Motor Age quote) "World's Racers Leave New York for Paris," *Motor Age,* Feb. 13, 1908, vol. 13, no. 7, p. 4.

There goes "Get There" (New York quote) "American Car Soon Leads," *New York Times,* Feb. 13, 1908, pt. 2, p. 2.

Barnard students "Autos Are Off in World Race," *Chicago Tribune,* Feb. 13, 1908, p. 5.

Never in the history (New York Times *quote*) "Great Gathering of Motors," *New York Times,* Feb. 13, 1908, pt. 2, p. 2.

By 10 o'clock (Tribune *quote*) "Globe Circlers Off," *New York Tribune,* Feb. 13, 1908.

Italian strategy "20,000 Mile Race Begun," *London Daily Mail,* Feb. 13, 1908, p. 5.

At Poughkeepsie (Scarfoglio quote) Antonio Scarfoglio, "20,000-Mile Race," *London Daily Mail,* Feb. 15, 1908, p. 5.

Crowds in Poughkeepsie "Make Reception Big One," *Poughkeepsie News-Press,* Feb. 12, 1908, p. 1; "Meet Auto Races Here," *Poughkeepsie Evening Star,* Feb. 12, 1908, p. 1.

Effect of cold "Autoists on Long Trip Linger Here," *Poughkeepsie News-Journal,* Feb. 13, 1908.

Condition of roads Joyce C. Ghee and Joan Spence, *Poughkeepsie, 1898–1998* (Arcadia, 1998), pp. 2, 60, 62.

River ice "Ice Harvest on the River at Its Highest," *Poughkeepsie News-Press,* Feb. 11, 1908.

Student on her way to exam "News of Week from Vassar," *Poughkeepsie Telegram,* Feb. 15, 1908, p. 3.

Crowd strains necks "Immense Crowd Greets Autoists," *Poughkeepsie Daily Eagle,* Feb. 13, 1908.

Züst rushes through "Immense Crowd Greets Autoists," *Poughkeepsie Daily Eagle,* Feb. 13, 1908.

Buffalo impressions "This Going Is Terrific," *Buffalo Express,* Feb. 14, 1908, p. 1.

New York impressions "Racing to Paris Pretty Slow Work," *New York World,* Feb. 14, 1908.

Intelligent native (Williams quote) "They're Drawing Near to Buffalo," *Buffalo Commercial,* Feb. 13, 1908, p. 4.

Mrs. Andrews and Frenchmen "Naudin Broken Differential," *New York Times,* Feb. 13, 1908, p. 2.

Description of Hudson Bruce Edward Hall, *Diamond Street: The Story of the Little Town with the Big Red Light District* (Hensonville, N.Y.: Black Dome Press, 1994), pp. 15–16.

Cockfight "Created Big Sensation," *Hudson Morning Republican,* Feb. 13, 1908.

Schuster sees to car "American Car First Here," *Hudson Morning Republican,* Feb. 13, 1908.

Chapter Seven

TOWPATH SPRINT

Race standings "They're Off to Paris," *New York Times,* Feb. 13, 1908, p. 1 n.b. All subsequent race standings at chapter headings are from the *New York Times* official race records, as published on the date specified.

Moto-Bloc in drift "Godard's Story of the Moto-Bloc," *New York Times*, Feb. 14, 1908, p. 2.

Three-dollar fine "Frozen Lake Crossed," *London Daily Mail*, Feb. 15, 1908, p. 5.

Thus we traversed (Scarfoglio quote) "20,000-Mile Race," *London Daily Mail*, Feb. 15, 1908, p. 5.

Thomas team helps De Dion "Four Cars Through This City," *Albany Argus*, Feb. 14, 1908.

After two hours (St. Chaffray quote) "St. Chaffray's Story," *New York Times*, Feb. 14, 1908, p. 2.

Sharp-shod horses "Verbank," *Poughkeepsie News-Telegraph*, Feb. 15, 1908.

Albany guides get stuck "This Going Is Terrific," *Buffalo Express*, Feb. 14, 1908, p. 1.

Bill outlawing 20 hp cars "Auto Bills May Cause Worry," *Albany Argus*, Feb. 14, 1908.

Banquet at Ten Eyck "New York to Paris Cars Here," *Albany Evening Journal*, Feb. 14, 1908.

Hansen's comments at banquet "The Autos Reach Fonda," *New York Times*, Feb. 14, 1908, p. 2.

We were received in triumph (Scarfoglio quote) Scarfoglio, *Round the World*, p. 35.

Railroad station opens "Schenectady's New Station," *Amsterdam Evening Recorder*, Feb. 17, 1908.

Bridge has to be built "Big Cars Came on Canal Towpath," *Utica Observer*, Feb. 14, 1908.

We call Capt. Hansen (St. Chaffray quote) "St. Chaffray's Own Story," *New York Times*, Feb. 15, 1908, p. 2.

What human forces can (Scarfoglio quote) Scarfoglio, *Round the World*, p. 36.

Koeppen went up the Hyde Park (Poughkeepsie quote) "Motorists Return Here," *Poughkeepsie Evening Star*, Feb. 13, 1908, p. 1.

Six-foot drift "Leaders at Utica," *Albany Evening Journal*, Feb. 14, 1908, p. 1.

Lieutenant Koeppen is making (Albany quote) "Driving Their Cars Along the Erie Towpath To-day," *Albany Evening Journal*, Feb. 15, 1908, p. 1.

The Protos stopped (Knape quote) "Naudin Broke Differential," *New York Times*, Feb. 14, 1908, p. 2.

The canal towpath does not (Utica quote) "Big Cars Came on Canal Towpath," *Utica Observer*, Feb. 14, 1908.

Schuster's wife improving "This Going Is Terrific," *Buffalo Express*, Feb. 14, 1908, p. 1.

Notes

As the Dutchman says (E. R. Thomas quote) "Driving Along Dangerous Roads," *Buffalo Commercial*, Feb. 15, 1908, p. 1.

Life is too short (Hansen quote) "Three Autos Reach Canastota," *New York Times*, Feb. 15, 1908, p. 1.

State speed limits John J. Walsh, "The Automobile Industry in Utica," *Vignettes of Old Utica* (Utica Public Library, 1982), p. 359.

But I simply had (Roberts quote) "Excellent 'Sport,' " *London Daily Mail*, Feb. 17, 1908, p. 5.

A slip of the wheel (quote) "They Longed for Syracuse," *Buffalo Express*, Feb. 15, 1908, p. 1.

Get after him, boy (canal quote) "Three Autos Reach Canastota," *New York Times*, Feb. 15, 1908, p. 2.

Italian population of Utica George Schiro, *Americans by Choice: History of the Italians in Utica* (Utica: Thomas J. Griffiths, 1940), p. 104.

It was easy to move (de Rosa quote) Schiro, *Americans by Choice*, p. 123.

It seemed to me (Van Denbergh quote) Schiro, *Americans by Choice*, pp. 9, 97, 102.

Floral horseshoe "Big Cars Came on Canal Towpath," *Utica Observer*, Feb. 14, 1908.

That peaceful, delicious town (Scarfoglio quote) Scarfoglio, *Round the World*, p. 38.

This way to see the egress (attorney quote) "Three Autos Reach Canastota," *New York Times*, Feb. 15, 1908, p. 2.

Everywhere they receive us (St. Chaffray quote) "Excellent 'Sport,' " *London Daily Mail*, Feb. 17, 1908, p. 5.

If those daring fellows (Utica quote) "Observed About Town," *Utica Observer*, Feb. 15, 1908, p. 3.

Race joke "Strenuous Day's Run Ended at Old Geneva," *Buffalo Illustrated Times*, Feb. 16, 1908, p. 1.

Scarfoglio loses temper "Auto Racers at Geneva," *Buffalo Express*, Feb. 16, 1908, p. 1; "Racing Autoists Due in Rochester This Morning," *Rochester Herald*, Feb. 16, 1908.

Hansen defends himself "Three of Automobilists in New York–Paris Race Arrive in Rochester," *Rochester Herald*, Feb. 17, 1908, p. 1.

Hansen's singing "Hansen Goes into a Dance," *New York Times*, Feb. 16, 1908, p. 2.

Chapter Eight
Act of War

Union veteran "Spirits of Rye; Spirit of 1861," *Buffalo Express*, Feb. 15, 1908, p. 1.

Roberts in Batavia "Two Racing Cars Here," *Buffalo Express*, Feb. 17, 1908, p. 1.

Williams holding on "Thomas First at Buffalo," *New York Times*, Feb. 17, 1908, p. 1.

Hansen's opinion of Roberts "Three of Automobilists in New York–Paris Race Arrive in Rochester," *Rochester Herald*, Feb. 17, 1908.

Choir boys cheering Schuster with Mahoney, *The Longest Auto Race*, p. 30.

Schuster lying in slush "Germans Fourth in Race," *Rome Daily Sentinel*, Feb. 15, 1908.

Hower "Henry [*sic*] B. Hower, Pioneer Auto, Oil Man, Dies," *Buffalo Courier-Express*, Oct. 6, 1932, p. 20.

Lewis's job "Dai H. Lewis, Auto Pioneer, Beloved Buffalonian, Dead," *Buffalo Motorist*, Sept. 1943, pp. 7–14.

Buffalo automaking companies Walter S. Dunn Jr., *History of Erie County* (Buffalo & Erie County Historical Society, 1972), p. 34.

Roberts in Williamsville "Leave for Erie Early Today," *Buffalo Courier*, Feb. 17, 1908, p. 8.

De Dion arrives on Main Street "Two N.Y.–Paris Cars Reach Buffalo," *Buffalo Courier*, Feb. 17, 1908, p. 1.

We want to help (Bull quote) "Endurance Run Becomes a Race," *Buffalo Commercial*, Feb. 18, 1908, p. 1.

An animated conversation began (Syracuse quote) "Fourth Machine Reaches City," *Syracuse Post-Standard*, Feb. 17, 1908.

Roads? What terrible roads (Koeppen quote) "Protos Looks like a Hencoop on Wheels," *Utica Observer*, Feb. 15, 1908, p. 1.

It looks to me (St. Chaffray quote) "St. Chaffray Enthusiastic," *New York Times*, Feb. 18, 1908, p. 2.

Protos covered with names "Germans Stop in Syracuse," *Syracuse Herald*, Feb. 16, 1908.

In every village (Scarfoglio quote) "Night Dash Across Frozen Snow," *London Daily Mail*, Feb. 20, 1908, p. 5.

Doctors, lawyers (Scarfoglio quote) Scarfoglio, *Round the World*, p. 43.

Car turned turtle (Ruland quote) "Message from Italian," *Buffalo Commercial*, Feb. 17, 1908, p. 1.

Even there, are the roads (St. Chaffray quote) "Thomas Machine Chasing Leaders," *Buffalo Commercial*, Feb. 17, 1908, p. 9.

Items stolen from Protos "Car Arrives and Departs," *Rochester Union & Advertiser*, Feb. 17, 1908, p. 1.

We will either reach Paris (Hansen quote) "Three of Automobilists in New York—Paris Race Arrive in Rochester," *Rochester Herald*, Feb. 17, 1908.

If we don't catch the Italians (Hansen quote) "Just a Bit of Feeling," *Buffalo Express,* Feb. 18, 1908, p. 1.

Schuster assures E. R. Thomas "Thomas Car Starts Off in Pursuit of the Italians," *Buffalo Evening Times,* Feb. 17, 1908, p. 1.

E. R. Thomas holds out flag "Just a Bit of Feeling," *Buffalo Express,* Feb. 18, 1908, p. 3.

The after-you-my-dear (Buffalo quote) "Just a Bit of Feeling," *Buffalo Express,* Feb. 18, 1908, p. 1.

Storms in Midwest "Great Blizzard Raging Out West," *Buffalo Courier,* Feb. 19, 1908, p. 1.

Chapter Nine
SNOW SPRAY

Wrapped in heavy (Clevelander's quote) Uncredited article, "American Car Leads Big Race," *Cleveland Press,* Feb. 18, 1908, p. 2.

Three o'clock alarm "American Auto Gets to Toledo," *New York Times,* Feb. 19, 1908, p. 2.

Operators as news source "Motobloc at Buffalo," *New York Times,* Feb. 19, 1908, p. 2.

Mockery of Williams's weight "American Auto Gets to Toledo," *New York Times,* Feb. 19, 1908, p. 2.

Unfortunately, Jim was in it (Loucks quote) Edna McMahon Loucks, "Thinking of Days Gone By—Conneaut," *Ashtabula County History, Then and Now* (Dallas, Tex.: Taylor Publishing Co., 1985), p. 59.

Description of Lake County Writer's Program of the WPA, *Lake County History* (Lake County: Western Reserve Historical Society, 1941), pp. 5–7, 45.

Farmwife with rifle "Feared Strategy of Italians," *New York Times,* Feb. 19, 1908, p. 2.

Cleveland as automaking capital George E. Condon, *Yesterday's Cleveland* (Miami, Fla.: E. A. Seemann Pub., 1976), p. 55.

Sperry returns home "Horses Tow Cars," *Norwalk (Ohio) Daily Reflector,* Feb. 24, 1908, p. 1.

Garford factory "Automobile Chasers Raced Through Public Streets," *Elyria Chronicle,* Feb. 19, 1908, p. 1.

De Dion in Norwalk "Big Cars Speeding Westward," *Norwalk (Ohio) Daily Reflector,* Feb. 19, 1908, p. 1.

Missing headlight "Two Cars Left Far in Rear," *Norwalk (Ohio) Daily Reflector,* Feb. 20, 1908, p. 1.

We are heroes (St. Chaffray quote) "Hunger Stops St. Chaffray," *New York Times,* Feb. 19, 1908, p. 2.

Description of Boody Hotel Randolph C. Downes, *Lake Port* (Toledo: Historical Society of Northwestern Ohio, 1951), pp. 416, 422.

Those who saw the Yankee (Toledo quote) "Auto Drivers in Real Race," *Toledo Blade*, Feb. 19, 1908, p. 6.

We set out from Cleveland (Roberts quote) "Auto Drivers in Real Race," *Toledo Blade*, Feb. 19, 1908, p. 6.

The weatherman has a right (Indianapolis quote) "Sports Thoughts of the Day," *Indianapolis News*, Feb. 20, 1908, p. 10.

Flyer's progress from Waterloo Untitled, *Albion (Indiana) New Era*, Feb. 26, 1908, p. 1.

Yer ahead of the Frenchy (farmer's quote) "Five Cars Are Left in Great Auto Race," *Chicago Post*, Feb. 20, 1908, p. 6.

Gwan, shovel your head off (St. Chaffray quote) "French Driver Laughed While Roberts Shoveled Snow," *Toledo Daily Blade*, Feb. 22, 1908, p. 16.

These drivers had a helper (McDonald quote) Archie McDonald, reminiscence, "Vignette 13-3," John Martin Smith, *History of DeKalb County, Indiana* (Auburn, Ind.: Natmus, 1992), p. 433.

Chapter Ten

COMBUSTION

Protos in last place "French Racer Comes at Noon," *Cleveland Press*, Feb. 21, 1908, p. 1.

It was equipped (Norwalk quote) "German Car in Town," *Norwalk Evening Herald*, Feb. 22, 1908, p. 1.

Protos breakdown "German Car Stays Here Sixteen Hours," *Norwalk Daily Reflector*, Feb. 22, 1908, p. 2.

Toledo Bee impression of Protos team "German Car Protos Passed Through Here," *Toledo News-Bee*, Feb. 22, 1908, p. 3.

It was all very nice (Maas quote) "German Car in Town," *Goshen (Indiana) Daily Democrat*, Feb. 26, 1908, p. 1.

Siberiana "Thomas Car Meets New Snow Barriers," *Chicago Evening Post*, Feb. 24, 1908, p. 8.

De Dion's broken transmission "Roberts Is Plucky in Fight with Snow," *Chicago Evening Post*, Feb. 21, 1908, p. 1.

Hansen's opinion of St. Chaffray's driving "Paris Auto Racers Still in Snow Fight," *Chicago Evening Post*, Feb. 22, 1908, p. 8.

I know the social life (St. Chaffray quote) "St. Chaffray Left Behind," *New York Times*, Feb. 23, 1908, p. 2.

I am tired of (Roberts quote) "American Auto Still in Lead," *Goshen Mid-Week News-Times*, Feb. 25, 1908, p. 3.

NOTES

Worst storm in twenty years "City Paralyzed by Storm: Worst Blizzard in 20 Years," *Michigan City Evening News,* Feb. 19, 1908, p. 1.

Size of drifts "Paged by Inter-Urban," *Elkhart Daily Review,* Feb. 22, 1908, p. 1.

Train stuck "Three Days on the Road," *Michigan City Evening News,* Feb. 21, 1908, p. 1.

Shovellers "Homeless Men Shovel Snow," *Chicago Tribune,* Feb. 19, 1908, p. 2.

Two miles out of that (Chicago quote) A Frozen Stiff Photographer, "Tour of Autoists Like Polar Trip," *Chicago Tribune,* Feb. 25, 1908, p. 1.

Pushing the car "American Car In; Italian Follows Close," *Michigan City Evening News,* Feb. 24, 1908, p. 1.

Digging the horses out A Frozen Stiff Photographer, "Tour of Autoists Like Polar Trip," *Chicago Tribune,* Feb. 25, 1908, p. 1.

Get there we must (Roberts quote) "Auto Racers Push on Through Snow," *New York Times,* Feb. 24, 1908, p. 1.

Size of horse teams "Italian Car in Late Today," *Michigan City Evening News,* Feb. 25, 1908, p. 1.

Züst record for horses "Chicago Greets Racers with Royal Reception," *Michigan City Evening News,* Feb. 26, 1908, p. 1.

Complaints about Indiana "American Car Is First to Chicago," *Ligonier (Indiana) Banner,* Feb. 27, 1908, p. 2.

Permission to use tracks withheld "World Race Cars Due Here Today," *Chicago Tribune,* Feb. 24, 1908, p. 3.

I will help only (Picard quote) "World Race Cars Due Here Today," *Chicago Tribune,* Feb. 24, 1908, p. 3.

Charles Coey Notable Men of Chicago (Chicago: Chicago Daily Journal, 1910), p. 81.

Is this Coey's (Coey quote) "Snow Chains Leader in Great Auto Race," *Chicago Record-Herald,* Feb. 25, 1908, p. 3.

Roberts smiles "Chicago Triumph for Leading Auto," *Chicago Tribune,* Feb. 26, 1908, p. 3.

It was an awful (Roberts quote) "American Car First; All Chicago Cheers," *Chicago Record-Herald,* Feb. 26, 1908, p. 1.

I got up speed (Sirtori quote) "Züst Races De Dion to Chicago Club," *New York Times,* Feb. 27, 1908, p. 2.

Cameras, films, guns (Godard quote) "Motobloc Car Looted," *New York Times,* Feb. 27, 1908, p. 2.

We are going on (Godard quote) "Motobloc Car Looted," *New York Times,* Feb. 27, 1908, p. 2.

Colonel Conn tries to help "Trouble for Motobloc," *Goshen (Indiana) Daily Democrat,* Feb. 27, 1908, p. 1.

Dwight leads Moto-Bloc "Automobile Was Attached," *Goshen Weekly News-Times,* Feb. 28, 1908, p. 1.

Besides telling you (Hansen quote) "Deserts French Auto," *Chicago Record-Herald,* Feb. 28, 1908, p. 8; "Arctic Explorer Quits French Car," *Chicago Tribune,* Feb. 28, 1908, p. 4.

Duel in snowdrift "Cuts De Dion for Thomas," *Michigan City Evening News,* Feb. 28, 1908, p. 1.

Chapter Eleven

GUMBO

Sirtori wishes Roberts luck "Paris Auto Race in Second Stage," *New York Times,* Feb. 29, 1908, p. 1.

It was the foreigners (Roberts quote) "American Car in City Sunday," *Cedar Rapids Daily Reflector,* Mar. 3, 1908, p. 7.

It's a cinch (Roberts quote) "Nearing the City," *Clinton (Iowa) Daily Advertiser,* Feb. 29, 1908, p. 1.

Banker drags roads "Run Across Iowa on Way to Paris," *Des Moines Register,* Mar. 2, 1908, p. 1.

Boone headline "The City of Boone Has Gone Nearly 'Automobile' Crazy," *Boone (Iowa) News-Republican,* Mar. 2, 1908, p. 1.

Iowans daffy on race "Auto Racers in Denison," *Denison Bulletin,* Mar. 3, 1908, p. 1.

Round-the-clock guards "Auto Tire Bursts," *Council Bluffs (Iowa) Daily Nonpareil,* Feb. 29, 1908, p. 1.

With a roar like that (Council Bluffs quote) " 'Slow Progress' in Iowa Mud," *Council Bluffs (Iowa) Sunday Nonpareil,* Mar. 1, 1908, p. 1.

I have to write (Lacey quote) "Army Car Flits By," *Council Bluffs (Iowa) Daily Nonpareil,* Mar. 2, 1908, p. 2.

Williams gave the town (Clarence quote) "Auto Ought to Be Canal Boat," *Des Moines Register,* Mar. 3, 1908, p. 7.

Roberts wants canal boat "American Car in City Sunday," *Cedar Rapids Daily Republican,* Mar. 3, 1908, p. 7.

Silence in Cedar Rapids "Auto Race Excitement," *Clarence Sun,* Mar. 5, 1908, p. 1.

Forward! Forward! (Scarfoglio quote) "Round the World Race," *London Daily Mail,* Mar. 4, 1908, p. 5.

Lascares joins De Dion Hy Gear, "French and Italian Cars on Road Again," *Chicago Post,* Feb. 29, 1908, p. 10.

The Frenchmen and the Italians (guide's quote) "Three of Racers Pass Through Clinton," *Clinton (Iowa) Daily Advertiser,* Mar. 2, 1908, p. 1.

Cedar Rapids for French and Italians "De Dion and Züst Motors Arrive," *Cedar Rapids Evening Gazette,* Mar. 3, 1908, p. 5.

Unofficial holiday "Italian and French Cars Are in Cedar Rapids," *Cedar Rapids Daily Republican,* Mar. 3, 1908, p. 8.

What a splendid building (St. Chaffray quote) "High Praise Given to Cedar Rapids," *Cedar Rapids Daily Republican,* Mar. 3, 1908, p. 6.

I have travelled a great deal (Scarfoglio quote) "High Praise Given to Cedar Rapids," *Cedar Rapids Daily Republican,* Mar. 3, 1908, p. 1.

Cost of telegram Untitled editorial column, *Cedar Rapids Daily Republican,* Mar. 4, 1908, p. 4.

De Dion broken frame "Frenchmen Were Guests at a Smoker," *Cedar Rapids Daily Republican,* Mar. 4, 1908, p. 1.

Puffed rice "Nebraska Mud Now for Auto Racers," *New York Times,* Mar. 6, 1908, pp. 1, 3.

Carmody's political campaign "St. Chaffray in Politics," *New York Times,* Mar. 7, 1908, p. 2.

Hansen is ze grand (St. Chaffray quote) "De Dion and Züst Motors Arrive," *Cedar Rapids Evening Gazette,* Mar. 3, 1908, p. 5.

De Dion in Carmody's shop "Will Not Come Here," *Cedar Rapids Daily Republican,* Mar. 5, 1908, p. 5.

St. Chaffray's mood "Frenchmen Were Guests at a Smoker," *Cedar Rapids Daily Republican,* Mar. 4, 1908, p. 1.

Take your car (Marquis de Dion cable) "Go Through If It Takes Three Years," *Cedar Rapids Daily Republican,* Mar. 6, 1908, p. 10.

Roberts in Ames "Auto Ought to Be Canal Boat," *Des Moines Register,* Mar. 3, 1908, p. 7.

Mayor can't speak "Hip! Hip! Ahmerikay Italian's Yell," *Ames Intelligencer,* Mar. 5, 1908, p. 1.

Use of hose "Doused the Crowd, Drove Them Back," *Nevada (Iowa) Evening Journal,* Mar. 6, 1908, p. 1.

Smiths' ride "Hip! Hip! Ahmerikay Italian's Yell," *Ames Intelligencer,* Mar. 5, 1908, p. 1.

Flag stolen "Hoodlumism Given Scoring," *Boone News-Republican,* Mar. 7, 1908, p. 5.

Adults' reaction "The Italian Autoists Like Boone and the People Reciprocate," *Boone News-Republican,* Mar. 5, 1908, p. 1.

Des Moines man in farmhouse "Across Iowa with the Racers," *Des Moines Register,* Mar. 8, 1908, sec. 4, p. 1.

Willie Johnson's disguise "Good Joke on the Public," *Boone News-Republican,* Mar. 5, 1908, p. 9; "Auto Owner Plays Prank," *Marshalltown Evening Times-Republican,* Mar. 2, 1908, p. 1.

Roberts experience on rough roads "Big Autos Hurry By," *Jefferson (Iowa) Bee,* Mar. 4, 1908, p. 5.

Bridge breaks in Belle Plaine "Cheers of Crowds Greet American Car," *Marshalltown Evening Times Republican,* Mar. 2, 1908, p. 7.

I don't like your roads (Roberts quote) "Montague Roberts Is Not Pleased with the Iowa Roads," *Boone News-Republican,* Mar. 3, 1908, p. 1.

Roberts on Jefferson Co. Roads "Big Autos Hurry By," *Jefferson (Iowa) Bee,* Mar. 4, 1908, p. 5.

Roberts opinions of Iowa Untitled article, *"Missouri Valley Times,* Mar. 5, 1908, p. 5.

A voice at the end (Boone quote) "The Italian Autoists Like Boone and the People Reciprocate," *Boone News-Republican,* Mar. 5, 1908, p. 1.

Italians unload car "Too Much by Night," *Council Bluffs (Iowa) Daily Nonpareil,* Mar. 6, 1908, p. 1.

We go straight (Sirtori quote) "An Iowa Welcome," *Council Bluffs (Iowa) Daily Nonpareil,* Mar. 8, 1908, p. 1.

It is one strange (Godard quote) "Moto-Bloc Reaches Chicago," *New York Times,* Mar. 4, 1908, p. 2.

Koeppen on use of trains "Protos Reaches Chicago," *New York Times,* Mar. 5, 1908, p. 2.

I feel that we have (Knape quote) "Change in Protos' Crew," *New York Times,* Mar. 6, 1908, p. 3.

Chapter Twelve

A SINGLE ROOM IN CHICAGO

The German and the other (Boone quote) "The Automobile Craze," *Boone County Democrat,* Mar. 6, 1908, p. 5.

Chicago is only America Edward Hungerford, "The Personality of American Cities" (1913), Bessie L. Pierce with Joe L. Norris, ed., *As Others See Chicago, 1673–1933* (Chicago: Univ. of Chicago, 1933), pp. 376, 435.

Godard invitation to chateau "Moto-Bloc Will Start Today," *New York Times,* Mar. 6, 1908, p. 3.

Kaiser's birthday celebrations Rudolph A. Hofmeister, *The Germans of Chicago* (Champaign, Ill.: Stipes Publishing, 1976), p. 63.

Condition of Protos "Will Leave Saturday," *Marshalltown (Iowa) Evening Times Republican,* Mar. 5, 1908, p. 1.

Snyder hired "Will Leave Chicago To-Day," *New York Times,* Mar. 7, 1908, p. 2.

They are last (Chicago quote) "German Car Stalled in Barn," *Chicago Tribune,* Mar. 8, 1908, p. 5.

Giant pretzel "It Was German Day," *Clinton (Iowa) Advertiser,* Mar. 10, 1908, p. 2.

First De Dion driveshaft to break "French Say They Will Win," *Omaha Evening Bee,* Mar. 9, 1908, p. 2.

What mattair if (St. Chaffray quote) "Frenchman Has Woe," *Council Bluffs (Iowa) Daily Nonpareil,* Mar. 13, 1908, p. 1.

As soon as we left (St. Chaffray quote) "St. Chaffray Here; Automobile Stuck," *Omaha World-Herald,* Mar. 10, 1908, p. 1.

I hope that no one (Hansen quote) "The Men Who Drive the American Car," *Omaha Record-Herald Sunday Magazine,* Mar. 8, 1908, p. 6-M.

I was glad to see (Roberts quote) "Omaha Crowds Meet Auto Race Leader," *New York Times,* Mar. 5, 1908, p. 1.

Description of Omaha Arthur C. Wakeley, *Omaha: The Gate City and Douglas County, Nebraska* (Chicago: S. J. Clarke Pub., 1917), p. 121.

Siren to blow "Auto Is Making 12 Miles an Hour," *Omaha Morning World-Herald,* Mar. 3, 1908, p. 1.

Mud-covered Thomas "American Car Spends Night at Logan, Iowa," *Omaha World-Herald,* Mar. 4, 1908, p. 1.

Smith's free clothes "American Car on Nebraska Soil," *Kearney (Neb.) Daily Hub,* Mar. 6, 1908, p. 3.

Col. William F. Cody (Roberts quote) "Omaha Crowds Meet Auto Race Leader," *New York Times,* Mar. 5, 1908, p. 1.

Roller-skating "American Car Gets a Great Reception," *Omaha World-Herald,* Mar. 5, 1908, p. 5; "American Car on Nebraska Soil," *Kearney (Neb.) Daily Hub,* Mar. 6, 1908, p. 3.

Democratic convention "Greatest Convention of Democrats Ever in State," *Omaha World-Herald,* Mar. 6, 1908, p. 1.

We hear nothing but (Roberts quote) "Roberts Answers Some of the Statements of Rivals," *Omaha Evening Bee,* Mar. 5, 1908, p. 1.

Mr. Roberts is a pleasant (Omaha quote) Untitled editorial article, *Columbus Telegram,* Mar. 6, 1908, p. 1.

Roberts on quality of guides Untitled editorial article, *Columbus Telegram,* Mar. 6, 1908, p. 1.

Listen for the whistle (Omaha quote) "Italian Car Is Coming," *Omaha Daily News,* Mar. 6, 1908, p. 1.

Züst's arrival "Italian Car Arrives After Hard Struggle," *Omaha World-Herald,* Mar. 8, 1908, p. 8.

The American car (Scarfoglio quote) "Omaha a Pleasant Surprise for Italians," *Omaha Daily News,* Mar. 8, 1908, p. 1.

Union Pacific repairs Züst "American Car at Cheyenne," *Nebraska State Journal,* Mar. 9, 1908, p. 2; "Italian Car Leaves Omaha on Its Long Trip to Paris," *Omaha Daily News,* Mar. 9, 1908, p. 7.

Chapter Thirteen
CHEYENNE

Clymer's experiences Floyd Clymer, "Announcement," *The Story of the New York-to-Paris Race* (Thomas Motor Car Co., 1908), reprinted by Clymer Publications; Floyd Clymer, *Henry's Wonderful Model T* (New York: McGraw-Hill, 1955), pp. 4–5.

Roads between Denver and Cheyenne "American Car Nearing Cheyenne," *Wyoming Tribune,* March 6, 1908, p. 1.

Next time, a Denver-built (Colburn quote) "American Car Due in Cheyenne Before Noon," *Cheyenne Daily Leader,* Mar. 8, 1908, p. 1.

Mathewson as Thomas agent "American Car Nearing Cheyenne," *Wyoming Tribune,* Mar. 6, 1908, p. 4.

Brinker to go along "Racing Car Will Change Drivers at Cheyenne," *Wyoming Tribune,* Mar. 5, 1908, p. 1.

Monte, You Winner (headline) "Monte, You Winner, The Town's Yours," *Cheyenne Daily Leader,* Mar. 9, 1908, p. 1.

Newsboys in Cheyenne "Newsboys of Denver Surprise Cheyenne," *Rocky Mountain News,* Mar. 9, 1908, p. 5.

I sail for Paris (Roberts quote) "Thomas Car at Sydney," *Cheyenne Daily Leader,* Mar. 6, 1908, p. 4.

You may just say for me (Roberts quote) "Thomas Car at Sydney," *Cheyenne Daily Leader,* Mar. 6, 1908, p. 4.

Thomas on trail to Cheyenne "Cowboys Welcome Race at Cheyenne," *New York Times,* Mar. 9, 1908, p. 1.

A majority of those pictures (Cheyenne quote) "American Car Delayed by a One-Man Strike," *Cheyenne Daily Leader,* Mar. 10, 1908, p. 1.

Roberts meets Mackenzie "Cowboys Welcome Race at Cheyenne," *New York Times,* Mar. 9, 1908, p. 1.

Atmosphere at banquet "Cheyenne Rises to the Occasion," *Wyoming Tribune,* Mar. 9, 1908, p. 1.

Houpt in Cheyenne "Thanks of Veteran Wheel Man in Paris Race," *Rocky Mountain News,* Mar. 10, 1908, p. 3.

I have never been west before (Roberts quote) "Cheyenne Rises to the Occasion," *Wyoming Tribune,* Mar. 9, 1908, p. 5.

Comparison to Roosevelt's visit "Welcome to American Car in Cheyenne Greatest Public Demonstration Since Famous Ride of President Roosevelt," *Wyoming Tribune,* Mar. 9, 1908, p. 1.

Chapter Fourteen
ON STRIKE

Schuster in bike business Schuster with Mahoney, *The Longest Auto Race,* p. 14.

Dai Lewis's business Dai H. Lewis, *America Bid Me Welcome* (Buffalo: 1943), p. 74.

Besides Roberts (St. Chaffray quote) Bourcier St. Chaffray, "De Dion to Go on To-Day," *New York Times,* Mar. 11, 1908, p. 2.

Mackenzie on car ride Katherine Mackenzie, "Only Girl to Ride in Auto," *Wyoming Tribune,* Mar. 11, 1908, p. 5.

Ordinarily we are quite (Scarfoglio quote) Scarfoglio, *Round the World,* pp. 87–88.

Nebraska farmers' boycott Margaret Curry, *History of Platte County (Nebraska)* (Culver City, Calif.: Murray & Gee, 1950), p. 486.

Park Miller as gas man Curry, *History of Platte County (Nebraska),* p. 518.

Wold ad "Wolf!" advertisement, *Keith County News,* Mar. 19, 1908, p. 3.

Scarfoglio on Indians Antonio Scarfoglio, "The Great Motor Race," *London Daily Mail,* Mar. 7, 1908, p. 5.

Gottberg volunteering to guide Untitled editorial article, *Columbus (Nebraska) Telegram,* Mar. 13, 1908, p. 1.

Gottberg's garage Untitled editorial article, *Columbus (Nebraska) Telegram,* Mar. 27, 1908, p. 1. In the 1920s Max Gottberg, the former sod-buster, built a public airport in Columbus, in hope of encouraging interest in aviation.

Mackenzie on Mathewson/Brinker pledge for speed Katherine Mackenzie, "Only Girl to Ride in Auto," *Wyoming Tribune,* Mar. 11, 1908, p. 5.

We intended to do (Schuster quote) "Banqueted the Autoists," *Laramie Boomerang,* Mar. 10, 1908, p. 1.

Owing to the bad roads (Schuster quote) "Thomas at Laramie, Züst in Hot Pursuit," *New York Times,* Mar. 10, 1908, p. 1.

I decided to ship (Mathewson quote) E. Linn Mathewson, "Auto Race Leader in Wyoming Snow," *New York Times,* Mar. 11, 1908, p. 1.

German headline in Des Moines "Die Protos Maschine Durch Dreck und Koth," *Des Moines Register and Leader,* Mar. 13, 1908, p. 8.

Young reporter in Cedar Rapids "German Contestants Entertained Last Evening," *Cedar Rapids Evening Gazette,* Mar. 12, 1908, p. 5.

Koeppen takes train west "German Car 'Protos' Arrived This Afternoon," *Cedar Rapids Evening Gazette,* Mar. 11, 1908, p. 2.

These automobilists should remember (Council Bluffs quote) "Iowa Mud," *Cedar Rapids Evening Gazette,* Mar. 16, 1908, p. 4.

Someone ought to start (Denison quote) Untitled editorial, *Denison Bulletin,* Mar. 25, 1908, p. 5.

It's debatable whether (Waterloo quote) "Looks as Though Team Would Have Won," *Cedar Rapids Evening Gazette,* Mar. 17, 1908, p. 4.

The machines should have (Boone quote) Untitled editorial notes, *Boone Standard,* Mar. 11, 1908, p. 1.

The New York to Paris endurance (Marshalltown quote) "Random Reflections," *Marshalltown Reflector,* Mar. 12, 1908, p. 4.

Cheyenne listens to Scarfoglio "Italian Car Starts in Pursuit of Thomas," *Wyoming Tribune,* Mar. 13, 1908, p. 1.

Haaga on Cheyenne "Hearty Welcome for Big Italian Car," *Wyoming Tribune,* Mar. 12, 1908, p. 1.

Chapter Fifteen

ROCKIES

Posse to search Wawaka "Motobloc's Stolen Articles Found," *Chicago Tribune,* Mar. 8, 1908, p. 5.

Items found Untitled editorial article, *Kendallville News-Sun,* Mar. 12, 1908, p. 1.

I expect that I will (Godard quote) "Motobloc Takes Back Trail," *New York Times,* Mar. 13, 1908, p. 2.

Godard on quick trip through Iowa "Motobloc Is Pushing On," *New York Times,* Mar. 15, 1908, p. 2.

Godard low on money "Trip Will Be Expensive One," *Boone (Iowa) News-Republican,* Mar. 20, 1908, p. 5.

Godard gets directions from stranger "Motobloc Loses Its Way," *New York Times,* Mar. 16, 1908, p. 2.

Protos called a threshing engine "The Last of the Autos," *Jefferson (Iowa) Bee,* Mar. 18, 1908, p. 5.

We have expected (Godard quote) "Motobloc at Ogden, Iowa," *New York Times,* Mar. 17, 1908, p. 2.

Moto-Bloc to be sent to Omaha "Motobloc Is Laid Up," *New York Times,* Mar. 18, 1908, p. 2.

Notes

Moto-Bloc photographed "Auto on Flat Car," *Council Bluffs (Iowa) Nonpareil,* Mar. 19, 1908, p. 3.

By rail to San Francisco (Nonpareil *quote*) Untitled editorial item, *Council Bluffs Nonpareil,* Mar. 19, 1908, p. 4.

St. Chaffray in Omaha "St. Chaffray Is Speeding West," *Omaha Daily News,* Mar. 17, 1908, p. 5.

The beginning of the Far West (St. Chaffray quote) "West Pleases St. Chaffray," *New York Times,* Mar. 15, 1908, p. 2.

Rehearsed Cheers "Fireworks for De Dion," *New York Times,* Mar. 18, 1908, p. 2.

Moonlight picnic Untitled article, *Columbus (Nebraska) Telegram,* Mar. 20, 1908, p. 1.

Farnam St. Margaret P. Killian, *Born Rich: A Historical Book of Omaha* (Omaha: Assistance League of Omaha, 1978), p. 41. n.b. One of Storz's employees was Frederick Austerlitz, the father of Fred Astaire, who spent his early years in Omaha with his sister, Adele. As young children, they are said to have entertained at parties held at the Storz mansion.

Storz's car "Adolph Storz Will Meet German Car," *Omaha Daily News,* Mar. 14, 1908, p. 7.

Parade for Protos "German Car Arrived 'midst Pandemonium," *Omaha World-Herald,* Mar. 18, 1908, p. 4.

Mayor's comment on women drivers "Our Jim Is for the Women," *Omaha Bee,* Mar. 16, 1908, p. 2.

St. Chaffray on dogs "De Dion Is in Trouble," *Grand Island Daily Independent,* Mar. 17, 1908, p. 1.

Prank with telegram "De Dion Still Delayed," *Grand Island Daily Independent,* Mar. 18, 1908, p. 1.

Gottberg as Guide "Last Car Leaves City," *Grand Island Daily News,* Mar. 19, 1908, p. 1.

No car in the New York to Paris Race (Grand Island quote) "Last Car Leaves City," *Grand Island Daily News,* Mar. 19, 1908, p. 1.

Koeppen at banquets "Protos Is Running Well," *New York Times,* Mar. 21, 1908, p. 2.

St. Chaffray's speech "Big Reception Here for German Autoist," *Wyoming Tribune,* Mar. 21, 1908, p. 1.

His wit "Felicitous Banquet to French Racers," *Cheyenne Daily Leader,* Mar. 21, 1908, p. 1.

Buckwalter's movie "Moving Pictures," *Wyoming Tribune,* Mar. 21, 1908, p. 1.

Movie is a hit "The Picture in Cheyenne," *Cheyenne Daily Leader,* Mar. 24, 1908, p. 4.

Mrs. Myers's menu "Big Reception Here for German Autoist," *Wyoming Tribune,* Mar. 21, 1908, p. 1.

I have not unlimited money (Koeppen quote) "Von Koppen [*sic*] in the Protos," *Cheyenne Daily Leader,* Mar. 24, 1908, p. 4.

Learning that the wagon (Mathewson quote) "Auto Races Through a Tunnel a Mile Long," *New York Times,* Mar. 14, 1908, p. 1.

We had gone only (Schuster quote) Schuster with Mahoney, *The Longest Auto Race,* p. 57.

Miller rejoins Thomas team "Utah Snows Halt the Leading Auto," *New York Times,* Mar. 15, 1908, p. 1.

Chapter Sixteen

PIONEER TRACKS
Züst stuck in bog "Car Stuck in a Marsh," *London Daily Mail,* Mar. 21, 1908, p. 5.

At 2 o'clock the springs (Scarfoglio quote) Scarfoglio, *Round the World,* p. 100.

Lamp-signallers questions Scarfoglio, *Round the World,* p. 107.

Züst rests on ravine "Züst's Narrow Escape," *New York Times,* Mar. 19, 1908, p. 1.

Züst refused permission to use tunnel "Racers Must Not Run on Railroad Tracks," *Wyoming Tribune,* Mar. 18, 1908, p. 1.

Damage caused by Thomas "Union Pacific Explains," *New York Times,* Mar. 22, 1908, p. 1.

Local motorists' opinion of road to Ogden "Autos Will Be Here Friday," *Ogden Standard,* Mar. 11, 1908, p. 6.

Schuster reeled like a man (Ogden quote) "American Racer in Ogden," *Ogden Standard,* Mar. 16, 1908, p. 8.

Trick played on Hansen "Captain Hansen's Bravery Was Put to a Test," *Ogden Standard,* Mar. 21, 1908, p. 5.

Route switched to southern Nevada "American Car Gets to Cobre on Time," *Salt Lake Tribune,* Mar. 18, 1908, p. 10.

Thomas crew nearly starves "Sandstorms Meet the Leading Racer," *New York Times,* Mar. 18, 1908, p. 2.

Army troops overseeing mines "Troops Leave the Camp of Goldfield," *Carson City Daily Appeal,* Mar. 7, 1908.

Students leave for mines "Rush to New Goldfields," *Carson City Daily Appeal,* Mar. 11, 1908.

Wealth of Nevada "A Great Bullion Yield," *Carson City Daily Appeal,* Mar. 11, 1908.

Stagecoaches in use A. Dudley Gardner and Juliet Cummings, *Midland Highway: A Historical Assessment of a Segment of the Midland Road from Ely to Tonopah* (Ogden, Utah: Sage Brush Consultants, 1993), p. 5.

NOTES

Editorialist on autos in mine country "Triumphs of the Automobile," *Salt Lake City Evening Telegram,* Mar. 17, 1908, p. 8.

Goldfield as boomtown Sally Zanjani, *The Last Gold Rush on the Western Frontier* (Athens, Ohio: Swallow Press/Ohio University, 1992), p. 89.

Thomas gets stuck "American Car Strikes Hard Luck, Bad Roads Put It in Hole at Veteran," *White Pine (Nevada) News,* Mar. 19, 1908, p. 1.

Yankee boy (Song lyrics) Goldfield Daily Tribune, Mar. 18, 1908, p. 1; excerpted in Phillip I. Earl, "New York-to-Paris via Nevada," *Nevada Historical Quarterly,* Summer 1976, vol. 19, no. 2.

Scarfoglio on Ogden in distance Antonio Scarfoglio, "Life in the Desert," *London Daily Mail,* Mar. 24, 1908, p. 5.

Sirtori on car swimming through creeks "Paris Racer Runs into California," *New York Times,* Mar. 22, 1908, p. 2.

Mrs. Ruland's affair "Divorce for A. L. Ruland," *New York Times,* Dec. 6, 1908, p. 13.

Chapter Seventeen

CALIFORNIA POSTCARD

Mrs. Hancock's villa "Modelled After Italian Villas," *Los Angeles Sunday Times,* Mar. 1, 1908, sec. V, p. 1.

Earle Anthony's radio station James J. Bradley, "A Gentleman's Car: Built by Gentlemen," in Beverly Rae Kimes, ed., *Packard: A History of the Motor Car and the Company* (Princeton, N.J.: Princeton Pub., 1978), p. 119–20.

Harper as banker Mayors of Los Angeles (Los Angeles: 1965), p. 55.

Allan Hancock in car "World Race Route Varied," *Los Angeles Times,* Mar. 19, 1908, p. 1.

Price of Thomases Western Motor Car Co. advertisement, *Los Angeles Sunday Times,* Mar. 22, 1908, pt. 8, p. 8.

E. L. Thomas's influence "Big Racer Will Follow the Leader Today," *Los Angeles Sunday Times,* Mar. 22, 1908, sec. 8, p. 2; "American Car Is Due Here Today," *Los Angeles Herald,* Mar. 22, 1908, pt. 3, p. 4.

Schuster considering connections to Alaska "Auto Racer Close to San Francisco," *New York Times,* Mar. 24, 1908, p. 1.

Schuster ignores telegrams "American Car Comes but Hastens On," *Bakersfield Californian* Mar. 23, 1908, p. 1.

Sontag as robber "Career of George Sontag Who Has Just Been Pardoned," *Bakersfield Californian,* Mar. 20, 1908, p. 1.

Bakersfield as boomtown Richard C. Bailey, *Heart of the Golden Empire, an Illustrated History of Bakersfield* (Woodland Hills, Calif.: Windsor Publications, 1984), p. 78.

NOTES

Although we had many trying (Schuster quote) "American Car Comes but Hastens On," *Bakersfield Californian,* Mar. 23, 1908, p. 8.

Fowler on auto enthusiasts "American Car Given Warm Greeting by San Francisco," *San Francisco Chronicle,* Mar. 25, 1908, p. 1.

Brinegar on American cars "Auto Notes," *Town Topics* (San Francisco), Mar., 1908, p. 28.

Thomas team jovial "Auto Enthusiasts Greet Thomas Car," *San Francisco Examiner,* Mar. 25, 1908, p. 5.

The trip across the continent (Schuster quote) George Schuster, "Racer Tells Story of Journey Across Continent," *San Francisco Examiner,* Mar 25, p. 4.

Storage compartments "Thomas Flyer on Trip to Alaska," Mar. 28, 1908, p. 12.

There is a delightful haziness (Fowler quote) "Thousands of Persons Inspect the American Racing Car," *San Francisco Chronicle,* Mar. 26, 1908, p. 1.

Sontag released from prison "Sontag Sees First Auto," *Bakersfield Californian,* Mar. 28, 1908, p. 6.

Flyer booked onto freighter W. H. B. Fowler, "Directors Believe the Thomas Can Negotiate Difficult Territory," *San Francisco Chronicle,* Mar. 27, 1908.

Brinker wants to continue Schuster with Mahoney, *The Longest Auto Race,* p. 73.

Chapter Eighteen
DEATH IN THE DESERT

L.A.'s enthusiasm for the Züst "Loses Way on the Desert," *Los Angeles Times,* Mar. 23, 1908, p. 4.

Southern Pacific rescues Züst "Railroads Aid the Züst," *New York Times,* Mar. 25, 1908, p. 2.

Estimate of delay "Italian Car Is Coming Back," *Ogden Standard,* Mar. 24, 1908, p. 6.

Sirtori back as driver "Züst May Catch Thomas," *New York Times,* Mar. 29, 1908, p. 5.

The road is fair (Scarfoglio quote) "Round the World Race," *London Daily Mail,* Apr. 6, 1908, p. 5.

L.A.'s greeting for Züst team "Los Angeles Wild over the Züst Car," *New York Times,* Apr. 1, 1908, p. 2.

Characteristics of Sirtori "Glad Greeting Here for Italian Racer," *Los Angeles Times,* Apr. 1, 1908, p. 1.

Sirtori on Aspen Tunnel "Glad Greeting Here for Italian Racer," *Los Angeles Times,* Apr. 1, 1908, p. 1.

Actual time overland Interview with A. L. Ruland, "Crew near Death on the Züst Car," *New York Times,* Mar. 29, 1908, sec. 4, p. 3.

Scarfoglio on beautiful California towns Scarfoglio, *Round the World,* p. 151.

She is disqualified (Sirtori quote) "Guilio Sirtori Is Tendered Ovation," *San Francisco Examiner,* Apr. 5, 1908, p. 48.

Italians book freighter "Second Auto Racer at San Francisco," *New York Times,* Apr. 5, 1908, pt. 2, p. 18.

Dog as De Dion guide "De Dion at Ogden," *New York Times,* Mar. 27, 1908, p. 1.

When small rivers (St. Chaffray quote) "De Dion's Wild Journey," *New York Times,* Mar. 25, 1908, p. 2.

Frenchmen leave bridges "French Auto Arrives in Ogden," *Ogden Standard,* Mar. 27, 1908, p. 1.

Hoboes commandeer train "Tramps Take Charge of a Train," *Ogden Standard,* Mar. 27, 1908, p. 6.

De Dion is stuck "French Auto Arrives in Ogden," *Ogden Standard,* Mar. 27, 1908, p. 1.

Lascares wields gun "De Dion Leaves Ogden," *New York Times,* Mar. 28, 1908, p. 2.

With six men on the rope (Ogden quote) "French Auto Arrives in Ogden," *Ogden Standard,* Mar. 27, 1908, p. 1.

Without news (St. Chaffray telegram) "French Auto Arrives in Ogden," *Ogden Standard,* Mar. 27, 1908, p. 1.

They say that the race proper (Tonopah quote) "French Racer Off for Goldfield," *Tonopah Daily Sun,* Mar. 31, 1908, p. 1.

The mere matter of racing (St. Chaffray quote) Goldfield Daily Tribune, Mar. 31, 1908, pp. 1, 4; quoted in Phillip I. Earl, "New York-to-Paris via Nevada," *Nevada Historical Society,* Summer 1976, vol. 19, no. 2, p. 115.

Substitute teamster "Sand Delays French Racer," *Los Angeles Times,* Apr. 3, 1908, p. 1.

St. Chaffray obeys speed limit "Auto Drivers to Be Arrested," *Bakersfield Californian,* Mar. 30, 1908, p. 1.

St. Chaffray gets to San Francisco "Fourth Car in Auto Race Reaches City," *San Francisco Examiner,* Apr. 8, 1908, p. 7.

Frenchmen lose tuxedos "French Racing Car Arrives in City," *San Francisco Chronicle,* Apr. 8, 1908.

Chapter Nineteen

SHARP TURNS

Sled traffic in Alaska "Auto Race Leader Arrives at Valdez," *New York Times,* Apr. 10, 1908, p. 1.

Description of Valdez "Valdez: Gateway to an Empire," in Hallock C. Bundy, ed., *The Valdez-Fairbanks Trail: The Story of a Great Highway* (Seattle: Alaska Pub. Co., 1910), pp. 23–25.

Description of the trail "The Story of a Great Highway," in Bundy, *Valdez-Fairbanks Trail,* p. 23.

Roadhouses Advertisement, Wortman's Roadhouse, *Alaska Prospector,* Apr. 9, 1908, p. 2; "The Story of a Great Highway," in Bundy, *Valdez-Fairbanks Trail,* p. 25.

Bachelor proprietor Advertisements, Teikhell House, Hotel Holman, *Alaska Prospector,* Apr. 9, 1908, p. 4.

Union Pacific helps Protos "French Car Making Speed," *Ogden Standard,* Mar. 28, 1908, p. 6.

Koeppen's mountain fever Koeppen, *Um Welt de Auto,* p. 158.

Mein Gott, it is no race (Snyder quote) "Last of the Racing Cars," *Ogden Standard,* Apr. 3, 1908, p. 8.

He then got possession (Odgen quote) "German Car Out of Luck," *Ogden Standard,* April 6, 1908, p. 5.

Protos has cracked cylinders "German Car Met with Another Accident," *Ogden Standard,* Apr. 7, 1908, p. 7.

Scarfoglio reading letters Scarfoglio, *Round the World,* p. 156.

Godard caught speeding "Godard Is Arrested," *San Francisco Examiner,* Apr. 8, 1908, p. 7.

Ours was the first car (Schuster quote) Schuster with Mahoney, *The Longest Auto Race,* p. 77.

Snow too deep for Thomas "Auto Race Leader Arrives at Valdez," *New York Times,* Apr. 10, 1908, p. 1.

All of the autoists are large athletic young men (Valdez quote) "Autoists Give Up over Trail," *Valdez Prospector,* Apr. 9, 1908, p. 4.

St. Chaffray on Alaska "Alaska Is Out of Auto Race," *Seattle Daily Times,* Apr. 14, 1908, p. 2.

I calculated the time (Koeppen quote) Koeppen, *Um Welt de Auto,* p. 149.

St. Chaffray wrote (Koeppen quote) Koeppen, *Um Welt de Auto,* pp. 150–52.

It is a big machine (Pocatello quote) "German Car on a Flat Car," *Pocatello Tribune,* Apr. 13, 1908, p. 1.

Imposter speeders "French Car Turns Turtle," *Portland Morning Oregonian,* Apr. 16, 1908, p. 1.

Koeppen sails on Glenlogan "Autos Will Sail for Yokohama Tuesday," *Seattle Daily Times,* Apr. 18, 1908, p. 2.

NOTES

Chapter Twenty
THE JAPANESE COUNTRYSIDE

Duc's overdose "De Chaulnes Dead After Honeymoon," *New York Times*, Apr. 25, 1908, p. 1.

Why fifteen servants (Street quote) Julian Street, *Mysterious Japan* (Garden City, New York: Doubleday, Page, 1922), p. 20.

In order to obtain this permit (Scarfoglio quote) Scarfoglio, *Round the World*, p. 169.

The three brave Frenchmen (Scarfoglio quote) "Round the World Race," *London Daily Mail*, May 18, 1908, p. 5.

New York Times *on Japan* "The Motorcars in Japan," *New York Times*, May 2, 1908, p. 8.

We were for twenty-four hours (Scarfoglio quote) "Round the World Race," *London Daily Mail*, May 18, 1908, p. 5.

St. Chaffray on width of roads "Wild Trip in Japan for Racing Autos," *New York Times*, May 13, 1908, p. 1.

Americans on Protos penalty "Allow Thomas Car a Lead of 15 Days," *New York Times*, May 8, 1908, p. 1.

Scarfoglio on status of women in Japan Scarfoglio, *Round the World*, pp. 197–98.

The guide sang their praises (Scarfoglio quote) Scarfoglio, *Round the World*, p. 204.

Our wheels were pulling (St. Chaffray quote) "Wild Trip in Japan for Racing Autos," *New York Times*, May 13, 1908, p. 1.

Lack of maps in Japan "It Was 'Banzai' Through Japan for the American Car in the Paris Race," *New York Times*, July 19, 1908, pt. 5, p. 11.

Mr. Mancini volunteers "It Was 'Banzai' Through Japan for the American Car in the Paris Race," *New York Times*, July 19, 1908, pt. 5, p. 11.

At the farther end (Schuster quote) Schuster with Mahoney, *The Longest Auto Race*, p. 88.

Crossing to the mainland Scarfoglio, *Round the World*, p. 214.

Chapter Twenty-one
SECOND START

Nevélski motto Karl Baedecker, *Russia* (New York: Scribner's, 1914; reprinted Arno Press, 1971), p. 538.

Koeppen meets teammates Koeppen, *Um Welt de Auto*, pp. 168–69.

Koeppen's initial opinion of teammates Koeppen, *Um Welt de Auto*, p. 354.

Perfectly roadless (governor quote) Koeppen, *Um Welt de Auto,* p. 170.

Fuchs and Neuberger had turned (Koeppen quote) Koeppen, *Um Welt de Auto,* p. 174.

One remembers that at Tokio (Scarfoglio quote) Scarfoglio, *Round the World,* pp. 214–15.

Germania Lord Frederic Hamilton *The Vanished Pomps of Yesterday* (London: Hodder and Stoughton, 1937), p. 139.

Züst is ordered to return "Italian Car Withdraws," *New York Times,* May 16, 1908, p. 1.

Thomas is trimmest "American Auto Crew Is at Vladivostok," *New York Times,* May 19, 1908, p. 1.

Protos parts lost Koeppen, *Um Welt de Auto,* pp. 174–75.

St. Chaffray's offer Scarfoglio, *Round the World,* p. 216.

He stated that he could (MacAdam quote) "St. Chaffray Halts American Autoists," *New York Times,* May 21, 1908, p. 1.

Chapter Twenty-two

SPORTSMANSHIP

Vladivostok weather Koeppen, *Um Welt de Auto,* p. 176.

[I] started the Thomas (Schuster quote) Schuster with Mahoney, *The Longest Auto Race,* p. 94.

After a while (Koeppen quote) Koeppen, *Um Welt de Auto,* p. 177.

In comradely fashion (Koeppen quote) Koeppen, *Um Welt de Auto,* p. 178.

It has now the lead (Koeppen quote) Koeppen, *Um Welt de Auto,* p. 178.

Bandit murders "Thomas at Chita Before Expected," *New York Times,* June 18, 1908, p. 1.

With the crew wading (MacAdam quote) "Protos Auto Takes Lead in Siberia," *New York Times,* May 26, 1908, p. 1.

We saw the uselessness (Koeppen quote) Koeppen, *Um Welt de Auto,* p. 180.

Bandits' interest in autoists "Thomas Car's Peril in Siberian Wilds," *New York Times,* May 29, 1908, p. 1.

We the car and the journey (Scarfoglio quote) Scarfoglio, *Round the World,* p. 219.

Baron to join Züst "Züst to Stay in Paris Race," *New York Times,* June 2, 1908, p. 1.

Manchurian tigers (Scarfoglio quote) Scarfoglio, *Round the World,* p. 240.

Chapter Twenty-three
WILD EAST

Makeshift campsite "Auto Racers Camp in Siberian Wild," *New York Times,* June 5, 1908, p. 1.

Soldiers arrive with watchdogs "Auto Racers Camp in Siberian Wild," *New York Times,* June 5, 1908, p. 1.

These Chinese or Korean (Koeppen quote) Koeppen, *Um Welt de Auto,* pp. 182–83.

The Second-Lieutenant (Koeppen quote) Koeppen, *Um Welt de Auto,* p. 190–91.

The bridge had disappeared (Koeppen quote) Koeppen, *Um Welt de Auto,* p. 194.

After photographs (Koeppen quote) Koeppen, *Um Welt de Auto,* p. 196.

The railroad insists (MacAdam quote) "Protos past Harbin, Thomas Following," *New York Times,* June 12, 1908, p. 1.

Protos stuck and Koeppen alone on steppes Koeppen *Um Welt de Auto,* pp. 209–19.

Chapter Twenty-four
BLUE WATER

Appearance of Tchita "Protos at Chita Wins $1,000 Trophy," *New York Times,* June 17, 1908, p. 1.

The prize was ours (Koeppen quote) Koeppen, *Um Welt de Auto,* p. 224.

Decembrists Benson Bobrick, *East of the Sun: The Epic Conquest and Tragic History of Siberia* (New York: Poseidon, 1992), p. 292.

Lt. Koeppen has displayed (von Albrecht quote) "Protos at Chita Wins $1,000 Trophy," *New York Times,* June 17, 1908, p. 1.

We passed a party (Schuster quote) Schuster with Mahoney, *The Longest Auto Race,* p. 103.

Description of Sryetensk John Fraser, quoted in W. Bruce Lincoln, *The Conquest of a Continent: Siberia and the Russians* (New York: Random House, 1994), p. 241.

Tag-along colt "Protos Two Days in Lead of Thomas," *New York Times,* June 20, 1908, p. 1.

Proud birds (Koeppen quote) Koeppen, *Um Welt de Auto,* p. 234.

Cleanliness of Baikal Lincoln, *Conquest of a Continent,* p. 247.

Like in a real ocean (Koeppen quote) Koeppen, *Um Welt de Auto,* p. 234.

There was nothing left (Koeppen quote) Koeppen, *Um Welt de Auto,* p. 237–38.

Fracas with villagers "Thomas Car Close Behind Protos," *New York Times,* June 22, 1908, p. 1.

I'll wait for you (Koeppen quote) "Thomas Car Close Behind Protos," *New York Times,* June 22, 1908, p. 1.

Chapter Twenty-five

FLASH FLOOD

Züst won't stop Scarfoglio, *Round the World,* p. 224.

They regard us as raving (Scarfoglio quote) Scarfoglio, *Round the World,* pp. 226–27.

We have been racing as if (Scarfoglio quote) "Züst Pushing on in Race to Paris," *New York Times,* June 19, 1908, p. 1.

Old Baikal saying Bobrick, *East of the Sun,* p. 29.

It was a crucial choice (Koeppen quote) Koeppen, *Um Welt de Auto,* p. 240.

Chapter Twenty-six

OUT IN FRONT

Picnickers in Irkutsk "Thomas Catches Protos at Tomsk," *New York Times,* June 28, 1908, p. 1.

Grim silence of the Thomas (MacAdam quote) "Thomas Catches Protos at Tomsk," *New York Times,* June 28, 1908, p. 2.

Half an hour later (MacAdam quote) "Thomas Catches Protos at Tomsk," *New York Times,* June 28, 1908, p. 2.

Air was thick with mosquitoes Schuster with Mahoney, *The Longest Auto Race,* p. 110.

Villagers, with wide-open eyes (MacAdam quote) "Thomas Catches Protos at Tomsk," *New York Times,* June 28, 1908, p. 2.

I was at a loss (Koeppen quote) Koeppen, *Um Welt de Auto,* p. 256.

As I tried to force the car (Schuster quote) Schuster with Mahoney, *The Longest Auto Race,* p. 114.

Neuberger became ill (Koeppen quote) Koeppen, *Um Welt de Auto,* p. 263.

Miller fixes Thomas "Racing Auto Sinks in Siberian Swamp," *New York Times,* July 5, 1908, p. 1.

I watched as one farmer (Koeppen quote) Koeppen, *Um Welt de Auto,* p. 267.

My patience was tested (Koeppen quote) Koeppen, *Um Welt de Auto,* p. 268.

If the Protos (Koeppen quote) Schuster with Mahoney, *The Longest Auto Race,* p. 119.

As long as the wheels (Schuster quote) Schuster with Mahoney, *The Longest Auto Race,* p. 120.

Chapter Twenty-seven

The Favor of the Czar

Schuster's telegram "Thomas Car Leads Racers into Europe," *New York Times,* July 10, 1908, p. 1.

The women were better behaved (MacAdam quote) "The Final Dash Across Europe in the Paris Race," *New York Times,* Aug. 16, pt. 4, p. 1.

Failing transmission "Thomas Car Halted by Broken Gear," *New York Times,* July 16, 1908, p. 1.

Suppose you go (Schuster quote) Schuster with Mahoney, *The Longest Auto Race,* p. 122.

Germans hear of Thomas position Koeppen, *Um Welt de Auto,* p. 272.

He greeted us cordially (MacAdam quote) "The Final Dash Across Europe in the Paris Race," *New York Times,* Aug. 16, pt. 4, p. 1.

I was too tired (Schuster quote) Schuster with Mahoney, *The Longest Auto Race,* 122.

We drove past mountains (Koeppen quote) Koeppen, *Um Welt de Auto,* pp. 278–79.

Externally, we had (Koeppen quote) Koeppen, *Um Welt de Auto,* p. 287.

Road to St. Petersburg Koeppen, *Um Welt de Auto,* p. 296.

While our car found room (Koeppen quote) Koeppen, *Um Welt de Auto,* p. 304.

Schuster loses 15 hours "Thomas Speeding Toward Protos Car," *New York Times,* July 23, 1908, p. 1.

Once, the car sank (MacAdam quote) "Thomas Speeding Toward Protos Car," *New York Times,* July 23, 1908, p. 1.

On German soil (Koeppen quote) Koeppen, *Um Welt de Auto,* p. 319.

A person who travels (Koeppen quote) Koeppen, *Um Welt de Auto,* p. 343.

Crowd in Berlin "Wild Reception in Berlin," *New York Times,* July 25, 1908, p. 1.

There must have been (Koeppen quote) "German Auto First in Paris," *New York Times,* July 27, 1908, p. 2.

Koeppen carried in building "German Auto First in Paris," *New York Times,* July 27, 1908, p. 2.

On the 26th (Ullstein quote) Koeppen, *Um Welt de Auto,* p. 328.

The great dash (Koeppen quote) "Protos to Arrive at Berlin To-day," *New York Times,* July 24, 1908, p. 1.

Chapter Twenty-eight

New York to Paris

Schuster catching up "Wild Reception in Berlin," *New York Times,* July 25, 1908, p. 1.

Monotony of magnificent roads (MacAdam quote) "Thomas past Berlin, Takes Road to Paris," *New York Times,* July 28, 1908, p. 1.

We have constantly (Schuster quote) "Thomas, Winner, Reaches Paris," *New York Times,* July 31, 1908, p. 2.

Schuster when Koeppen gets to Paris "Thomas past Berlin, Takes Road to Paris," *New York Times,* July 28, 1908, p. 1.

It was only by good luck (MacAdam quote) "Thomas Car Is Delayed," *New York Times,* July 30, 1908, p. 1.

Nobody knew our schedule (Schuster quote) Schuster with Mahoney, *The Longest Auto Race,* p. 132.

Cheered them to the echo (Paris quote) "Thomas, Winner, Reaches Paris," *New York Times,* July 31, 1908, p. 1.

Performance the most remarkable (Paris quote) "Thomas, Winner, Reaches Paris," *New York Times,* July 31, 1908, p. 1.

Chapter Twenty-nine

Young Men in the Morning

Thoreau about train "Human Brawn vs. Autos," *New York Evening Mail,* Aug. 1, 1908.

New York Times *on Thomas* "Return of the Victors," *New York Times,* Aug. 18, 1908, p. 6.

St. Chaffray in Paris "Thomas Car Has Completed Its Long Route," *Buffalo Evening News,* July 31, 1908, p. 5.

Most interesting and exciting "Return of the Victors," *New York Times,* Aug. 18, 1908, p. 6.

Suffering the agony (Scarfoglio quote) Scarfoglio, *Round the World,* p. 328.

It was hurled at me (Scarfoglio quote) Scarfoglio, *Round the World,* p. 332. [Note that Scarfoglio's phonetic Russian phrases are not entirely correct, as printed in the English translation of his book.]

We have been travelling (Scarfoglio quote) Scarfoglio, *Round the World,* p. 327.

Acknowledgments

The origin of this book is the same as that of many of the better opportunities in my career: *American Heritage,* the historical magazine that is about to celebrate its fiftieth anniversary. The idea for an article on the 1908 New York-to-Paris Automobile Race belonged to Richard F. Snow, the editor of the magazine (see "The Longest Race," *American Heritage,* November 1996). I am even more indebted to Richard for his invaluable support at the outset of the writing of this book.

For the article in *American Heritage,* I depended almost solely on the daily reports carried in the *New York Times,* back in 1908. They were basic to the book, too, but accounts were also drawn from newspapers all along the race route (except in Siberia). It is well worth noting that many of the American papers needed would have been lost for all time if not for the U.S. Newspaper Program, the long-term object of which has been to microfilm historical newspapers, from the most obscure to the most famous. It is funded by the National Endowment for the Humanities, which has to be thanked for preserving the voices, the days, and all of the gossip contained in local newspapers, and so making a book like this one possible.

The majority of the microfilms was ordered for me from local libraries around the country through Inter-Library Loan. I am indebted to the ILL department of the Onondaga County (New York) Public Library, Betsy Burton in particular, for keeping the microfilms coming to me, despite the fact that I used to bring her request slips by the hundred, or nearly so. Betsy was never anything but obliging throughout. The ILL department at the Buffalo & Erie County Library was also helpful and very productive in the same vein.

The state of Iowa offered so many newspapers of interest that I didn't think that even ILL could handle the load, but at the time, I wasn't able to make a long research trip. I asked one of my oldest friends, Dr. Karen Haslett, who teaches anthropology at the University of Iowa, if she would find and photocopy articles, assuming that I supplied the names of newspapers and the dates. Working at the Iowa State Historical Society repositories at Iowa City and Des Moines, she did a superb job. I shouldn't have been surprised. Karen is smart enough to do anything and sensitive enough, by far, to see how much those old newspaper articles meant to my project. I later found out that Karen's mother, Jean Haslett, joined in the searching and deserves credit for being a five-star researcher. I am grateful to them both.

A second major focus of the research for this book were the memoirs written by several of the participants. A crucial one was *Im Auto Um Die Welt,* written in 1908 by Hans Koeppen. It was never translated into an English edition. Since my knowledge of German is limited to two words *mit Schlag*—("with whipped cream"), I tried to find someone to translate it for me, but with very little luck. It is a fairly long book, written in the old-fashioned fraktur lettering that few people can read these days. Dr. Gerlinde Ulm Sanford, chairman of the German department at Syracuse University, was extremely helpful in the early going, translating important passages. She was, however, involved with a time-consuming task of her own, transcribing previously unpublished letters by Goethe, and so she could not take on the entire translation for me. Other people took the book with good intentions but could do nothing with it, for one reason or another. More than a year passed, and I was getting the feeling that Oberlieutenant Koeppen and I were in grave trouble.

Through a mutual acquaintance, I met Mr. Richard Harfmann. Though I did not know it at the time, Richard has only one standard: he makes an excellent job of everything he does. Without further ado, he prepared a meticulous translation of Koeppen's work. There is a great deal of Richard's indomitable spirit in these pages. He is, in every sense, a godsend.

I filled in some of the gaps in the newspaper search and found many foreign titles at the New York Public Library and the Library of Congress. In other cases, local libraries and historical societies were instrumental in supplying articles or other background material.

The Buffalo & Erie County Historical Society is a fine repository for material on the Thomas Motor Car Company. Deborah D'Ambrosio of the Nutley Free Library in Nutley, New Jersey, helped to find local obituary notices for Montague Roberts. I would like to thank the Morley Library in Painesville, Ohio, for finding material on Lake County for me. Paul L. Beck at the Kendallville Public Library in Kendallville, Ohio, and Karis Lyon at the Hicks Library in Elyria were very helpful, as were Theresa Schmidt at the Historical Society of Porter County in Valparaiso, Indiana; Diana Zornow at the Elkhart County Historical Museum in Bristol; Curt McConnell at the Goshen (Indiana) Historical Society; and Cindy Messenger at the Kearney Public Library in Kearney, Nebraska. The Dawson County Historical Society in Lexington, Nebraska, the Columbus (Nebraska) Public Library, and the Louis E. May Museum in Fremont, Nebraska, also supplied original newspaper articles.

I would like to thank the Wyoming State Archives for sending several batches of excellent material. In the same state, Norma Jean Robins at the city of Rock Springs Historical Museum, the Carbon County Museum in Rawlins, the Uinta County Museum in Evanston, and the Rock River Museum in Rock River each sent very interesting packets of clippings. The White Pine County (Nevada) Historical and Archaeological Socity in Ely, where Donna Frederick found articles, and the Central Nevada Museum in Tonopah were both very cooperative.

Finally, my parents went, as usual, to any length to help me research this book. Paul Birchmeyer was interested in the topic from the first. My good friend Douglas Brinkley was encouraging at junctures especially important to this book, and I will always be grateful to him. And as ever, I cannot forget Neddy.